A Fistful of Icons

A Fistful of Icons
*Essays on Frontier Fixtures
of the American Western*

Edited by Sue Matheson

McFarland & Company, Inc., Publishers
Jefferson, North Carolina

LIBRARY OF CONGRESS CATALOGUING-IN-PUBLICATION DATA

Names: Matheson, Sue, editor.
Title: A fistful of icons : essays on frontier fixtures of the American western / edited by Sue Matheson.
Description: Jefferson, North Carolina : McFarland & Company, Inc., Publishers. 2017 | Includes bibliographical references and index.
Identifiers: LCCN 2017024469 | ISBN 9780786498048 (softcover : acid free paper) ∞
Subjects: LCSH: Western films—United States—HIstory and criticism. | Western television programs—United States—HIstory and criticism. | Motion pictures—Art direction—United States. | Motion pictures—Setting and scenery—United States. | Television—Art direction—United States.
Classification: LCC PN1995.9.W4 F55 2017 | DDC 791.43/65878—dc23
LC record available at https://lccn.loc.gov/2017024469

BRITISH LIBRARY CATALOGUING DATA ARE AVAILABLE

ISBN (print) 978-0-7864-9804-8
ISBN (ebook) 978-1-4766-2943-8

© 2017 Sue Matheson. All rights reserved

No part of this book may be reproduced or transmitted in any form or by any means, electronic or mechanical, including photocopying or recording, or by any information storage and retrieval system, without permission in writing from the publisher.

Front cover: poster art from *The Good, the Bad and the Ugly*, 1966 Italy (MGM/Photofest)

Printed in the United States of America

McFarland & Company, Inc., Publishers
  Box 611, Jefferson, North Carolina 28640
    www.mcfarlandpub.com

*For Stuart and Rebecca
who have watched many Westerns*

Acknowledgments

I would like to thank Ray Merlock, Virginia Goulet, Dan Smith, Harvey Briggs, and Rod Nabess for their encouragement and outstanding support of this project. I must also thank Andrew Patrick Nelson for his contribution to this project in its early stages. I am particularly grateful to all the contributors whose enthusiasm, dedication, and hard work brought this collection to life. Most importantly, I would like to thank Stuart and Rebecca Matheson who kept the home fires burning and warded off skunks while this collection was completed.

Table of Contents

Acknowledgments vi

Preface 1

Introduction 3

Performing the Iconic West: Wild West Shows 9
    CYNTHIA J. MILLER

Buckskin Fringe and Cavalier Culture in the Hollywood Western 23
    SUE MATHESON

The Urbanized West of Cecil B. DeMille 36
    DAVID BLANKE

"They taught us to be men": Cigarettes, Westerns 51
and (Mostly) John Ford
    RICHMOND B. ADAMS

The Good Bounty Hunter: Steve McQueen in *Wanted:* 62
Dead or Alive
    KELLY C. MACPHAIL

Racialized Markers of Gender and Gendered Markers of Race 74
in 1950s Westerns
    DEBORAH L. KITCHEN-DØDERLEIN

"Mister, this is cattle country": Livestock and Gender 86
in Western Films
    JIM DAEMS

Ride 'Em Cowboy: Equine Representations in the Western 99
    STELLA HOCKENHULL

Table of Contents

Horses for Ladies, High-Ridin' Women and Whores MARIA CECÍLIA DE MIRANDA N. COELHO	113
The Sexual Signification of the Gun in Western Film FRAN PHEASANT-KELLY	124
Rifles and Things in *Winchester '73* KATHERINE A. JOHNSON	142
The Cowboy Brew: Coffee and Conflict in the Westerns of Budd Boetticher, Jr. CHRISTOPHER MINZ	152
Cowboy Accommodations: Plotting the Hotel in Western Film and Television MONICA MONTELONGO FLORES	166
When Worlds Collide: Town and Country, Mise-en-Scène in *Have Gun, Will Travel* ROBERT E. MEYER	177
Executioner, Judge and Priest: The Desert Sublime in Westerns HELEN M. LEWIS	188
Machines in the Garden: Technology and the Western in the 1960s and 1970s MARTIN HOLTZ	198
"Dynamite blows two ways": Dynamite in Western Films GILLES CHAMEROIS	213
Trippy Pictures: Iconicizing the American Acid Westerns ALEXANDER DAVIS	231
"Reach for the sky": Western Iconography, the American Frontier and the Story of Pixar in *Toy Story* ASHLEY SUFFLÉ ROBINSON	244
Burying the Past: Cemeteries, Burials and Remembrance in the Western ANDREW HOWE	257
The Four Archetypes of the Three Burials (of Melquiades Estrada) WICKHAM CLAYTON	271
About the Contributors	285
Index	289

Naturally, Hollywood is not history and nobody believes the West was like a Western. But if Westerns are fantasy, why so consistent a fantasy?
—David Hamilton Murdoch, *The American West: The Invention of a Myth*

"The world is what you make of it, friend. If it doesn't fit, you make alterations."
—Lawrence and Mark Kasdan, *Silverado: The Screenplay*

Preface

Richard Slotkin remarks in *Gunfighter Nation* that the American Frontier ceased to be simply a "geographical place" in 1893—with the help of writers like Frederick Jackson Turner and Theodore Roosevelt, it became a set of symbols, a *mythic space* with "its own peculiar geography, politics, and cultures," later adopted by Hollywood and further converted into "a landscape known through and completely identified with the fictions created about it" (61). In this landscape, on the leading edge of westward expansion, the Hollywood Western houses Turner's dream of a collective democracy *and* Roosevelt's fictional frontier heroes, natural aristocrats dressed in buckskin. Embodying Roosevelt's notions about the invigorating life close to Nature in simpler times, the cowboy owes his cool to the largest and richest iconography of all film genres.[1] It is remarkable that much of Gene Autry's success is due to his horse, Champion, Roy Rogers' celebrity to fringed shirts, and Clint Eastwood's fame to a stubby cheroot.

This project grew out of my keen interest in the unchanging nature of the Western's iconography despite its genre's many revisions. As Marshall McLuhan points out in *The Mechanical Bride: Folklore of Industrial Man*, celluloid images become more and more vivid as historical accuracy becomes dimmer (156). Firmly fixed in the American psyche, the Western's consistency does not seem to be conscious in its origin or effect, because its cohesion and unity resides in its highly familiar forms. Because of its frontier fixtures, the Western continues to speak a language we all recognize. *A Fistful of Icons: Essays on Frontier Fixtures of the American Western* is the first collection of scholarly essays to pioneer these dynamic patterns belonging to Hollywood's oldest and most popular genre. Showcasing the work of scholars from the United States, Canada, France, Germany, the United Kingdom, Norway, and Brazil, *A Fistful of Icons* offers 21 opportunities to examine selected topics, among them Buffalo Bill, the bounty hunter, buckskin jackets, the Winchester rifle, the horse, the cup of coffee, the cigarette, dynamite, and cemeteries, while enjoying the Western's proclivity for self-generation (and self-promotion). Forged over the genre's century of invention, reinvention and reinterpretation, the Western's icons and archetypes celebrate *and* deconstruct the American character while continuing to transmit its complicated cultural coding. A spoiler alert is necessary here: space and time constraints have made it impossible to explore every facet of the Western's mythic subtext. There are no investigations of American Indian attire, inimical card games, innumerable Union suits, outrageous moustaches, or creaking covered wagons in this volume. It is my hope and expectation that these (and other) notable absences will stimulate more insights (and publications) about Western film.

NOTE

1. See Gary Johnson's entertaining and instructive introduction to Western film in his article "The Western: An Overview."

WORKS CITED

Johnson, Gary. "The Western: An Overview." *In Focus* 10 at http://www.imagesjournal.com/issue06/infocus/western.htm.

McLuhan, Marshall. *The Mechanical Bride: Folklore of Industrial Man*. Berkeley, CA: Gingko Press, 1951.

Slotkin, Richard. *Gunfighter Nation: The Myth of the Frontier in Twentieth-Century America*. Norman: University of Oklahoma Press, 1998.

Introduction

A branch of art history, iconography identifies, describes, and interprets the content of images. As anyone who has attempted to examine the Western knows, recognizing its icons is one matter—writing about and attempting to categorize them quite another. Marshall McLuhan remarks in *The Mechanical Bride* that "the world of the frontier is a focus of numerous feelings and emotions" which "loom larger and larger imaginatively" (156). Since McLuhan's pioneering work on Western iconography in "Horse Opera and Soap Opera" has been published, little critical attention has been directed to the iconic images found in the Western films even though they are generic fixtures, unifying elements on a diverse and changing body of work. In short, the Western's iconography, consistent and consistently coherent, is its genre's aesthetic mean. Appearing at first straightforward, and even simplistic, these self-referencing signs signify the American experience in dynamic patterns that are at once multi-faceted *and* multi-layered. In every Western, these icons contain hundreds of inter-related and inter-linking texts and connect in an incredibly active and complex synergy of popular American forms and norms. Constituting an enormous symbolic nexus, they express social, political and cultural concerns with heroism, personal individualism, freedom and independence, masculinity, and other matters near and dear to the heart of America.

Self-contained *and* self-generating, this iconography's performative value lies in its self-referencing nature. However, attempting to classify or categorize one of its icons is like trying to box a hydra. Just when its heads have been severed and the torso tucked safely away, the beast grows several more trunks—and then each severed head produces two or three others. Perhaps this is why the Western, pronounced dead several times since the 1970s, has resurrected itself at regular intervals and proven to be self-sustaining—why its cinematic language still survives today. Simply put, Westerns are not created *ex nihilo*. Because every Western draws its essence from earlier "oaters" (inspired by even earlier horse operas), the tradition of the Western is what

T.S. Eliot would recognize as a simultaneous order, one that embodies a historical timelessness in which the past and the present, fiction and fact, are fused—and as a canon in which objects, events, and situations act as objective correlatives. Expressing and evoking the American experience, the innovative Western's greatness and individuality lies in its adherence to *and* its departure from the tradition to which it belongs. Every director of a Western, be he John Ford or Gore Verbinski, recognizes and pays tribute to the norms and forms of the nineteenth century's dime novel, to the frontier life depicted in Wild West shows, and to the aesthetic ideal of the West found in the works of American painters like Frederic Remington, Charles Schreyvogel, Charles Russell, and Henry Farny (often found earlier Westerns). The introduction of every Western into its canon alters the cohesion of its elements and causes the old to adjust to accommodate the new. These adjustments change the way the genre itself is realized and understood, and create its dynamic and progressive workings.

Paradoxically, the Western, an organic, constantly developing tradition, is identified and defined by its consistent, consistently coherent, frontier fixtures. In 1964, for example, Sergio Leone's *A Fistful of Dollars*, a rank European interloper, became a blockbuster at the American box office and spawned the Spaghetti Western—using cinematic grammar from the classic hero-tale found in *Shane* (1953) and *My Darling Clementine* (1947), scoring from *Rio Bravo* (1959), and a cobra-handled Colt, a gunbelt, and spurs from *Rawhide* (1959–1965); released in 1990, Kevin Costner's *Dances with Wolves* won seven Academy Awards and the Golden Globe Award for Best Motion Picture and has been credited with revitalizing Western filmmaking—while employing cinematic grammar regarding American Indians found in *The Last of the Mohicans* (1936), *Broken Arrow* (1950), and *Devil's Doorway* (1950); released in 2010, Joel and Ethan Coen's remake of *True Grit* grossed over $25.6 million during its first weekend—recycling much of the dialogue and the cinematic grammar attending the good badman in Henry Hathaway's earlier Oscar-winning *True Grit* (1969). Clearly, the Western's cultural dynamics continue to be rooted in a deep nostalgia for its past.

This collection begins with Cynthia J. Miller's "Performing the Iconic West: Wild West Shows." While tracing William F. Cody's career as a showman and considering the influence of his Wild West show on the American imagination, Miller argues that the West on screen "may be considered a 'meta icon'—not only an icon of the West in its own right, the frontier's wilderness, also encompasses an array of mutually reinforcing Western icons and characters" (9). Following, Sue Matheson's "Buckskin Fringe and Cavalier Culture in the Hollywood Western" examines the nature of Buffalo Bill's trademark, the iconic buckskin jacket, an important marker of the Western hero. Considering a number of buckskin-wearing, befringed frontiersmen in the Hollywood West, Matheson identifies a complicated and compelling cultural code linking primitive masculinity with the Western hero. Not all directors, however, use Western iconography to assert the natural superiority of Roosevelt's rugged individualist. The Western's complexity is aptly examined in David Blanke's "The Urbanized West of Cecil B. DeMille." Blanke's investigation of DeMille's Westerns concludes that they do not glorify the genre's typical semantics of male individualism and the natural world. The iconography of DeMille's Westerns, he argues, highlights instead the importance of civilization, the women's sphere, a shared consensual culture, and particularly the spread of a benevolent modernity.

As markers of masculinity, Western icons vary greatly. Ongoing and constantly renewed questions in the Western about the nature of American masculinity form the basis of Richmond B. Adams' "'They taught us to be men': Cigarettes, Westerns and (Mostly) John Ford." Adams identifies a recent and important cultural shift that has occurred in the Western's representations of masculinity offered by the presence and absence of cigarettes and tobacco. The height and age of the hero is another gender-specific and significant trope. Masculinity's inherent contradictions underpin Kelly C. MacPhail's study of the American anti-hero that propelled Steve McQueen to international stardom in "The Good Bounty Hunter: Steve McQueen in *Wanted: Dead or Alive*." Reconsidering markers of interracial marriages in *Broken Arrow* (1950), *Across the Wide Missouri* (1951), *High Noon* (1952), *Broken Lance* (1954), *The Far Horizons* (1954), and *The Searchers* (1956), Deborah L. Kitchen-Døderlein's "Racialized Markers of Gender and Gendered Markers of Race in 1950s Westerns" concludes that the Western's white masculinity not only celebrates but also mediates a future in which race and gender are subsumed in their service to hegemony.

In the Western, animals are also important signifiers. Jim Daems' "'Mister, this is cattle country': Livestock and Gender in Western Films" traces how representations of masculinity during 60 years of filmmaking—in *Marked for Murder* (1945), *The Sheepman* (1958), *The Ballad of Josie* (1967), *Rustlers' Rhapsody* (1985), and *Brokeback Mountain* (2005)—have been transmitted via livestock, specifically by cattle and sheep. Stella Hockenhull's "Ride 'Em Cowboy: Equine Representations in the Western" explores the centrality of the horse to Western iconography as well as that animal's essential function of enhancing the cowboy's masculinity. Celebrity animals, like Roy Roger's Trigger, Hockenhull argues, are not only star vehicles, but also symbols, because the cowboy's competent horsemanship signifies the freedom and power associated with a winner. The horse is associated with women as well as men in the Western. In "Horses for Ladies, High-Ridin' Women and Whores," Maria Cecília de Miranda N. Coelho also finds the horse a complex signifier, acting as an equalizer that gives women as much freedom and power as men *and* as a symbol of the submission and objectification of women in a world subject to male codes of morality, sexuality, and heroism.

6   Introduction

When examining firearms in the Wild West, Ernest Hemmingway's quip that points out "a stone is a stein is a rock is a boulder is a pebble" is apt. In "The Sexual Signification of the Gun in Western Film," Fran Pheasant-Kelly judges the Western's representation of the gun to be fetishtic and the gun to be a symbol of male power and homoerotic relationships that is limited by what can be put up on screen. Then in "Rifles and Things in *Winchester '73*," Katherine A. Johnson points out that the gun in the West is not always gender-coded, arguing that Lin McAdam's rifle is a device drawn from filmic-it narrative. Johnson finds in *Winchester '73* (1950) a scathing Cold War critique of America's obsession with the new atomic bomb.

A central marker of frontier masculinity, alcohol figures prominently in most Westerns, but Christopher Minz's "The Cowboy Brew: Coffee and Conflict in the Westerns of Budd Boetticher, Jr." investigates what happens when the Western hero drinks coffee. Minz reveals that the act of drinking coffee in Boetticher's films is a melodramatic means of signaling and bridging conflict, both internal and external—as well as a way to create domestic space in a genre long seen to be inimical to the feminine. Coffee in Boetticher's films, Minz argues, plays with and disrupts the viewer's understanding of etiquette and domestic protocol—especially in *Seven Men from Now* (1956). The hotel is also known for its connotations of domesticity in the Western. In "Cowboy Accommodations: Plotting the Hotel in Western Film and Television," Monica Montelongo Flores views the hotel as a marker of domesticity, capitalism, criminality, sexuality, civilization, and the progress associated with America's westward expansion. Flores argues the hotel, coded as a gate keeping authority in 1969 and then as a site for discussions of race and sexuality, has helped create more complex narratives, images, and associations in the Western's landscape.

Binary presentations of America are found in many Westerns. Accordingly, Robert E. Meyer's "When Worlds Collide: Town and Country, Mise-en-Scène in *Have Gun, Will Travel*" carefully investigates the visual representations of the two worlds that the inveterate hotel-dweller Paladin (Richard Boone) inhabits while arguing that changes in this character's milieu do not signal changes in his identity and rugged masculinity. In other Westerns, however, the relationship between Man and Nature is presented differently. Helen M. Lewis' "Executioner, Judge and Priest: The Desert Sublime in Westerns" finds that milieu *is* all-important because of the sublime implications of the desert landscapes that inform and develop character in the West. According to Lewis, it is the presence of the sublime in Monte Hellman's *The Shooting* (1966), King Vidor's *Duel in the Sun* (1946), John Ford's *Three Godfathers* (1948), and Ray Milland's *A Man Alone* (1955) that makes these films American morality plays.

Although trains, planes, and automobiles are usually considered novelty items in the Western, Martin Holtz's "Machines in the Garden: Technology and the Western in the 1960s and 1970s" argues that the machine is an important element of Western iconography. The Western's complex relationship with industrial America, Holtz concludes, is much more than simple escapism, because the genre has always contained traces of the industrialism that it defines itself against. Then, re-examining genre conventions as the Western moves into the 1960s, Gilles Chamerois' "'Dynamite blows two ways': Dynamite in Western Films" reads this explosive as an apt metaphor for 1960s cinema's breaking away from traditional codes and the destruction of the Western frontier.

In the 1960s, Westerns underwent a number of modifications. Alexander Davis' "Trippy Pictures: Iconicizing the American Acid Westerns" traces good and bad "trips" which renegotiated Americans' rapidly changing relationship with their national identity via representations of American Indians or "Others" and the figure of the cowboy. Then, in the 1990s, the classic Western returned, remade for children. Ashley Sufflé Robinson's "'Reach for the sky': Western Iconography, the American Frontier and the Story of Pixar in *Toy Story*" determines that the true appeal of John Lasseter's film comes from its engagement with the Old West. Robinson concludes that Pixar's deliberate use of tropes from the nineteenth-century American frontier and Western films not only revitalized the Western but also reconnected contemporary America with one of its foundational myths and its archetypical identity.

Aptly, two discussions of Western necrology conclude this collection. Alexander Howe's "Burying the Past: Cemeteries, Burials and Remembrance in the Western" examines the Western's obsession with the cemetery, an extremely complicated trope that reminds its viewers of the price of Manifest Destiny, offers personal and communal loss as markers of masculinity, provides its revenge narratives with sites of contemplation and closure, and extends graveyards as expressions of missed opportunity, gender and self-sufficiency, race and exclusion, and the passage of time. Then, in "The Four Archetypes of the Three Burials (of Melquiades Estrada)," Wickham Clayton maps the iconographic tensions created by the temporal displacement of the classic Western into the present day.

In the present day, the resurrected Western continues to capture the American public's imagination—most recently, HBO's *Westworld* (2016), a smash hit, has proven to be a bigger draw with audiences than *The Walking Dead* (2010–) or *Game of Thrones* (2011–)—averaging over 11.7 million viewers to date (Alexander). Charting moments in the complicated (and often conflicted) self-sustaining trajectory of the Western, *A Fistful of Icons* does not attempt or claim to be a comprehensive or exhaustive work about Western iconography. The ideas and concepts contained in its commentaries, offered by a wide range of contributors in a variety of approaches on selected topics, are not conclusions on which the reader is expected to rest but points of departure for futher study. We are looking forward to the critical conversations this book will generate and hope that more opportunities for further study in this field will continue as long as Western movies are made and enjoyed.

Work Cited

Alexander, Julia. November 15, 2016. "Think HBO May Have a Hit on Its Hands." At http://www.polygon.com/tv/2016/11/15/13640916/westworld-game-of-thrones-walking-dead-ratings.

Performing the Iconic West
Wild West Shows

Cynthia J. Miller

"It is safe to say that the Western movie would not have been the same without Buffalo Bill" (Carter 454). That observation, made by author Robert A. Carter, resonates with many film historians and scholars studying the West in popular culture. Images of "Buffalo Bill" Cody, particularly those bound up with his Wild West show, have influenced popular conceptions of the American West for well over a hundred years. Cody's Wild West shows, along with all those that followed—headed by colorful figures of the day such as Buck Taylor, the Miller Brothers, Dr. W.F. Carver, Tim McCoy, and even women like the Kemp Sisters—crafted a spectacular West, one that was full of sights and sounds and animated by bold, vibrant characters that embodied the spirit of the frontier. From Indian wars to trick shooting, Wild West shows offered a glimpse of the American West that was a far cry from the hardships, disease, and disappointments experienced by most who were drawn to the new territories, yet the notions that these shows conveyed to their audiences almost immediately became part of the stories that America told about itself, on the pages of both novels and history, in theatrical performances, and perhaps most significantly, on screen.

In many ways, the Wild West show may be considered a "meta icon"—not only an icon of the West in its own right, but also encompassing an array of Western icons and characters in its many performances and tableaus. Mutually reinforcing, the cowboys, Indians, dance hall girls, and sharpshooters all infuse the shows in which they are featured with an air of authenticity, while the shows, in turn, bestow an air of romance and adventure on the characters, artifacts, and scenes they present. Not only speaking to those intimately familiar with the American West, images of Wild West shows—taken either as a whole or in part—are effective across genres and cultures, as

Memorabilia from Buffalo Bill's Wild West Show.

metonyms for the freedom, bravery, and adventure of a West that never really was. This essay, then, will examine Wild West shows and the personalities drawn together on their programs as significant and complex icons of both the fantasy and reality of the American West that have continued—and in many ways, increased—in relevance into the present day through their appearance on screen, as well as the ways in which these shows serve to reinforce many other Western icons through their spectacular visual displays and breathtaking performances.

Thinking About the Wild West

> Imagine wild buffalo, Indians and cowboys together in an arena right before your eyes! With stagecoach attacks, gunfight showdowns, shooting demonstrations, horse-riding displays ... this will be a night to remember!
> —McNenly 3

Wild West shows were part of the traveling show tradition in the three decades leading up to the twentieth century, and for several decades thereafter. Don B. Russell's "Checklist of Wild West Shows" indicates that, from 1883 to 1940, there were approximately 116 of these shows in existence, employing thousands of performers, many of whose names are still familiar today (Russell 121–127). Their iconic power to instill fascination and wonder continues to the present day, in fact, in productions such as the Great American Wild West Show from Branson, Montana; Montie Montana, Jr.'s Wild West Show from Springville, California[1]; the Great Wild West Revue in Greenbush, Wisconsin, and many others—including Disneyland Paris.

Promising "action, history, and thrills," these shows offered audiences an idealized depiction of the American West, and with it, a celebration of courage, independence, patriotism, the domination of nature, violence, and masculinity. Showcasing the exotic and dangerous, Wild West shows featured displays of skill, such as trick riding, roping, and fancy shooting; competitions, such as rodeo events and races; theatrical reenactments of historical moments and battles, such as Custer's Last Stand; along with celebrated and exotic figures, such as well-known Western personalities, Indian chiefs, and costumed performers from all over the world. These shows brought the danger of the West back to the East—and beyond—in a carnivalesque setting, framing them as both entertainment and education, at once neutralizing and mythologizing the perils and glories of the frontier for popular consumption. They provided women with otherwise unavailable outlets for displays of skill traditionally thought of as masculine, such as riding, roping, and shooting, as well as allowing female audience members the opportunity to see these performers departing from socially accepted behaviors.

Like most traveling shows of the era—medicine shows and circuses, in particular—Wild West shows were conceived and run by flamboyant figures with a talent for promotion and the creation of spectacle. These larger-than-life personalities, such as Pawnee Bill, Colonel Jack, Indian Bill, and of course, Buffalo Bill, were iconic of the American pioneering spirit of the late nineteenth century that was so critical to the national identity. Surrounded by cowboys, Indians, lawmen, and animals, they simultaneously celebrated and exploited Native American culture, wildlife, and the frontier environment. When Pawnee Bill's Wild West hit the road in the spring of 1888, the show boasted, in addition to its headliners—which, for a few months, included Annie Oakley—"Indians from five different tribes, 165 people, 165 animals, and Pawnee Bill, himself" (Farnum 8). Arriving by train, these elaborate traveling shows featured dozens of ornate wagons, steam calliopes, and an entourage of Mexican, Russian, Arab, and Asian riders, tumblers, and acrobats.

The original, and best-known, of the Wild West shows was, of course, founded by "Buffalo Bill" Cody, first in the 1870s, as the Buffalo Bill Combination, and then reformed in 1883, as Buffalo Bill's Wild West Show. It was the "gold standard" of Western traveling shows, as the *Denver Post* lauded: "There never was anything like Buffalo Bill's Wild West show before; there will never be anything like it again" (*Denver Post*, 1913). Cody sought, through his Wild West shows, to produce a recreation of border life on a scale grander than the walls of a theater could ever accommodate. Billed as "America's National Entertainment" (Cody xvi), the show, which included a cast of hundreds, toured the United States, England, and Europe for 20 years, including a landmark performance nearby the 1893 Chicago World's Fair. Its passage required three railway trains of 75 cars each.

Authenticity was the lifeblood of the Wild West shows such as Cody's, whether presenting feats of extreme skills, such as sharpshooting, roping, or trick riding, or portraying events and occurrences, such as buffalo hunts, Indian raids, or cattle round-ups. A key element in making audiences feel as though they had witnessed "the real thing," was the casting of as many Indians as possible in the shows' performances. Great chiefs, whose names, thanks to the press, were household words were, as theatrical managers would say, "good box office." Sitting Bull participated in Buffalo Bill's show for four months in 1885, appearing for a brief horseback ride through the arena; Geronimo similarly lent his notoriety to Pawnee Bill's show in 1906. They, along with others such as Black Elk and Standing Bear, were showcased as dramatic foils—exhibited as curiosities, and advertised with colorful banners resembling those found in carnival sideshows.

Alongside this emphasis on authenticity, however, entrepreneurs of Wild West extravaganzas frequently thrived on the fascination created by ambiguous pasts in the "real" Old West, and in this, no better example exists than Cody.[2] Some called into question Buffalo Bill's heroic history and the realism of his shows, such as a reporter for the *Detroit Free Press* who quipped, "Buffalo Bill has at last found a manager willing to take him to England, but what the public will next want to know is whether he is to be left there or not" (Cody xvi). Others, however, such as this Londoner visiting New York, reported that the Wild West show he attended was "an entertainment in which the whole of the most interesting episodes of life on the extreme frontier of civilization in America are represented with the most graphic vividness and scrupulous detail ... no one can exaggerate the extreme excitement and 'go' of the whole performance" (Burke 214–215).

As historian Louis S. Warren observes, these contemporary arguments about the truthfulness or fabrication of Buffalo Bill's heroics were commonplace and "mirrored much wider debates about the meaning of the Far West and the trustworthiness of the organs of popular culture through which most Americans learned about it: newspapers, advertising, literature, painting, and theater." Warren explains that Cody, a showman on par with P.T. Barnum, mingled his real-life adventures with "colorful fictions," creating for himself an image that was the embodiment of public fantasy—indistinguishable from the very myths created by his Wild West shows (Warren 2015). And while Cody, like his fellow showmen, had his detractors, others were steadfast in their faith in the man behind the spectacle:

> To see him in his trimmins, he can't hardly look the same,
> With laundered shirt and diamonds, as if "he run a game."
> He didn't wear biled linen then, or flash up diamond rings;
> The royalties he dreamed of then were only pasteboard kings;
> But those who sat behind the queens were apt to get their fill,
> In the days when Cody was a scout and all the men knew Bill [Burke 190].

Buffalo Bill's "trimmins"—along with the show's headliners and cast, horses and buffalo, wagons and tents, weapons and banners—became such potent icons of the Wild West that for many, particularly audiences in Eastern cities and across the Atlantic, they *were* the American West. And as the Wild West, along with the men and women who became synonymous with it, made its way into film, that legacy would persist and deepen.

The Wild West on Film

While the commemorative and promotional power of art was used to its full advantage in the traveling show tradition, still images—whether painted or photographed—lacked the power of moving pictures for conveying the vibrancy of Wild West performances. The larger-than-life spectacle of Wild West shows was a perfect fit for cinematic adaptation—film's potential for both recording staged history and self-promotion was immediately recognized by Cody—and in the fall of 1894, Buffalo Bill and members of his Wild West show appeared in more than a dozen films produced by Thomas Edison in his kinetoscope studio, known as the "Black Maria" due to its resemblance to a police patrol wagon; these included *Buffalo Bill* (1894), *Sioux Ghost Dance* (1894), *Annie Oakley* (1894), and *Bucking Bronco* (1894) (Mathews et al 27). Each of these precursors to the Western film, as it came to be known, reinforced the iconic status of the "wild" West and its cast of characters, as they performed idealized versions of themselves.

Edison's first encounter with Cody was five years earlier, at the Exposition Universelle, outside Paris, in 1889. The program announced that the Wild West Show was "More than an exciting and realistic entertainment for public amusement, our object is to PICTURE TO THE EYE, by the aid of historical characters and living animals, a series of animated scenes and episodes which had their existence, in fact, in the wonderful pioneer and frontier life of the Wild West of America" (Baldwin 206).

When the pair finally met at dinner that evening, Edison was struck with the full force of the showman's spectacle as Cody entered the room, "glittering in his well-known costume of white and gold, topped by his white ten-gallon hat, which he removed with a sweep that comprehended the whole audience" (Tate 238). The two met again four years later, in Chicago, during the World's Columbian Exposition—an encounter that, as historian Sandra Sagala points out, was in perfect synergy with Frederick Jackson Turner's presentation of his "frontier thesis" in the city during the same period.[3] "The historian and the showman," she notes, both shined a spotlight on the significance of the frontier in American history and the American character (Sagala 11). As the scholar declares the end of an era and questions what will become of the American character in the years that follow, the frontiersman-turned-promoter shines a spotlight on reenactment, remembrance, and commemoration. Wild West shows, such as Cody's, would be the only way to experience the now-closed frontier.

Edison and Cody went on to partner for their series of one-minute nickelodeon films, but the Wild West became increasingly of interest to other early filmmakers, as well, and many honed their craft, and their equipment innovations, on Cody's Wild West show, eager to take advantage of its iconic appeal: the Lumiére Brothers produced *La Cirque Buffalo Bill: Peaux Rouges* (*The Circus of Buffalo Bill: Redskins*); James White (of the kinetoscope company) and William Heise filmed *Buffalo Bill and Escort*; Frederick Armitage, Sigmund Lubin, and William Selig all shot footage of their own, for Biograph, Selig Polyscope, and other motion picture production companies.[4]

As the fledgling medium developed, Cody (like many theatrical entrepreneurs and performers in vaudeville and burlesque) lamented that motion pictures were putting live performances out of business. The cost, convenience, and variety of offerings in the new medium caused an explosion in moviegoing across the country, and Western films were headed down the trail toward supplanting Wild West shows as canonizers of Western icons. An additional complication was new competition by a different sort of Wild West production, the Miller Brothers 101 Show, which emphasized more sophisticated ranch skills—roping and trick riding—over rough and tumble frontier life and its grisly violence.

In the face of these multiple threats to his livelihood, wisdom suggested that Cody align himself with the new cinematic medium, and in 1910–1912, the first Western biopic, *The Life of Buffalo Bill*, was produced by the team of Pliney Craft and William Powers (as the Buffalo Bill and Pawnee Bill Film Company), in an attempt to bring the stories of the man and the myth together on one screen. While fraught with discord and legal battles, the film's commercial success highlighted the power of Buffalo Bill as a Western icon in the newly emerging star system.

By 1913, Buffalo Bill's Wild West was bankrupt and being sold at auction, and what may be considered the Golden Age of the Wild West Show had passed; but at age 67, Cody, now experienced with motion picture performing and production, embarked on one final venture to record and promote the icons and events of the historic West (and himself) in *The Indian Wars* (1913), making full use of the stature he had achieved in America's culture of the West during the course of his career as a Wild West showman. Cody envisioned his legacy, however, to be one of authenticity and education, rather than the manufactured spectacle that had made him a household name. He would depict three great battles of the Indian wars: Summit Springs, Warbonnet Creek, and Wounded Knee, with himself as the star, seizing the opportunity to not only set the record straight about the battles, but once again, highlight his daring deeds.

Audiences, however, were far less fascinated by the reality of the frontier than they were by its myths. In spite of calls for "accuracy in Indian subjects" by *Motion Picture World*, which emphasized the value of "education on such subjects" (Sagala 132), box office draw for *The Indian Wars* was not the landslide Cody or his financiers had hoped. As one exhibitor complained, his patrons wanted something "not too deep for them" and did not consider documentaries to be entertaining (Sagala 132). As Sagala notes, while Cody intended *The Indian Wars* to be instructive, many filmgoers viewed its history with intrinsic disinterest (132). For many, there was truth to film historian Kevin Brownlow's observation that "no one goes to a Western for a history lesson" (Brownlow 223). It would not be long, however, before Buffalo Bill—

and Wild West shows, in general—were the stuff of both history and Westerns. "Stampedes" and rodeos had arisen from the Wild West show's exhibition of cowboy skills[5] and would persist to the present day as "live" Western entertainment, while film would reproduce and extend Western spectacle for the masses. But before film took over as the purveyor of Western imagery, millions of people experienced the "reality" of the frontier at various Wild West shows. As S. Matthew DeSpain illustrates, the Wild West shows "moved Western life from the realm of history into mythology and popular culture and shaped ideas and images of America's frontier past that persist today" ("Wild West Shows").

Real to Reel

As film took over the role of chronicling the lives and times of the Wild West, showmen like Buffalo Bill and their productions provided natural and ready subjects, as Cody's early films had illustrated. In some instances, the Wild West show provides a colorful, nostalgic backdrop for genre stories. In the Canadian television crime drama series *Murdoch Mysteries*, for example, in the episode "Mild, Mild West" (2009) a traveling Wild West show, featuring Buffalo Bill and Annie Oakley, becomes the setting for a murder that Detective Murdoch and his team must solve. In others, such as in the feature film *Hidalgo* (2004), based on the legend of Western performer and distance rider Frank Hopkins, the spirit of the Wild West show—the lifeways of its performers, the mythic proportions of its claims, and its fervent promotion of a vanishing way of life—is critical to the atmosphere of the action that follows.

Annie Oakley, Sitting Bull, "Wild Bill" Hickok, and others lent their characters to an array of motion pictures for decades to come, such as *Annie Get Your Gun* (1950) and *Wild Bill* (1995), and to television programming as diverse as *Doctor Who*, *Voyagers!*, and *Bones*. A wide range of adaptations of these character archetypes can also be found on screen, from Melody Patterson's skilled and savvy Wrangler Jane in the television series *F Troop* (1965–1967) to Owen Wilson's whimsical character Jedediah Smith in the *Night at the Museum* trilogy (2006, 2009, 2014).

As Sandra Sagala notes, after his death in 1917, Western filmmakers continued to particularly capitalize on Cody's glamorous, larger-than-life persona—both as a showman and an authentic frontiersman—in their representations of the frontier (151–162). From *The Last Frontier* (1926) to *Cody of the Pony Express* (1950), Cody's iconic status was invoked again and again in tales of the West, his later Wild West fame drawing new interest in even the earliest days of his frontier career. Cody's stature as a Western personality—and his transformation from frontiersman to showman—could not be more apparent than in the opening narration for the 1944 Twentieth Century–Fox production *Buffalo Bill*, which related: "In 1877, a young man rode of out the West and overnight his name became a household word ... Buffalo Bill" (Twentieth Century–Fox).

The Wild West show's iconic power came full circle when, in 1940, cowboy crooner Roy Rogers, whose own Western persona had been shaped, in part, by the legacy of Cody's glittering Wild West stage image, played Cody in *Young Buffalo Bill*. Not surprisingly, the Wild West show has been credited by some as the origin of the cowboy hero archetype—the most recognized icon of the West—noting that Cody and the other Wild West showmen made the cowboy a saleable figure, eventually surpassing Native Americans and scouts as main attractions, and setting the stage for the cowboy heroes of the Silver Screen (Despain). Several of the Wild West show cowboys, such as Tom Mix and Bill Pickett, learned much of their cowboy stagecraft while performing with the shows, and carried those performance skills and polished sagebrush images with them into motion pictures as some of film's earliest Western stars. Thus it might well be said that all of the traditional cinematic cowboy heroes that followed owed a debt to Wild West shows for their iconic status. Rogers—who, along with Gene Autry was part of the succeeding generation of popular B Western cowboys—became one of the most beloved motion picture cowboys and was, like Cody, a consummate showman, entrepreneur, and artful purveyor of the cowboy hero persona.

In more recent years, Cody and the Wild West have been the subjects of more complicated revisionist narratives, calling into question the images constructed around both. In 1974, the now-cult film *This Is the West That Was* satirized Cody as an inept frontier figure, whose envy of Wild Bill Hickok's prowess as a gunfighter leads to a showdown on the streets of Deadwood. Moving beyond the comedic, Robert Altman's caustic *Buffalo Bill and the Indians* (1976) juxtaposed the showman's public image—"brave, considerate, and handsome"—with an unflattering behind-the-scenes image of an aging man who was bitter, prejudiced, drunk, and unfaithful (Sagala 162). In this, both are taking aim at not only the showman himself and the world of the Wild West show, but at something larger—the myths of national history and identity that both created, embodied, and engrained in the popular imagination—the notion that the winning of the West was glorious, valiant, and honorable, something to be celebrated. In a similar fashion, Clint Eastwood's *Bronco Billy* (1980) reveals the sad realities of Wild West show life for a down-and-out showman and his cast, none of whom are real cowboys. Schemes, scams, drunkenness and desperation abound as Bronco Billy tries to keep his show on the road. Yet even these challenges suggest the large-scale cultural work that not only Cody and his fellow showmen, but Wild West spectacle and all those involved have performed, not only in their own time, but over half a century later.

In the decades that have passed since these interrogations of the foundational myths of the Wild West show, the frontier spectacles, as well as the icons and archetypes they gathered together, have continued to serve as vehicles for messages of identity, bravery, freedom, artistry, and wonder in film and television narratives, often as an antidote to settings where those elements are at risk. From the comic to the fantastic, stylized cowboys, spectacular feats of frontier daring, and Barnum-esque promotion emerge in both traditional and unexpected places.

The Wild West: Icon and Meta-Icon

Even before its inception as live performance in Buffalo Bill's Combination, the urge (or multiple urges) that brought Wild West shows into being—to capture, create, collect, and display exotic icons of the frontier—was visible. Artist George Catlin (1796–1872) spent eight years visiting well over 50 Native American tribes. These forays into the frontier resulted in some 500 paintings and "a substantial collection" of artifacts, which the artist assembled into a panoramic touring Indian Gallery and lecture, to educate the public on Indian life in the Wild West.[6] As an outgrowth of efforts such as this, the Wild West show may be seen as having a complex, multi-layered role in the construction, representation, commemoration, and understanding of the frontier and the actions, events, and characters that animated it. It may be seen simultaneously as an icon, a constellation of icons, and also a maker of icons.

Frontier imagery was the stock-in-trade for these outdoor spectacles of Western pageantry. Six-shooters, bows and arrows, boots and spurs, saddles, and other practical artifacts already strongly identified with frontier life were in constant view in Wild West shows, in performances and tableaus of Western life, and were all marshaled together as part of the greater whole. Their appearance, however, like that of the iconic wagon, was heightened to a glamorous sheen—brighter, more colorful, and more ornate—and transformed into breathtaking spectacle. In a similar fashion, these frontier pageants mobilized the star power of already-famous icons of the West: scouts like Buffalo Bill and Pawnee Bill, Western actors like Tim McCoy and Ken Maynard, Indian chiefs such as Sitting Bull and Geronimo, to draw crowds eager to see these already established icons. Under the Wild West shows' tents and within their arenas, casts of thousands of unknown cowboys and Indians *became* archetypes of exotic frontier life for enthusiastic audiences, and in some cases, new icons were made, such as sharpshooter Annie Oakley and cowboy heroes William Levi "Buck" Taylor, Bill Pickett, and Tom Mix.

In keeping with Cody's drive for "authenticity," Wild West shows, much like their urban counterparts, dime museums, clung to a premise of educating the general public about the exotic and unfamiliar, and as a result, tutored audiences on "reading" the West and provided what may be thought of as a sort of "Western literacy" for those who would never otherwise experience frontier life. The authoritative voice of the showman mediated popular knowledge of, and reactions to, not only the nature of life on the Great Plains, but the American Character, as it was shaped by the frontier, Manifest Destiny, and the events that influenced control of the Western territories, such as the Indian Wars. This sort of historical "curation" not only instructed audiences about the past, but also, how to *think* about the past—in simple binary oppositions that have long been associated with Western narratives prior to the revisionist era: right/wrong, victim/aggressor, hero/villain, winners/losers—removing the messy complexities of human existence.

Thus, in their roles as chronicles and commemorations of a vanishing way of life, these productions themselves became artifacts of a bygone era, and increasingly, as the decades passed, Western icons themselves. The image of the Wild West arena, the trick riders and sharpshooters, the recreated raids and battles, and the figure of the showman, himself, all came to serve as shorthand for the constellation of ideas, values, and adventures inherent in a West that never was.

In many ways, this is the multilayered legacy of the Wild West show in contemporary film and television—its ability to speak a particular truth about American views of the West at the century, even if that truth is somewhat hidden beneath gold plating, or in the wings, just off-stage. As many film historians have argued, the historical value of images such as those of the Wild West show and its key figures does not rest in the accuracy of detail, but in their ability to capture the essence of the era—the adventure, the arrogance, the hopefulness, the struggles.

Audiences' shared cultural understandings of late nineteenth and early twentieth century traveling frontier shows are engaged not only by large-scale representations of Wild West shows on screen, but also by countless combinations of the icons and archetypes they encompassed. The bucking bronco was, perhaps, the first iconic component of Wild West shows to make the transition to a key role on the Silver Screen, initially as the subject of one of Edison's kinetoscope shorts, and then in countless Western sagas. The bucking bronco's association with both Cody's style of frontier pageantry and the Millers' ranch-focused shows made it a particularly apt symbol to transition to the screen, but others rapidly followed suit.

The "predictable" connections to the Wild West shows are, of course, in Westerns or Western-influenced narratives where direct representations of frontier pageantry occur, such as *Bronco Billy* or *Hidalgo*; or even history-focused programming, such as *Time Squad* episodes "Keepin' It Real with Sitting Bull" and "Where the Buffalo Bill Roams,"[7] in which a trio of hapless "time cops" travel back in time to correct the course of history. But the more telling are those that arise in other genres or settings, such as *Fantasy Island*'s "The Last Cowboy,"[8] in which a middle-aged executive (Stuart Whitman) who wishes to experience the "real" Wild West arrives on the island in bedazzled frontier finery with fantasies of Wild West heroics, but finds himself on a dusty, failing farm as a hired hand, in well-worn cowhand's clothes. Here we see the impact of Wild West show glamour and spectacle, in taken-for-granted notions of the "gentleman cowboy hero" that have persisted for generations—a thread beginning in live Western performance and continuing through films of the Golden Age of the B Western in the 1930s and post-World War II "oaters," as well as narratives of the Western revival—life attempting to mimic art.

Conclusion

Taken together, these examples begin to illustrate the complexities of Wild West shows in the iconic construction of the West. At their inception, they drew on existing icons, archetypes, historical events, and other performance genres for their lifeblood. Buffalo Bill Cody was already part of the popular imagination thanks to Ned Buntline's dime novels; battles such as Wounded Knee and Little Bighorn were legendary moments in the history of the Indian Wars; Phineas Taylor Barnum and Benjamin Franklin Keith had already demonstrated the drawing power of variety and spectacle, in both circus and vaudeville; and the national focus on westward expansion had already bestowed symbolic meaning on an array of Western artifacts like six-shooters, buckboards, teepees, boots and spurs, bucking broncos, and so much more. The cultural "magic" of the Wild West show, however, was its showmen's ability—owed largely to Cody—to draw these together into a cohesive narrative pageant of national identity, and then magnify the whole to mythic proportions, becoming iconic, itself, in the process.

A century later, the Wild West show and the cast of characters associated with it are seldom in the forefront of cultural consciousness, but they—and the values, ideals, and identities that they represent—are still called upon in film and television for their evocative power. The stories they convey, whether through fully developed narratives or simply their visual presence, speak to the ebb and flow of our continuing relationship with the lore of the West. While traditional Western prowess and spectacle continues to fascinate, images of the "show cowboy" in films such as *Bronco Billy*, Robert Redford's *The Electric Horseman* (1979), and even music videos like Glen Campbell's

"Rhinestone Cowboy" (1975) often present troubling counterpoints, as they highlight the façade of staged Western glamour.

But whether serving as an anachronistic backdrop that emphasizes the performative nature of the Wild West (much like the traveling circus or tent show); as a romantic homage to the turn-of-the-century, celebrating frontier values and simplicity; or as cultural critique of westward expansion, Manifest Destiny, and military-political injustices of race, class, and gender, the images, artifacts, events, and characters associated with the Wild West show resonate immediately and broadly across genres and generations. The parades, banners, showmen, displays of daring, historical recreations, and ethnographic entertainment all stand in much simpler relationship with our era than they perhaps did with their own.

Notes

1. Montana's final show was in 2009. Eulogized as "the last of the cowboy showmen," Montie Montana, Jr., died in 2013.
2. Cody was already something of a legend, thanks to the dime novels of Ned Buntline.
3. Turner's presentation was made at the meeting of the American Historical Association in downtown Chicago. See Sandra K. Sagala, *Buffalo Bill on the Silver Screen: The Films of William F. Cody* (Norman: University of Oklahoma Press, 2013), 11. See also Louis S. Warren, *Buffalo Bill's America*, 431.
4. Some of this footage, such as Lubin's and White and Heise's, is available for viewing at the Library of Congress.
5. In the 1940s, in fact, cowboy crooner Gene Autry would head his own Western stampede.
6. For more on Catlin and his Indian Gallery, see www.georgecatlin.org.
7. October 19, 2001; March 1, 2002
8. Season 5, Episode 4, 1981.

Filmography

Annie Get Your Gun. Dir. George Sidney, Busby Berkeley. Metro-Goldwyn-Mayer Studios, 1950.
Annie Oakley. Dir. William K.L Dickson (uncredited). Edison Manufacturing Company, 1894.
Bronco Billy. Dir. Clint Eastwood. Warner Bros., 2000.
Bucking Bronco. Dirs. William K.L. Dickson and William Heise. Edison Manufacturing Company, 1894.
Buffalo Bill. Dir. William K.L. Dickson. Edison Manufacturing Company, 1894.
Buffalo Bill. Dir. William A. Wellman. Twentieth Century–Fox, 1944.
Buffalo Bill and Escort. Dir. James H. White and William Heise. Edison Manufacturing Company, 1894.
Buffalo Bill and the Indians. Dir. Robert Altman. Dino DeLaurentiis Company, Lions Gate Films, 1976.
La Cirque Buffalo Bill: Peaux Rouges (*The Circus of Buffalo Bill: Redskins*). Dir. Lumiére Brothers, 1896–1897.
Cody of the Pony Express. Dir. Spencer Gordon Bennet. Columbia Pictures Corporation, 1950.
The Electric Horseman. Dir. Sydney Pollack. Wildwood Enterprises, 1979.
F Troop. Richard M. Bluel, creator. Warner Bros Television, 1965–1967.
Hidalgo. Dir. Joe Johnston. Touchstone Pictures, 2004.

22 A Fistful of Icons

The Indian Wars. Dirs. Vernon Day and Theodore Wharton. Col. Wm. F. Cody Historical Picture Company, 1913.
"Keepin' It Real with Sitting Bull," *Time Squad* (TV Series 2001–2003). Dir. David Wasson. Cartoon Network Studios, October 19, 2001.
"The Last Cowboy," *Fantasy Island* (TV Series 1977–1984). Dir. Don Chaffey. Columbia Pictures Television, 31 October 1981.
The Last Frontier. Dir. George B. Seitz. Metropolitan Pictures Corporation of California, 1926.
The Life of Buffalo Bill. Dir. Paul Panzer. Buffalo Bill and Pawnee Bill Film Company, 1912.
"Mild, Mild West," *Murdoch Mysteries* (TV Series, Season 1, 2009). Dir. Paul Fox. Bell Broadcast and New Media Fund, 2009.
Night at the Museum trilogy (2006, 2009, 2014). Dir. Shawn Levy. Twentieth Century–Fox, 2014.
Sioux Ghost Dance. Dirs. William K.L. Dickson and William Heise. Edison Manufacturing Company, 1894.
This Is the West That Was. Dir. Fielder Cook. Public Art Films, 1974.
"Where the Buffalo Bill Roams," *Time Squad* (TV Series 2001–2003). Dir. David Wasson. Cartoon Network Studios, March 1, 2002.
Wild Bill. Dir. Walter Hill. United Artists, 1995.
Young Buffalo Bill. Dir. Joseph Kane. Republic Pictures, 1940.

Works Cited

Baldwin, Neil. *Edison: Inventing the Century*. New York: Hyperion, 1995.
Brownlow, Kevin. *The War, the West, and the Wilderness*. New York: Alfred A. Knopf, 1979.
Burke, John M. *Buffalo Bill from Prairie to Palace*. Lincoln: University of Nebraska Press, 2012.
Carter, Robert A. *Buffalo Bill Cody: The Man Behind the Legend*. New York: John Wiley and Sons, 2000.
Cody, William F. *The Wild West in England*. Lincoln: University of Nebraska Press, 2012.
Denver Post, July 13, 1913.
DeSpain, S. Matthew. "Wild West Shows" in *Encyclopedia of the Great Plains*, David J. Wishart, ed. http://plainshumanities.unl.edu/encyclopedia/doc/egp.ii.061.
Farnum, Allen L. *Pawnee Bill's Historic Wild West*. Westchester, PA: Schiffer Publishing, Ltd., 1992.
Mathews, Nancy Mowil, et al. *Moving Pictures: American Art and Early Film, 1880–1910*, Volume 1. Manchester, VT: Hudson Hills, 2005.
McNenly, Linda Scarangella. *Native Performers in Wild West Shows: From Buffalo Bill to Euro Disney*. Norman: University of Oklahoma Press, 2012.
Russell, Don B. *Wild West: A History of Wild West Shows*. Austin: University of Texas Press, 1970.
Sagala, Sandra K. *Buffalo Bill on the Silver Screen: The Films of William F. Cody*. Norman: University of Oklahoma Press, 2013.
Tate, Alfred O. *Edison's Open Door: The Life Story of Thomas A. Edison, a Great Individualist*. New York: E.P. Dutton, 1938.
Warren, Louis S. *Buffalo Bill's America*. New York: Knopf, 2005.

Buckskin Fringe and Cavalier Culture in the Hollywood Western

SUE MATHESON

In *Pony Express* (1953), Buffalo Bill Cody (Charlton Heston) is dressed in buckskin, befringed from his shoulders to his toes. Heston's shoulder blades, pectorals, and the inside seams of the arms of his jacket drip four-inch strands of leather. In this truly terrible movie, frontier fringe makes Charlton Heston (of all actors) the sort of hero that women simply can't resist—awarding him a heroic masculinity—at once paradoxically primitive and sophisticated—which enables him to transcend the association of buckskin with the backwardness of the backwoods. In part, the origin of the frontiersman's garments in the dynamic, westward movement of the changing American frontier accounts for Heston's charismatic machismo. James Fenimore Cooper's Natty Bumpo's buckskins align him with Native Americans in the popular imagination and identify him as a natural gentleman, a knight-errant in the wilderness. Later, as the American frontier pushed westward, the figure of frontiersman altered, adapted to new surroundings, and became associated with the life style and horse culture of the Great Plains. Throughout *Pony Express*, Heston's Buffalo Bill is very much a horseman, a figure associated with the tall grass prairie of the American West, not its wooded Wilderness. Blending popular notions about the noble savage and Cavalier culture, the thin strips of leather that decorate the jacket of the mounted frontiersman on the Plains carry cultural coding that is at once complicated and compelling. Combining and reconciling the martial attributes of two figures who at first appear incompatible—the cavalryman and the Indian—frontier fringe is an important Hollywood icon of masculinity in the Western, whether it appears in films like George B. Seitz's 1936 production of *The Last*

24 A Fistful of Icons

Denny Russell (Jan Sterling, left) and Evelyn Hastings (Rhonda Fleming) find a buckskin-clad Buffalo Bill Cody (Charlton Heston) irresistible in *Pony Express* (Paramount, 1953).

of the Mohicans or Walt Disney's *Davey Crockett: King of the Wild Frontier* (1955).

On the large screen, buckskin jackets enhance the attractiveness of romantic male leads. Thirties heartthrob Henry Wilcoxon, for example, may have played the lead role of Marc Anthony in Cecile B. DeMille's *Cleopatra* (1934), but two years later in George B. Seitz's 1936 production of *The Last of the Mohicans*, as Major Duncan Heyward, he is unable to capture and hold the attention of the fort commander's daughter or the women in the audience when placed beside the buckskin-befringed colonial scout, Hawkeye (Randolph Scott). Because he is a British officer, Heyward is unable to win Alice's hand even though he later offers to be burnt alive at the stake in her place. Without fringe, he is not a woodsman and proves to be either helpless or a liability in the wilderness. Even when masquerading as a masculine primitive in Hawkeye's buckskins, Heyward is unable to attract Alice's attention and respect.

Natural leaders on the frontier, men in buckskin are alpha males who ensure the survival of others. Davey Crockett, in Walt Disney's *Davey Crockett: King of the Wild Frontier* (1955), like Hawkeye, is an effective leader in the wilderness. Like Hawkeye, he takes command of the situation in which the British army finds itself, telling Major Norton: "From here on we make no more noise'n we got to. No talkin', no stragglin', an' everybody keep close up." With Crockett the frontiersman in charge, natural law eclipses military regulations: as he points out to Jackson after a skirmish with Redstick, he and his neighbors "ain't quitting the war," they'll "be back directly" but before they spend a year hunting for the Indian chief, they have to "see if [their] families is still cared for." Crockett and his men they leave for home in spite of Norton's objections and best efforts to keep them in camp. And then they return when they think it fit to do so. In The *Last of the Mohicans*, agency also belongs to the frontiersmen, who, like Crockett, come and go as they please to ensure the safety of their families.

Throughout both these films, the frontiersman is portrayed as a rugged individualist whose fringe reveals a significant and martial complication of his character. Identifying and displaying the individual wearer's relationship with the natural world—that is the more elaborately trimmed the buckskin garment, the more primitive and therefore more noble the character of its wearer is—Hawkeye's and Crockett's leather trimmings also distinguish their wearers, announcing their martial status and their rank among their peers. The longer a frontiersman's fringe, the more prestigious his position in his community. As the generous length of their fringe suggests, Crockett and Hawkeye are high-ranking members of a buckskin army of volunteers who all dress in variants of leather outerwear, according to their means and preferences—producing an effect that is very much like that found among European officers of the seventeenth century who resisted standardization by designing their own uniforms. Emphasizing Hawkeye's and Crockett's distinctiveness and rugged individualism, costume designers Franc Smith and Norman Martien assign simplified, standardized uniforms to the frontiersmen's "allies"—thereby devaluing the British.

In *The Last of the Mohicans*, when Chingachook, Alice and Heyward (still dressed in Hawkeye's buckskins) encounter General Abercrombie's scouts and soldiers, Heyward, the most ornately decorated of the frontiersmen, becomes a man of consequence by organizing Hawkeye's rescue. He, the other frontiersmen, and the general's men join forces to free Hawkeye from the Hurons. Morally and ethically redeemed by his change of attire, Heyward leaves the artificiality and corruption of the colonial army's patronage system and enters the meritocracy of frontier society—having earned his fringe as *The Last of the Mohicans* ends, he is a reformed character, an Americanized "colonial" officer who argues effectively against military protocol and obtains Hawkeye a pardon for refusing to obey orders. Their differences reconciled, the noble savage (Chingachook), the "American" frontiersman, and Heyward the British officer march off to war together, natural aristocrats all.

Of course, the complicated, iconic nature of buckskin was not manufactured solely in Hollywood. Actual frontiersmen and Indian Scouts, like Texas Jack Omohundro, William F. Cody (Buffalo Bill), and Wild Bill Hickok all capitalized on popular nineteenth-century notions about men who wore buckskin and its fringe and made successful stage careers for themselves by appealing to the public's nostalgia for the vanishing frontier. Studio portraits show Omohundro, Cody, and George Custer striking heroic poses and reinventing themselves as rugged Plainsmen in their beautifully and extravagantly fringed tunics and jackets to further the public's perception of the innate nobility of the frontiersman, be he a buffalo hunter or an Indian Scout. Almost all their contemporaries, it seems, found the lifestyle of those of wearing buckskin in the Wild West attractive. Russian royalty, the Grand Duke Alexis, vacationing in America in 1872, acted out an atavistic fantasy, hunting buffalo on the Plains with Custer, Cody, and a band of Sioux Indians (provided by Phil Sheridan); in America and Europe, audiences flocked to see Buffalo Bill's Wild West shows; and the rich and famous vacationed at Cody's dude ranch in Colorado. Caught up in the general passion for primitivism, Theodore Roosevelt ordered from a local seamstress in the Dakota Badlands in 1884 buckskin clothing that he wore throughout his time spent in the Badlands and on hunts into the 1900s. For Roosevelt, buckskin was "the most picturesque and distinctively national dress ever worn in America. It was the dress in which Daniel Boone was clad when he first passed through the trackless forests of the Alleghanies and penetrated into the heart of Kentucky, to enjoy such hunting as no man of his race had ever had before; it was the dress worn by grim old Davy Crockett when he fell at the Alamo" (17).

Before Theodore Roosevelt dressed like a Plainsman, George Armstrong Custer and Buffalo Bill Cody also capitalized on the romance of buckskin, transforming and updating the frontiersman's leather hunting tunic into the horseman's leather jacket. The style and popularity of the buckskin jacket in the twentieth and the first part of the twenty-first centuries may be traced back to Custer's post-bellum modifications of his Civil War uniforms. Combining the martial and aristocratic traditions of the Old *and* the New Worlds to further his reputation as a brilliant Civil War cavalry commander, Custer's publicity photos as a "buckskin cavalier" on the American Plains borrow from the cavalier culture of the Southern States, in general, and the state of Virginia, in particular. Before the Civil War, cavalier culture in the Southern States and "the legend of the Virginia cavalier" embraced a whole range of attitudes and behavior patterns derived from the English gentry class' emphasis on status, hierarchy, privilege and the symbolic primacy of landownership. Aptly the Southern Cavalier dressed like his elegant and romantic English and European counterparts, wearing knee-length leather boots, tunics and plumed, broad-brimmed hats that were often cocked. During the Civil War, dashing officers on horseback personified the virtues of the Virginia cavalier and Southern chivalry. Renowned as an outstanding horseman and a gentleman, J.E.B. Stuart, for example, was considered to be an exemplary Southern cavalier: his patriotic example and self-sacrifice during the Civil War expressed many of the South's most important cultural values—among them, honor and chivalry, self-discipline, civic duty, martial skill, and horsemanship.

In the Union cavalry, George Custer painstakingly created his professional persona as Stuart's Yankee opposite. A Yankee Cavalier, he designed his own unconventional, gentrified uniforms, boasting shoulder straps, brass buttons, red neckerchiefs, and cocked, broad-brimmed sombreros. Lionized by the Third Division, many of whom complimented their commander by also wearing "braided jackets and red ties," Custer was considered the Union's "model of a light cavalry officer, quick in observation, clear in judgment, resolute and determined in execution ... [and] brave as a lion" (Utley 40). On the Western Plains after the Civil War, Custer continued to live out the North and the South's fascination with the cavalier found in the novels of Sir Walter Scott and Southern plantation literature, dressing in "a handsomely embroidered buckskin suit, with his red neck-tie" (Pratt 43), and hunting buffalo with a retinue of admiring followers, a group often likened to that of a cavalier court—a lifestyle which he had fostered while stationed after the Civil War in Elizabethtown, Kentucky, that was completed by a stable of thoroughbred horses and a large pack of hunting dogs. In *Tenting on the Plains: Or, General Custer in Kansas and Texas*, Elizabeth Custer includes a romantic illustration of a buckskin-clad Custer dripping leather fringe and communing with "his horse Vic, staghounds and deerhounds" (333), on the open prairie.[1]

In the press, Custer was identified as being at once a chivalrous gentleman, a natural aristocrat, and a masculine primitive. Noted for his panache on the battlefield and often sketched by battlefield artist Alfred Waud, Custer appeared on the cover of *Harper's Weekly* on March 19, 1864, and continued to be a darling of the press until the Civil War ended. For instance, he was noted for "another brilliant and successful dash" and his "indomitable energy and great daring" on April 20, 1865, in the *New York Times*. At Sailor's Creek, he "was in the front at all times directing, rallying and encouraging the officers and men," directing what the *Times* correspondent deemed "another brilliant affair" ("GRANT'S ARMY"). Waud continued to produce dramatic illustrations of Custer in action until his demise at the Little Bighorn. In "Custer's Last Fight," Waud depicts the light cavalry officer dressed in his buckskin jacket and directing the course of the battle. Edgar Samuel Paxson's "Custer's Last Battle on the Little Bighorn" is an equally romantic rendition of Custer's defeat—and again, Custer appears dressed buckskin. Tellingly, when Paxson copyrighted this picture in 1900, he may have been thinking of Waud's work, for he, like Waud, named his rendition of the Battle of Little Bighorn "Custer's Last Fight." Waud's depiction of Custer facing death had captured the public's imagination, and his buckskin jacket became a popular culture icon, repeated in numerous illustrations of the Last Stand, adopted by cigarette trading cards at the turn of the century, and later appearing in comic books.

Thus, in the Hollywood Western, it is not surprising that Custer's heroics in numerous Last Stands also depict him wearing buckskin, when, according to his contemporaries and Edward S. Godfrey, Custer actually rode to the Little Big Horn with his buckskin outer garment tied behind his saddle and most likely died in his Army blouse. After all, it was a very hot day on June 25, 1876. Allegedly, six other men rode to the Last Stand also dressed in buckskin. Custer, however, is generally presented in the movies as the only cavalryman wearing his fringed jacket during the action that took place at the Little Bighorn—portrayed by Francis Ford (twice in 1912), Ned Finley (1916), Dustin Farnum (1926), John Beck (1926), Clay Clements (1933), John Miljan (1936), Frank McGlynn (1936), Paul Kelly (1940) Addison Richards (1940), Ronald Reagan (1940), Errol Flynn (1941), James Millican (1942), Sheb Wooley (1952), Douglas Kennedy (1954), Britt Lomond (1958), Philip Carey (1965), Leslie Nielsen (1966), Robert Shaw (1967), Wayne Maunder (1967 and 1990), Richard Mulligan (1970), Marcello Mastroianni (1974), James Olson (1977), Gary Cole (1991), Josh Lucas (1993), Peter Horton (1996), William Shockley (1997), and Bill Hader (2009).

Notably, Custer's on-screen relationship with Native Americans has experienced a conflicted trajectory (during which a number of excellent revisionist Westerns have revised his heroic status), but his relationship with buckskin has not. In *They Died with Their Boots On* (1941), for example, Custer expires nobly, first with his six guns blazing, then brandishing his gleaming saber, and finally standing with his jacket firmly buttoned against the onslaught of Crazy Horse (Anthony Quinn) and hordes of attacking Sioux. In buckskin, his death is portrayed as a moral and ethical triumph as the 7th Cavalry is "sacrificed" in "a dirty deal" as they nobly protect Terry's infantry. Crucified on the cross of "a ruthlessly advancing civilization that spelled doom to the red race," Custer is heroically absolved of any responsibility for his actions during Sheridan's Total War against the Plains Indians (even the Washita tragedy which immediately comes to mind) and forgiven for the massacre of his men at the Little Big Horn. Almost 30 years later, the cultural coding conveyed by Custer's jacket had not changed. In *Little Big Man* (1970), Custer (Richard Mulligan) is depicted as a madman, and, as such, cannot be considered a cavalier, whose salient characteristic is always that of self-control. On foot at the Little Big Horn, Custer tellingly removes his jacket while addressing the President and Congress on the battlefield and is then shot in back. In this movie, his buckskin jacket is not shot full of arrows. It survives the massacre intact—the romantic legend of the cavalier Plainsman survives him, as does his penchant for buckskin. Today, one of his jackets, donated by his wife in 1912, remains on display for public consumption, enshrined in the Smithsonian.

William F. Cody was not a cavalryman, but he too adopted the popularized cavalier persona of the Plains. Following in Custer's footsteps, Cody also wore a van Dyke, cocked his broad-brimmed hat, and updated his buckskin garments. A buffalo hunter, a guide for the Grand Duke Alexis, and a civilian scout awarded the Medal of Honor while working with the 3rd Cavalry Regiment, he rode a horse named Buckskin Joe and posed for studio portraits in fringed tunics and Kit Carson coats. As the chief scout for the 5th Cavalry, he carefully dressed for the opportunity to be the first man to kill an Indian (Chief Yellow Hand) to avenge Custer's death, sporting a cavalier costume that he had worn while performing in Ned Buntline's "The Scouts of the Prairies." After this widely publicized act, Cody's public image became identified with his buckskin jacket which resembled Custer's updated outerwear.

It was as a theatrical costume that the buckskin jacket made its appearance and became Buffalo Bill's trademark in the Wild West Show. An icon of the West and a signifier of the natural aristocrat, the buckskin jacket quickly became identified with Cody, appealed to the ladies, and contributed to the meteoric social rise of the farm boy from Iowa. Dressed in buckskin, Cody was admitted to the courts of Europe and the company of Queen Victoria. As Christopher Corbett points out in *Orphans Preferred: The Twisted Truth and Lasting Legend of the Pony Express*, Buffalo Bill's Wild West show mesmerized the British public and bewitched the nation: Victoria "had been so enchanted with Buffalo Bill's Wild West that she demanded an encore and on June 20 royalty from all over Europe attending her golden jubilee were entertained by the American cowboy and Indian troupe" (Corbett 165). Cody took "the reins of the Deadwood stage with young Prince Albert Edward riding shotgun and racing about the performing grounds with the kings of Denmark, Greece, Belgium and Saxony in the back of stage while Indians firing blanks and shouting bloodcurdling war whoops chased the royal caravan" (Corbett 165). As Corbett remarks, Custer's Last Stand may have been supplanted by the Roughrider's Charge up San Juan Hill in Buffalo Bill's Wild West (166), but buckskin jackets proved irreplaceable, remaining an important element in the Show's acts.

Because Buffalo Bill's Wild West show set the standard by which the paying public judged the look of the Hollywood Western, it is not surprising that 11 movies have been made about one of the West's most popular protagonists: Cody played himself in *The Indian Wars* (1914). In *Buffalo Bill* (1894); *In The Days of Buffalo Bill* (1922); *Fighting with Buffalo Bill* (1926); *Battling* with *Buffalo Bill* (1931); *The Plainsman* (1936); *Young Buffalo Bill* (1940); *Buffalo Bill* (1944); *Buffalo Bill Rides Again* (1947); and *Buffalo Bill, l'oeroe del far west* (1965), actors dressed in buckskin portrayed the showman. Throughout ten of these adventures, Buffalo Bill, dressed in fringe, embodies the high moral standards and sterling ethics belonging to both the natural aristocrat and the dashing cavalier. In *Buffalo Bill* (1941), for example, William F. Cody chivalrously rescues a U.S. senator and his beautiful daughter; he admires and respects Indians; he is a good friend to Yellow Hand, the Cheyenne chief whom he then is forced to kill. In 1944, the buckskin-clad Cody in *Buffalo Bill* rights wrongs: he is not only portrayed as a good friend of Yellow Hand, he also attacks those who maltreat Native Americans. In 1965, Buffalo Bill's high moral standards and sterling ethics are again put to the test. In *Buffalo Bill, l'oeroe del far west*, he is sent to stop arms trading and avert an Indian War.

In the fifties, existential heroes in Westerns also wore buckskin while addressing social and political imbalances and repairing their communities' equilibrium. A reliable indicator of a "good" man, fringe graced the jackets of Shane (Alan Ladd) and Hondo (John Wayne), who appeared in 1953 and 1955, characters cut from the same cinematic cloth as the Davey Crockett who fell defending freedom and wearing buckskin at the Alamo and the George Custer who sacrificed his command dressed in buckskin to protect Terry's infantrymen. Like Crockett and Custer, Shane and Hondo are rugged individualists and masters of their own moral centers. Ignoring warnings, Shane corrects Ryker's bullying, reaffirming the sanctity of the American family via his support of the Starretts' marriage and defense of homesteading; Hondo also stabilizes and promotes the family unit by protecting and caring for Angie and Johnny Lowe. In the revisionist comedy, *Cat Ballou* (1967), even Kid Shelleen (Lee Marvin), a parody of the buckskin-wearing outlaw found in Penny Dreadfuls, still manages to do "the right thing," righting social wrongs by administering natural law, in a most unnatural way, by killing his own brother. Finally, in 1976, Robert Altman's cynical revision of Buffalo Bill in *Buffalo Bill and the Indians, or Sitting Bull's History Lesson* presented viewers with a cynical, swaggering, wig-wearing, immoral charlatan, who dons buckskin to exploit American Indians and seduce young women. At last, in this movie, a century after the death of Custer, the frontiersman's clothes failed to make the man a hero.

Buffalo Bill and the Indians, or Sitting Bull's History Lesson is the exception rather than the rule when one considers the nature and uses of buckskin garments on Hollywood sets. In general, buckskin announces the transcendent nature of the man who wears it. After all, Davey Crockett, the king of fringe, was also the *King* of the Wild Frontier. A marker of the American Character, buckskin defines protagonists who wear it as natural aristocrats.

Davy Crockett (John Wayne) died nobly in his fringe during the filming of *The Alamo* (1960). Tom Dunstan (John Wayne), at first a romantic, sympathetic character, is dressed in buckskin at the beginning of *Red River* (1948). When Dunstan abandons his buckskins, he descends into madness driving cattle north clad in a cattleman's plain leather vest and leather chaps. More recently, in *The Last of the Mohicans* (1992), Uncas the Last Mohican (Eric Schweig) is remarkable for his nobility, self-restraint, gentleness, and fringed leather tunic. The savage Magua (Wes Studi), on the other hand, is never dressed in buckskin fringe. In *The Lone Ranger* (2013), Johnny Depp, like Jay Silverheels in *The Lone Ranger* (TV Series 1949–1957), *The Lone Ranger* (1956) and *The Lone Ranger and the City of Gold* (1958), plays Tonto befringed, albeit from the waist down.

Throughout the twentieth century, a handful of Westerns with fringe-wearing women have been made, but such characters should be considered anomalies, as in these movies, their buckskin jackets, tunics, trousers, and skirts are not symbols of social transcendence. *Annie Oakley* (1935) and *Calamity Jane* (1955) are romanticized biographies in which their female protagonists dressed in buckskin *appear* to be breaking the strict gender codes of the Wild West, but these women leave their Wild West personas behind to find "happiness" in marriage. In short, Annie (Barbara Stanwyck) and Calamity (Doris Day) are characters designed to appeal to female chauvinists, not feminists. A better marksman than Toby Walker (Preston Foster), Oakley, in her fringed skirt is a natural aristocrat: Sitting Bull (Chief Thunderbird), whom she befriends, calls her "Little Sureshot." Calamity, an Indian-fighting stagecoach driver, drinks and plays cards beating the boys. Neither woman, however, finds living like a man with men emotionally fulfilling. Each transcends her unhappy, stifled condition by falling in love: Barbara Stanwyck sharpshoots her way into Preston Foster's arms; Doris Day stops fighting Indians, drops her bullwhip, and exchanges her buckskin tunic and trousers for a wedding dress—in the end, she learns how to keep house and happily marries Howard Keel's Wild Bill Hickok.

In Hollywood Westerns, women are not presented as cavalier figures, but, on television, young girls like Buffalo Bill, Jr.'s little sister, Calamity can be. In *Buffalo Bill, Jr.*, a televised series that ran from 1955 to 1956, the innocence of childhood returns a ten-year-old Calamity, dressed in a fringed skirt and riding a white pony, to the paradisal condition of the natural world. Innately good, she (and her brother, the Buffalo Bill, Jr., after whom the series is named) round up villains, who invariably are corrupt adults, to be tried and sentenced every week by Judge Ben "Fair and Square" Wiley. Calamity and her brother's cavalier values (of honor and civic duty) enable them to succeed where well meaning, but corrupted adults fail. Calamity's buckskins also signal her affinity with the natural world and Native Americans. As Jackila, her buckskin-wearing Mescalero mentor, points out in "The Fight for Geronimo," Calamity hears of Geronimo's capture before her brother does, because Native American wisdom (and girl power) are superior to science and technology: Buffalo Bill, Jr., discovers that smoke signals (and Calamity) can travel faster than the telegraph and prove themselves to be superior to Western ways and the Western's masculine status quo. Jackila, always a gentleman, points out that the "white man's ways" are often the "primitive" ones.

In the adult Westerns of the sixties, the problems of the frontier are not so easily solved. Professional Westerns, remarkable for their gritty deconstructions of Old West romanticism, exhibit an astounding dearth of cowboy cavaliers and buckskin jackets. There is not a strand of leather festooning the arms and legs of Gil Westrum (Randolph Scott), Steve Judd (Joel McCrea), or Heck Longtree (Ron Starr) in *Ride the High Country* (1962) as they and Elsa accompany a gold shipment. Completely lacking in heroic masculinity and its flamboyant fringe, Dolworth (Burt Lancaster), Fardan (Lee Marvin), Ehrengard (Robert Ryan), and Jake (Woody Strode) in *The Professionals* (1966) even eschew leather jackets and leggings when returning an errant wife to her husband. In *True Grit* (1969) and in *The Wild Bunch* (1969), there is also no fringe to be found. Like the protagonists of *Ride the High Country* and *The Professionals*, Rooster Cogburn (John Wayne) and LaBoeuf (Glen Campbell), in *True Grit* and Pike (William Holden), Dutch (Ernest Borgnine) and the gang in *The Wild Bunch* are fringeless "professional fighters, willing to defend society only as a job they accept for pay or for love of fighting, not for any commitment to the ideals of law or justice" (Wright 85). In *True Grit*, Rooster joins forces with LaBoeuf for more reward money. Mattie Ross (Kim Darby) is told, "A fellah's got to think of himself once in a while, baby sister. We'll get your man. That's the main thing." In *The Wild Bunch*, Dutch also abandons a man who saved his life to be murdered. Angel is "a thief," Dutch says, when Mapache complains that a case of rifles is missing, "You take care of him."

A subset of the professional Western, the Spaghetti Western is also notable for the absence of heroes dressed in buckskin. In the *Dollar* trilogy, Sergio Leone's antiheroes who kill for their own gain are defined not only by their repellant actions. In *For a Few Dollars More* (1965), neither Douglas Mortimer (Lee Van Cleef) nor El Indio (Gian Maria Volonte) wear buckskin. Both are violent, psychopathic killers. The Man With No Name (Clint Eastwood) sports only a debased variant of the buckskin jacket, for his serape is made of wool. Like the sense of justice that this character lives by, the fringe that this character sports is sparse. It remains unclear at the movie's end whether The Man With No Name's ambivalent morality will prompt him to return the money that was stolen from the Bank of El Paso. In *The Good, the Bad and the Ugly* (1967), what fringe there had been disappears from Eastwood's serape with his character's ethics. As Tuco (Eli Wallach) informs his audience, the fringeless Blondie is a "son of a b----!"

To date, buckskin garments have not lost *their* aristocratic cachet, *their* cavalier character, or *their* iconic identification with frontier individualism which transcends collective norms and forms despite the influence of the professional Western on the genre and Hollywood's current pessimistic critique of the Western's mythology and iconography. Even today, the buckskin-wearing figure of the transplanted Southern horseman continues to convey its cultural coding. Unwilling or unable to return home, he still seeks to re-establish a prelapsarian garden (perhaps that antebellum garden of the South), continuing to correct the corruption of the civilized world only to move further westward as the frontier becomes "civilized." In the Cohen brothers' remake of *True Grit* (2010), the buckskin jacket continues to brand the man who wears it a cavalier. Even though Mattie Ross (Hailee Steinfeld) accuses the befringed LaBeouf (Matt Damon) of being "a rodeo Clown" and Rooster Cogburn (Jeff Bridges) declares him "a nincompoop ... [who] can wander the Choctaw Nation for as long as he likes," the Texas Ranger's cavalier sense of honor and adherence to civic duty rescues his comrades. It is LaBoeuf who prevents Mattie from being raped by Tom Chaney (Josh Brolin). It is LaBoeuf who shoots Lucky Ned Pepper (Barry Pepper) as he tries to kill Cogburn. It is LaBoeuf who hauls Mattie and Cogburn out of the rattlesnake pit. Mattie, who thinks LaBoeuf a buffoon, and Cogburn, who cannot claim to have any of the natural aristocrat's qualities, leave Indian Territory owing their lives to the Texas Ranger, who, lying dead on the ground, is last seen in his buckskin jacket.

At the end of her story, Mattie relates her knowledge that Cogburn has died while working in a Wild West show to the viewer. She also reports that she has been unable to discover whether there has been any closure to Laboeuf's adventures. At first Mattie's interest in LaBoeuf seems unusual at the conclusion of the Coen brothers' *True Grit*, until one remembers that at the end of Henry Hathaway's *True Grit* (1969), a fringeless LaBeouf lies dead and it is Cogburn who turns down Mattie's awkward offer to lie beside her for eternity. In the Coen brothers' later version, however ludicrous the spurred and befringed Ranger's actions may look to Mattie (and the viewer), LaBoeuf embodies not only the cavalier's martial nature but also that figure's emotive power and appeal. Aptly, Mattie's last words to the viewer express her regret for his absence and remind us that cultural phenomena, be they icons or myth, may change because of the passage of time: "I heard nothing more of the Texas officer LaBoeuf," she remarks nostalgically. "If he is yet alive, I would be pleased to hear from him, I judge he would be in his 70s now, and nearer 80 than 70. I expect some of the starch has gone out of that cowlick." LaBoeuf's befringed charismatic durability, however, indicates how deeply the Southern

34 A Fistful of Icons

cavalier and heroic masculinity remains embedded in the Hollywood Western and the American psyche. Putting the issue of the amount of starch in a cowboy's cowlick aside, it is evident that frontier fringe has survived into the twenty-first century—and that buckskin continues to act as an important marker of the American Character in the Hollywood Western.

NOTE

1. As Utely points out, George Armstrong Custer was consistently identified as wearing buckskin after the Civil War by the press. A typical description of the sportsman by a young woman who accompanied one of his hunting parties depicts him in pursuit of antelope, "with his long, golden hair flying in the wind, his heavily fringed buckskin suit matching the color of his hair" (79).

FILMOGRAPHY

Annie Oakley (1935). Dir. George Stevens. Warner Home Video, 2007. DVD.
Battling with Buffalo Bill (1931). Dir. Ray Taylor. VCI Entertainment, 2007. DVD.
Buffalo Bill. Dir. William K.L. Dickson. Black Maria Studio, 1894.
Buffalo Bill (1944). Dir. William Wellman. Twentieth Century Fox, 2005. DVD.
Buffalo Bill and the Indians, or Sitting Bull's History Lesson (1976). Dir. Robert Altman. MGM Home Entertainment, 2001. DVD.
Buffalo Bill, l'eroe del far west. Dir. Mario Costa. Filmes Cinematographica, 1965.
Buffalo Bill Rides Again. Dir. Bernard B. Ray. Jack Schwarz Productions, 1947.
Calamity Jane (1953). Dir. David Butler. Warner Home Video, 2005. DVD.
Cat Ballou (1965). Dir. Elliot Silverstein. Sony Pictures Home Entertainment, 2000. DVD.
Davey Crockett: King of the Wild Frontier (1955). Dir. Norman Foster. Walt Disney Home Entertainment, 2004. DVD.
Fighting with Buffalo Bill. Dir. Ray Taylor. Universal Pictures, 1926.
For a Few Dollars More (1965). Dir. Sergio Leone. MGM Canada, 2006. DVD.
The Good, the Bad and the Ugly (1967). Dir. Sergio Leone. Fox Video (Canada) Limited, 2003. DVD.
Hondo (1953). Dir. John Farrow. Paramount, 2005. DVD.
In the Days of Buffalo Bill. Dir. Edward Laemmle. Universal Film Manufacturing Company, 1922.
The Indian Wars. Dirs. Vernon Day and Theodore Wharton. Essanay Film Manufacturing Company, 1914.
The Last of the Mohicans (1932). Dir. George B. Seitz. eOne Films Distribution, 2012. DVD.
The Last of the Mohicans (1992). Dir. Michael Mann. Twentieth Century Fox Home Entertainment, 2010. DVD.
Little Big Man (1970). Dir. Arthur Penn. CBS, 2003. DVD.
The Lone Ranger (1956). Dir. Stuart Heisler. Vci Video, 2004. DVD.
The Lone Ranger: Legends Collection. Dirs. Morse, Seitz, Jr. et al. Allegro Media Group, 2013. DVD.
The Lone Ranger: 25 Thrilling Episodes. Dir. Morse, Seitz, Jr. et al. Classic Media, 2013. DVD.
The Lone Ranger and the Lost City of Gold (1958). Dir. Stuart Heisler. Vci Video, 2004. DVD.
The Plainsman (1936). Dir. Cecil B. DeMille. Universal Studios Home Entertainment, 2013. DVD.
The Pony Express (1953). Dir. Jerry Hopper. Olive Films, 2012. DVD.
The Professionals (1966). Dir. Richard Brooks. Sony Pictures Home Entertainment, 2005. DVD.
Red River (1948). Dir. Howard Hawks. Criterion, 2014. DVD.
Ride the High Country. (1962). Dir. Sam Peckinpah. Warner Bros. Home Video, 2006. DVD.
They Died with Their Boots On. (1941). Dir. Raoul Walsh. Warner Bros. Home Video, 2005. DVD.

True Grit. (1969). Dir. Henry Hathaway. Paramount Pictures, 2007. DVD.
True Grit. (2010). Dir. Joel and Ethan Coen. Paramount Pictures, 2011. DVD.
The Wild Bunch. (1969). Dir. Sam Peckinpah. Warner Bros. Home Video, 2006. DVD.
Young Buffalo Bill (1940). Dir. Joseph Kane. Alpha Video, 2003. DVD.

WORKS CITED

"GRANT'S ARMY. Record of the Operations of Our Cavalry. Another Brilliant Affair by Gen. Custer Capture of Three Railway Trains, 25 Pieces Artillery, 200 Wagons, &c., by the Third Division. Details of the Surrender of Lee's Army. After the Surrender Order from General Custer." *The New York Times* 20 April 1865 http://www.nytimes.com/1865/04/20/news/grant-s-army-record-operations-our-cavalry-another-brilliant-affair-gen-custer.html?pagewanted=2). Cited parenthetically as GRANT'S ARMY.
Corbett, Christopher. *Orphans Preferred: The Twisted Truth and Lasting Legend of the Pony Express.* New York: Broadway Books, 2003.
Custer, Elizabeth Bacon. *Tenting on the Plains: Or, General Custer in Kansas and Texas.* New York: Charles L. Webster & Company, 1889.
Pratt, Adam. "'A Curious Compound of the Hero and the Dandy': George Armstrong Custer, the Cavalier Image, and White Masculinity in the Postwar South." *Black and White Masculinity in the American South, 1800–2000.* Eds. Lydia Plath and Sergio Lussana. Newcastle upon Tyne: Cambridge Scholars Publishing, 2009: 37–55.
Roosevelt, Theodore. *Ranch Life and The Hunting Trail.* New York: The Century Co., 1911. Available at https://archive.org/details/ranchlifehunting00roos.
Utely, Robert M. *Custer: Cavalier in Buckskin.* Norman, Oklahoma: University of Oklahoma Press, 2001.
Wright, Will. *Sixguns and Society: A Structural Analysis of the Western.* Berkeley: University of California Press, 1975.

The Urbanized West of Cecil B. DeMille

DAVID BLANKE

The study of iconography and archetypes through generic film holds within it great scholarly promise. Certainly, Rick Altman's (1984) functional definition whereby genre (a) announces itself through recurring semantic elements—the so-called building blocks of genre—and (b) gives meaning through a recognizable syntax—or the ideological arrangement and purpose to which these building blocks are set—provides scholars with a consistent methodology and comparative baseline from which to begin any serious analysis of genre. But more recent criticism, exploring the role that commercial producers and the audience play in the material construction and reception of genre, suggest a more contingent and historicized interplay between iconography and meaning. As Steve Neale writes, in *Genre and Hollywood*, genre serves less as a definitive tool for aesthetic canonization and more as a framework to "a multi-dimensional" process "that encompasses systems of expectations, categories, labels and names, discourses, texts ... and the conventions that govern them all" (68). As such, any study of iconography which fails to historicize a film's material production and reception threatens to yield a self-referential and brittle account of the overall significance of genre. Neale notes this "empiricist's dilemma," whereby the motifs and images studied bereft of their historical context tend merely to validate that certain producers—and often only commercially successful producers—effectively express a meaningful style across any particular theme. Taking from Tom Ryall, Neale cautions that the pursuit of genre must recognize that meaning is constructed through "a triangle composed of artist/film/audience" (12). Genre exists through visual semantics and syntax, certainly, but these icons are supervised through "both their construction by the film maker, and their reading by an audience" (18).

This essay examines the iconography and archetypes employed by Cecil B. DeMille during two phases of his career in an effort to frame and explain the relative efficacy of his use of the Western genre. It argues that DeMille used the Western not to glorify the typical semantics of the genre—including rugged male individualism and nature, for example—but rather to highlight the importance of civilization, the women's sphere, a shared consensual culture, and particularly the spread of a benevolent modernity. As such, his films represent a path not widely travelled by others in Hollywood; one that suggests a genre which extended new meaning to female and other Eastern urban consumers not proscribed by traditional frameworks of the Western. Mindful of the cautionary note struck by Neale, the analysis is rooted in both the unique circumstances of commercial film production as well as the conditions through which many movie-goers received these works. As such, it tries to explain why DeMille—whose Westerns were quite popular and commercially successful—twice abandoned the genre in favor of newer and, to his reading, more flexible generic models.

DeMille's over-sized persona, of course, makes the process of historicizing his work problematic. Derided for his art, his politics, his melodramatic sentimentality, and his gargantuan ego, DeMille's public image has served for decades as a convenient whipping boy made to suffer for the ills of American commercial cinema. While these faults are evident throughout his long career—spanning nearly 50 years and 70 feature films—such criticism shifted widely over these years. His deft use and even development of cinematic spectacle and mise-en-scène make his films particularly useful for those examining spectatorship. On a more materialist level, DeMille survived the ever-changing commercial landscape fashioned by financiers and the marketplace. His career careened through multiple "Hollywoods," including the wildcat years before the studio system, the rise of these integrated behemoths (when he unsuccessfully challenged the studios as an independent producer), the Great Depression and War years, into finally into the twilight of Classical Hollywood Cinema. Arriving in Los Angeles with little more than a famous surname and the faith of his best friend and financier (Jesse Lasky), DeMille dominated, was bankrupted, and then regained cultural relevancy within the industry at least three times over his lifetime. Such endurance speaks to the empiricist warnings raised above. While one may not like the man or his cinematic methods, it remains clear that he embodied the dominant Hollywood "systems" of the 1910s, 1930s, and 1950s.

DeMille's impassioned ideological battles—first against the rising studio and star systems and later as a shrill supporter of Senator Robert Taft's anti-union legislation—are noteworthy too. If his Lazarus-like commercial success represents a man who could adapt to the changing business climate of his industry, then these ideological skirmishes suggest someone far less willing to employ trendy popular notions in his films. Meaningful here strictly for their influence on his Western iconography, DeMille could best be described today as a social libertarian. While barely excusing his vicious attacks on partisan opponents in the immediate post-war years, these values led him to a life-long opposition to content censorship, labor blacklisting (which he accused the unions of abetting), and dogmatic representations in film of gender, race, sexuality, consumer culture, and especially religion. These elements of his personality are largely ignored today because the aesthetics of his films are deemed by critics to be "passé, naïve, unsophisticated, [and] a degradation of the true sacrality" of cinema (Louvish 270). Such attitudes impede our appreciation of the methods that he did employ, however, and his films deserve an analysis free of (or at least within the historicized context of) such strict aesthetic values. DeMille's prickly demeanor and ideological crusading produced two series of Western films—the first in the 1910s and the second in the 1930s—that relied on these personal precepts yet also highlight decided unique aspects of the genre. In both phases his Westerns were wildly popular and commercially successful.

In his earliest days in Hollywood, DeMille relied almost exclusively on the Western genre. His first, *The Squaw Man* (1914), was soon joined by four others (including *The Virginian*, *The Call of the North*, *Rose of the Rancho*, and *The Girl of the Golden West*) that he released that same year. This decision to highlight the Western—made primarily in New York when acquiring the rights to successful Broadway plays, particularly those of David Belasco—proved decisive for the financial success of the fledgling Jesse L. Lasky Feature Play Company, the studio for which DeMille was the leading director.[1] Costing, in aggregate, more than $81,000 to produce, the five films generated more half a million dollars in profit. Moreover, DeMille's rapid pace of production—releasing nearly 30 feature films in his first four years in California—allowed his technical team to learn their craft and to develop a distinctive chiaroscuro visual style that Demille would retain well into the 1920s (Birchard 17).

DeMille brought a unique sensibility to the Western, influenced by his earlier association with the Broadway stage. He, his father, and his brother had worked closely with David Belasco, the "Wizard of Broadway," in a relationship that stretched back to the 1890s and which carried a significant amount of emotional baggage. DeMille felt he was abandoned by Belasco (who, conversely, helped DeMille's older brother's New York career to thrive). Accordingly, DeMille's early commercial success in film often carried with it a whispering chorus of detractors who questioned the director's artistic merit and ability to attain the artistry of the "legitimate stage." Lasky felt the same pressures, and the pair worked feverishly to sign well-known Broadway actors and the rights to Belasco's more famous plays. Their assumption (which proved accurate) was that the remote yet still culturally curious national audience cared less for originality and artistry than in seeing the works and actors that were discussed by the theater set. In terms of this analysis, these worries convinced DeMille that "authentic" settings, familiar faces, and Belasco-like plot twists—not a stable Western genre with an integrated set of visual semantics and syntax—were the keys to their success.

With these production and reception qualifiers in mind, DeMille's early Westerns did display patterns that hinted at his unique conception of the genre. Production for both *The Squaw Man* (1914) and *The Virginian* (1914) was separated by a mere four months, and as such it is useful to analyze the two in tandem. Dustin Farnum starred in both Broadway productions. His leading role in DeMille's film versions offered Paramount the name recognition necessary to entice exhibitors to book a showing. *The Squaw Man* is the story of an English aristocrat, James Wynnegate (Farnum), who is forced to flee to America to preserve his family's honor; save his cousin, the Earl of Kerkill, from a lengthy jail sentence; and to impress the Earl's wife, Lady Diana (who shared a far more meaningful emotional relationship with James than with her spouse). James' travails in England and his travels to America share almost as much screen time as those scenes set in the west. Once there, the Englishman buys a ranch, forces his workers to adopt a more cultured (or at least less alcoholic) lifestyle, and then falls in love with the daughter of the local Indian chief ("Nat-U-Rich" played by Red Wing aka Lillian St. Cyr, a full-blooded Winnebago). Upon the accidental death of the Earl, and his deathbed admission of James' innocence, Wynnegate is proclaimed the legitimate heir to the estate. Informed of his good luck, James struggles to reconcile his obligations to his American wife and his desire to return home (or, as the intertitle reads, "HOME!"). Vowing at least to send his American son off to claim his inheritance, the tensions spark a potential Indian uprising. All is settled, however, when Nat-U-Rich commits suicide and frees James and his son to return to the loving and welcoming arms of Lady Diana.

Less convoluted yet equally melodramatic, *The Virginian* tells the tale of two cowpokes, The Virginian (Farnum) and his friend Steve (J.W. Johnston), faced with adapting to the male freedoms presented on the frontier. The film's first inter-title explains that "in the heart of the West, when cattle pastured in every valley, and solitary horsemen rode the ranges, there reigned supreme that romantic figure—the cow-puncher." The film then follows two narrative trajectories. The Virginian's romanticism leads to marriage (to "Molly Wood," a newly arrived schoolmarm played by Winifred Kingston), civilization, and a life lived happily ever after. By contrast, Steve, feeling abandoned by his friend (who begins taking basic education classes with Molly), falls in with a local outlaw and commits crimes that lead him inexorably to the hangman's noose.

Visually, both films offer the raw materials required of the Western, including rustic cabins, teepees, and raucous saloons. The interior staging of *The Squaw Man* is fairly primitive and no doubt the product of DeMille's limited production resources. His staff, and particularly cinematographer Alvin Wyckoff, helped ease these deficiencies in *The Virginian* by adding visual depth that included off-stage back rooms, open windows, and more realistic furnishings. While DeMille used stock footage of the English Derby in *The Squaw Man*, the remaining reels were all shot in California either on location or at the Lasky barn. Exterior shots focused almost exclusively on natural perils, including white-out blizzard conditions and geyser "death holes" for *The Squaw Man* and dangerous river crossings and spooky nighttime wilderness for *The Virginian*. The central characters in both works conformed to the conventional semantics of the Western genre described by Neale, acting either as agents of civilization and community, threatening savages and outlaws, or as lone male heroes torn between two worlds (140).

Still, and in spite of DeMille's inexperience, it was clear that the director was fashioning a unique visual representation of the west; one that contrasted sharply with the emerging syntax of the genre featuring the challenges of untamed wilderness and unbridled masculinity. For *The Squaw Man*, this was accomplished through an extensive prequel to the Western scenes that including a luxurious English estate, numerous parlors and meeting halls, Jim's efforts to book ship passage and then survive an onboard fire, and his fortuitous meeting with "Grouchy Bill Cowan," where he prevents the rancher who would take him west from being pickpocketed in a posh New York restaurant. *The Virginian* did not require such an extensive backstory, yet DeMille's camera luxuriated not on the majestic buttes and wide open plains of the West but the schoolhouses, saloons, town shops, and depots that would later come to define his work. While not yet the "spectacle" that we came to associate with the director, clearly he saw the west in terms of what is was not (i.e., civilized) and strove to identify what Easterners would bring with them in their cross-country pilgrimage. These images placed women in a more "natural" setting for his audience. In perhaps the most affective scene of *The Virginian*, the two male friends decide to mix-up the sleeping children at a community party for Molly. The families all leave with the wrong kids before discovering the boys' prank and high-tailing it back to the ranch. The scene does a wonderful job of showing both the unbridled (and immature) male culture of the west, the nascent threat it poses to home and family, and sets up the dramatic differences between the fates of the Virginian (domesticated) and Steve (executed).

Both of these early visual trends—favoring the spectacle of civilization over nature and the potency of female agency in the west—found their fullest expression in *A Romance of the Redwoods* (1917). A rewriting of Belasco's original *The Girl of the Golden West* (which DeMille filmed in 1915), the screenplay and cinematography reflect the rapid maturation of commercial feature films and its ability to tell compelling, complex, cross-cut stories free from the aesthetic burdens of Broadway. Notably, the historical context of the film's production and reception can be summed up in two words: Mary Pickford. By 1917 "America's Sweetheart" was already in the process of turning her unprecedented cinematic stardom into creative and financial freedom. Signing with Paramount in 1916 (under the Artcraft Pictures Corporation) for a then-astronomical sum ($10,000 a week with a $300,000 signing bonus and guarantee of 50 percent of all profits), Zukor teamed the star with DeMille in an effort to recoup his losses from her first two contract films (*Less that the Dust*, considered one of the worst films Pickford ever made, and *The Pride of the Clan*, a contrived costume drama situating "Little Mary" amid feuding Scottish fishermen). Space does not permit a full rendering of the odd relationship between DeMille and Pickford—who both had deep roots in Broadway—but suffice it to say that one of the director's prime responsibilities was to force Pickford to complete her films on time and under budget (more than 70 percent of the production costs for *Redwoods* came from Pickford's salary alone). Notably, and in spite of her profoundly popular public role as the perpetual pre-teen, in both of their collaborations the director cast Pickford as a fully-grown, sexually active woman. Such casting against type—and certainly a type not demanded by the Western—was a risky gamble for DeMille. As sales manager Al Lichtman later told Lasky, while *Redwoods* might be "considered an excellent picture from a technical viewpoint, is not especially pleasing to motion picture patrons. Most Pickford fans are disappointed in this film because it is so different from the usual type of play in which Miss Pickford appears." Regardless of these early reports, the grosses from both Pickford films exceeded all of DeMille's work to date, with the exception of *Joan the Woman*.[2]

Typical of DeMille and his now-battered artistic reputation, the novelty and popularity of *A Romance of the Redwoods* stems from his now-dated melodramatic plot construction. Here, Jenny Lawrence (Pickford) travels west to live with her uncle. Unknown at the time, the uncle has been killed by Indians and his identity stolen by a highwayman, "Black" Brown (Elliott Dexter), as a way for him to elude arrest. Jenny arrives, discovers the ruse, and threatens to expose Brown only to learn that the tough guy is needed to protect her on the frontier. The two fall in love and Brown secretly plans one last heist to use as their re-location dowry. But Brown is identified and a posse captures him at their cabin. Threatening to lynch him, Jenny uses a doll's clothes to convince the posse that she is pregnant, to let the couple marry, and then leave the county for good (while sending the ill-gotten gains to a murdered young man's mother). Robert Birchard effectively summarizes the delicious ironies contained within DeMille's tortured screenplay: "In the primitive environment of the West, Jenny is [transformed into] a sex object. Just as the outlaw offers the appearance of respectability, the 'respectable' male citizens [portrayed in the town scenes] would be just as content to pay for her favors at the dance hall. Although Jenny and 'Black' Brown are genuinely in love, she symbolically traps him into marriage—and wedded bliss is presented as the only alternative to a necktie party" (Birchard 106). It is little surprise, then, that immediately after concluding his contractual obligations with Pickford—who learned to trust his direction—DeMille shifted his métier to the fascinating "marriage/sex" films of the 1920s.

Unlike his initial Westerns where DeMille seemed interested in striking a balance between the traditional Western iconography—including open vistas, Native Americans, and men on horseback—in *Redwoods* the director makes a firm commitment to Eastern and urban tropes to tell the tale. As Birchard notes, the typical "innocent Easterner" motif establishes the film's initial context. DeMille shows Jenny packing for her trip west by filling stacks of suitcases filled with her choicest ballroom gowns! Both in disembarking from the train and in travelling by mule to Brown's cabin, the director reinforces the humor of the woman's materialism and vanity. Yet later, after Brown falls in love with the girl and seeks a suitable present to give her (in the form of a dressed china doll), it is the intricate and formal clothing of the toy that proves to the men that the couple has indeed committed to domesticity. While unnoted by the posse, the audience cannot fail to notice the "woman's touch" applied throughout their home, including cleanliness, order, fresh flowers, and a tablecloth. As the sheriff watch the two ride off towards the county line—now aware of the trick that had been played on them—he tells his posse "when twenty men are fooled by one small woman, they'd better take their medicine." So too seems to be the lessons that DeMille preaches of the West.

More importantly, for this phase and the ones yet to come, in *A Romance of the Redwoods* DeMille's Western iconography takes a decidedly urban shift. While the typical fare is offered, using now more mature cinematography and clever camera placements to highlight nature, it is the urban west that tells the story. Suggesting the visual smorgasbord to come in the 1930s, his street scenes teem with a host of extras—including miners, farmers, women, and children—all busy preparing for lives that the audience will never know. The saloon/dancehall scenes sparkle not because of the rowdy and drunken men—which are to be expected—but the brazen (and drunken) women who set the gauge for the level of hedonism allowed at any time. When Jenny is accosted, the other women just smile. It is Brown who is forced to step in and place her back onto a gendered pedestal. Notably, the crowd settles and denotes a sense of mutual respect once the postman arrives with the day's mail. In a theme he returns to in his later Westerns, DeMille uses these letters almost as a Greek chorus, or at least as a window to the ethical consciousness of his characters. Here, a young man begins feeling remorse for his lifestyle in the prospecting fields because it means he abandoned his aged and ailing mother.

In sum, it remains clear that DeMille—while interested in the west as an iconic and liminal experience rooted deep in the American experience—saw the genre more as an opportunity to explore the limits and influences of civilization over that of nature. His earliest work clung to Eastern rituals and meaning, using them to advance and conclude his plot structures. By the time he released *A Romance of the Redwoods*, a film that directly preceded his (in)famous "sex films" on marriage, these rituals existed at the heart of his Western syntax. Here "America's Sweetheart" acts a sexually charged and intelligent woman who could fully express the hegemonic power of her gender—still potent even in the male culture of the saloon—largely through urban institutions and under the rational (if improbable) enforcement of the law. These urban settings not only conveyed the dominant influences of Eastern culture over the West but also (for DeMille the libertarian) the intelligent and consensual needs of the marketplace for a society that is balanced between male and female, order and hedonism, freedom and respectability. As the opening intertitle of *The Virginian* hints, while the venerable Western "cow-puncher" once "reigned supreme," it will be the railroads, the towns, and governments that would give structure and significance to the region.

After *A Romance of the Redwoods* DeMille abandoned the Western until 1936, when he began production on *The Plainsman*. That year saw a minor revival of the genre—including *The Three Godfathers* and *Ramona*, fully three years before *Stagecoach*—and a consistent shift in DeMille's oeuvre towards historical topics. Between 1934 and 1949, all but one of his 11 films (including *Land of Liberty*, a compilation film commissioned for the 1939 World's Fair) featured historical subjects and seven of these focused exclusively on the American frontier. As with his early phase, the director's relationship to his production resources mattered greatly. DeMille faced professional oblivion in 1932—having left the protection of Paramount, in 1924, he failed as an independent and then, in 1929, produced three commercial failures for MGM—but worked his way back into the good graces of Zukor's Paramount Pictures by producing *The Sign of the Cross* (1932), which re-established him as a reliable box-office favorite. By 1936, his commercial reputation restored, DeMille could rely on the studio's outstanding technical staff, its deep roster of acting talent, and four-walled promotion department. By that time DeMille had also branched out into radio by hosting the weekly Lux Radio Theatre and developing his acclaim as the venerable "Mr. Hollywood." The weekly broadcast anchored the director in Hollywood and led him to rely more fully on second-unit production staff—especially Art Rossen—to capture his location shots.

Similarly, by the 1930s the national audience's reception to Westerns had changed profoundly from the 1910s. While the genre was still not revered, the Great Depression opened an opportunity for film-makers to relate the historical struggles of the past as a type of metaphor for those facing unemployment and dispossession. Moreover, the rise of content censorship—much of it derived from the Catholic Church's reaction to *The Sign of the Cross*—limited the types of social criticism and realism that Hollywood could employ. History and the West offered a safer home than films featuring gangsters or licentious Romans by which to explore the dark hearts of mankind. As Lary May notes, the films of this era often highlighted consensual themes driven by grass-roots democracy—not the cultured values of the economic elite—as the nation's surest path to recovery (176–80). DeMille's ideological biases favored such a view and formed the backbone of his most famous films. Consensus paces the plot development of all three of the films considered here—*The Plainsman*, *Union Pacific* (1939), and *Unconquered* (1947)—but notably the post–World War II brand of consensus had taken a decidedly political and partisan shift. DeMille's own opposition to closed shop laws—which forced him to resign from his beloved radio broadcasts, in 1944—embittered the aging director and led to a four-year stretch when he stood as a partisan conservative champion in Hollywood. While he never opposed unionization, never testified before HUAC, nor joined the more militant Motion Picture Alliance for the Preservation of American Ideals, DeMille's infamous efforts to impose loyalty oaths at the Screen Director's Guild sealed his reputation as an elitist seeking to force his brand of economic liberty down the throats of the less powerful.

Within this bifurcated context—separating the revived "Mr. Hollywood" and the consensual Depression-era audience from the partisan DeMille and the post-war ideological battles that raged throughout the country—the iconography between his earlier modern Westerns, *The Plainsman* and *Union Pacific*, and *Unconquered* stand in sharp contrast. *The Plainsman*, starring Gary Cooper as Wild Bill Hickok and Jean Arthur as Calamity Jane, revolved around the lives of enterprising frontiersmen who opened the west to white settlement. *Union Pacific*, starring Barbara Stanwyck, Joel McCrea, Robert Preston, and Brian Donlevy in wholly fictional roles, tells the story of the race to complete the trans-continental railroad. Both films were commercial hits for DeMille and both offer a consistent set of semantics elements that amplified DeMille's urban conception of the Western. Notably, both films began with rolling credits, later emulated by George Lucas in the *Star Wars* franchise, that provide detailed narration about the meaning of the west to the American experience. A sample from *Union Pacific* reads: "the legend of the Union Pacific is the drama of a nation, young, tough, prodigal, and invincible, conquering with an iron highroad the endless reaches of the West. For the West is America's Empire, and only yesterday Union Pacific was the West." Clearly, both films offered the West loaded with presentist historical messages.

The similarities do not end there. Both films begin their narratives in Washington, D.C., featuring convincing portrayals and striking images of known historical figures, including Abraham Lincoln and his Cabinet, as well as leading Senators and industrialists. In both, Lincoln's death is portrayed as a form of martyrdom for Western expansion and the films' protagonists serve as Lincoln's knights-errant. Combined, the films' extended opening scenes lend a sense of intellectual *gravitas* to what was, effectively, mindless fun.

Significantly, too, both films set up their visual dramas as acts of individual volition. In scene after scene, the lead characters are required to choose between clearly articulated alternatives of the west. For *The Plainsman* this choice involves the continued sale of armaments following Appomattox. For *Union Pacific*, the choice is whether one would support the legitimate business enterprises tasked with building a transcontinental railroad or speculate in shady stock options that could reap millions if scoundrels could undermining the nation's progress. Robert Preston's character ("Dick Allen") in *Union Pacific*, for example, was typical of DeMille's Cain-and-Abel method (presaged in *The Virginian*). A sympathetic character and close friend of the film's hero, Preston had the choice to side with McCrea ("Jeff Butler"), domestication, and the UP or enjoy the easy pleasures offered him by corrupt male speculators. He chose the latter and died in the final reel for his sins. As a result, both films rely on lifestyle choices to highlight the difference between "good" and "bad" capitalism, practiced both on the Western plains as well as in the halls of Congress.

Finally, both films portray women and Native Americans as sympathetic, even heroic characters; more often than not the vessels of decency or, at worst, the innocent victims of these larger battles. In *The Plainsman* it was the corrupt Bureau of Indian Affairs that led Indians astray through lies and corruption. In a telling early scene from *Union Pacific*, the speculator's henchmen (although not Preston) shoots and kills an unarmed, friendly Indian simply to relieve their boredom when traveling west. The crime—and it was portrayed as a cold-blooded murder—serves as the opening salvo between the agents of the UP (McCrea) tasked with defending the rule of law over those who used the west as a place of reckless Social Darwinism.

Beyond these thematic elements, DeMille's cinematic depiction of the west serves as an important reminder of his new use for the genre. Throughout his long career, DeMille retained a remarkably talented eye for visual editing. In lively street scenes—particularly notable where the ferryboat landing in *The Plainsman* and the saloon and mail depot in *Union Pacific*—his ability to capture the promise and peril of Western expansion was impressive. DeMille's Westerns clearly lacked the characteristic and unhurried natural scenery that gave Ford or Hawks their true brilliance. But while his Westerns lacked an eye for nature they excelled at depicting the profoundly human thrill of life on the frontier. Both films depict a complicated world, an active world, one that hinted at dozens of ethical dilemmas similar to those faced by the main characters. As in *Redwoods*, the street, saloon, and mail depot images of *Union Pacific* crackle with kinetic energy as the eye is drawn to small but telling details about the characters and the alien (yet familiar) world they inhabit. DeMille consciously injected these cinematic footnotes into even his most insignificant characters. As Martin Scorsese once told Kevin Brownlow, DeMille "had an extraordinary skill with crowds, for the truth of what a crowd is about.... It's the people around the main actors, it's the people in crowd scenes, in the foreground, three in the back, five on the side," that give his work legitimacy. "That is why the name DeMille meant that I was going to see a real movie" (Eyman 324–25).

The stated purpose behind such an attention to detail in his Westerns was to give his audience verisimilitude, or in DeMille's words "authenticity" (Kozlovic 74). He sought "authentic" Native American clothing and tools; his white ethnics used "authentic" and historically accurate colloquialisms; he built "authentic" train depots, saloons, wigwams, and telegraph stations; and featured "authentic" depictions of historical figures—such as Lincoln and Ulysses S. Grant. His studio produced numerous booklets and other promotional materials that highlighted the cost of historical research—typically exceeding $50,000—to further support these claims. Of course, a sense of authenticity did not always translate into historical accuracy. Adolph Zukor was "appalled" by what he saw in *The Plainsman*. "I've spent my whole life in Plains history," he remarked, "and if the main characters hadn't been named I shouldn't have recognized a one of the three [of them]" (Kozlovic 83). While Zukor's sensibilities were, no doubt, assuaged by the nearly $2 million profit that *The Plainsman* generated in 1937, others tended to dismiss DeMille's semantics on this point alone: in contrast to other Westerns, his were simply bad history.

But few asked why DeMille relied on such willful visual deception. While the director's response was complex and spread out over a long career, he answered with an astoundingly modern, even post-structural answer. Writing in a promotion piece for *Union Pacific* titled "Hollywood, the Greatest Historian," DeMille concluded,

> It is trite, but pertinent, to observe that history is not written in the form of a [film] scenario. Many of the facts unearthed in research for films cannot be used. They do not "belong" [because] they break the unity and continuity of a scenario [as experienced by an audience]. It is the obligation of the producer and his aides, however, to

know everything there is to know about a period before trying to put any part of it on the screen.... This is imperative because the chances are the picture is going to be *seen* and believed by more people than the average history book has readers.... Furthermore, the historical characters *presented on the screen* are afterward known to millions not as the history book pictures them, but *as they appear in film*. That is the power of cinema.[3]

Predating scholars' analysis of "Film as History" by a generation, DeMille believed that his powerful and dynamic iconography "often goes farther beneath the surface of events than" historians and "give a [more] accurate picture of what motivated men" like Lincoln, Custer, Grant, Hickock, or Cody.[4]

The combination of his visual, cinematic acuity and his fascination with "the little man"—about which his production notes are exceedingly detailed—suggests that DeMille viewed the west optimistically: as a promise of redemption through the open choices offered by unregulated freedoms. While far from Franklin Roosevelt's "nothing to fear" reassurances, DeMille's Western imagery championed a strong sense of national optimism that clearly orbited around the free choices made by his audience. Of course, DeMille's ideological purposes behind these portrayals were often less than democratic. As the early narration of *Union Pacific* makes clear, "the west is America, and [the] Union Pacific was the west." Rather than portray organized business as the source of America's ills—as many in the Depression years came to believe—DeMille held that honest economic competition offered the country its best path forward. Again, in his production notes the director wrote how the Great Pyramids were built for vanity, the Great Wall of China for fear, but that the Union Pacific was built to unite a nation. When promoting the picture's premiere, in Omaha at the Headquarters of the UPRR, DeMille spoke to the assembled workers and patrons of the corporation. It was "a thrilling experience," he later wrote to UP president William Jeffers, for "I felt that I was looking America in the eye—and I liked what I saw."[5]

If *The Plainsman* and *Union Pacific* stand as the twin pinnacles of DeMille's urbanized, progressive, and rational West, then *Unconquered* surely represents his nadir. Ironically, just as scholars such as André Bazin and Francois Truffaut were learning to value the Western as evidence of the American auteur, DeMille had reached the end of the generic line. An erstwhile tale of White Slavery on the Pennsylvania frontier—technically, not a transMississippi "Western," but still steeped in the traditional themes of rugged masculinity and the tensions between the wilderness and civilization—given its thematic content and proximity to the Lux Radio Theater-AFRA crisis, *Unconquered* served as DeMille's own version of *Intolerance* (1916), D.W. Griffith's response to the public controversy caused by *The Birth of a Nation* (1915). Writing to Sidney Bidwell, the promotions manager for DeMille

Productions—almost a year before production began, but less than six months after he lost his battle with the unions—the director claimed this film would serve as his definitive statement about "the struggle for freedom" in America. To make matters worse, and to possibly excuse some of the old man's most crotchety attitudes, during production DeMille suffered the tragic loss of two of his closest friends, Jeanie Macpherson and Wilfred Buckland.[6]

Some still defend *Unconquered* for its rich visuals and almost nostalgic celebration of cinematic frontier lore, but the film struggles as both a work of fiction and history. Paulette Goddard chews up the scenery as an indentured servant freed on the pre–Revolutionary Pennsylvania frontier. Gary Cooper both looks and sounds like an authentic trailblazer, but the drama is poorly paced and lacks even a hint of unresolved tension. Bosley Crowther generously noted that DeMille's "unblushing employment" of nearly every "dime-novel cliché" gave the work "a strange magnetic pull." But as a work of visual art it served no better than an old codger's cracker barrel reminiscences of bygone days. One could "pick it up or leave it whenever you want to," Crowther marveled, "and still not miss a thing." The film fared poorly at the box office and proved to be the director's last American historical epic (Crowther 11). In *Unconquered*'s pivotal scene, Cooper buries the bodies of a homespun frontier family, the Salters, slaughtered by Native Americans stirred up by rival economic factions. Using Cooper's natural cadence to perfection, his character eulogizes, "The Salters *are* the New World: Unconquered. Unconquerable. Because they're strong and free. Because they have faith in themselves, and in God." Cooper's frontiersman and the dead Salters, shown in silhouette under a fading sun, represent the country's collective will, its shared destiny realized only through consensual cooperation. While understated (largely because of how frequently DeMille relied on this narrative device), the villain of the film, fur trader Martin Garth (Howard Da Silva), creates the crisis of Ft. Pitt purely because of his economic greed. Garth's motives are parasitic to the natural economic cornucopia to be shared by an expanding frontier population.

The public rejected *Unconquered* largely because DeMille's focus on visual "authenticity" separated so widely from the narrative verisimilitude required of genre. His visual cues—including a ridiculous escape scene whereby Cooper and Goddard jump from a canoe as they plunge down a waterfall—no longer supported the audience's broader expectations for an "exceptional" Western experience, a key rhetorical signifier of American freedoms during the Cold War. Licking his wounds and, significantly, stepping away from contemporary political controversies, DeMille retreated to cinematic spectacle for his remaining three works.

Taken collectively, the two phases of DeMille's Western iconography clearly establish the director's intentions for the genre. Unlike more successful, stable, and (to be honest) more mature cinematic deliberations on the West, like *Stagecoach* or *The Covered Wagon*, DeMille's images were arranged to serve the forces of cultural consensus and civilization. Institutions and urban environments showed more plainly than nature the limits and possibilities for personal freedom. Characters unable to modify or compromise in their cultural expressions were excised from the community and lost to the democratic promise that propelled progress in the director's fictional worlds. Villains existed in the West, but they were the product of choices presented to them through society and the marketplace rather than character flaws exposed by endless mesas, deserts, or confrontations with nature. DeMille's West was a mirror intended to justify the present, not a blank slate which could highlight the roads not taken.

Notes

1. The Jesse L. Lasky Feature Play Company, founded in 1913, merged with Adolph Zukor's production firm to produce the Famous Players-Lasky Company in 1916, which included W.W. Hodkinson's Paramount Pictures distribution company. Adding two other production studios the following year (and summarily firing Hodkinson), Zukor took financial control of Paramount Pictures while Lasky served as the head of studio production and DeMille as their leading director. This essay uses "Paramount Pictures" as a convenient shorthand method to reference these changes.

2. Al Lichtman quoted in Cecil B. DeMille Archives, Harold B. Lee Library, Brigham Young University, Provo, Utah (Box 240, Folder 1). For grosses, see Birchard, 105.

3. DeMille quoted in Cecil B. DeMille Archives, Harold B. Lee Library, Brigham Young University, Provo, Utah (Box 332, Folder 11); emphasis added. For similar attitudes stated by DeMille, see Kozlovic, 79.

4. Ibid.

5. DeMille's production notes for *Union Pacific* found in Cecil B. DeMille Archives, Harold B. Lee Library, Brigham Young University, Provo, Utah (Box 547 Folder 2).

6. DeMille to Sidney Bidwell found in Cecil B. DeMille Archives, Harold B. Lee Library, Brigham Young University, Provo, Utah (Box 390, Folder 6).

Filmography

The Call of the North. Dir. Cecil B. DeMille. Jesse L. Lasky Feature Film Company, 1914.
The Girl of the Golden West. Dir. Cecil B. DeMille. Jesse L. Lasky Feature Film Company, 1915.
The Plainsman. Dir. Cecil B. DeMille. Paramount Pictures, 1937.
A Romance of the Redwoods. Dir. Cecil B. DeMille. Artcraft Pictures, 1917.
Rose of the Rancho. Dir. Cecil B. DeMille. Jesse L. Lasky Feature Film Company, 1914.
The Sign of the Cross. Dir. Cecil B. DeMille. Paramount Pictures, 1932.
The Squaw Man. Dir. Cecil B. DeMille. Jesse L. Lasky Feature Film Company, 1914.
The Virginian. Dir. Cecil B. DeMille. Jesse L. Lasky Feature Film Company, 1914.
Unconquered. Dir. Cecil B. DeMille. Paramount Pictures, 1947.
Union Pacific. Dir. Cecil B. DeMille. Paramount Pictures, 1939.

Bibliography

Altman, Rick. A Semantic/Syntactic Approach to Film Genre. *Cinema Journal* 23:3 (1984): 6–18.
Birchard, Robert S. *Cecil B. DeMille's Hollywood*. Lexington: The University Press of Kentucky, 2004.

Cecil B. DeMille Archives. Harold B. Lee Library. Brigham Young University, Provo, Utah.
Crowther, Bosley. "'Unconquered,' Typical De Mills Extravaganza on Era Before Revolutionary War at Rivoli." *The New York Times* 11 October 1947. Web. http://www.nytimes.com/movie/review?res=9502EFDB123AE233A25752C1A96 69D946693D6CF
Eyman, Scott. *Empire of Dreams: The Epic Life of Cecil B. DeMille*. New York: Simon & Schuster, 2010.
Hayne, Donald (ed.). *The Autobiography of Cecil B. DeMille*. Englewood Cliffs, New Jersey: Prentice-Hall, 1959.
Kozlovic, Anton. "The Plainsman (1937): Cecil B. DeMille's Greatest Authenticity Lapse?" *Kinema* (Spring 2003): 73–86.
Louvish, Simon. *Cecil B. DeMille: A Life in Art*. New York: St. Martin's Press, 2007.
May, Lary. *The Big Tomorrow: Hollywood and the Politics of the American Way*. Chicago: University of Chicago Press, 2010.
n.a. "An Interview with Rick Altman." *The Velvet Light Trap* 51:1 (2003): 67–72.
Neale, Steve. *Genre and Hollywood*. New York: Routledge, 2000.
Pratt, George C. "Forty-Five Years of Picture Making: An Interview with Cecil B. DeMille." *Film History* 3 (1989): 133–145.

"They taught us to be men"
Cigarettes, Westerns and (Mostly) John Ford

RICHMOND B. ADAMS

As he reveals who shot Liberty Valance (Lee Marvin), Tom Doniphon (John Wayne) tells a shocked Ransom Stoddard (James Stewart) to "think back, pilgrim. You were coming out of the saloon when Valance fired his first shot. Remember?" After the climactic scene of *The Man Who Shot Liberty Valance* (1962) during which Stoddard meets Valance in the main street of Shinbone, Doniphon instructs Stoddard to keep Hallie, his former girlfriend, soon to be Mrs. Stoddard (Vera Miles), happy by giving "her something to read and write about" before he retreats into broken-hearted obscurity. If the film's director, John Ford, had transmitted the revelation that Doniphon, not Stoddard, had killed Valance simply through words, it would have proven a powerful enough ending on its own. Ford, however, has Doniphon begin his tale by removing a cigarette from his mouth and literally blowing a cloud of smoke in the direction of Stoddard, who has just been nominated as a delegate to argue for the territory's statehood application in Washington, D.C., solely on his falsely gained reputation as having killed Valance. Once Doniphon leaves the scene, Ford flashes forward to Stoddard, a United States Senator, telling reporters in present-day Shinbone the story of his return to bury a man none among them had ever known. Deciding to "print the legend" rather than the facts of the story, these reporters leave the Stoddards to travel aboard the train back to Washington. The train sequence brings the film to its end with Senator Stoddard's pipe hanging from his mouth, despairing over the magnitude of the lie that stands at the heart of his cultural reputation and political rise to power. The cigarette, and its relationship with cigars and pipes as forms of tobacco, cultural icons of the American late nineteenth century, stands alongside the gun, the hat, the horse, the saloon, the duel, the romance, the conflict with Native Americans, and other more prominent elements associated with the Western. Cigarettes in the actual West, however, did not have the same cultural prominence as they came to have in the films that mythologized them. As historian Allan M. Brandt outlines in *The Cigarette Century: The Rise, Fall, and Deadly Persistence of the Product that Defined America* (2007), this form of tobacco only began to be manufactured during the Civil War and "apparently" did not reach noticeable sales until the economic crisis of 1873 made their "relatively inexpensive" cost more attractive to smokers with limited funds (26). Despite their rise in popularity, Brandt notes that as late as 1900, "cigarettes still made up less than 2 percent of the thriving tobacco market, dominated by chew, cigars, and pipes" (26).

Given the dearth of cigarette consumption among Americans as they moved west after the Civil War, the cigarette's prominence in Western films across the first two-thirds of the American century points to other questions other than those having to do with the literal history of the period (26). Expressed by film directors John Milius and Martin Scorsese, these questions center on Americans' understanding of masculinity ("John Ford/John Wayne: The Filmmaker and the Legend"). Milius says, referring to the working combination of John Ford and John Wayne, "in a politically incorrect way ... taught us to be men" ("John Ford/John Wayne"). Following Milius, Scorsese remarks that "the issue for me is ... what is a man" ("John Ford/John Wayne"). In four of John Ford's best known Westerns, *Stagecoach* (1939), *My Darling Clementine* (1946), *The Searchers* (1956) and *The Man Who Shot Liberty Valance* (1962), American masculinity is defined through lenses of almost everything from clothes, to personal etiquette, to gun fights, and to Ransom Stoddard's role as a "hash slinger" in Shinbone's days of pre-civilization. The iconic combination of cigarettes and tobacco in these films also contributes to the ongoing and constantly renewed question of American masculinity.

In Westerns, cigarettes did not necessarily serve as advertisements for the ever-growing power of the tobacco industry across American life, but their presence in these films functioned with virtually the same result (Brandt 53; 63; 77; 87). In them, cigarettes and tobacco play a noticeable, if not always central role in shaping the American masculine persona during the period of America's unquestioned post–World War II national hegemony. In ways that are appropriate and troublesome, Ford's Westerns equated masculine hegemony with the use of tobacco, and especially the cigarette. Notably, however, within two years of Ford's finishing of *Valance*, the United States Surgeon General's released findings that cigarette smoking bore a strong link to the development of lung and other cancers (224). While "confirming the worst fears" of "seventy million regular smokers in the United States," the report also began a process that severed the link between the cigarette and masculinity (224). Accompanied by the decline of the traditional Western as a central American film genre, the removal of the cigarette as a marker of masculinity signaled a transformation of the image of American masculinity, which, according to Milius' words, had explicitly taught how "[men] were going to have to measure up [and that] [s]omething was going to be expected of us" ("John Ford/John Wayne"). As the mid-century evolved into its latter half, the cultural wisdoms transmitted by the images associated with the cigarette and tobacco underwent significant changes, primarily due to the Surgeon General's Report in 1964 (Brandt 229; 308), and expressed themselves in newer adaptations of the Western on film.

One recent representative film that reflects these cultural shifts involving cigarettes, tobacco and the Western is Ed Harris' *Appaloosa* (2008). Adapted from the Robert B. Parker novel of the same name, Harris' portrayal, as lead male star, of Virgil Cole undermined previous American notions of masculinity signified to a large degree by the use of cigarettes and tobacco. From its opening to ending, *Appaloosa* virtually avoids any sequence during which cigarettes, or smoking more generally, are used. While exceptions exist, the use of cigarettes and tobacco throughout tends to center on the activities not of the hero, but one Randall Bragg (Jeremy Irons), who had murdered the sheriff (Robert Jauregui) of Appaloosa, New Mexico, at the start of the film. The response of Cole, the film's hero and an independent lawman hired by the town fathers to restore order after the sheriff's murder, is that he "doesn't smoke" to Bragg's offer of a cigar immediately prior to the climactic gunfight in which Cole does not participate. Harris' film, set during America's move west and duplicating many features of a traditional Western, shifts the cultural link of smoking. In *Stagecoach* when Doc Boone (Thomas Mitchell) is castigated by the gambler Hatfield (John Carradine) for using tobacco "in the presence of a lady," Mrs. Lucy Mallory (Louise Platt); in *Appaloosa*, the hero refrains from tobacco use entirely. The manner in which Harris portrays (and directs) the hero as someone who does not fight in the showdown with his principal adversary and even, as the film ends, watches his friend Everett Hitch (Viggo Mortensen) walk into the desert wilderness rather than leaving civilization behind himself, as Ethan Edwards (John Wayne) did in Ford's *The Searchers* (1956), opens a set of new questions concerning the manner by which American masculinity has developed over the last 70 years (*Appaloosa*).

Adapted from Ernest Haycox's story "Stage to Lordsburg," *Stagecoach* was Ford's first Western since 1924. In it, John Wayne plays the "bighearted outlaw" Ringo Kid (John Wayne) alongside Dallas (Claire Trevor), the occasionally virtuous, but ultimately flawed leading lady (McBride 278–279; 286; 281). Beginning in Tonto, Arizona, as the stage stops for new horses while on its way to Lordsburg, *Stagecoach* showcases Dallas being exiled from town by the "Law and Order League" of local women who ensure that she is placed

Doc Boone enjoys his cigar in *Stagecoach* (Warner Bros., 1939).

in a stagecoach bound for Lordsburg (Eyman 194). Once underway, the stage becomes a battlefield of sorts over how and when tobacco is properly used. Those social distinctions reveal perceptions of American masculinity during the early to late nineteenth century. Hatfield corrects Doc Boone as he smokes a cigar in the coach that he shares with Mrs. Mallory (*Stagecoach*). As Hatfield puts the matter in as blunt a manner as he can in Mrs. Mallory's presence, the doctor is reminded that "a gentleman doesn't smoke in the presence of a lady" (*Stagecoach*; Duffey 37; 47). Complicating matters still further, Hatfield pointedly does not include Dallas in his definition of "lady." Knowing well her line of work, Hatfield, as well as Doc Boone and everyone else aboard the stage other than the Ringo Kid, associates Dallas with smoke-filled bordellos. Even after Dallas begins to gain a measure of respect from Mrs. Mallory by assisting in the delivery of her baby, Hatfield does not accord her the same protection during the Apache chase scene that he does the daughter of his former commanding officer in the Confederate Army. As it appears the Apache will overtake the stagecoach and capture the women aboard, Ford focuses his camera on Hatfield's pistol pointing toward Mrs. Mallory's head. As a gentleman protecting ladies from the ravages of miscegenation, Hatfield intends to kill her. He makes no similar effort to prevent Dallas from being captured by the closing Apaches. Ford's earlier presentation of the conflict between Hatfield, Doc Boone, and to a lesser degree, the Ringo Kid over smoking in the stage reflects more than an argument between an alcoholic physician, a ruthless gambler, and a still-naïve escaped convict (Kasson 44; *Stagecoach*). As a man of both the nineteenth and twentieth centuries, Ford knew well that manners and etiquette, especially in gender relations, helped to create images of self- and social understanding (Duffey 3–4; Hartley 87; Eyman 20–21).

The cultural relationship of tobacco also offers another, and more complicated, set of ways to examine Ford's first talking Western (McBride 165; 285; Eyman 113; 194). Simply put, while Doc Boone's smoking of a cigar, "a powerful symbol of social authority and power" across the nineteenth century, augments his status as a member of the triumphant Union Army, Hatfield's insistence on proper etiquette "in the presence of a lady," complicates Ford's notion of what price victory seems to have exacted (Brandt 25; *Stagecoach*). In *How to be a Lady: Useful Hints on the Formation of Womanly Character* (1850), Harvey Newcomb wrote that while men will occasionally partake of "tobacco," it is nonetheless a "filthy, poisonous plant, a little bit of which you could not be persuaded into [a woman's] mouth" (83, Newcomb's italics). Some 27 years later, but only 17 years before Ford's birth, Eliza Bisbee Duffey remarked that "no man has any right to smoke in a public place where there is any woman present" (93; McBride 21). By smoking a cigar in a lady's presence, Doc Boone suggests to both Hatfield and Mrs. Mallory that their recent loss in the war has resulted in nothing short of a slap across their faces (*Stagecoach*). In short, this scene reflects a growing tension found within American society during the post bellum era. Expressed in both fiction and film, this tension between propriety and power escalated and, in part, reshaped how Americans understood themselves as a distinct people (Adams 1–24). At its center stood how American men understood themselves and the manner in which they attempted to fulfill their expected gender roles of provider, protector, and, at least concerning temporal matters, the final authority figure (Stearns 83; Hartley 33; 43).

All Ford's Western films exhibit this tension between propriety and power. Ford's use of cigarettes and tobacco in *My Darling Clementine* (1946) conveys a similar manner he employs throughout *Stagecoach*. Tombstone is a ruthlessly wild and uncivilized place when the Earp brothers arrive at its outskirts. In it, Ford almost totally removes tobacco and cigarettes as central, or even near-central, signifiers. That is not to say that tobacco smoke is absent or downplayed: far from it. From almost the moment Wyatt and his brothers assume the role of sheriff and deputies, cigar and cigarette smoke permeates the atmosphere. Rather than visually locating its central source as one form of tobacco between the lips of given characters, however, Ford's smoke in *Clementine*, almost without exception, is mixed. The scene in which Granville

Thorndyke (Alan Mowbray) recites Hamlet's "to be or not to be" soliloquy from 3.1 to Doc Holliday, Sheriff Earp, and the Clantons, takes place within a saloon full of smoke, but its source is generalized. A second instance occurs prior to Doc Holliday's return from down south when Ford situates the new sheriff at a gambling table with, not coincidentally, several unidentified men in Tombstone's principal saloon. Unlike the other seated men, and certainly a singing Chihuahua (Linda Darnell), Sheriff Earp is the only person in the scene clearly seen smoking some form of tobacco, in his case, a cigar. Even as the sheriff dangles his cigar while concentrating on his poker hand, Ford establishes that the saloon is almost smothered in smoke.

During the game, as Earp plays his hand, two visual details add degrees of complexity to the scene. While centering on the sheriff catching Chihuahua sending signals to another player at the table and his forcibly throwing her into the water pool meant for horses, Ford augments these sequences via a small, but notable, shot of another man standing directly behind the sheriff. Unlike any other character present, he is clearly smoking a cigarette. No one knows if he, like Chihuahua, has tried to assist any of the other gamblers. It is not explained to which side of the Clanton/Earp feud the unnamed, cigarette-smoking man belongs. Yet his singularity as a cigarette smoker connects him to the sheriff, the new enforcer of legal proprieties. During Earp's historical tenure as sheriff, cigars, of course, held predominance over the cigarette signifying both overt, and, as in the case of the gambling scene, covert power (26; 37). By the 1940s, cigarettes had come to supplant cigars as the most popular form of American tobacco and had achieved almost simultaneously had achieved a type of functional equality (Brandt 37; 42; 49; 53). By the mid–1940s and *My Darling Clementine*, cigarettes were not only smoked in larger numbers, they became more acceptable signs of proper masculinity (121). The unnamed man standing directly behind Earp, the emblem of cultural power and smoking a product heretofore viewed with near unanimity as a repugnant sign of ill-breeding, signifies the respectability that cigarette smoking had come to attain.

The growing respectability of tobacco as an emblem of American masculinity expressed by the Western becomes more apparent in what is perhaps Ford's most un-civilized film, *The Searchers* (1956). Rampant with racism, sexism, and strains of American imperialism, Ford's tale of Ethan Edwards (John Wayne), on the hunt for five years to find his niece Debbie (Lana and Natalie Wood) across the barren Texas landscape, constituted an exploration of "racial and sexual issues [for] most people in 1956 would have been considered 'unspeakable'" (McBride 558). As the film portrays issues reaching far back into the darkest parts of America's history, Ford implants sequences that simultaneously create images of coming civilization that imply a tepidity that he found nearly as troubling as Edwards' monstrosity. Ford portrays this tepidity in the earliest scenes of the film. On the night of Ethan's return from three years of Mexican exile following the Confederate surrender at Appomattox, his brother Aaron (Walter Coy) sits by the fireplace, smoking a pipe. Echoing the Colonial era, Aaron Edwards' pipe represents a form of "individual moral character, honor, and reputation" that had been transferred from the quality of the type of tobacco leaves to the vehicle through which it is consumed (*The Searchers*; Brandt 21). As Brant notes, by the early 1900s, "unlike cigarettes," "smoked in the array of settings," pipes and cigars "were typically used in parlors and drawing rooms" (49). In 1868, cigarettes denoted a type of masculinity capable of an animal ruthlessness which the peaceable pipe-smoking Aaron needed to defend his hearth (*The Searchers*; Brandt 25–26). Viewed in terms of method by which his tobacco is consumed, Aaron is ill-equipped to contend with the looming danger hanging over his home, and a sense of helplessness and doom hovers over what soon follows. Once Ethan leaves the next morning with the Texas Rangers to investigate earlier Comanche raids, it is only a matter of time before Chief Scar (Henry Brandon) and his warriors destroy the Edwards family. As the differing and complex forms by which tobacco is consumed through *The Searchers* suggest, American men, who saw themselves as Victorians in "battle" with one another for the protection of hearth, home, and family, lost their ability to defend those same institutions as they became civilized (Brandt 25; 33; 46–47; Stearns 83).

Ford, however, does not simply place a cigarette in Ethan's mouth. Reflecting the growing complexity within American life after 1865, Ethan, when in the company of others, even his travelling companion Martin Pawley (Jeffrey Hunter), smokes mostly cigars. While doing so, Ethan stands virtually alone among the other men, who, Ford demonstrates, nearly always partake of their tobacco through the use of pipes. From Aaron's scene the night before his family is massacred to the last scene of *The Searchers* when his daughter (Natalie Wood) is brought to her uncle's home, and met by the pipe-smoking neighbor Jorgensen (John Qualen) with his wife (Olive Carey) standing by his side, pipes are the choice for men found in refined social situations. Such a growing difference, even between cigars and pipes, to say nothing of cigarettes, also provides a vehicle by which to understand *The Searcher*'s iconic ending. Given the setting of the film in isolated Texas, and cigarettes as a form of tobacco still in its infancy, Ethan's choice of cigars stands in noted contrast to the pipes used by his brother, Mr. Jorgensen, and, for example, the U.S. military captain during the fort scene which portrayed the consequence of young white girls kidnapped by native tribes for their own use. Ford created scenes, in short, where pipes were viewed as signs of masculine domesticity and weakness while cigars were consumed by those men, like Ethan, who could not live within what they saw happening around them. As Ethan approaches the Jorgensen home with Debbie in his arms, he sees its male protector holding a pipe in his right hand, and, with a rather stunning lack of masculine self-sufficiency, making no effort even to come off the porch to greet his niece. It is certainly plausible that seeing such a picture, with a pipe signifying domestication in its formative matrix, contributes significantly to Ethan's decision not to enter the Jorgensen home once he gave, on the porch of course, Debbie to the care of her other relatives. Much like cigarettes came to represent, as they gained cultural preeminence in the twentieth century, the power of a restrained, but at times necessarily wild form of masculinity, cigars, at least for a time, served that same purpose in the late nineteenth century, especially across areas well past the shaping power of civilization's more confining influences (Brandt 27; 33; 51; 53; *The Searchers*). Simply put, Ethan cannot live within a culture fast becoming respectable, but at the same time losing its physically protective and emotionally self-sufficient sense of defining what it means to be an American man.

Ford's portrayal of America after World War II, as many critics have noted, did indeed become progressively darker (Davis 178; Gallagher 467; McBride 559). Ethan did not stumble away from the Jorgensen porch with contempt in his demeanor. Rather, his apparent stumbling more broadly suggests, along with perhaps an uncertainty about his destiny, an ambiguity about America's grasp of its place in the post war world even at the height of its political, economic, social and military hegemony. Renouncing the predominance of domesticated masculinity transmitted via the primacy of pipes, Ethan stumbles away from the Jorgensen porch, which is itself another sign of American post-war prosperity rooted in home ownership, into a wilderness that he neither can nor wants to control. Simultaneously, however, when threats arise against these domesticated and soft Americans who cannot be protected by their men, Ethan realizes that he may well be called upon once more to rekindle the fires of "battle" within his fellows in order to preserve the still ambiguous "blessings of civilization" within which he cannot live (Stearns 83; *Stagecoach*). Arguably, such rekindling took on new forms of complication in Ford's last great film some seven years later, *The Man Who Shot Liberty Valance*.

Since *My Darling Clementine* and *The Searchers* had been released, tobacco had come under siege (Brandt 166; 173; 264) and, by the time *Valance* came into theatres in 1962, the relationship between tobacco, and especially the industry that sold it to the American public, had undergone significant change. Brandt describes Paul Hahn, the American Tobacco President, writing a 1953 press release designed to combat "'loose talk'" concerning the harmful effects of tobacco, when "'no one has yet proved that lung cancer in any human being is directly traceable to tobacco or its products in any form'" (qtd. 264; qtd. 264). Hahn's comments, however, had "no scientific basis for such optimism," and growing bodies of research had begun to "cast an ominous shadow over the cigarette's future" (Brandt 264). While the Surgeon General, Dr. Luther Terry, did not issue the official report linking cigarettes with lung and other forms of cancer until early January of 1964, the tobacco controversy grew after World War II. As scenes from *Valance* suggest, problems associated with tobacco use are expressed in Ford's last great film. Ford's use of tobacco, culminating with Doniphon's seeming to blow it into Stoddard's face, becomes is a complicated and pessimistic part of the "physical milieu" of the film, supporting what McBride sees as a "profoundly skeptical ... reexamination of American history and mythology [and offered] a[n] anticip[ation of] the public's loss of faith in government" (622).

Those complications express themselves in almost the first sequence of the film. Ransom and Hallie Stoddard have returned to Shinbone to bury Doniphon after having received news of his death from the long-time retired Marshall Link Appleyard (Andy Devine). As local reporters, led by Maxwell Smart (Carleton Young), insist on their right of the backstory from a United States Senator leaving his national political duties to attend the funeral of a man who had died "in obscurity," Stoddard agrees, and begins to unfold his tale with a pipe noticeably in his hand. Stoddard's pipe signals how the story will unfold. His story describes a decline in traditional forms of American masculinity (McBride 624; *The Searchers*). Adding even more poignancy to the scene and what will follow is the presence of an ashtray. Not only, Ford suggests, does a United States Senator, ostensibly a man of great power who knows how to use it, lack the masculine strength of Doniphon with his cigarettes and even of the founding editor of *The Shinbone Star* local newspaper, Dutton Peabody (George O'Brien) and his cigars, he even needs an ashtray to dispose of his burned byproducts.

Ford also uses tobacco to complicate his portrayal of Liberty Valance. Characterized as "among the screen's most flamboyant villains," and a "mad gunman," Valance's basic role is to protect the interests of cattle barons "opposed to statehood," and he demonstrates no limits whatsoever in his willingness to enforce the desires of his paymasters (Davis 308; McBride 624). Without limitations, witnessed in the savage whippings of Stoddard and Peabody early and late in the film, Valance would be expected to be accompanied by emblems that reinforce his amorality. Among these, especially by the early 1960s, one would expect to find cigarettes (Brandt 166; 173; 264). Valance, however, is never seen with a cigarette, and certainly not a cigar (denoting cultural power in the late nineteenth century) or a pipe (signifying domesticated, weakened masculinity) (Brandt 25; *The Searchers*). Valance simply does not smoke, a marker which, complicating matters of character, places him in the same cultural matrix as Stoddard, who wears an apron as he washes dishes in Peter's restaurant. When these images from Ford's film are juxtaposed against Scorsese's statement from the PBS production: "the problem is teaching us how to be men. The issue for me is … what is a man" ("John Ford/John Wayne"), it seems that domestication has linked with the consequences of the growing cultural, medical, and political consensus against the use of tobacco following the 1964 report within the United States. By the time of *Appaloosa*, such domestication of what was a self-sufficient American hero has resulted in so little force of personality that a sheriff cannot even overrule the desire of his sidekick and draw against the villain in the climactic gunfight. The non-smoking Virgil Cole stays behind to live in marriage while Everett Hitch enters the wilderness to wander in it, as Ethan Edwards does in *The Searchers*. Perhaps to paraphrase Milius' sentiments, almost *nothing* is expected of men today beyond a near hubris of self when the exact opposite is "required," reinforcing what is an already deep cultural anxiety "John Ford/John Wayne"). At the same time, it is not in question here that the tobacco companies first marketed, then delayed, then misled, then outright lied for decades in order to protect the sales of their product (Brandt 56; 61; 67; 81; 139; 261; 262; 376). There also have been too many early and agonizing cancer-related deaths that were all too connected with the consumption of tobacco, including the present author's paternal uncle in 1979 at the age of 41. For Milius and Scorsese, the link between masculinity and sacrifice for something greater than oneself in Western films stands as a constant. Given how Ford and other directors use the genre to explore questions of American identity, his employment of tobacco, through both its presence and absence, remains an important cultural marker for American men in the post-war and post–September 11 eras. In that sense, the difference between Tom Doniphon, a smoker, committing "cold-blooded murder" so that his girlfriend can be "happy" with *another* man and Virgil Cole, a non-smoker, remaining with a woman whom he knows all but certainly has betrayed him, and no less with the man just killed by his partner, is stark indeed. One might suggest that such a difference is not only stark, but also awkwardly troubling.

Filmography

Appaloosa. Dir. Ed. Harris. New Line Cinema, 2008.
The Man Who Shot Liberty Valance. Dir. John Ford. Paramount, 1962.
My Darling Clementine. Dir. John Ford. Twentieth Century Fox, 1946.
The Searchers. Dir. John Ford. Warner Brothers, 1956.
Stagecoach. Dir. John Ford. United Artists, 1939.

Works Cited

Adams, Richmond B. *Harold Frederic's Social Drama and the Crisis of 1890s Evangelical Social Drama*. Lewiston, Queenston and Lampeter: Mellen Press, 2013.
Brandt, Allan M. *The Cigarette Century: The Rise, Fall, and Deadly Persistence of the Product that Defined America*. New York: Perseus, 2007.
Davis, Ronald L. *John Ford: Hollywood's Old Master*. Norman: University of Oklahoma Press, 1995.

Duffey, Elizabeth Bisbee. *The Ladies' and Gentlemen's Etiquette: A Complete Manual of the Manners and Dress of American Society*. Facsimile Ed. 1877. White Fish, MT: Kessinger, 2008.
Eyman, Scott. *Print the Legend: The Life and Times of John Ford*. New York: Simon & Schuster. 1999.
Fite, Gilbert C. *Richard B. Russell, Jr.: Senator from Georgia*. Chapel Hill: University of North Carolina Press, 1991.
Gallagher, Tag. *John Ford: The Man and His Films*. Berkeley: University of California Press, 1986.
Hartley, Cecil B. *The Gentlemen's Book of Etiquette and Manual of Politeness: Being a Complete Guide for a Gentleman's Conduct in All His Relations Toward Society*. Facsimile Ed. 1873. White Fish, MT: Kessinger Press, 2007.
"John Ford/John Wayne: The Filmmaker and the Legend." *American Masters*. PBS. May 10, 2006. Dir. Samuel D. Pollard. Perf. John Wayne, Joseph McBride, and John Milius.
Kasson, John F. *Rudeness and Civility: Manners in Nineteenth Century Urban America*. New York: Hill and Wang. 1990.
Newcomb, Harvey. *How to Be a Lady: Useful Hints on the Formation of Womanly Character*. Facsimile Ed. 1850. Dahlonega, GA: Crown Rights, 2005.
Stearns, Peter N. *Be a Man! Males in Modern Society*. New York: Holmes and Meier, 1979.

The Good Bounty Hunter
Steve McQueen in Wanted: Dead or Alive

Kelly C. MacPhail

The bounty hunter is an invention of America's Old West. Necessitated by the scarcity of law enforcement and the problem of jurisdiction, bounty hunters were contracted to find wanted criminals and to perform other jobs that the law was too shorthanded to carry out on its own. Often cited in this respect is an 1873 U.S. Supreme Court ruling, *Taylor v. Taintor*,[1] which, among other things, allows those to whom a person has been remanded to pursue that individual into another state and forcibly enter into his or her private residence to capture and detain the individual if he or she has become a fugitive.[2] When *Wanted: Dead or Alive* (1958–61) appeared on CBS, it cleverly reinvented the figure of the bounty hunter as a specifically American archetypical antihero within the greater narrative of the civilizing of the Western frontier and in so doing propelled Steve McQueen to international stardom.

The late 1950s witnessed a reinvention of the Western genre that transformed the popular television drama into a more complex and developed narrative; in line with this revitalization, *Wanted* rejected earlier characterizations of the bounty hunter as bloodthirsty, cruel, and one-dimensional and instead presented a conflicted hero with intelligence, mercy, honor, humor, and emotional depth. McQueen's character, Josh Randall, is indeed a study in contradiction: armed with the "Mare's Leg," a sawn off repeating rifle invented for the show, Josh is clearly tough and fast enough to defeat the fiercest of villains, but he is also a Confederate Civil War veteran who believes in goodness and the sanctity of human life. Although law enforcement officers may mistake him for a greedy vigilante, he is shown in the first episode anonymously giving up most of his bounty money to help others in need. He commits to difficult moral decisions that put his own life in jeopardy, and he consciously relies on a code of honorable conduct that puts him in conflict with wanted fugitives, lawmen, women, a short-term partner, and rival bounty hunters. Undoubtedly, the series offers the prototype for the more fully realized figure of the bounty hunter that would be later developed and repeated in Westerns such as *For a Few Dollars More* (1965); *The Good, the Bad, and the Ugly* (1966); and *The Great Silence* (1968). Modern incarnations of the bounty hunter are found in popular reality shows and biopics as well as classic science fiction and speculative fiction that includes *Blade Runner* (1982), the *Star Wars* franchise (1977–present), and the series *Supernatural* (2005-present). The complex and humanized figures found in these latter films and TV shows would not have been possible but for the resignification of the bounty hunter accomplished by Steve McQueen[3] in *Wanted: Dead or Alive*.

McQueen appeared as himself in a promotional message for the series that aired after the episode of *Trackdown* that launched *Wanted* as its spinoff.[4] As he remarks, *Wanted: Dead or Alive* was meant to provide "a new approach to Westerns" because Josh is not a lawman but nonetheless fights on the side of justice without the limitations often imposed on lawmen: "Since Josh doesn't wear a badge, he can take the shortest distance between two people. On these occasions, his lawmen friends kinda turn their heads and wish they could use the same method." As McQueen asserts, "There's a lot of stories on *Wanted: Dead or Alive*, and they've all got one thing in common: they all happen to people—honest and dishonest ones; all with a problem; all with an empty space they wanted Josh to fill for them" (*Trackdown*, "The Bounty Hunter" 1.21). From the beginning, it is clear that the show wants to present an altered bounty hunter who serves America's national and cultural story. According to McQueen's description, *Wanted* aims to depict the bounty hunter as often more effective than lawmen who are in fact limited by the law and wish that they too could operate freely. The bounty hunter is necessary because he solves difficult problems and "fills an empty space" because he is flexible enough to get any job accomplished.

The historical concept of the bounty hunter is complex. The word "bounty" comes to English through French from the Latin *bonitatem*, meaning "goodness," and from the cognate group of *bonum*, meaning "good," which is also the root of the term "bonus." The *Oxford English Dictionary* traces the first usages of bounty in English to the moral virtues of goodness and valor in war ("Bounty"). The term took on the connotation of generosity given to people by God or by a sovereign, both in general and specific senses, and in the 1700s under Queen Anne, the sovereign's bounty referred to a financial bonus paid to military men who were newly enlisted or who distinguished themselves in battle. An early use of bounty in the sense of hunting for individuals arose in America's early colonial period, when bounties were offered to whites for the scalps of Native Americans deemed to be enemies

("Bounty"). Bounties were later offered proof of killing wild animals seen as dangerous or as nuisances, such as wolves or coyotes. In more modern parlance, bounties refer to specialist work in many different fields, from business to politics to sports.[5] From this basis, the logical assumption is that Americans in the Wild West then extended the concept to include hunting wanted fugitives from justice. However, the roots of the concept are in fact rooted in the bail surety system that dates back to medieval English common law instead of the Western sense of locating and arresting wanted individuals. When bail surety was transported to the American colonies, it changed significantly given the much greater mobility of the colonists, eventually leading to what is now estimated to be a $4 billion industry in the United States.[6]

Fictional representations of bounty hunters have done much to distort historical reality or, in fact, to invent a new archetype based on a small amount of historical fact. Thus, the designation of "bounty hunter" is now mainly misapplied in most uses of the term. Although there were men in the Old West who were paid upon the capture or killing of wanted fugitives, there were actually very few people who did so as a regular occupation of any type. Bill O'Neal, in his comprehensive study of the biographies and exploits of 255 individual Western gun-fighters, lists only three men who qualify as bounty hunters, although his exact definition of the term is left unclear (8). Without question, however, the role of rewards was essential to the development of this judicial system in England and in both Eastern and frontier America. Certainly in the context of the Old West, the general populace scorned such figures as despicable and motivated by blood money. Exceptions were lawmen, deputies, or employees of federal agencies accepting a bounty as reward money; this was seen as an acceptable connection between justice and reward (Traub 294, 300), although federal and state legislation frequently barred lawmen from accepting bounties. Nonetheless, such rewards happened frequently, especially when such bounties were offered by private citizens or businesses instead of the state.[7] One byproduct of these bounty rewards was a greater level of cooperation and communication between lawmen, who circularized information about wanted criminals including pictures, physical descriptions, details of the crime, and the reward (Traub 299–300).

Modern "bounty hunters" work on a different system than in the Old West, and their use of the name appears to be more in the service of marketing than reality. Now, bounty hunters, better termed bail enforcement agents, work on contract for bail bondsmen. In such cases, the fugitives had already been apprehended by police and charged with a crime, at which point a court judge determined whether to hold the individual in custody or allow them to leave jail after paying a specified amount of bail money that would be forfeited were they to fail to appear for their trial. This system of surety dates back at least to pre-Norman England. Whereas in the older English system a family member or acquaintance would put up the bail or indeed would have their own freedom put in jeopardy, as the surety necessitated them serving the person's sentence if the accused did not appear for trial, the American form allowed for the creation of independent bail bondsman. As many people are unable to put up large sums of money, bail bondsmen accept such people as clients, put up the cash for them, and take a percentage as payment. If the clients fail to appear for trial, the bail bondsman has a set period in which to compel them to appear or else lose the full amount of the bail. The modern bail enforcement agent or "fugitive recovery specialist" is then contracted by the bondsman for a commission or a percentage to find the individuals and bring them to the police.[8] Notions common to Josh Randall in the context of *Wanted: Dead or Alive* do not apply: most obviously, killing a fugitive except in self-defense would be considered a groundless murder that would be prosecuted. Likewise, many literary or cinematic "bounty hunters," so called, are in fact bounty killers: hired assassins intended primarily to murder specific individuals on someone else's behalf. Typically, such bounty hunters work outside the law or are fighting on behalf of an oppressive entity against the heroes, as in the case in the *Star Wars* franchise. Likewise, although many Western films feature show bounty hunters as hired guns, such characters are frequently represented as on the wrong side of the law, unlike Josh Randall.

Nonetheless, *Wanted*'s bounty hunter is situated in an ambiguous relation to society and to the law. In the decades since *Wanted*, and partly because of it, the icon of the bounty hunter has significantly expanded from a simple gun-for-hire motivated solely by payment. The figure, in many incarnations, is presented as a mysterious liminal character who upholds social values, protects mores, and acts in a capacity similar to that of the established officers of the law. There is still a motive in making profit, but the typical rhetoric of straight-and-narrow bounty hunters in popular media insists that they work alongside the police to bring criminals to justice, and this contributes to their romanticized image as tough and honorable loners. *Wanted* further appeases its audience by having Josh take on cases that are frequently not dangerous or do not involve criminals. What is essentially a warm-hearted portrayal of Josh escalated as the series gained more of a following. Indeed, the only such episode in the first season, a Christmas themed episode that aired on December 20, 1958, has Josh helping a little boy who offers him eight cents to bring in Santa Claus (1.16). By Season 3, Josh is more often pictured as a straightforward do-gooder to balance the more violent, crime-ridden episodes. For example, he helps a young couple elope (3.22), aids a Japanese woman in finding her betrothed (3.24), assists a thief in returning a large sum of stolen money against the wishes of his accomplice (3.23), and even locates a missing pet sheep for a distraught couple in one of the oddest but funniest episodes of the series (3.15).

Josh's core motivation to become a bounty hunter was his need for freedom. In one episode,[9] Josh recounts that there was not a lot of thought behind his decision: "Just happened. Working in a bank back home. One day I looked out at a customer and it hit me—I was living in a jail. Quit that afternoon" (1.11). Following his epiphany, all he really wants is freedom and just enough money to get by; as he puts it, he "don't want to work that hard. As long as I got a handful of beans and the makin', that's all I need" (1.11). Considering the series as a whole, it becomes apparent that the production staff took some time to decide what the icon of the bounty hunter would mean for their show. The show's theme music is comprised of martial sounding brass and percussion instruments over a shot of Josh Randall walking along a boardwalk, tearing down a wanted poster, and glaring at the camera. The opening focuses on the striking appearance of the threatening Mare's Leg. McQueen's humor and easy smile are nowhere apparent. This opening instead offers a serious tone with a serious protagonist. By Season 3, this opening had been replaced with a much darker sequence in which a black screen is interrupted by three gun flashes aimed directly at the viewer; Josh Randall then steps out of the dark with the camera's focus again on the threatening Mare's Leg. The effect emphasizes the threatening aspects of the bounty hunter although the mood of the series itself has noticeably lightened from that of the first season as Josh's good nature has become more evident. This relatable bounty hunter is often referred to in a friendly manner simply as "Josh"; he is a man known by his first name, which, perhaps not incidentally, invokes a cool and carefree attitude of joking or "joshing" around. Likewise, Josh's regional accent, although uneven as the series progresses, also becomes more homespun. Folksy remarks enter his speech along with a Southern drawl especially found in his catch phrase, "let's goo."

The first episode of the series, "The Martin Poster,"[10] introduces the ambiguous role that Josh plays throughout in relation to the Law. This episode opens with Josh riding his black horse out of a wild wind blowing sand and dirt. As he enters the Western town of La Tunas, the camera shifts to the interior of the marshal's office and focuses first on the badge of the marshal before pulling out to reveal two armed men,[11] the Martin brothers, who are in the process of breaking Carl out of prison. Josh enters and a gunfight ensues that kills the marshal, leaving him to track the two villains and bring them to justice. Thus, in the just first two minutes of the series, a paradigm is established in which the bounty hunter is seen to represent Justice, if not Law, and to stand in for lawmen who are unable to contend with the onslaught of evil men.

Again and again, Josh shows that he believes in the law and must act not only as a quasi-lawman but also as an investigator, lawyer, judge, and jury in order to understand the true and often hidden facts of a situation.

Several of his cases involve tracking down people accused of serious crimes who fear they will be hanged and who have decided to take their chances on the run instead. Frequently in these cases, it is close relatives or friends who hire Josh, pleading with him that they know that the person he seeks is innocent or has been framed. Josh, as a champion of justice, brings these individuals back to civilization to stand trial. Indeed, he often takes an active hand in proving their innocence and restoring the balance of truth to improve a barely civilized society where the powerful sometimes use the legal system to their own advantage.

Notably, Randall's good nature is often over emphasized by producers and viewers alike. Several descriptions of the program refer to him frequently giving away half or all of the bounty that he earns to help those in need, thus presenting him as a purely socially minded figure who brings evil doers to justice without a thought of reward. In the actual diegesis, however, this rarely happens. The reason for the discrepancy is that the first episode of the series, "The Martin Poster" (1.1), shows Josh giving up most of his bounty to aid the family of a murdered sheriff. Given the need to portray Josh as a morally upright and generous individual, the series early on shows him to be giving, empathetic, and kind hearted. Throughout the series, however, Josh is actually very insistent about being paid the full amount of the bounty for the jobs he completes. Josh regards his work as difficult and dangerous, so he not only takes but also insists on his full pay. Thus, despite the reality that Josh is in effect a private contractor, the first episode in particular so fully portrays him as selfless and generous that a popular perception continues to see Josh as the Robin Hood of the Old West.

Josh's freedom, independence, and deadly efficiency is revealed in another of the show's trademarks, the Mare's Leg (or Mare's Laig), a sawn off 1892 Winchester carbine that Josh carries like a pistol, thus blending the characteristics of a pistol's fast draw and a rifle's power. The Mare's Leg was designed especially for *Wanted* and remains the subject of much discussion. There are notable continuity errors in reference to the gun itself that arise from the bullet caliber, the barrel shape, the size of the lever loop, and the use of more than one of the series' three prop guns in single scenes. The weapon itself is an 1892 Winchester model, although the series is set in the late 1860s. However, McQueen wielded the weapon well after considerable practice and modifications, as he told interviewer John Lachuk in a 1961 interview for *Guns Quarterly*. In the same article, McQueen even recounts winning a fast draw contest with the Mare's Leg by a 2/5s of a second draw in a friendly competition at a Palm Springs fair against other TV stars including James Arness from *Gunsmoke*, John Payne from *The Restless Gun*, and Peter Brown from *Lawman* (Lachuk 12). The gun itself has inspired tributes from sources as diverse as the Sergio Leone Spaghetti Western classic *Once Upon a Time in the West* (1968) to Joss Whedon's space Westerns *Firefly* (2002) and *Serenity* (2005) to the apocalyptic comedy *Zombieland* (2009). As a symbol of continuity, the Mare's Leg even reappears on display in the office of Josh's bounty hunter grandson in the film *Wanted: Dead or Alive* (1987). Without question, the Mare's Leg is a fitting weapon for the bounty hunter, joining the power and speed necessary for Josh to survive and to defeat his opponents. Likewise, the anachronous weapon points to the curious overlaps between fiction and reality in which TV stars play make-believe in fast draw competitions and McQueen's legendary cool and easy demeanor is translated back into the public's ideal of the bounty hunter created by *Wanted*.

A part of the allure in *Wanted*'s presentation of the bounty hunter is Josh's cherished solitude and independence. As a bounty hunter, Josh is a nomad who cannot or will not settle down although he may desire to do so. The solitary bounty hunter is thus placed in a position to judge the worth—and the monetary value—of human life despite the fact that others often disparage his own worth because of his job. As one character, a sheriff's daughter named Julie Taggart, laments in "The Hostage" (2.6), "Are you really worth it, Mr. Randall? My father gets paid forty dollars a month for capturing men like Jumbo Kane. Forty dollars. You collect a thousand for doing the same thing," to which Josh replies, "Yes, ma'am. That's why I do it." When Jumbo Kane (Lee Van Cleef) escapes, shoots her father, and demands another hostage, questions of nobility and humanity arise. Josh is urged to do "the noble thing" by the townspeople (of the aptly named Rogue City) by volunteering to be the hostage. When he refuses, they have no problem in coercing him to do so at gunpoint. The townspeople, who minutes before had applauded Josh for bringing in Kane, now debate the value of his life. The town's judge, who fears for his life because it was he who sentenced Kane, insists, "Julie, what's more important? Your father's life of the life of a ... bounty hunter?" to which she replies, "That doesn't even need an answer, and you know it." Later, Julie realizes that Kane, who is holed up in the sheriff's office, must be stalling because her father is already dead. To verify this, she shouts to Josh, whom the townspeople have forced to become Kane's new hostage. Josh knows that he will likely die if he admits that her father is dead because the judge will order the townsmen open fire to kill Kane without regard for Josh's life. However, he tells the truth, and Julie grudgingly changes her mind about him and argues against the judge that they cannot allow Josh to die because he told the truth when he could have lied to save himself. The judge demands, "Now how often does a foot scrapin' bounty man get a chance to die a hero's death?" but Julie insists that it is "A martyr's death. There's a difference." Josh's honorable actions thus give Julie a clearer idea of what true humanity means. In the process of making his escape, Kane takes Julie hostage, but a shackled Josh fights Kane until Julie is able to shoot and kill

Kane. The judge immediately offers Josh the sheriff's job, which he rejects with the remark that enemies are sometimes much easier to recognize than friends.

Love is also restricted for this bounty hunter. In an early episode, "The Fourth Headstone," Josh must transport a beautiful woman to stand trial despite her claims that she was falsely accused of murdering her husband, her lover, and a ranch foreman (1.9). As the two travel across the county, the woman charms Josh, who appears to believe her and to fall in love with her. Consequently, he is nearly murdered, and the woman is revealed to be classic femme fatale in an episode that is a decidedly cross-genre *noir* Western. The episode title, "The Fourth Headstone," refers to the possibility that Josh would become her next victim. Likewise, in a late episode, Josh again appears to fall in love, this time with a young woman who is deaf and mute. After successfully helping her, he rides off but is emotionally torn while doing so ("The Voice of Silence," 3.20). In an early episode, a young nun proves to be a match for Josh. In "Ransom for a Nun" (1.7), Josh is transporting a violent criminal but hands him over to his outlaw gang in exchange for Sister Grace, the 17-year-old nun whom they are holding prisoner. The feisty young nun hinders Josh's efforts to recapture the criminal, despite the possibility that he will go to prison himself for making a deal to allow the man to go free. One scene in which Josh ties up Sister Grace inside a church so he will be free to protect her and fight the criminals shows the sexual tension between the two. Indeed, it is the young woman's status as a nun that makes her so attractive next to Josh; though she is his match in bravery, intelligence, and fortitude, any connection between the two remains a pure and impossible fantasy that cannot ultimately threaten Josh's independence.

The complicated relationship between pay, love, and honor is raised again in "Journey for Josh" (3.3). In this episode, the town sheriff argues that Josh does the same work that he himself does but for twice the pay. However, as the episode demonstrates, this is not true. Besides the obvious difference that the town's sheriff does not endure the constant exposure to danger that Josh endures, he also has a steady income, lives in the town, and presumably has a set residence; he may even be married and have a family. Josh, on the other hand, has no opportunity for such stability or safety. Indeed, it is in this episode that Josh falls deeply in love with a prisoner he is transporting named Susan Marno (Lisa Gaye). She too has little respect for the bounty hunter at first. Their first impressions become complicated on the road when Susan saves Josh's life from an attacker and he saves her from a poisonous rattlesnake. Nevertheless, Susan adamantly maintains that Josh is subhuman and even less honorable than a criminal like herself because he is a bounty hunter: "You think we're even, don't you? Well, we're not. There's a difference between you and me—a big difference, and I'm going to tell you just what it is. No matter what you've done or what you are, to me you're another human being. But what am I to you—nothing—a package or something to be delivered. My life is just a dollar sign to you, money in the bank, something on the open market, so don't you dare think we're even. Don't you dare!" (3.3).

Nonetheless, they soon reconcile and fall in love, with Josh claiming that he has never felt this way about a woman before. Notably, they turn back from the town where Josh has to deliver Susan, and it is clear that he is going to plan a way around taking her in at all. He and Susan, however, are being tracked by Susan's former partner, who attacks them. Tragically, Susan is shot and killed. The episode does not cohere well because it attempts to do too much; it has, in fact, the emotion and plot of a full length movie squeezed into a 25-minute episode. In terms of character, however, the series is here echoing the earlier sequence with Sister Grace. Romance plots in the show only work temporarily and simply cannot or do not work in the long term. Although Josh's desires for female companionship are dashed in the short term, the series thrives in the long term because he maintains his freedom, an element that is vital to the fictional image of the independent and solitary bounty hunter.

An opportunity for Josh to find friendship is offered by Jason Nichols (Wright King), a character who adds a new dimension to *Wanted* in 11 late episodes of Season 2. A former deputy, he becomes a sidekick and friend for Josh. Jason is young, enthusiastic, very handy with a gun, and steps in when Josh is gravely injured during their first episode. A partnership and friendship develops between the two, and Josh teaches Jason the skills necessary to survive and make a living as a bounty hunter. Without explanation, however, the two eventually part ways. The first episode of this story arc is "Jason" (2.21), in which Josh turns in a small-time criminal "Doc" Phillips (Sean McClory) in order to capture Clell Fanning, using, as he puts it, a "little fish" to catch a "big fish." When Josh meets Jason, Jason seems right away to admire Josh. Likewise, Jason is immediately likeable; he is friendly, humorous, and even keeps a small dog that drinks beer. However, he acts brusquely with women and is seen pressing a prisoner for information by beating him. Although Josh appears to like Jason and takes him under his wing, Jason does not have the same sense of justice, level of intelligence, or deductive reasoning ability that Josh exhibits as necessary for a bounty hunter. Yet when Josh is seriously injured and the sheriff killed in a raid by Fanning's gang, it is Jason who steps in to calm the townsfolk, to protect Josh, and to help apprehend Fanning. Craftily, he feigns drunkenness and claims that he alone in the town has seen Fanning. After a night of thinking, he comes to the conclusion that "Doc" Phillips actually invented the persona of Clell Fanning as a scapegoat should he ever be caught. Jason again reveals his violent nature when he fights "Doc" in the jail cell to get the truth. He then splits the $5000 bounty with Josh. Realizing that he made more money that way than he would in three years as a sheriff's deputy, Jason asks to team up with Josh, who is very reticent to do so; he values his freedom too highly to be connected either with a wife or with a male buddy.

An explanation for the end of Josh and Jason's already tenuous partnership is never given in the series.[12] However, Jason's last episode could provide some clues about his disappearance. In "Prison Trail" (2.31), he helps Josh transport a woman and three men to Leavenworth Prison in Kansas. The bounty hunters soon find themselves being trailed by a man who is after a large quantity of stolen money whose location is known only by the female prisoner. Josh rides this man off, but he returns at night to attack the camp. When Jason notices that two Pawnee now accompany the man, Josh, in his typically cool demeanor, observes, "Oh, that's fine. From what I understand, all you got to do to get them to work for you is to promise 'em a scalp." Jason, who appears particularly scared by the threat of the Pawnee, remarks, "Well, we got three good ones under that wagon; put them on the market and throw in the squaw to boot"; when he later learns that the woman is the one their attacker is after, he says, "Maybe we could trade her, Josh. Doesn't sound like she'd be much of a loss to the human race." Josh, however, thinks only of his duty and does not respond to Jason's cowardly remarks. Nonetheless, Jason does fight honorably in the ensuing gunfight and in fact saves Josh's life when one of the Pawnee is about to shoot him. Although the end of the episode shows the group progressing to Leavenworth, there is no discussion of the events of the night before or of Jason's cowardly suggestion to sacrifice the prisoners to save themselves. Clearly, Jason lacks Josh's sense of duty and honor as well as the courage under pressure that Josh regards as essential to the life of a bounty hunter.[13]

It is with such ideals of duty, honor, and courage in mind that *Wanted: Dead or Alive* remolds the Western archetype of the bounty hunter. With the King of Cool, Steve McQueen, as its star, the series not only portrayed the bounty hunter as more vital to the Old West than it really was but also cast the figure as a benevolent, justice-oriented character who could deal single-handedly with any situation. Thus, *Wanted* celebrates the bounty hunter as a chivalric hero motivated by the civilizing mission of the frontier and by the enduring American spirit of individualism and independence.

Notes

1. *Taylor v. Taintor* (1872) 83 U.S. 366 [21 L.Ed. 287].
2. However, the claim that the passage in question actually establishes the wide swath of rights claimed by bounty hunters is debatable, as it was an *obiter dictum*, meaning the passage was not a ruling intended to establish a legal precedent but simply an aside for clarification of the case at hand in which an individual out on bail had refused to appear for trial. Notably, the industry is not federally regulated by any legislation similar to that which limits

police officers, such as the necessity for search warrants or Miranda warnings, despite attempts to do so.

3. McQueen's last two movies, *Tom Horn* (1980) and *The Hunter* (1980), would both be fictionalized accounts of real life bounty hunters, while a 1987 film, also named *Wanted: Dead or Alive*, would star Rutger Hauer as Nick Randall, Josh's grandson who makes a living as a bounty hunter in present day Los Angeles.

4. *Trackdown*, "The Bounty Hunter" 1.21.

5. One such usage arose in 2011 with "Bountygate," in which it was found that some New Orleans Saints players were being paid illegal bonuses for injuring opposing players.

6. Bounty hunting, now called bail enforcement, remains an American industry, and even there it is limited or even illegal in some states. The Philippines, as a former U.S. commonwealth, is the only other country with a similar system although it has existed in different forms in other countries or in rare instances.

7. Such bounties, usually more lucrative than state bounties, were offered by institutions such as railway companies, banks, or cattlemen's associations (Traub 297–98).

8. For further information on the development of the bail industry in the United States, see Porcello's "International Bounty Hunter Ride-Along," Johnson and Warchol's "Bail Agents and Bounty Hunters," or Burns, Kinkade, and Leone's "Bounty Hunters: A Look Behind the Hype."

9. This episode was written by John Robinson, who was also the producer for 68 of the series' 94 episodes.

10. Though "The Martin Poster" (1.1; 6 Sept. 1958) was the first episode of the series, the pilot episode is actually "The Bounty Hunter" (1.21; 7 March 1958), an episode of another Western series *Trackdown* (1957–59) that focused on a Texas Ranger.

11. One of the villains is played by a young Michael Landon, who would go on to star in such classic TV Westerns as *Bonanza* (1959–73) and *Little House on the Prairie* (1974–83).

12. In reality, the end of this storyline was likely simply caused by the end of Season 2 or because the show employed several different writers, which led to an occasional lack of continuity.

13. In an earlier episode, "The Partners" (2.22), Josh and Jason quarrel for a similar reason after Jason shoots and kills three fugitives that Josh believes could and should have been taken in alive.

Filmography

"The Bounty Hunter." *Trackdown*. Perf. Robert Culp and Steve McQueen. CBS. 7 Mar. 1958.
The Hunter. Dir. Buzz Kulik. Perf. Steve McQueen and Eli Wallach. Paramount, 1980.
Tom Horn. Dir. William Wiard. Perf. Steve McQueen, Linda Evans, and Richard Farsworth. Warner Bros., 1980.
Wanted: Dead or Alive. Dir. Gary Sherman. Perf. Rutger Hauer, Gene Simmons, and Robert Guillaume. New World Pictures, 1987.
Wanted: Dead or Alive. 1958–61. Perf. Steve McQueen. Mill Creek Entertainment, 2009. DVD.

Works Cited

"Bounty, n." *OED Online*. Oxford University Press, May 2015. Web. 10 May 2015.
Burns, Ronald, Patrick Kinkade, and Matthew C. Leone. "Bounty Hunters: A Look Behind the Hype." *Policing: An International Journal of Police Strategies & Management* 28.1 (2005): 118–38. Print.
Johnson, Brian R., and Greg L. Warchol. "Bail Agents and Bounty Hunters: Adversaries or Allies of the Justice System?" *American Journal of Criminal Justice* 27.2 (2003): 145–65. Print.
Lachuk, John. "The Gun That Brings 'Em Back 'Dead or Alive.'" *Guns Quarterly* 5 (1961): 10–13, 61–62. Print.
O'Neal, Bill. *Encyclopedia of Western Gun-Fighters*. Norman: University of Oklahoma Press, 1979. Print.

Porcello, Ryan M. "International Bounty Hunter Ride-Along: Should U.K. Thrill Seekers Be Permitted to Pay to Experience a Week in the Life or a U.S. Bounty Hunter?" *Vanderbilt Journal of Transnational Law* 35.953(2002): 953–987. Print.

Traub, Stuart H. "Rewards, Bounty Hunting, and Criminal Justice in the West: 1865–1900." *The Western Historical Quarterly* 19.3 (1988): 287–301. Print.

Racialized Markers of Gender and Gendered Markers of Race in 1950s Westerns

Deborah L. Kitchen-Døderlein

In the 1950s, Western movies became focal points for the collision between the America that had been and the hopes of the nation that America could become. With the United States and Hollywood embroiled in the Cold War, McCarthyism, HUAC hearings and the blacklist, the Westerns' screen action (set in the historical past) provided an emotional distance from its audience's present fears and offered a measure of safety for its viewers from the political conflict at home and abroad that began after the end of the Second World War.[1] During the 1950s, domestic friction and civil challenges in America were equally prevalent and potent. Post-war veterans returned to women who had successfully taken on the mantle of authority within the workplace and at home. African Americans returned from the battlefield ready to fight for victory against racism at home. As a popular mode of storytelling, movie Westerns were well-poised to assuage the anxieties of white males about their civil authority by presenting iconic celebrations of white masculinity. Some Westerns did so by incorporating aspects of love and romance into the plot, in order to tie the lone hero to a larger culture. While celebrating white masculinity, some even imagined the possibility that love could cross racial boundaries. Production Code bans against portraying miscegenous couples, however, ensured that such a white male hero would never be entirely domesticated. Interracial romances were instead used to highlight the traits which made the hero "heroic" because the romance could be brushed aside in the end as various plot devices punished such lovers for their romantic transgressions. The death of one character, for example, ensured misery for the other who suffered the loss. The assimilation of non-white characters in Westerns released during the 1950s assured audiences that whiteness was worth the loss of one's native culture, family and identity. In another plot option, the non-white character accepted defeat sadly, leaving his or her white love interest to a white rival. Tragic endings like these were somehow less tragic in a Western than in a melodrama, because the larger theme was not about romance and love but self-reliance within and for a larger community or purpose. In this way, Hollywood movie Westerns envisioned and mediated a future for the nation which subsumed race and gender in service to hegemony.

This essay examines a subset of Hollywood Westerns of the 1950s which includes interracial romance or sexual interaction: *Broken Arrow* (1950), *Across the Wide Missouri* (1951), *High Noon* (1952), *Broken Lance* (1954), *The Far Horizons* (1954), and *The Searchers* (1956). Meeting points for discussions about race and gender, these movies showcase the West as being inherently multi-racial—with long-standing Mexican populations, African American cowboys, Asian workers, and immigrants from throughout the world acting as an occupying force to take American Indian lands. Imbalanced sex ratios of the westward movement also created a hyper-masculine environment on screen. Specifically, this essay investigates how the racialized markers of gender and the gendered markers of race used in these movies present a nuanced view of Western iconography and archetypes.

Theory

Despite the multi-cultural, multi-racial reality of the western frontier, Hollywood Westerns released before the 1950s generally portray a boundary land that is white to its core. Rarely foregrounded, non-white characters provide a backdrop for the action in these movies. They are a part of the scenery of the West—and the plot "problem" to be resolved by the hero. They exist as "others" to display white masculine power. Although blood-thirsty "savages" might scalp a few innocent settlers, as "others," such non-white characters perish, when white settlers overtake them under the leadership of a white, male hero.[2] Here it should be noted that in Westerns, the "gaze" is not just male. It is also specifically and unself-consciously white. In general, Westerns released before the 1950s were made by men and for men. If, as Judith Butler notes, "'doing whiteness'" as a performance is an act designed to "'achieve and maintain dominance for white people,'" considerations of performance should also be applied to Westerns. In the 1950s, however, presentations of identity in Westerns became more complex as white masculinity contrasted with other race's masculinities as well as the femininity of women. This is particularly true of Westerns that included interracial romances. A romance between characters of the same race tends to assume white as normal/human, but a romance between characters of different races is inherently more complex because every character must display two categories at the same time, as both gender and race are central to the romance.³

Racialized and Gendered Markers

In the 1950s, markers of race and sex continued to serve as basic markers for power in Westerns. Legitimate power and authority were generally reserved for white, male heroes. Other raced male characters could express certain limited kinds of power. For example, Indian braves could demonstrate physical strength and courage in battle. Indian chiefs could be noble and demonstrate a sense of honor. However, notions of Manifest Destiny ensured that however noble the "savage," such characters would ultimately die or live as a conquered race. White male heroes could express a three-dimensional identity with more nuances of trustworthiness, honor and courage—and still survive or pass on their heroic attributes to a son, as in *Broken Lance*.

Beyond basic markers of race and sex, other physical markers came into play. Casting decisions separated the truly masculine from the ordinary lower level of masculinity and those who performed as white, male heroes shared certain markers that set them apart from the other men on screen. For example, most of the white men who starred in these movies were tall—taller than the average man of the time and certainly taller than other men in these productions. Clark Gable was 6'1", while James Stewart, Fred MacMurray, and Gary Cooper were all 6'3" and John Wayne was 6'4." Because of their bodies, these men could easily stand out in a crowd—a necessity in movies filled with crowds of men. Only Spencer Tracy was of average height at 5'9½", but camera angles and blocking allowed him to stand out as well. White, masculine power was also marked by age. The stars ranged from age 42 to 54 when their movies were released. They were mature, but not elderly and frail. Although Gary Cooper was in pain while filming *High Noon*, he had to manage the fight scenes to prove he still had masculine prowess. The choice of mature men who were already well established movie stars in casting the heroic leads was in part a function of their drawing power at the box office. Additionally, they were able to bring the gravitas of age into their characterizations.

Age and height differences served also as markers of inferior status among men. Supporting male characters (white and non-white) were generally shorter than the white male leads, although there were some exceptions to this rule. Hank Worden, who played the simpleton, Mose Harper, in *The Searchers*, was 6'1½". Jeff Chandler, as Cochise (in *Broken Arrow*) was actually an inch taller than James Stewart. To allow for Cochise to appear as a physical equal made sense in a plot that declared equal respect between the two characters. However, James Stewart clearly demonstrates more power than Chandler's Cochise. His character is the one to initiate all talks and demonstrate fearlessness by riding into the Indian camp alone.

Secondary male lead characters were younger versions of the stars physically. As young potential heart throbs, they needed to share markers of masculine power with the stars. Charlton Heston was 31 years old and 6'2½" when *The Far Horizon* was released. Robert Wagner was 24 years old and just shy of 6 feet tall when *Broken Lance* was released. Jeffrey Hunter, of *The Searchers*, was 30 years old and 6 feet tall. Both Wagner and Hunter played mixed offspring of interracial couples. Wagner's character was allowed markers of respect for masculinity as the rising son of Tracy's character. He could perform a younger version of the hero—one who would grow into such a roll though he was not quite there yet. Still Wagner's and Hunter's bodies could not be allowed to upstage the stars. Clever blocking allowed them to stand beside the star briefly, and then to retreat.

Age difference, as a physical marker, also clearly delineates the female lead characters as inferior to the male leads. As Table 1 illustrates, in almost every case the male star is noticeably older than the female love interest. The most powerful portrayals of the main romantic couples paired established male stars with female ingénues. Age differences between the male and female leads in *Broken Arrow*, *Across the Wide Missouri*, *High Noon*, and *Broken Lance* ranged from 23 to 28 years. This is equally true of white couples and interracial couples. *The Searchers* pairs a young Natalie Wood with Henry Brandon, 26 years older. However, this relationship is that of a captive forced into marriage, rather than a love affair. Only *The Far Horizon* marks less age difference between MacMurray and either Donna Reed or Barbara Hale. Both of these women are slightly older that Charlton Heston in forming the secondary couples.

Table 1: Ages at the Time the Movie Was Released

	Male Star	Female Love Interest	Age Difference: Male–Female
Broken Arrow			
James Stewart & Debra Paget*	42	17	25
Across the Wide Missouri			
Clark Gable & Maria Elena Marques*	50	25	25
High Noon			
Gary Cooper & Grace Kelly	51	23	28
Gary Cooper & Katy Jurado*	51	28	23

	Male Star	Female Love Interest	Age Difference: Male–Female
The Far Horizons			
Fred MacMurray & Donna Reed*	46	33	13
Fred MacMurray & Barbara Hale	46	32	14
Charlton Heston & Donna Reed*	31	33	-2
Charlton Heston & Barbara Hale	31	32	-1
Broken Lance			
Spencer Tracy & Katy Jurado*	54	30	24
Robert Wagner* & Jean Peters	24	28	-4
The Searchers			
Jeffrey Hunter* & Vera Miles	30	27	3
Henry Brandon* & Natalie Wood	44	18	26

*Indicates a non-white character in a relationship with a white character
Source: www.imdb.com

In *Broken Lance* and *The Searchers*, the younger, secondary couples are reasonably close in age. These secondary couples seem more equal in terms of romantic interactions also, in that there tends to be parity in who leads in flirtation and setting the parameters of the romance. However, the couples with great age differences demonstrate extreme power differences between the pair. Therefore, age parity indicates parity in romantic power, while age distance serves as a marker of significant difference in power.

Height differences between male and female romantic leads are also significant markers of masculine authority and power over women in these movies. (See Table 2.) Except for *Broken Lance*, the male leads are 8½–17 inches taller than their female counterparts. This difference in the heights of male and female leads allows for gestures and embraces that serve to mark protectiveness, as the man is at least a head taller than the woman. Combined with age differences, some of the female leads look like children next to the men they are supposed to marry. The most extreme example of this is Debra Paget, who is both a 17-year-old teenager and 13 inches shorter than 42 years old James Stewart. In many of their scenes, the two are positioned standing close together in romantic embraces, highlighting these differences.

Table 2: Height Differences

	Male Star	Female Love Interest	Height Difference: Male–Female
Broken Arrow			
James Stewart & Debra Paget*	6'3"	5'2"	13"
Across the Wide Missouri			
Clark Gable & Maria Elena Marques*	6'1"	unknown	unknown

	Male Star	Female Love Interest	Height Difference: Male–Female
High Noon			
Gary Cooper & Grace Kelly	6'3"	5'6½"	8.5"
Gary Cooper & Katy Jurado*	6'3"	5'6½"	8.5"
The Far Horizons			
Fred MacMurray & Donna Reed*	6'3"	5'3½"	11.5"
Fred MacMurray & Barbara Hale	6'3"	5'5½"	9.5"
Charlton Heston & Donna Reed*	6'2½"	5'3½"	11"
Charlton Heston & Barbara Hale	6'2½"	5'5½"	9"
Broken Lance			
Spencer Tracy & Katy Jurado*	5'9½"	5'6½"	3"
Robert Wagner* & Jean Peters	5'11"	5'5½"	5.5"
The Searchers			
Jeffrey Hunter* & Vera Miles	6'	5'3½"	8.5"
Henry Brandon* & Natalie Wood	6'5"	5'0"	17"

*Indicates a non-white character in a relationship with a white character

Source: www.imdb.com

Racial markers were complicated when casting Westerns that included interracial romances. First, it was difficult to hire enough Native American actors for the large crowd scenes if the studio required racial accuracy and so whites, Mexicans, Filipinos, and other "raced" actors, were regularly cast as Indians. Second, box office draw depended upon the use of recognized stars, which explains the casting of older, white men as the male romantic lead. His star power could ensure financial success for the picture. Handsome, young, white men such as Robert Wagner (in *Broken Lance*) and Jeffrey Hunter (in *The Searchers*) could be marketed as the next generation of stars—or even heartthrobs—whether they played white characters or mixed-race characters. The same considerations of star power and box office draw led to white men often playing Indian chiefs, such as Jeff Chandler in *Broken Arrow*.

For Westerns that included interracial romances, racial markers were even more complicated. Until the revisions of 1954, the Production Code specifically forbade "miscegenation." Some versions of the Code specified that miscegenation was defined as mixing between black and white, however other versions did not limit the definition. Even as challenges mounted against the Code in the 1950s, race remained a touchy subject that studios feared. Southern theaters often threatened boycotts of movies that suggested racial equality, and interracial sex and romance were particularly risky topics. In order to avoid controversy, the Breen office often required that a white female actor be cast as the romantic partner so that audiences would not have to view any level of intimacy between real men and women of different races. Additionally, female stars could also affect the box office. For these reasons, Debra Paget (in *Broken Arrow*, 1950) and Donna Reed (in *The Far Horizons*, 1954) played Indian women in love with white men. The exceptions were Katy Jurado (in *Broken Lance*, 1954 and *High Noon*, 1952), and Maria Elena Marques (in *Across the Wide Missouri*, 1951), both of whom were Mexican.

Once the basic physical markers of the actors—race, sex, height, and age—are taken into account, other markers define differences among characters. These include plot actions that explicitly mark power differences, costuming, makeup, confidence, success, and sacrifice among other markers. Each are used to differentiate between white, male heroes and other white men, all white men and Indian men, white men and white women, white men and non-white women, Indian men and Indian women, and Indian women of status and other Indian women. Mixed race individuals and even immigrant families on their way to becoming Yankee white are also marked in particular ways.

For example, the range of emotions a character is allowed to express is an important marker in the performance of race and gender. Of all the white male heroes, John Wayne's Ethan is particularly stoic. He expresses some anger, but holds even that in check and does what needs to be done. After finding his niece, Lucy, raped and murdered, he buries her, and the only suggestion that he feels something is that he gallops his horse as if he is running away from something when he meets Martin and Lucy's boyfriend. Then and earlier when he finds his brother and sister-in-law murdered, he is moved but holds his anguish inside, only making snide comments at the funeral. In *Broken Lance*, Matt Devereaux (Spencer Tracy) expresses some anger, though even this is displayed as determination and control of the situation. *High Noon* was criticized by many at the time for allowing the hero to display fear. Yet even when expressing his fear, Marshall Will Kane (Gary Cooper) maintained control of himself. His powerful performance served as an example to many, including President Bill Clinton, that bravery is not the absence of fear, but rather the ability face one's fears and do what is right, honorable, and necessary—even if it means sacrificing oneself (Hoberman).

The use of emotions to mark the difference between the mature hero and the immature son/nephew who will grow into heroic manhood is also significant. Both Joe (Robert Wagner) and Matt Devereaux (Spencer Tracy) in *Broken Lance*, express a wide range of emotion—anger, regret, grief and love. Joe is somewhat quicker to anger than his father (Spencer Tracy) and expresses more compassion for his half-brothers, trying to reunite them with Matt. He combines the Indian spiritual understanding of his mother with the grit of his Irish immigrant father. His love for his father leads him to sacrifice himself, accepting a jail term himself, rather than see Matt convicted. His white half-brothers are less three-dimensional, with the oldest expressing mostly anger and resentment both at his father and at Joe. The other two brothers lack intelligence and all three lack honesty and compassion. They are willing to steal from their own father. On the other hand, Robert Wagner sacrifices himself to save his father's reputation—taking the blame even when it means he spends three years in prison for a crime he did not commit. Compared to his white brothers, he is the only one with the sense of honor necessary to grow into a real man. In *The Searchers*, Martin (Jeffrey Hunter) is similarly endowed with a sense of honor and commitment to justice regardless of the personal cost. Yet he, too, shows considerably less self-control and more emotion than Ethan (John Wayne). Both of these younger men are clearly on the path to heroic identities. Yet because of their mixed race origins and youth, they struggle to learn the self-control of white masculinity. Both Joe Devereaux and Martin express hurt at being called "half-breeds." In this way, emotional outbursts seem to be both markers of maturity and of race. Through the loss of contact with their mothers, both Martin and Joe have the opportunity to fully assimilate into white, heroic masculine culture and they are rewarded with the ultimate prize—white wives.

Posture also serves as both a racialized marker of gender and a sexualized marker of race. Among the male heroes, sitting tall and upright in the saddle contributes to their identity as men of power. Among the Indian men, sitting tall in the saddle is a mark of bravery—especially just before they ride out to die in battle. Otherwise, Indian men tend to lean in and move with the horse. Chiefs consistently maintain erect posture. For example, Cochise (Jeff Chandler) in *Broken Arrow* stands as tall as Tom Jeffords (James Stewart) throughout all of their interactions. This is a marker of mutual respect between the two. Cochise's (Jeff Chandler) personal power is also marked by a wide stance, with feet firmly planted and shoulders squared. The white hero, Tom Jeffords (James Stewart) stands erect but more relaxed. These posture markers suggest a greater need for the Indian chief to mark his claim to power, while the white hero assumes his own right to power. Posture is also an important marker among female characters. Proud and upright posture is a marker of the Indian princess. White women tend to have good posture, though not as stiff and forced as the Indian princess. In general, erect posture marks pride and a sense of authority for both men and women and for Indians and Whites.

The physical ability to overpower others is another marker of racialized gender. Each Western shows multiple examples of the white men overpowering Indian men in battle. John Wayne's Ethan also picks up his niece both as a child and as an adult. He also pushes Martin aside regularly. Gender power differentials are also performed when a romance is added to the plot. For example, in *Across the Wide Missouri*, Flint (Clark Gable) puts Kamiah (Marie Elena Marques), his Indian wife, over his knee and spanks her. That action convinces the grandfather that Flint is in fact her husband. *Across the Wide Missouri* uses other markers of childishness to set aside Kamiah as female. After buying her, Flint (Clark Gable) falls in love with her because of her playfulness and childish voice as she imitates his singing of "Skip to My Lou." He gives her elks' teeth "to play with" while he is gone. He also does not allow her to challenge male assumptions of superiority by outriding the men (he catches up and reins in her horse) and further proves his authority by restricting her independent movement.

Differentials among non-white, female characters are also signified by markers that distinguish "Indian princesses" from other Indian women referred to pejoratively as "squaws." These markers define different levels and varieties of femininity. The trope of the Indian princess is used regularly in these films. Only she is worthy of the white man's love. Femininity in the 1950s was defined as inherently submissive. In *Broken Lance*, however, Katy Jurado's character, named Princess, departs from this convention. Like the Western's leading males, she holds herself tall with a straight back. Of all the female romantic leads, she is the only one to portray maturity and inner strength. Her marriage with Matt Devereaux (Spencer Tracy) seems to be one of greater mutual respect than the marriages in *Broken Arrow* and *Across the Wide Missouri*.

Another marker of the princess is that she seeks out the "civilized," white man over a man of her own people. Other female characters lack interest in the outsider. This interest, however, does not enable her to pursue the man openly. In *The Far Horizons*, Sacajawea (Donna Reed) asks Lt. William Clark (Charles Heston) "How does a white woman get a man?" He answers, "She waits until he asks her to marry him." Just as she had accepted Indian markers of gendered inferiority by not objecting to being given to a man, she accepts the white man's markers by agreeing to wait for his proposal.

Sacrifice serves as another marker of both race and gender. A white female character expects men and non-white women to sacrifice themselves for her. Conversely, Indian female characters become the embodied sacrifice. In most of these movies, the non-white female character either ends up dead or broken-hearted. In both *Broken Arrow* and *Across the Wide Missouri*, the Indian women who fall in love with and marry white men are killed. In *Broken Arrow*, white men shoot Sonseeahray (Debra Paget) as she grabs her unconscious husband's knife to attack them in his defense. Her sacrifice "put(s) a seal on the peace" as both sides honored her loss and agreed to keep peace between them. In *Across the Wide Missouri*, Kamiah is shot with an arrow. She is honored only in death, because her son grows up assimilated into both cultures. In *The Searchers*, Martin (Jeffrey Hunter) treats Look (Beulah Archuletta) as a "squaw"—an unworthy, accidentally-collected nobody. However, when she runs away and is murdered after Martin kicks her down the hill while she is trying to sleep, he realizes that she was in fact a woman of value. Her death marks her femininity. It also marks her racial position in that she could not live as an equal to the white or even the mixed man. Lesser sacrifices are also required of non-white female love interests. In *The Far Horizons*, Sacagawea earns Clark's love by running after the boat until she drops from exhaustion. She sacrifices her name as he prefers to call her Janie. In the end, she sacrifices her happiness by stepping aside so Clark can be with Julia, a white woman (Barbara Hale).

Costumes too are important visual markers of both race and gender identities. Despite common perceptions that the hero is always the man with a white Stetson, these films do not make such obvious distinctions when costuming the men. Their heroes have black hats or light hats. None wear stereotypical white hats. Looking gritty and dirty helped to create performances that are nuanced, acknowledging a mixture of good and bad in these characters. The best example of costuming to differentiate between white and non-white women can be found in *High Noon*. The white wife, Amy (Grace Kelly) is dressed in light colors. The neckline of her dress is high and everything about the dress is modest and unassuming. Her demeanor assumes value as a white woman, but she leans into Gary Cooper in a somewhat submissive pose. Helen's (Katy Jurado) dress is very different from Amy's (Grace Kelly). It is designed as a corset with a skirt attached. The fabric strips on the skirt called attention to every curve of her legs and hips. The neckline is plunging and shows much cleavage. As a Mexican woman, Helen (Katy Jurado) stands straighter and taller. She has a strong, haughty look on her face. Both her posture and the distance she maintains to Cooper are a performance of strength and independence, while her dress announces a sexuality that is denied to a white woman.

The Far Horizons marks race and gender with costumes even more obviously. In the early scenes, the white women dancing are wearing costumes that are essentially long versions of the 1950s silhouette. The men's costumes look like out-of-date marching band uniforms. When Sacajawea (Donna Reed) wants to get Clark's (Charlton Heston) attention, she tries to fashion a white woman's dress, and which Clark cuts very short. This action marks his masculine power and authority and her interest in him as she accepts his authority over her. The difference in racialized gender costumes clearly calls attention to Sacajawea as a sexualized "other."

Classic Westerns often illustrate a tension between the individual and the community. In them, heroes are loners at the start, but love or common struggle brings them into community with others. Yet, despite his growing acceptance of his need for community, the white, male hero does not depend on others to achieve his ends. He may get assistance, but he remains willing to walk away and follow his own path if others do not want to follow him.

In *The Searchers*, Ethan (John Wayne) joins the posse, for example, but refuses to be sworn in. He allows the official leader to give orders—once. When those orders prove foolhardy, he goes off on his own. Martin (Jeffrey Hunter) insists on following him, marking Martin's ability to recognize greatness and competence and ally himself with the man most likely to achieve their goal.

Ultimately, this self-confidence and independence in dealing with other men, as well as women sets white masculinity apart from other masculinities. According to Peek, the mark of the true hero in Westerns is that in the end, he overcomes all challenges to achieve his goal. He is a winner (208–211). The marker for this trait is success. White male heroes were portrayed as the natural overlords of a sweeping landscape of sky, prairie, flora and fauna. Thus, Ethan (John Wayne) rescues his niece and finds his own humanity in *The Searchers;* Flint (Clark Gable) raises an admirable and assimilated son who honors the heritage of both his white and Indian parents in *Across the Wide Missouri;* Lt. Clark (Charlton Heston) returns East safely to marry a respectable white woman; Tom Jeffords (James Stewart) brokers peace between the Apaches and white settlers in *Broken Arrow;* Marshall Kane survives his lone battle to save an ungrateful town from a gang of killers in *High Noon*. *Broken Lance*, alone, seems to break this mold as Matt Devereaux (Spencer Tracy) dies while Joe (Robert Wagner) goes to prison in his stead. However, Joe's development into a righteous man capable of facing half-brothers who would murder him and walking away the better man suggests that there has been a moral victory for Matt.

Broken Arrow (1950), *Across the Wide Missouri* (1951), *High Noon* (1952), *Broken Lance* (1954), *The Far Horizons* (1954), and *The Searchers* (1956) spoke to audiences of the 1950s. *High Noon* did particularly well at the Box Office (in part because it was a low budget film). *Broken Arrow* was nominated for three Academy Awards, while *Broken Lance* was won an Academy Award for Best Writing and Katy Jurado was nominated for Best Actress in a Supporting Role. *High Noon* won three Academy Awards and was nominated for three others, including Best Picture. *Broken Arrow, High Noon, Broken Lance*, and *The Searchers* (1956) all won Golden Globe Awards. The popularity of these Westerns in which strong white male heroes won over Indians, other white men, and women can be seen as celebrating and justifying the power of the United States in the world in a time of fear. In all these Westerns, racialized gender markers and gendered race markers are also important, for they marked the authority of white male heroes in an earlier era and suggested that, despite wartime advances and independence for veterans of color and women in the 1950s, it was possible, desirable, and right for white men to rightfully reassert their cultural hegemony in post-war America.

Notes

1. For example, *Broken Arrow* has been interpreted as an allegorical tale challenging popular perceptions in the United States of the Cold War with the Soviet Union and *High Noon* has been seen as critiquing the blacklist in McCarthy era Hollywood.

2. In referring to characterizations within movies, the term Indian is used because even when film makers used the names of specific nations/tribes, the facts that would distinguish that nation from other nations are missing or at best loosely applicable. The stock character was merely a generic Indian. In Westerns, all Indian men were horseback riders who killed buffalo, stole horses, and sought glory on the battlefield.

3. Here it should be noted that some recent romantic comedies in other genres have challenged this assumption of white normativity by showcasing African American stars. However, Bowdre argues that these portrayals still lack complex identities consisting of both race and gender. Rather, they equate hyper-sexuality of both men and women as normatively black (113–114). Performances of gender and race therefore require conscious stylized acts which signify gender and race identities. These are achieved through various archetypes and tropes. Markers of these performances can be the specific bodies of the actors, costumes, makeup, gestures, physical movement, posture, use of space, the timber and quality of the voice, and the staging of one among multiple actors. Examining these markers used by multiple films within a genre reveals how such archetypes and tropes are used—particularly in Westerns from 1950s Hollywood in which race and gender lines are drawn very clearly.

Filmography

Across the Wide Missouri. Dir. William Wellman. Warner Archive. 1951.
Broken Arrow. Dir. Delmar Daves. Twentieth Century Fox, 1950.
Broken Lance. Dir. Edward Dmytryk. Twentieth Century Fox Film, 1954.
The Far Horizons. Dir. Rudolph Maté. Paramount Pictures, 1954.
High Noon. Dir. Fred Zinnemann. 1952. Lionsgate, 1952.
The Searchers. Dir. John Ford. Warner Bros., 1956.

Works Cited

Bogle, Donald. *Bright Boulevards, Bold Dreams: The Story of Black Hollywood.* New York: One World Ballantine Books, 2006. Print.
Bowdre, Karen. "Romantic Comedies and the Raced Body," in Stacey Abbott and Deborah Jermyn, eds., *Falling in Love Again: Romantic Comedy in Contemporary Cinema.* New York: I.B. Tauris, 2009. Print.
Hoberman, J. "Film; It's Always 'High Noon' at the White House." *New York Times.* 25 April 2004. Web. 6 February 2016. http://www.nytimes.com/2004/04/25/movies/film-it-s-always-high-noon-at-the-white-house.html.
Peek, Wendy Chapman. "The Romance of Competence: Rethinking Masculinity in the Western." *Journal of Popular Film & Television* 30.4 (2003): 206–219. *International Index to Performing Arts.* Web. 15 September 2015.
Yancy, George and Judith Butler. "What's Wrong with 'All Lives Matter'?" *New York Times.* 12 January 2015. Web. February 6, 2016. http://opinionator.blogs.nytimes.com/2015/01/12/whats-wrong-with-all-lives-matter/?rref=collection%2Fcolumn%2Fthe-stone&action=click&contentCollection=opinion&region=stream&module=stream_unit&version=latest&contentPlacement=101&pgtype=collection.

"Mister, this is cattle country"
Livestock and Gender in Western Films

Jim Daems

"'Heroes shouldn't be holier-than-thou and namby-pamby,'
[John Ford] concluded early"[1]

One powerful icon of the Western genre, understandably, is livestock. Cattle are the predominant symbol of the wide-open frontier and the self-made man. As such, cattle are strongly linked to notions of masculinity. In this essay, I will focus on the connections between livestock and gender. In particular, I want to examine critically how the representation of gender is fashioned through the conflict between cattle and another form of livestock, sheep. My primary focus will be on *Marked for Murder* (1945), *The Sheepman* (1958), *The Ballad of Josie* (1967), *Rustlers' Rhapsody* (1985), and *Brokeback Mountain* (2005). Spanning 60 years, these five films exemplify this conflict and demonstrate how it has been used in Westerns to explore changing norms of masculinity. In *Marked for Murder*, Tex Haines (Tex Ritter) and a couple of Texas Rangers—Dave Wyatt (Dave O'Brien) and Panhandle Perkins (Guy Wilkerson)—attempt to find the cattleman responsible for escalating a range war with the sheep herders, most notably Ruth Lane (Marilyn McConnell). Similarly, the introduction of sheep into cattle country creates a conflict of masculinities in *The Sheepman* between Jason Sweet (Glenn Ford), and the corrupt cattleman, "Colonel" Steven Bedford (Leslie Nielsen), who was known to Sweet in his past as the gambler and gunfighter Johnny Bledsoe, and is engaged to the tomboyish Dell Payton (Shirley MacLaine). *The Ballad of Josie* plays more with gender-bending than the preceding films. Here, widowed Josie Minick (Doris Day) sets up a sheep farm in order to try to provide for herself and regain her son from his grandfather, setting off a conflict with neighboring cattlemen. In *Rustlers' Rhapsody*, the range war between the corrupt cattle baron, Colonel Ticonderoga (Andy Griffith), and the sheepmen provides a context for a brilliant parody of the conventions of earlier B Westerns. Finally, in *Brokeback Mountain*, the sheep relate to conflict in much more figurative ways that problematize the cowboy masculinity represented by the rodeo circuit and ranch life in the latter half of the twentieth century. Perhaps ironically, I will argue that, for all the backlash that *Brokeback Mountain* created, the movie is actually truer to the western genre's roots in classical bucolic and pastoral—that the cowboy's masculinity and homosocial bonds on the range have always been tenuously defined against his relationship to livestock.

From the first time I saw *Brokeback Mountain*, the pastoral tradition was prominently in my mind. The film was an extension of the literary tradition moving from Theocritus and Virgil's *Eclogues* through Edmund Spenser's *Shepheardes Calendar* and beyond. As Rictor Norton states, "If any particular genre can be called a homosexual genre, the evidence would point most convincingly to the pastoral tradition." *Brokeback Mountain* also, in my mind, clicked into place amongst the hundreds of western movies and television series that I had grown up watching with my father—suddenly, that intense dislike of sheepmen in westerns (if they were even recognized as men) took on a whole new meaning that lay submerged within the western genre. *Brokeback* is the return of the repressed of both the pastoral tradition and the western.[2] This is clear if we trace the cattle-sheep battles of a selection of western films.

Some, however, may insist upon the distinction of pastoral and bucolic—

Ennis Del Mar (Heath Ledger, left) and Jack Twist (Jake Gyllenhaal, under the trees) tend a herd of sheep in *Brokeback Mountain* (Focus Features, 2005).

that the western and its primary focus on cattle is bucolic rather than pastoral. I am not particularly concerned in this essay about the characteristics that distinguish the two genres, particularly because of the interplay between the two types of livestock that the western films I am focusing on involve. I am more interested in the hierarchy that is established in western films and how that relates to classical generic conventions, gender, and conflict. Commenting on the hierarchy of herders in Theocritus' work, for example, Daniel W. Berman notes, "Whether a pastoral hierarchy—that cowherds or oxherds … are somehow superior to shepherds … who are in turn superior to goatherds … exists within the poems of Theocritus has been a debated question for some years. Real-life economic concerns certainly could play a role in the perception of such a hierarchy, since cattle were more expensive to purchase and raise than sheep or goats (as they still are). But a strict system of ordering within the bucolic poetry of Theocritus is difficult to trace without controversy" (228). Berman argues that the herder hierarchy is a later critical construct: "by the fifth century commentators believed that a hierarchy, whether real or fictional, existed in the poetic pastoral world of Vergil. Since Theocritus' bucolic poetry is the unchallenged progenitor of Vergilian pastoral, many have concluded that the hierarchy in fact originated with the Alexandrian poet" (230). Whether or not the hierarchy originates in Theocritus' work or in later commentaries on Virgil, even a cursory exposure to western films affirms a hierarchical relationship between cattlemen and sheepmen that bears some similarities to classical distinctions. Sheep are just not welcome in cattle country.

The interactions between cowherds, shepherds, and goatherds (at the bottom of the hierarchy in classical pastoral) are also important: "Interpersonal contact between herdsmen is also brought to bear [… in the hierarchy]; critics have noted that conversation between two cowherds is polite (*Idyll* 6), but that between a shepherd and a goatherd vulgar and abusive (*Idyll* 5)" (Berman 230-1). We can note that the interaction between cattlemen and sheepmen is marked by abuse, as cattlemen talk down to sheepmen. This is usually marked by cattlemen representing sheep as smelly and stupid, thereby degrading any person that associates with sheep as being themselves smelly and stupid. As Jason Meredith (Peter Graves) states to Josie Minick in *The Ballad of Josie*, any "idiot" with a Winchester and a dog can tend to sheep. Meredith's point is evident in terms of economics, intelligence, and gender. Josie keeps sheep rather than cattle because it is less expensive to start a sheep ranch; she is, obviously, female, and sheep herding does not involve the same sort of physical labor as cattle; and, finally, the two hands she hires to tend her sheep are rather shabby looking fellows from the deep south. This last point is another significant way in which sheep are marked off from cattle—there is, quite often, an ethnic distinction or some other characteristic that marks those tending sheep as other. While southerners are American, there are a number of stereotypes involved that mark them as below northerners in a way similar to the Latino shepherd in *The Sheepman*, the, apparently, eastern European shepherds in *Rustlers' Rhapsody*, and the queer shepherds of *Brokeback Mountain*.

Steers are closely related to the mythos of virile masculinity in both the B- and the studio-Western—one's association with steers (down through the hierarchy of cattle baron to cowboy, or even camp cook), in particular, confirms one's masculinity. Steers symbolize the "self-made" and successful man—the cattle baron. Lower down, the cowboy symbolizes a rugged individualism and independence working on the range free from domestic entanglements, often desiring to one day have his own small ranch. Dairy cattle and sheep, however, are associated with significant masculine slippage. In *Colorado Sunset*, a 1939 Gene Autry B-entry, Autry and his pals pool their money together to buy a cattle ranch; however, the comic sidekick character entrusted with the transaction ends up buying a dairy farm. As Lynette Tan points out, "An expression of disgust is clear in their reaction to this turn of events, and to the notion that they might soon be 'playing nursemaid to some cows.' The frequent distinction between cattle ranching and dairy farming is important, associating Autry and his group with a notion of masculinity that excludes the domestic, overcompensating to the extreme that even the animals they deal with cannot be female" (96). The more settled lifestyle of dairy farming is not amenable with the masculine ideal—it domesticates the cowboy, feminizing him as a "nursemaid," indicating a hierarchical sub-category within cattle. The link is furthered, as Tan notes, by the "overcompensating" critique of the sex of the cattle tended which essentially implies that males are not meant to "care" for anything female in this way without jeopardizing their masculinity. One might note that there is something particularly curious in this equation in an Autry film, as there is in other B Westerns from the 1930s and 1940s. Autry, like Tex Ritter and Roy Rogers, is a "singing cowboy" and generally wears overly elaborate and embellished "western" clothes, breaking into songs while sitting around the campfire, or just sitting around. This, in itself, potentially undercuts his claim to masculinity—he is not the rugged male in a plaid shirt, blue jeans, a sweat-stained hat, and dusty boots (like the later John Wayne or the Marlboro Man), although he can shoot and fight, and he does uphold a strong moral code.

What does, however, maintain the singing cowboy's masculinity is the content, the lyrics, of the songs he sings. The songs are generally concerned with two topics—cattle (or life on the range) and courting women. In her analysis of the singing cowboy within the context of the Depression, Stephanie Vander Wel argues, "Autry's early cowboy tunes told sympathetically morose tales of the cowboy's vulnerability to the dangers and hardships of the open range. Yet his Tin Pan Alley cowboy songs provided lush soundscapes that framed the intimate sounds of his vocal delivery over the airwaves of radio. Crooning to his audience, the singing cowboy soothed the concerns of the era as he presented a principled version of masculinity that took the risk of being perceived as effeminate" (209). If we add the singing cowboy's appearance to Vander Wel's insights, the sympathy and "vulnerability" of the lyrics of the songs doubles the "risk of being perceived as effeminate." Ultimately, however, songs about the rugged life on the range and songs about courting women manage to save the "principled version of masculinity" that the singing cowboy portrays. We see this in Tex Ritter's *Marked for Murder*. The movie consists of a conventional range war plot between cattlemen and sheepmen. *Marked for Murder* employs another interesting plot element to preserve the singing cowboy's masculinity as he sides with the sheepmen—the largest sheep herd is owned by a woman. This legitimizes Ritter's siding with the sheepmen against the evil machinations of the cattlemen. Ritter's songs—the conventional mix of life on the range with cattle and courting women—tied to the love interest subplot that brings him and Ruth Lane, the female "sheepman," together allow him to do what is clearly morally right without being tarred as effeminate through association with sheep. But the potential of misreading the masculinity within that contrast of "lush soundscapes" and rugged setting remains latently present.

The Ballad of Josie enacts a similar movement without the singing element—even Doris Day does not sing in the film. Here, the newly widowed Josie Minick, who accidentally kills her abusive, drunken husband, searches for a way to make a living for herself and her son. Along the way, the movie employs a battle-of-the-sexes plot line that no doubt reflects late-1960s feminism, culminating in Josie becoming a sheep rancher—importantly, Meredith talks her out of becoming a cattle rancher, as women are incapable of the required work. What is implied here is that becoming a sheep rancher, while transgressive of gender roles, is not as transgressive as a woman becoming a cattle rancher. Josie's transformation into a sheep rancher is significant as she rushes into the general store and buys male clothing and cowboy boots.[3] She also eventually buys a handgun as the range war, or rather siege at her ranch begins. The gender inversions presented by the Wyoming statehood subplot essentially culminate in Josie starting her sheep ranch, and the challenges it poses to the alpha-male cattle rancher, Arch Ogden (George Kennedy). Significantly, the plotting resolves the gender issues of both the main and the subplot. In order for the Wyoming territory to gain statehood, the women of the territory have to willingly agree to give up the voting rights that they have, but would not be allowed in a state joining the union. The women of the town, throughout the movie, are shown to be politically active—rousing support for Josie both when she is put on trial for the murder of her husband

and when she is jailed for arming the town's women with pool cues to attack Ogden and the men he is rallying together to drive her sheep off. The issue about the women giving up their voting rights is quietly passed over as a parade at the end of the movie celebrates Wyoming becoming a state; however, Josie's transformation parallels the implied loss of women's rights culminating in statehood.

In addition, throughout the film a relationship has been developing between Josie and Meredith. When Ogden lays siege to Josie's ranch, Meredith and his cowboys (while initially wanting to drive off the sheep like Ogden) defend the sheep by characterizing Ogden as an autocratic threat to their way of life as well as to potential statehood. Following Ogden setting Josie's barn on fire, he and Meredith fight. With Ogden's loss, a less violent solution is sought. Ogden offers to buy Josie's flock and give her a deal on cattle to start a cattle ranch. But, much like the silence on women's issues and statehood at the end, what Josie does is unclear. She burns her men's clothing and apparently marries Meredith; hence, if she does accept Ogden's offer, the cattle would likely become part of Meredith's herd. What this implies is that, in disposing of the sheep, Josie's return to her traditional gendered role as a wife rights the gender balance, now centered on Meredith (we can also only assume at the end that her remarriage to a well-off cattleman may reunite her with her son). Her independence, initially driven by her desire to find some way to support herself and convince her father-in-law that she could support her son, is essentially mocked by its association with sheep. Meredith "gets the girl" and in the process has tempered the autocratic masculinity of Ogden by first defeating him in a fist-fight and then, as a consequence, forcing him to buy Josie's herd.

The Sheepman, released nine years before *The Ballad of Josie*, also reestablishes gender roles through livestock. Here, Jason Sweet's masculinity is not questioned as much because he wins his flock of sheep in a poker game. In other words, he is a reluctant sheepman. However, his actions upon arriving in the middle of cattle country prior to his flock's arrival are designed to assert his masculinity. Almost immediately upon arriving, Sweet asks Milt Masters (Edgar Buchanan) who the toughest guy in town is. Sweet then proceeds to find Jumbo McCall (Mickey Shaughnessy) and pick a fight, which he handily wins. In addition, Sweet also demonstrates his ability with a gun. The fact, too, that Dell Payton is almost immediately attracted to him, despite being, as we later learn, engaged to the cattle baron, suggests he is not, to recall *The Ballad of Josie*, just some "idiot" with a gun and a flock of sheep. When his sheep arrive we do see something familiar—a Latino shepherd, Angelo (Pedro Gonzalez Gonzalez). The shepherd is an other in more ways than just ethnicity, as he provides more comic relief and is not good with a gun. The shepherd is almost the complete opposite of Jason Sweet's masculine prowess. Much like the male protagonists' maintenance of masculinity through the dangerous association with sheep in *Marked for Murder* and *The Ballad of Josie*, *The Sheepman* releases its gendered tensions by making Sweet the moral center of the tale. This is accomplished as Sweet silences resistance to his sheep by first defeating Bedford's hired gun, Chocktaw Neal (Pernell Roberts) and then Bedford. This, in turn, saves Dell from marrying the villain, and she, like Josie Minick, puts on a dress and will apparently marry Sweet. Sweet also, to Dell's surprise, gets rid of the sheep—claiming all the conflict was merely to demonstrate that no one can push him around.

In each of the preceding films, gender relations between men and between men and women are constructed through hierarchical associations between cattle and sheep. These are all heteronormative. But we can begin to extend these relations in another direction by turning to a parody of B Westerns, *Rustlers' Rhapsody* (1985). Employing the same plot of a range war between sheepmen (here, from their accents, of eastern European descent) and an evil cattle baron, *Rustlers' Rhapsody* pries apart what was noted above as preserving the hero's masculinity. Hired by the sheepmen to protect them from the cattle baron, "Good Guy" singing cowboy Rex O'Herlihan (Tom Berenger), appropriately over-dressed and travelling with an extensive wardrobe, must eventually and paradoxically confront the "Good Guy" hired by the cattle baron, Bob Barber (Patrick Wayne).[4] Rex's masculinity is questioned from the moment he arrives in town—one person asks, "What in the hell are you? Where the hell did you get that shirt?"—openly questioning the masculinity of over-dressed singing cowboys like Autry, Ritter, and Rogers. Rex is also oblivious to both Miss Tracy's (Marilu Henner) and Ticonderoga's daughter's (Sela Ward) interest in him, writes letters to his mother, and spends his evening carefully ironing his fancy, elaborately monogrammed shirts. When it comes to the first meeting between the two "Good Guys," Rex is thrown off by Bob's questioning of his sexuality—Bob notes that Rex is 31 years old, single, doesn't date or even kiss the girls, and, finally, asks Rex if he is "a confident heterosexual." Rex pauses, and finally says, "Confident? ... Not *just* heterosexual?" Rex, sulking, withdraws, returns to camp, and tells his stereotypical former town drunk sidekick, Peter (G.W. Bailey), that he needs to get new clothes: "understated stuff, lots of browns." *Rustlers' Rhapsody* deliberately interrogates the signs that marked out the B Western singing cowboy's "vulnerability" and borderline effeminate appearance, transforming Rex into the pejorative term used by Ticonderoga's foreman Blackie (Jim Carter) to describe a minor character he briefly encounters in the town saloon—a "Prairie fairy."[5]

But the critique of the hero's masculinity in the movie is also furthered by its representation of, at the very least, a repressed homoeroticism between the cowboys and between Ticonderoga and his foreman. While the cattle baron's main hired hand, Blackie (signaling his moral standing in conventional 1930s through 1950s means of white and black hats, of which he obviously wears the latter color) uses the pejorative just mentioned, his death scene is quite blatantly homoerotic. *Rustlers' Rhapsody* indeed widens its scope by employing the conventions of Italian, or "Spaghetti" westerns to challenge the rugged, individualist masculinity of the genre. Horses in Italian westerns usually prance, rather than gallop. Here, Rex's horse does dressage in order to attract the attention of Ticonderoga's and his new ally's, an Italian colonel and railway man (Fernando Rey), heavily armed supporters and prevent a massacre of the sheepmen. This is used simultaneously to affirm our questions about Rex's sexuality and also to draw the cattle men and cowboys further into that questioning. The bad guys are entranced by Rex and his horse Wildfire's dressage abilities, so much so that one cowboy states, "Wish my horse could do that," and another responds, "Me, too." What is occurring here is that Rex's association with the sheepmen is manipulated in order to split the unity of the singing cowboy—pulling apart the problematic appearance and singing from the masculine action of gun and fist fighting that supports a strong, over-simplified moral code of good vs. evil symbolized by white and black hats. The parody suggests that Rex's lack of confident heterosexuality is only blatantly visible through taking the side of the sheepmen, thereby forcing him to confront another "good guy" and his own sexuality; however, what is made manifest by association with a form of livestock below cattle in the genre, is also represented as being latently present all along in the more macho, masculine cattlemen and cowboys. The homoerotic subtext is again present when, at the final showdown between Rex and the sheepmen versus the colonels and their henchmen, Rex shoots Barber, is wounded himself, and is held lovingly in Peter's arms. Gender order is reestablished with Colonel Ticonderoga's apology to the sheep herders, and Rex's statement that, while having his wound treated he finally kisses Miss Tracy—"We were in the doctor's office and did more than talk. I'm getting better." However, not to be tied down to the feminine (perhaps because she is the conventional "whore with a heart of gold"), Rex rides off into the sunset with Peter chasing after him.

Much like Peter's pursuit of Rex, an action that performs the nostalgic gaze of the viewer's longing for a more simplistic life-on-the-range—motioned to by the black-and-white opening of *Rustlers' Rhapsody*—*Brokeback Mountain* extends the nostalgic and conventional western homosocial ending. While ostensibly a desire for rugged individualism and independence in the genre, the male gaze in *Brokeback* is sexualized. However, I want to first consider what the film appropriates from pop culture and the western genre before turning to the sexualized masculine gaze. *Brokeback Mountain* opens in 1963, quite significantly, considering the appearance of the leads and the panoramic shots of them in the mountains, the year after the Marlboro Man ads became solely fixed upon the cowboy and the re-creation of the range as Marlboro Country.[6] In a sense, *Brokeback* is nostalgically appropriating the nostalgia evident in the Marlboro Man campaign—both, in effect, look back at an essentially vanished era that by the 1960s only existed in advertising, films, television, and rodeos. Yet this is opposed to the reality of Ennis and Jack tending sheep dressed like cowboys, which marks them as the other, outside of the traditional masculine hierarchy symbolized by cattle from the very beginning of the film and even before their first sexual encounter. As Sue Brower states, "'Cowboy' has become a signifier of an ironic twentieth-century (and now twenty-first-century) perspective on the genre's tradition as it has been commercialized" (48).

Shepherding makes this stand out. But it is important to note how homophobic responses to *Brokeback* avoid the irony and hold to the myth by denying that the film is a western: "One thing is clear, which is that homophobic responses to *Brokeback Mountain* often resist viewing the film as a Western, opting instead to see it as completely antithetical to, more often than not a perverted mockery of, the Western. Such a reading perceives *Brokeback Mountain* as a straight-up attack on 'American values,' a perverse film neatly summed up in the title of one widely-read virulent response subtitled 'Rape of the Marlboro Man'" (Needham 31). Gary Needham is referring to David Kupelian's "'Brokeback Mountain': Rape of the Marlboro Man." In that review, Kupelian argues that *Brokeback* is "gay propaganda," an advertisement for what he sees as a deadly "life choice" like smoking: "The 'Marlboro Man' campaign launched 50 years ago. Today, the powerful cowboy image is being used to sell us on another self-destructive product: homosexual sex and 'gay' marriage" (Kupelian). The view here is ironic because, arguably, *Midnight Cowboy* (1969) had already put an end to the nostalgia of the western genre and its association with the American idyllic symbols of mom, apple pie, and the simplistic morality of the preceding Cold War era symbolized by white and black hats. Joe Buck's (Jon Voight) appearance is itself a nostalgically bizarre mix of cowboy signifiers—a throwback to the ornate clothes of the singing cowboy. Even Buck's boots, in their ornamentation, serve no practical purpose beyond displaying the commodified nature of the "cowboy." Indeed, with *Urban Cowboy* (1980) the cowboy achieved its final overtly commercialized form.

While Kupelian is homophobic, the connection between *Brokeback* and the Marlboro Man is important. The sexualization of the gaze in *Brokeback* can be seen through the Marlboro Man campaign. *Brokeback* returns to what the herder and gender hierarchy represses through range-war conflict, landing it firmly in the classical pastoral tradition. Now, I have not seen any comments by Annie Proulx, Larry McMurtry, or Diana Ossana of an awareness of classical pastoral homosexuality, but a familiarity with both that tradition and the western pushes it to the fore, forcing us to locate the film and its protagonists outside of what has become commercialized. This is nowhere more apparent than in the sexualization of the male gaze and how the viewer is made to see the film through that framework. Only three minutes into the film, for example, we view Ennis Del Mar (Heath Ledger) through the side-view mirror of Jack Twist's (Jake Gyllenhaal) truck as he shaves. This type of frame is frequently employed in the film. For example, only ten minutes later we have a shot past Jack with Ennis in the background nude washing, followed next by a shot past Ennis as Jack urinates in the background. These shots deliberately move from the homosocial to the homoerotic potential of life on the range. These shots switch to the negative when we see Ennis and Jack rough-housing around camp—the scene shot/reverse shot shifts to Joe Aguirre (Randy Quaid) as he lowers his binoculars. These force the viewer to see the relationship through not only the mixed feelings of the protagonists, but also the homophobic view of Aguirre, as well as Alma's (Michelle Williams) confusion as she watches Jack and Ennis through the screen door.

These alternate perspectives also highlight the self-hatred that Ennis embodies and relate directly to the story of the homophobic killing that he tells Jack, a killing that, Ennis says, his father may have been involved in: "Hell, all I know he done the job." The film already foreshadows the tale immediately following the first sex scene between Ennis and Jack. Their instructions from Joe are that one man remain in camp and the other tends the sheep. The consequences are clear when Ennis returns to the flock and discovers an eviscerated sheep that has been attacked by wolves. The scene can be allegorically aligned with Aguirre's homophobic voyeurism, which also makes it significant in terms of the silence of the scene—it stands for many things that cannot be said, certainly not by Ennis and his internalized homophobia: "Representations of masculinity and emotional reticence are often allied to a strong silence in men. For the cowboy, it would seem too that reticence is one instance of how masculinity gets constructed in relation to silence, introspection and mystery. Masculinity becomes invisible and unknowable because men in movies do not talk about being men. Too much talk can be revealing and can lead to emotions" (Needham 53). We can recall, here, that a key component of the parody of *Rustlers' Rhapsody* is the fact that men do talk about masculinity and sexuality. In addition, this relates to the singing cowboy—a way of allowing emotional expression within a heteronormative frame that attempts to sidestep any possible homoerotics within the homosocial world of the range. Significant, too, is the fact that, although a solitary presence on the range, The Marlboro Man ads had also played off of this: "The most striking feature of the Marlboro campaign was its use of a single, bold, photographic image with hardly any copy" (White, Oliffe, and

Bottorff). His silent solitude prompts no questioning of a "confident heterosexuality."

However, like the eviscerated sheep that Ennis finds—and its allegorical link to the homophobic killing that occurred in his childhood, and, of course, Jack's murder—*Brokeback* falls into a rather conventional mainstream queer scenario. As in the other films discussed, that eviscerated sheep signifies the violence of the cattle-sheep hierarchy where cattlemen threaten or actually do kill sheep or shepherds in order to drive them away from cattle country. Jack's murder and Ennis' internalized homophobia force homosexuality to remain closeted or face death. Paradoxically, it is Ennis' repressed homosexuality, which prompts him to violently act out, that saves him—indicating, as in the conflicts between sheepmen and cattlemen, that violence is a key component of masculinity, allowing Ennis to pass in the aggressive heteronormative world. But the protagonists' fates are also important for another reason. Some critics suggest that the suffering and death of *Brokeback*'s queer protagonists allowed it to achieve its mainstream success. This is obviously not the severe homophobic response of a critic like Kupelian, but, as Ara Osterweil argues, "by presenting this story through the established codes of Hollywood melodrama, *Brokeback Mountain* ultimately contains the radicalism of its subject matter through generic conservatism. In a way that recalls John Schlesinger's *Midnight Cowboy* (1969)—another 'breakthrough' film—the same-sex protagonists in *Brokeback Mountain* are required to *suffer* for their love" (38). Similarly, D.A. Miller argues, "Here is the contradiction under which *Brokeback Mountain* 'happens to be' well crafted. On the one hand, homosexuality is only interesting (marketable) if it is the occasion for rehearsing a fantasy of the Homosexual as thrillingly, pointlessly antisocial, a *bête noire* who must die. On the other hand, this fantasy is neither compatible with, nor even tolerable to, the liberal politics of homosexuality as we know them and as *Brokeback Mountain* would espouse them" (55).

Generic denials seek to push the film outside of the western, maintaining a strictly bucolic masculinity while treating the queer characters as dysfunctional individuals, thereby denying the socio-cultural reasons that have made LGBT characters "suffer" and die. In doing so, however, it affords Jack and Ennis the only marginalized space that the genre permits since classical times—the idyllic otium of shepherding on Brokeback Mountain. If *Brokeback* is radical in its representation of the queer shepherds it is so only in creating that pastoral space where desire, however troubling, can be at least physically expressed. In the end, as with the other films, it restores the heteronormative vision of gender which, in this case, rather than seeing the protagonists ride off into the sunset, is trapped within Aguirre's view through the binoculars. There is, then, much more at stake in how the western represents livestock.

Notes

1. Ronald L. Davis, "Paradise among the Monuments: John Ford's Vision of the American West," 50.
2. Though *Brokeback Mountain* focuses on the homoerotic relationship of the pastoral tradition, one can see this as an extension of a homosocial *philia* in the western. Andrew C. Isenberg, for example, in his analysis of masculinity in the 1950s television series *Wyatt Earp*, sees the homosocial bonding of Earp and Doc Holliday in this non-sexualized way. Isenberg cites Bat Masterson's comment on that relationship: "Noting how Holliday put his life at risk in the service of Earp in Arizona in 1881 and 1882, Masterson wrote, 'Damon did no more for Pythias than Holliday did for Wyatt Earp'" (153). For another analysis of *philia* in westerns, see Sue Matheson "'When you side with a man, you stay with him!' *Philia* and the Military Mind in Sam Peckinpah's *The Wild Bunch* (1969)." Male-male relationships based on this classical Greek model, however, do not entirely preclude homoeroticism. In Plato's *Symposium*, for example, Socrates states, "And if there were only some way of contriving that a state or an army should be made up of lovers and their loves, they would be the very best governors of their own city ... and when fighting at each other's side, although a mere handful, they would overcome the world" (130).
3. Frances Pheasant-Kelly looks at another gender-bending Day western in "Outlaws, Buddies, and Lovers: the Sexual Politics of *Calamity Jane* and *Butch Cassidy and the Sundance Kid*." She argues that some of the transgressive nature of this is deflated by Day's overexaggerated performance of masculinity, which can also be seen in *The Ballad of Josie*.
4. Patrick Wayne is, of course, John Wayne's son—the masculine ideal in western movies from the 1930s through to the 1970s.
5. The Hays Production Code had prevented any overt queer content in movies, so, in part, the naïve representation of the singing cowboy in the 1930s and 1940s, when played for laughs in the 1980s, allows the repressed and censored to emerge. It is interesting to note that just prior to a more rigorous enforcement of the Hays Code in 1934, when it became "exceptionally effective in regulating what people saw in theatres" (Vaughn 64), queer content did occur. In Bob Steele's *The Man from Hell's Edge* (1932), a B-Western directed by Robert N. Bradbury, Bob Williams (Steele), aka "Flash" Manning, is put in prison to infiltrate the gang that killed his father. As he closes in on the gang's leader, El Lobo (Julian Rivero), Manning is covertly joined by Shamrock (George "Gabby" Hayes) and Half-Pint (Gilbert Holmes) (all three are actually Secret Service). What is most interesting in the context of the parody of *Rustlers' Rhapsody*, is that Manning shoots the guns out of the hands of "bad" guys, much like O'Herlihan. In addition, there is one curious scene, although it is played for comic relief, where Shamrock and Half-Pint are admonished by Manning, undercover as a deputy, for causing trouble in a saloon (Manning even shoots the gun out of Half-Pint's hand in this scene). As they leave the saloon, Shamrock and Half-Pint start skipping down the street, hand-in-hand. They are "effeminately" waved at by a cowboy on the street, who they shoot at to run-off. There is an ambiguity here as to whether the wave is meant as a queer acknowledgement or as mockery.
6. The Marlboro Man ads began in 1955. Philip Morris had introduced the brand in 1924, and, as Cameron White, John L. Oliffe, and Joan L. Bottorff state, "It was initially manufactured with an ivory tip or a red 'beauty tip' and marketed as 'a fancy smoke for dudes and women.'" Leo Burnett's Marlboro Man campaign was specifically undertaken to revise the branding of the product. Jack Twist's moustache later in *Brokeback* brings him visually closer to the Marlboro Man, but it also marks the distance between the Marlboro Man and reality nostalgically, linking his appearance, in turn, to Jack and Ennis' nostalgia for Brokeback Mountain.

Filmography

The Ballad of Josie. Dir. Andrew V. McLaglen. Universal Pictures, 1967.
Brokeback Mountain. Dir. Ang Lee. River Road Entertainment, 2005.
Colorado Sunset. Dir. George Sherman. Republic Pictures, 1939.
The Man from Hell's Edge. Dir. Robert N. Bradbury. Sono Art-World Wide Pictures, 1932.

Marked for Murder. Dir. Elmer Clifton. Alexander-Stern Productions, 1945.
Midnight Cowboy. Dir. John Schlesinger. United Artists, 1969.
Rustlers' Rhapsody. Dir. Hugh Wilson. Paramount Pictures, 1985.
The Sheepman. Dir. George Marshall. Metro-Goldwyn-Mayer, 1958.
Urban Cowboy. Dir. James Bridges. Paramount Pictures, 1980.

Works Cited

Berman, Daniel W. "The Hierarchy of Herdsmen, Goatherding and Genre in Theocritan Bucolic." *Phoenix* 59.3-4 (Fall-Winter 2005): 228-45. Web.

Brower, Sue. "'They'd Kill Us if They Knew': Transgression and the Western." *Journal of Film and Video* 62.4 (Winter 2010): 47-57. Web.

Davis, Ronald L. "Paradise among the Monuments: John Ford's Vision of the American West." *Montana: the Magazine of Western History* 45.3 (Summer 1995): 48-63. Web.

Isenberg, Andrew C. "The Code of the West: Sexuality, Homosociality, and Wyatt Earp." *The Western Historical Quarterly* 40.2 (Summer 2009): 139-57. Web.

Kupelian, David. "'Brokeback Mountain': Rape of the Marlboro Man." Dec. 27, 2005. www.calvarypo.org/HANDS/0252.pdf. Accessed August 15, 2015. Web.

Matheson, Sue. "'When you side with a man, you stay with him!'—*philia* and the Military Mind in Sam Peckinpah's *The Wild Bunch* (1969)." In *Love in Western Film and Television: Lonely Hearts and Happy Trails*. Ed. Sue Matheson. New York: Palgrave Macmillan, 2013. 225-37. Print.

Miller, D.A. "On the Universality of *Brokeback*." *Film Quarterly* 60.3 (Summer 2007): 50-60. Web.

Needham, Gary. *Brokeback Mountain*. Edinburgh: University of Edinburgh Press. Ebook.

Norton, Rictor. "The Era of Idylls." *The Homosexual Pastoral Tradition*. 20 June 2008. http://rictornorton.co.uk/pastor00.htm. Accessed May 19, 2015. Web.

Osterweil, Ara. "Ang Lee's Lonesome Cowboys." *Film Quarterly* 60.3 (Summer 2007): 38-42. Web.

Pheasant-Kelly, Frances. "Outlaws, Buddies, and Lovers: the Sexual Politics of *Calamity Jane* and *Butch Cassidy and the Sundance Kid*." *Love in Western Film and Television: Lonely Hearts and Happy Trails*. Ed. Sue Matheson. New York: Palgrave Macmillan, 2013. 141-60. Print.

Plato. *Symposium*. In *The Portable Plato*. Ed. Scott Buchanan. Trans. Benjamin Jowett. Rpt. Harmondsworth: Penguin, 1977. Print.

Tan, Lynette. "The New Deal Cowboy: Gene Autry and the Antimodern Resolution." *Film History* 13.1 (2001): 89-101. Web.

Vander Wel, Stephanie. "The Lavender Cowboy and 'The She Buckaroo': Gene Autry, Patsy Montana, and Depression-Era Gender Roles." *Musical Quarterly* 95.2-3 (Summer-Fall 2012): 207-51. Web.

Vaughn, Stephen. "Morality and Entertainment: the Origins of the Motion Picture Production Code." *The Journal of American History* 77. 1 (June 1990): 39-65. Web.

White, Cameron, John L. Oliffe, and Joan L. Bottorff. "Masculinity, Race, and Style in the Consumption of Cigarettes, 1962-1972." *American Journal of Public Health* 103. 4 (April 2013): e44-e55. Web.

Ride 'Em Cowboy
Equine Representations in the Western

Stella Hockenhull

"The horse is central not only to the Western but to the whole culture of the West" (Buscombe *BFI Companion to the Western* 150).

From early films such as *Cupid's Round Up* (LeSaint, 1918) starring Tom Mix and his mount, Tony, to *All the Pretty Horses* (Thornton, 2000), horses have played a major part in the Western genre, in particular in their contribution to the cowboy's iconography and that of his adversary, the Native American. Not only does the horse connect the cowboy to nature, it enhances his persona and masculinity, providing a noble and enduring quality to his character. Further, the horse serves to represent speed, loyalty and liberty. As John Cawelti argues, "The hero is a man with a horse and the horse is his direct tie to the freedom of the wilderness, for it embodies his ability to move freely across it and to dominate and control its spirit. Through the intensity of his relationship to his horse, the cowboy excites that human fantasy of unity with natural creatures" (57).

Invariably, horses play a special role in the affections of their masters in the Western, and customarily the central protagonist/hero retains the same, often eye-catching, animal throughout the narrative. Sometimes they are awarded dashing names, such as Silver, Raider, Trigger or Champion; at times they are marketed as star vehicles which, as Edgar Morin argues, encourages a "mythic quality and the star becomes heroic" (29–30). Celebrity animals often appear at the top of the billing, with the industry realizing their value through guest appearances and merchandise; moreover, they are accorded agency and motivate the plot through the attribution of anthropomorphic characteristics to enable them to intercept danger or to encourage romance.

In *Dallas* (Heisler, 1950), for example, the horse helps his rider, Blayde Hollister (Gary Cooper), to find his way home and in *Riders of Destiny* (Bradbury, 1933) romance blossoms because Singin' Sandy Saunders (John Wayne) loans his horse to love interest Fay Denton (Cecilia Parker), whose own animal has been shot.

Equine representation in the Western also serves other purposes. In *Shane* (Stevens, 1953), the central character and cowboy, Shane (Alan Ladd), is romanticized through his harmonious relationship with his horse. When he first emerges from the mountains astride his mount, he is watched by the young boy Joey Starratt (Brandon de Wilde), the child openly expressing admiration for this magical apparition. Alternatively, a number of films destabilize the genre's iconography, particularly in respect of the cowboy/horse relationship. One example, termed the "post-heyday Western" by Jean-Christophe Cloutier, is *Unforgiven* (Eastwood, 1992). In this film, aging gunslinger William Munny (Clint Eastwood) has uncharacteristically settled down to homestead dwelling, and is now physically unable to even mount his horse. Even so, ultimately it is the horse that separates the cowboy from other mortals, operating as a symbol of his heroism and masculinity, and, furthermore, as a link with American patriotism and the wilderness.

The Western Horse as Celebrity

It is not only the cowboy that operates as the leading character of the Western; frequently, the horse becomes a star in the film, adopting heroic qualities, while acting to save his master and emerging as a moral envoy. Such animals include Champion the Wonder Horse, who was Singing Cowboy Gene Autry's ride, and Trigger, Roy Rogers' palomino horse that was eventually immortalized at the Roy Rogers Museum in California. This notion of animal as star is a fairly new concept, although the study of stars has been a cornerstone of film studies since Richard Dyer's seminal work *Stars* (1979). Dyer's construction of stardom entails an understanding of the role of publicity and marketing as well as stars as symbols of morality. However, his influential work does not encompass the concept of non humans, despite the fact that animals such as Trigger and Champion are long-established screen celebrities, and animal stars have been in existence for some considerable time. More relevant to the notion of animals as stars is the work of Dyer's predecessor, French philosopher and sociologist Edgar Morin. His study focuses on the mythical aspects of venerated film individuals, and this concept is more easily translated into a framework for animal analysis.

As early as 1957, in his pioneering study entitled *Les Stars*, Morin argues that stars function as myths within contemporary urban society and that these new luminaries "spring from their characters as heroes or heroines" (6). For Morin, the idols adopt mythic and divine status, yet they are also normal beings participating "in the daily life of mortals: they are no longer inaccessible: they are mediators between the screen-heaven and earth" (23). This mythic quality operates as a tension between the actor and the role they play, and the star takes precedence over the character they are performing. As he observes, the myth occurs as "an ensemble of imaginary situations and behaviours. These behaviours and situations may have as their protagonists superhuman beings, heroes, or gods [who] attempt to deliver mortals from their infinite misery.... The star is the actor or actress who absorbs some of the heroic—that is, divinized and mythic—substance of the hero or heroine of the movies, and who in turn enriches this substance by his or her own contribution" (Morin 29–30). The star therefore becomes the icon of the audience, and this mythical, divine status, which Morin refers to, can also be bestowed upon animals.

Fans are a further important element of star construction. As Morin explains, gossip columnists and journalists, who are as much interested in the stars as the films, enable spectator identification and empathy with them, and therefore encourage imagined familiarity. Stars are regularly photographed by the press, and this might adopt the form of official and unofficial media coverage. Through such a process, they become superindividuals, which, in the case of animals, invariably involves an anthropomorphic treatment.[1] In the public domain, animals have become personified and frequently described as human characters, given human names, and their feelings and thoughts explained in some detail. Categorizing elements of personification identified as human attributes further blurs the boundaries between human and animal, such a personalized centrality aiding emotional connection and intimacy on the part of the spectator.

"Trigger,"[2] American actor, singer and cowboy Roy Rogers' trusty horse, is conferred with all of the above qualities, and was anthropomorphized in the films in which he starred. These were B Westerns, which were lower budget than their A counterparts, and were predominantly fantasy, and targeted at children. For this reason, the B Western cowboy had a special affinity with his horse, which was capable of heroic deeds, and usually able to assist and save his master.

As mentioned, Dyer's criterion to qualify as a star includes publicity and promotion, specifically marketing and critical reviews of the films at the time of their release. The credits for Roy Rogers' films nearly always provide the horse a special mention and, more often than not, Trigger is featured in the billing. Moreover, critical reviews of the films acknowledge the horse, assigning him human characteristics by referring to his valiant gallantry and intelligence. *To-Day's Cinema*, for example, observes not only the "dashing heroics" of Roy Rogers in *Susanna Pass* (Witney, 1949), but also the way in which Trigger "uses his horse sense" (6). One reviewer for the *Monthly Film Bulletin* writes of the same film that Rogers and Trigger "come to the rescue of the town" (315). In a marketing campaign for *Son of Paleface* (Tashlin, 1952), *The Motion Picture Herald* makes special mention of the equine star, informing the reader that "Bob Hope and Jane Russell are playing with Roy Rogers and Trigger, and all deserve equal billing" (W.H. 46).

If the publicity surrounding Trigger signals his celebrity status, then his onscreen performance further consolidates his stardom. James Naremore, writing in *Acting in the Cinema* (1988), distinguishes between three aspects of characterization: role in terms of the fictional character, actor as the being performing the character, and star image which he proposes is an intertextual occurrence derived from the actor's previous roles. For Naremore, stars become associated with a gamut of performance signs recognizable by the audience, and this links with Morin's notion of star as mythical and superhuman. In all of the Roy Rogers and Trigger films, Trigger is represented as a fearless and feisty animal, clever and cunning with the ability to not only detect, but also outwit, his master's adversaries. Further, he is represented as tireless and capable of endurance.

At his first outing in *Under Western Stars* (Kane, 1938), Trigger receives no mention by name, and his appearance is not particularly prominent. However, as Rogers became more renowned, the horse is developed as a motivating character in plot development. In *Come On, Rangers* (Kane, 1938), for instance, the horse resists theft, and in *Frontier Pony Express* (Kane, 1939), he is the speediest horse on earth. By the end of the film, he acts as a decoy for the Confederates pursuing Rogers by jumping off a cliff and into a lake. Here, not only does Trigger appear to behave fearlessly and heroically, he is also a symbol of American patriotism. In the later *Heldorado* (Witney, 1946), Trigger is mainly used as a means of transport, although he is also heralded as a local celebrity in the film. Indeed, at one point, Rogers parades Trigger into a rodeo arena where he performs the favorite trick of rearing up onto his hind legs. Shot from a low angle, he appears majestic and spirited, and ennobles his rider in the process. This pose is Trigger's trademark and is significant in equine visual representation as Roderick McGillis notes: the rearing horse has long been used in the Western to connote "victory, power, strength, bravery, control, and confidence; this is the heroic pose par excellence" (106).

By the release of *My Pal Trigger* (McDonald, 1946), Trigger is awarded superindividual status and he is furnished with a history. The film commences with Rogers riding his mare, Lady, into the Golden Horse Stud, a breeding farm for palomino horses. Rogers is cast this time as a travelling horse trader, and the narrative is structured as a Trigger origin story. On arrival, he encounters the daughter of the ranch owner, Susan Kendrick (Dale Evans), performing a public dressage display. Watched by the locals, she sits astride the palomino stallion Golden Sovereign, but when Lady arrives the mare distracts him, the suggestion being that a relationship develops between the animals. Ultimately, the pair mate, although Golden Sovereign is shot in error and dies. Even so, Lady is now in foal and the result is Trigger, a beautiful palomino colt. That the film is a vehicle for Rogers' horse is therefore not in question, and Trigger the foal occupies much of the film's screen time.

In the later *Under California Stars* (Witney, 1948), Trigger becomes a significant motivating character. He is kidnapped and a ransom demanded, but is predictably rescued, gaining his revenge in the final chase sequence. At the outset of the film, Trigger is billed immediately beneath the name of Roy Rogers, and described anthropomorphically as "The Smartest Horse in the Movies." When Rogers and his men learn of the miscreants at the neighboring cattle farm who are trying to steal their horses to sell to local crook Pop Jordan (George Lloyd), he ably leaps astride Trigger to take appropriate action. Subsequently, the pair appears framed under the sign of Rogers' ranch, the horse, viewed from a sideways perspective for effect, once more rearing majestically in the air. Later, Trigger's stable companions are stolen by Jordan and his accomplice, Lige McFarland (Wade Crosby), and the horse tirelessly pursues them alone, fast on their trail. Seen from a variety of angles, galloping towards the camera, and from a side view in the distance, he demonstrates the attributes of power and intelligence as, riderless, he gives chase. Eventually captured and held to ransom for a figure of $100,000, Trigger is shown center frame, albeit roped by his kidnappers on either side. As though fighting his captors, he rears upwards in signature pose, subsequently attacking one of the reprobates by striking him with his front legs. Nonetheless, he is overpowered and led back into his stable. Rogers fails in his mission to recover him, and Trigger's stable goes on fire. Eventually, however, following a shootout, Trigger is rescued and Rogers and his horse are reunited. At the end of the film, the horse saves his master's life, and, in line with the notion of Trigger as star, not only does he exhibit fearless characteristics, he is a mythical animal and unmistakably the hero of the story.

Rogers and Trigger went on to make a number of other films together but, by the mid–1940s, fan interest in the B Western, and indeed Westerns in general, was diminishing. By 1951, along with stars such as Gene Autry, Roy Rogers moved into television with *The Roy Rogers Show*. Before the premiere of the first episode on December 30 an introductory half hour was devoted to *Son of Paleface* "interviewing and introducing" Bob Hope and Trigger. However, the horse did not receive the same attention in the TV shows as he had in the films, although in episodes such as *Ghost Town Gold* he produces his characteristic posture opening the show by rearing up in front of the Double R Bar ranch sign. In line with Dyer's notion of stardom, Trigger also made guest appearances on programs such as *The Gabby Hayes Show* and the *Roy Rogers Rodeo: TV Special*. Additionally, both horse and rider became widely merchandised, with the manufacture of model cowboy characters and related miscellaneous toys and books. When Trigger died, his fame was such that he was preserved and mounted at the Roy Rogers Californian museum for display.[3]

The Horse as Symbol of Masculinity

Whereas the star horse has a name, is given a history, anthropomorphized and operates as a crucial character in the narrative, the working horse generally does not have such a prominent role. Nonetheless, in general the central cowboy protagonist is attuned to his mount, and even favors one particular steed. The early Westerns were filmed in black and white and therefore the color of the animal was significant. A bright chestnut or palomino horse stood out, and therefore, for practical reasons, the hero's horse usually has a striking appearance. Also, with some exceptions, the archetypal cowboy in the Western is the quintessential hero. He is physically powerful, competent and experienced in the ways of the land. Living in the wild, he is content and at home with nature. Above all he is an icon of manliness, either "possessing a robust, virile heterosexuality [where] the privileged coupling is normally between brave men and beautiful, strong women" (Freedman 18), or a private sufferer, who possesses the ability to rebuff female company and live a life of self-denial. Often the hero cowboy demonstrates his masculinity through taming and breaking his horse, thus displaying his prowess, manliness and expertise although, according to Henry Nash Smith, this Wild West hero did not appear until the late 1880s in the wake of Buffalo Bill. As he points out, the American hired man on horseback was not a celebrated individual before this date, and was previously viewed as a "semibarbarous laborer who lived a dull monotonous life of hard fare" (Nash Smith 122). The Western, however, succeeded in glamorizing the cowboy, representing him as an expert pugilist and horseman, whose job it is to fight evil and Native Americans. As Roderick McGillis indicates, the cowboy's mount "draws attention to the body. Horses are beautiful to look at and so are horse and rider together" (111). Likewise, the Western hero wears spurs and chaps and has an elaborate saddle and clothing to correspond with this riding expertise. Further, the horse is both free spirited and courageous, traits that are transferable to the rider.

Wendy Chapman Peek argues that scholarly views on the cowboy hero are often divided into two opposing character types. One is the masculine hero, who is linked to power as a symbol of American courage, strength, freedom and the wild. Alternatively, she argues, the second is the man committed to family and community. She takes issue with the concept that these two are distinct from each other, contending that the true Western hero must embrace both worlds, not in conflict, or negative terms, but as complementary to one another. As she indicates, "Viewed diachronically, to be at one time dominant and at another deferential is not a contradiction but a strategy, one that several Western protagonists use to achieve their goals" (Peek 208). Moreover, as she purports, the Western is not primarily about masculinity, but about competence which is arguably derived from the mastery of horsemanship.

Sandy Saunders' competence as a rider in *Riders of Destiny* (Bradbury, 1933) is one such example, and he embraces the two worlds described by Peek. Government agent Saunders is brought in to control local land baron James Kincaid (Forrest Taylor). He first appears as a distant figure in the backwoods astride a pure white horse with flowing mane and tail. As Jenni Calder argues, "The screen hero is not likely to ride just any old pony. He is going to be partly identified by his horse" (97), and Saunders' mount is easily recognizable, mobilizing a memorable and romantic impression for the spectator. Additionally, the cowboy appears in harmony with his animal, and reciprocity is achieved between the two and "communicated not through language but through relaxed and rhythmical movements" (Tompkins 95). To achieve this effect, the camera alternates between medium shots of Saunders singing as they traverse the plains, and distance shots of the horse prancing as if choreographed to the tune. Soon after, the cowboy discovers a young woman, Fay Denton, whose horse has been shot. He gallantly offers her his mount, and she rides home to safety. Now on foot, Saunders appears diminished and temporarily vulnerable.

After Saunders has escorted Fay home, he puts his horse in the barn (notwithstanding Fay's advice), first taking the animal for a drink of water. He thus corresponds with Peek's notion that the cowboy hero can incorporate complementary spheres. Indeed, Saunders shows himself to be caring and competent, and also tough. More importantly, his fine beast stands out from the other horses ridden by the wrongdoers, Kincaid and his men. These are comprised of predominantly bays (brown with black manes and tails), which appear insignificant, particularly as the film is monochrome. This is a point reinforced by McGillis who claims, "Most bad guys ride indistinguishable bays.... Only the hero rides a thick-necked distinctively coloured stallion. And this horse and this man need only each other for company and companionship" (109). Saunders is undoubtedly the hero, even if this is only identified through the color of his mount. In addition, the horse sports an elaborate studded bridle and saddle, equipment that distinguishes his rider from Kincaid's horses which are not endowed with such finery.

Later, when Saunders gallops into town to assess the damage that Kincaid has wrought, he arrives among the locals, who stand around horseless. According to Calder, the man on foot is usually represented in the Western as a debased character: "The unhorsed cowboy standing precariously on his high heeled boots has been deprived of half his power and several feet of his stature" (94). The weakness associated with the "unhorsed" has its roots in the U.S. cavalry and the inferiority of the foot soldier to the mounted combatant. Indeed, providing not only height for its rider, the horse also enables speed for a quick chase or retreat in times of conflict. As Calder argues, "The horse transforms the man, adds something to his personality and his presence as well as his stature and his speed" (94). Thus, in most of the classical Westerns the hero is an excellent horseman and dresses appropriately for this role. Seen in medium shot, Saunders is the only mounted person in the entire group, with even Kincaid now on foot. Thus, at this juncture, Saunders towers above the other men, both in stature and decency. At the end of the film, he chases the enemy out of town on horseback in stylish and proficient mode, and the camera frames him in medium shot to enable the spectator to witness his sprint towards the animal followed by an effortless vault onto its back. From this spectacular and impressive feat of riding he then rapidly pursues his quarry at a fast gallop. Not only does Saunders' horse ennoble his owner, he also presents a spectacle by means of his swiftness and appearance.

If Saunders epitomizes the caring, yet masculine cowboy, then Shane also fulfills a similar role in George Stevens' seminal film, *Shane*. In a similar vein to Saunders' horse, Shane's mount is striking: a gleaming chestnut color with flaxen mane and tail. This film is shot in color, yet the horse stands out, thus distinguishing its rider. Shane is a mysterious character whose background is never explained and who emerges from the wilds carrying all his possessions with him. He arrives at the Starrett ranch, a solitary figure astride his eye-catching mount, and is immediately invested with a sense of mystery and allure. Indeed, "Shane's only union is with his horse and this adds a mythic aura to his presence, raising his status to that of an inscrutable free spirit. He retains this mystery throughout, and neither the characters in the film, nor the spectator are privileged to any information about him" (Hockenhull 166). As mentioned in the introduction, Shane is first seen through the young Joey Starrett's eyes whereby "the glowing chestnut of Shane's horse is an inseparable part of the initial impact" (Calder 96). The boy idolizes him because he is strong, able with a gun and a capable horseman, and this idealization commences from the outset.

Throughout the film, Shane is contrasted with the boy's father, Joe Starrett (Van Heflin). He unstintingly helps on Joe's farm, is strong, competent and capable on the land and has mastery over horses. His homestead counterpart, on the other hand, struggles with the physical aspects of hard labor

Shane (Alan Ladd) and his eye-catching companion in *Shane* (Paramount, 1953).

and is not an accomplished horseman. At the end of the film, Shane rejects security and leaves the Starrett household, returning to his solitary existence on the prairie alone. Again, seen from Joey's point of view, and repeating the opening scene in reverse, he rides away towards the mountains, and he and his mount become specks on the horizon. Shane has chosen the wilderness and isolation above family life, a point noted by Buscombe who claims that "when Shane's attraction to Marian, the wife of his friend Joe Starrett, threatens their friendship Shane buries his feelings for her and rides off alone" ("Man to Man" 35) returning to the mythical open space and a solitary existence. This image of the horseman riding into the landscape is symbolic of the country he must conquer, and his return to the wilderness is motivated by a search for new adventure. Corresponding to Saunders, and in line with the genre, Shane's bridle is elaborately studded and his saddle is large and well equipped with all he needs to survive. As Jane Tompkins argues, when the hero leaves town on his horse "he is not unaccommodated. The saddle he sits on is large and comfortable, and usually ornamented; to it are appended all sorts of gear—canteens, rifles, ropes, knives, bags of food, blankets, articles of clothing…. When he leaves the girl at the end of the movie, the hero isn't going off into the wild blue yonder all by himself; he is coming home to his horse, and together they are going to seek new adventures" (97).

The Horse in the Post-Heyday Western

In *Unforgiven*, Clint Eastwood as William Munny is initially represented as atypical of the Western hero, particularly in relation to his inadequacies in horsemanship. The narrative centers on ex-expert criminal/gunfighter turned pig farmer, Munny, whose legendary skills as a ruthless gunman are called upon to avenge a savage attack on prostitute Delilah Fitzgerald (Anna Levine). Munny is, at this point, older and has lost many of his previous skills such as gun handling and riding, nowadays a homesteader with two dependent children and no wife. Indeed, the film offers an aging man ill at ease with his body in what Jean-Christophe Cloutier describes as a "post-heyday Western." As he puts forward, cowboys of the post-heyday Western contravene "the Western form. Aged Westerners violate the genre because their bodies are ill fitted for the job, plagued by frailty, ineptitude, and illness" (Cloutier 113).

When the spectator first encounters Munny, he is represented as inept, and horses play a large part in this characterization. At the start of the film he is on foot and a settler as opposed to a roamer, thus, in Calder's vocabulary, deprived of power. We only learn of his past through the Schofield Kid (Jaimz Woolvett), who wants to enlist his help in gaining the reward put out in revenge for Delilah's mutilation. The Schofield Kid's verbal description of Munny imbues the latter with a heroic, mythical status, a factor not matched by the present-day figure we encounter. Initially, he refuses the offer of money, but later makes the decision to claim the reward, and commits the gaffe of being unable to mount his horse.[4] Seen from a low angle, the horse spins quickly around, and Munny eventually loses his balance and falls to the ground. Informing his children that "this horse is getting even with me for the sins of my youth.... I used to be weak and given to mistreating animals" implies that not only is he incapable of climbing aboard, he is also admitting to past brutalities. This is unusual in that the hero cowboy figure is not normally associated with cruelty, particularly with animals.

Munny's inability to mount becomes a repeated motif in the film, and is incongruous with the mythic status of the Western hero and his mastery of horses. This situation occurs again later in the narrative when Munny and the Schofield Kid attempt to escape following a shootout; he again struggles to get on his horse, albeit it is imperative that he does so to save his own life. It is only at the end of the film, after he has successfully shot and killed the sheriff, Little Bill Daggett (Gene Hackman) and a number of his henchmen because they murdered his friend Ned Logan (Morgan Freeman), that he successfully mounts. This time he does so with ease and, as a result, appears manly and in control. Indeed, Munny has redeemed his reputation as cowboy as shown in the final scene, which reveals him astride his horse, trotting confidently along the main street, while shouting threats to the surviving townspeople.[5] His new eminence is reinforced through the appreciative looks of Delilah and the townswomen, their facial expressions seen in close-up indicating admiration and veneration for the man who has defended their honor.

Conclusion

Horses have always played a major part in the iconography of the Western, and the classical Western in particular has distinct rules. One of these is its incorporation of the horse as a mode of transport for the cowboy who must display equine expertise thus symbolizing his masculinity.[6] However, the cowboy's mount has other subtexts. It not only identifies him as manly and heroic, but also stands as a symbol of American courage. Further, the horse signifies freedom from societal constraints and links its rider with nature and the wilderness over domesticity. If the horse functions to demonstrate masculinity, then it also signifies the caring aspects of the cowboy, and as a man committed to community. The hero cowboy has a special relationship with his mount which is usually pale in color and strikingly beautiful to separate him out from the other, usually unsavory, characters.

Not only are horses essential to the iconography of the Western, they are also highlighted as heroic characters in their own right, often awarded celebrity status, and provided human qualities to motivate the narrative. In some films we see a destabilization of the cowboy myth, yet, as in *Unforgiven*, the horse continues to play a part, ultimately redeeming Munn, and restoring him in the eyes of the community to his previous stature. In sum, as Tompkins comments, horses represent "the fact that the body of the horse stands beneath the body of the rider, between the human being and the earth. Horses express a need for connection to nature, to the wild. But it is nature in a particular form.... It is the physical existence of horses above all that makes them indispensible in Westerns" (93–94).

NOTES

1. See Hockenhull, "Celebrity Creatures: the 'Starification' of the Cinematic Animal."
2. Trigger was played by a number of palomino doubles. The original, named Golden Cloud was reportedly purchased in 1938 for $2500 although this date has been disputed and it transpires that Rogers borrowed the horse from Hudkins Stables, until he purchased him five years later. See Pando, *An Illustrated History of Trigger*.
3. It is beyond the scope of this essay to discuss other examples such as Gene Autry and Champion. For further reading see Stanfield, "Dixie Cowboys and Blue Yodels: The Strange History of the Singing Cowboy."
4. This is a repeated motif in *The Wild Bunch* (Peckinpah, 1969). Sykes (Edmond O'Brien), the oldest member of the group, has difficulty mounting his horse. The cowboy unable to mount, or, as poor horseman, has links with the comedy Western. See Turner,

110 A Fistful of Icons

"Cowboys and Comedy: The Simultaneous Deconstruction and Reinforcement of Generic Conventions in the Western Parody."

5. Horses also play a part in the narrative in *Unforgiven*. Little Bill Daggett, the sheriff (Gene Hackman), orders the perpetrators of the crime to deliver a string of ponies to the brothel owner as payment for loss of one of his girls. Further, the women are feisty and allude to their own treatment as animal-like: "Just because we let them smelly fools ride us like horses don't mean we got to let them brand us like horses," says Strawberry Alice (Frances Fisher).

6. There are horseless Westerns such as *High Noon* (Zinnemann, 1952) and *The Man Who Shot Liberty Valance* (Ford, 1962) but, as Calder claims, "these are dramas of the gun rather than the horse" (99) and are uncommon.

Filmography

All the Pretty Horses. Dir. Billy Bob Thornton. USA. Miramax, 2000.
Come On, Rangers. Dir. Joseph Kane. Republic Pictures, 1938.
Cupid's Round Up. Dir. Edward Lesaint. Fox Film Corporation, 1918.
Dallas. Dir. Stuart Heisler. Warner Bros., 1950.
Frontier Pony Express. Dir. Joseph Kane. Republic Pictures, 1939.
The Gabby Hayes Show (1950–1954, 1956) Dir. Vincent J. Donehue. NBC, ABC.
Ghost Town Gold (Broadcast 25 May 1952) Dir. Robert G. Walker. Roy Rogers Productions, 1952.
Heldorado. Dir. William Witney. Republic Pictures, 1946.
My Pal Trigger. Dir. Frank McDonald, Yakima Canutt (uncredited). Republic Pictures, 1946.
Riders of Destiny. Dir. Robert N. Bradbury. Paul Malvern Productions, 1933.
Shane. Dir. George Stevens. Paramount Pictures, 1953.
Son of Paleface. Dir. Frank Tashlin. Paramount Pictures, 1952.
Susanna Pass. Dir. William Witney. Republic Pictures, 1949.
The Roy Rogers Rodeo: TV Special (1955) Dir. Unknown. NBC.
The Roy Rogers Show (1951–1957) Dir. George Blair, John English, Leslie Martinson, Don McDougall, Christian Nyby, Robert G. Walker. NBC.
Under California Stars. Dir. William Witney. Republic Pictures, 1948.
Under Western Stars. Dir. Joseph Kane. Republic Pictures, 1938.
Unforgiven. Dir. Clint Eastwood. Warner Bros., 1992.

Works Cited

Basinger, Jeanine. *The World War II Combat Films*. New York: Columbia University, 1986. Print.
Benshoff, Harry M. and Sean Griffin. *America on Film: Representing Race, Class, Gender and Sexuality at the Movies*. Oxford, Chichester: Wiley Blackwell, 2009. Print.
Bruzzi, Stella. *Men's Cinema: Masculinity and Mise-en-Scène in Hollywood*. Edinburgh: Edinburgh University Press, 2013. Print.
Buscombe, Edward. (ed.) (2nd edition). *The BFI Companion to the Western*. London: BFI, 1993. Print.
_____. "Man to Man." *Sight and Sound*. 16. 1 (2006): 34–37. Print.
_____. "Photographing the Indian." *Back in the Saddle Again*. Eds. Edward Buscombe and Roberta E. Pearson. London: British Film Institute, 1998. 29–45. Print.
Calder, Jenni. *There Must Be a Lone Ranger*. London: Hamish Hamilton, 1974. Print.
Carter, David. *The Western*. Harpenden: Kamera Books, 2008. Print.
Cawelti, John. *The Six-Gun Mystique*. Bowling Green, OH: Bowling Green Popular Press, 1970. Print.
Clarke, Roger. "Lonesome Cowboys." *Sight and Sound*. 16. 1 (2006): 28–33. Print.
Cloutier, Jean-Christophe. "A Country for Old Men: *Unforgiven*, *The Shootist*, and the Post-Heyday Western." *Cinema Journal*. 51 4 (2012): 110–127. Print.

Dyer, Richard. *Stars*. London: British Film Institute, 1979. Print.
Frayling, Christopher. *Spaghetti Westerns*. London, New York: I.B. Tauris, 2006. Print.
Freedman, Carl. "Post-Heterosexuality: John Wayne and the Construction of American Masculinity." *Film International*. 5 1 (2007): 16–31. Print.
Gaines, Jane Marie and Charlotte Cornelia Herzog. "The Fantasy of Authenticity in Western Costume." *Back in the Saddle Again*. Eds. Edward Buscombe and Roberta E. Pearson. London: British Film Institute, 1998. 172–181. Print.
Hintz, Harold. *Horses in the Movies*. South Brunswick, New York: A.S. Barnes and Company, 1979. Print.
Hockenhull, Stella. "Celebrity Creatures: the 'Starification' of the Cinematic Animal." *Revisiting Star Studies*. Eds. Sabrina Q Yu and Guy Austin. Edinburgh: Edinburgh University Press, 2016, forthcoming. Print.
_____. "Horse Power: Equine Alliances in the Western." *Love in Western Film and Television: Lonely Hearts and Happy Trails*. Ed. Sue Matheson. New York: Palgrave Macmillan, 2013. 161–177.
Horrocks, Roger. *Male Myths and Icons: Masculinity in Popular Culture*. Macmillan, 1995. Print.
_____. *Masculinity in Crisis: Myths, Fantasies and Realities*. London: Macmillan, 1994. Print.
Hughes, Howard. *Spaghetti Westerns*. Harpenden: Kamera Books, 2010. Print.
Jenkins, Jennifer L. "Framing Race in the Arizona Borderlands." *Moving Image*. 14. 2 (2014): 68–95. Print.
Krapp, Peter. "Unforgiven: Fausse Reconnaissance." *The South Atlantic Quarterly*. 101. 3 (2002): 589–606. Print.
Langford, Barry. "Revisiting the 'Revisionist' Western." *Film and History*. 33. 2 (2003): 26–34. Print.
Lusted, David. *The Western*. Harlow, England: Pearson/Longman, 2003. Print.
McClain, William. "Go Home! Sergio Leone and the 'Death of the Western' in American Film Criticism." *Journal of Film and Video*. 62. 1–2 (2010): 52–66.
McDonald, Paul. "Why Study Film Acting?" *More Than a Method*. Eds. Cynthia Baron, Diane Carson and Frank P. Tomasulo. Detroit: Wayne State University Press, 2004. 23–41. Print.
McGillis, Roderick. *He Was Some Kind of a Man: Masculinities in the B Western*. Waterloo, Ontario: Wilfrid Laurier University Press, 2009. Print.
Morin, Edgar. *The Stars*. [1957, translated 1972 by Richard Howard]. Minneapolis: University of Minnesota Press, 2005. Print.
Naremore, James. *Acting in the Cinema*. Berkeley: University of California Press, 1988. Print.
Nash Smith, Henry. *Virgin Land: the American West as Symbol and Myth*. New York: Vintage Books, 1950. Print.
Neale, Steve. "Prologue: Masculinity as Spectacle." *Screening the Male: Exploring Masculinities in Hollywood Cinema*. Ed. Steve Neale. London, New York: Routledge, 1993. 9–20. Print.
Pando, Leo. *An Illustrated History of Trigger*. Jefferson, NC: McFarland, 2007. Print.
Peek, Wendy C. "The Romance of Competence: Rethinking Masculinity in the Western." *Journal of Popular Film and Television*. 30. 4. (2003): 206–219. Print.
Pheasant-Kelly, Frances. "Outlaws, Buddies and Lovers: The Sexual Politics of *Calamity Jane* and *Butch Cassidy and the Sundance Kid*." *Love in Western Film and Television: Lonely Hearts and Happy Trails*. Ed. Sue Matheson. New York: Palgrave Macmillan, 2013. 141–160. Print.
"Review: Hands Across the Border." *Kinematograph Weekly*. March 3 (1944): 33. Print.
"Review: Susanna Pass USA 1949." *Monthly Film Bulletin*. (1951): 315. Print.
Roberts, Shari. "Western Meets Eastwood: Genre and Gender on the Road." *The Road Movie Book*. Eds. Steven Cohan and Ina Rae Hark. London: Routledge, 1997. 45–69. Print.
Saunders, John. *The Western Genre: From Lordsburg to Big Whiskey*. London: Wallflower Press, 2001. Print.
Stanfield, Peter. "Dixie Cowboys and Blue Yodels: The Strange History of the Singing Cowboy." *Back in the Saddle Again*. Eds. Edward Buscombe and Roberta E. Pearson. London: British Film Institute, 1998. 96–118. Print.

Tasker, Yvonne. *Spectacular Bodies: Gender, Genre and the Action Cinema*. London: Routledge, 1993. Print.
Tompkins, Jane. *West of Everything: The Inner Life of Westerns*. Oxford: Oxford University Press, 1992. Print.
Turner, Matthew. "Cowboys and Comedy: The Simultaneous Deconstruction and Reinforcement of Generic Conventions in the Western Parody." *Film and History*. 33 2 (2003): 48–54. Print.
W.H. "Campaign Catalog: 'Son of Paleface' Flexes His Box Office Muscles." *Motion Picture Herald*. July 19 (1952): 46. Print.
W.J. "Review: Susanna Pass." *To-Day's Cinema*. 12 July (1951): 6. Print.

Horses for Ladies, High-Ridin' Women and Whores

MARIA CECÍLIA DE MIRANDA N. COELHO

In his preface to Jean-Louis Rieupeyrout's book *Le Western: Ou le cinéma américain par excellence* (Paris: Éditions du Cerf, 1953), André Bazin remarks,

> Galloping horses, fights, strong and brave men in a wildly austere landscape could not add up to a definition of the genre nor encompass its charms.
> Those formal attributes by which one normally recognizes the western are simple signs or symbols of its profound reality, namely the myth.... Let us take one example, that of woman ... because of the scarcity of women and the perils of a too harsh existence in this burgeoning world, make it imperative to safeguard its female members and its horses.... These myths, of which we have just examined what is the most significant example [being that of the woman] (the next is the myth of the horse) may ... be reduced to one even more essential principle ... the great epic Manicheism [142; 144].[1]

Within the sphere of "myth," the horse is a complex symbol. In a number of Westerns films in which it is associated with female characters, the horse acts as both an equalizer that gives women as much freedom and power as men, and as property that can be branded, tamed, and used according to male codes of morality, sexuality, and heroism. Bazin's use of the terms "*Odyssey*," "epic" and "myth" in regard to the association that exists between women and horses in Westerns is especially pertinent (he also finds similarities between the Trojan War and the American Civil War as the latter was represented within Westerns[2]). Homer's heroes often serve as archetypes for characters in later literature and film.[3] The close association of the horse with women, which in classical literature begins with the construction of the Trojan Horse and the rescue of that most beautiful of women, Helen, is widely known and often appears in Western films.[4] That horses are one of the important icons in the Western seems to leave little room for doubt.[5] However, when one considers women as icons, matters are more complex. As Anthony Mann once put the matter: women are both necessary and absent. In his 1957 interview with Charles Bitsch and Claude Chabrol in *Cahiers du cinéma*, he said:

> He [Borden Chase] studied the history of West extensively, he is passionate about it, and above all, he is without equal in his ability to describe relationships between men—and as you know, that's westerns.... In fact, we always throw a woman into the story, because without a woman, a western wouldn't work. Even though she isn't necessary, everyone appears to be convinced that you cannot do without a woman.... So then you have to come up with a clever trick to send her somewhere, so she won't be in your way, and you won't need to film her. It is sad to say, but women do not have much importance in westerns [22].[6]

Mann's statement reflects what spectators seem to see when they watch Westerns. Although women are important insofar as they motivate and direct men's actions, often as wife or sister, kidnapped, murdered or raped and so cause for revenge, their presence in the narrative tends to be ephemeral since protagonists are almost always male.

In the 1950s, a number of Westerns showcased the horse as an instrument of freedom and power for the woman who rode it but also functioned as a symbol of submission and objectification of women in a world controlled by men. Here I will focuses on scenes in which the horse is closely associated with women in five films: *Forty Guns*, *The Furies*, *Unforgiven*, *The Professionals*, and *The Ballad of Little Jo*. *The Furies* (Anthony Mann, 1950) and *Forty Guns* (Samuel Fuller, 1957) are paradigmatic for my topic. Their protagonists, both played by Barbara Stanwyck, are strong women who defy gender conventions. In addition to being good riders and wearing male attire, they are smart and witty and run ranches with the same competence as the men who admire and fear them.[7] Through the theme song of *Forty Guns*, the expression "high-ridin' woman" gained fame and familiarity.[8] Each of these female characters is powerful and feared and moves around freely just as the men do, on horseback or driving their buckboards, but if "someone big, someone strong, someone tall" that can "break her" happens to appear, "the woman with a whip is only a woman after all." Paradoxically, this does not invalidate the fact that, at least for some moments, the horse becomes a vital element in the making of female characters independent and powerful.

In the long and famous opening scene of *Forty Guns*, protagonist Jessica Drummond appears dressed in black, mounted on a galloping white horse, and leading a group of men mounted on dark horses. As they ride by, they pass a buckboard in their path, and the three men inside it are forced to protect themselves from the cloud of dust that the galloping horses have stirred up. The driver, Griff Bonnell (Barry Sullivan), struggles to control the two horses who are pulling the carriage and are frightened by the group that is thundering by. He is there with his two brothers, Wes (Gene Barry) and Chico (Robert Dixan). Griff is an ex-gunman who has come to Cochise County under the orders of the Arizona state prosecutor, with the mission to arrest one of the men who works for Jessica. Jessica leads a private posse of 40 men and rules over the entire city, but her real source of trouble is her reckless younger brother Brockie (John Ericson). When Jessica and Griff meet for the first time, the attraction they feel for each other is palpable. Also evident is a power struggle: when Jessica invites Griff to work for her and he refuses, Jessica's sharp retort, "I'm not interested in you, Mr. Bonnell. It's your trademark," is followed by her (Freudian?) request to hold his gun, asking, "May I feel it?" and his (de)negation, "It might go off in your face." The dialogue, laden with double entendre (as elsewhere), reveals Jessica's degree of command over the city as well as over language itself. Yet she relinquishes both power and irony as she falls in love with Griff, whose is similarly attracted to her. In the middle of a thick drama involving parallel plots and murders that make her relationship with Griff difficult, Jessica ends relinquishing both wealth and power to follow him. The last scene shows Griff leaving in the same buckboard in which he had arrived, even though he had just confessed his love for Jessica to his brother Chico. Jessica, now wearing a white dress—and thereby standing out as had her white horse in the film's opening scene—runs after Griff, calling out his name. We then hear the verses of the aforementioned ballad, as she climbs into the buckboard and is off to California at the side of the tall, strong man, who we could say has "broken her."[9]

As its title indicates, Greek mythology underpins *The Furies*, mainly through the Electra myth that is the archetype for the relationship between Vance (Barbara Stanwyck) and her beloved father, T.C. Jeffords (Walter Huston), cattle baron and owner of the eponymous ranch.[10] Vance rides alongside her father and other men and usually appears wearing male attire. Their relationship, fragile to begin with, is complicated by the arrival of a future stepmother, Flo Burnett (Judith Anderson), whose face, Vance disfigures. After seeing her best friend, the Mexican Juan (Gilbert Rolland), hung by order of her father for having stolen a horse, Vance abandons The Furies. She and her father, however, are reconciled in the end, after an ingenious feat that Vance orchestrates to save the ranch with the help of Rip Darrow (Wendell Corey), who is an old enemy of her father and who has fallen in love with her.

In the first scene of the film, Clay (John Bromfield), T.C.'s son, is shown arriving at The Furies on horseback. He finds his sister in the room that had belonged to their mother and is kept as a shrine after her death. Vance is trying on an evening gown that had been her mother's, an act that provokes her brother's fear and his musings on how lonely their mother must have felt there, being treated merely as another one of T.C.'s possessions. Clay also speaks of financial difficulties that are plaguing T.C. The conversation between brother and sister illustrates the son's conviction that he is unimportant to his father. Vance attributes this to the fact that her brother always submitted to T.C., something she herself never did. Vance's strong personality, associated with horses, becomes more evident throughout the film, in which her brother has little presence; it is Vance, not Clay, who is heir to T.C.'s name and legacy.[11] After T.C. is murdered by the mother of the Mexican he killed, Vance and Rip, arriving on horseback and returning T.C.'s corpse, stop before the ranch gate as in the first scene, when Clay arrived at The Furies. Rip announces his plan to build a splendid tomb for T.C., for whom he will provide a grandson. Vance, in turn, announces she will name the child T.C. Vance may be a strong woman who rides with the men, but her true role is not to replace them or run the ranch. Her life revolves around her father and then her husband; later, her role is that of a mother who ensures the continuity of the family name. Aptly, Jim Kitses regards this film as a "more matriarchal than patriarchal western."[12]

In both *Forty Guns* and *The Furies*, Barbara Stanwyck plays women who have to demonstrate their strength in order to belong to the world of men. A major element of this strength lies in their equestrian skills and ability to deal in business with men as their equals. Yet, as they reaffirm the values of the male world of the West, these "high-ridin' women" later hand their power over to the men they choose to follow.

The *topos* of women and horses further revises the traditional Western in terms of gender in the more recent *Unforgiven* (1992).[13] Its protagonist is William Munny (Clint Eastwood), who, accompanied by an old friend, Ned Logan (Morgan Freeman), and an inexperienced youth, "The Schofield Kid" (Jaimz Woolvett), has accepted the mission of killing two men who cut the face of the prostitute Delilah (Anna Levine), in the town of Big Whiskey, controlled by sheriff Little Bill (Gene Hackman). The film's action begins and ends in the same kind of somber scene of a rainy night. The beginning shows a cowboy, aided by a friend, attacking Delilah as he slaps her several times on the face because she laughed at the size of his penis. His aggression is interrupted only when saloon owner Skinny (Anthony James) gets there and then calls for the sheriff. One of the prostitutes, Alice Strawberry (Francis Fisher), asks the sheriff, who had planned to subject the cowboys to no more than a whipping, to hang them. What makes Little Bill change his mind is not Alice's request, which carries little weight, but Skinny's claim that Delilah was a "capital investment" that has now been reduced to "damaged property." The sheriff's solution is that her aggressor pay for his crime with five colts and that the one who aided him give two more to Skinny, on their return to the city. This arrangement infuriates the women, who get together and hear Alice's complaint: "Just because we let them smelly fools ride us like horses don't mean we gotta let 'em brand us like horses. Maybe we ain't nothing but whores but we, by god, we ain't horses." Convinced that they must act, the prostitutes decide to offer a bounty on the two cowboys. When the cowboys return with seven horses and an additional colt for Delilah, the women are further angered and chase them out of town.

Although *Unforgiven* centers on a conflict between men, the film provides a prime illustration of Anthony Mann's observation that women are both necessary and absent in Westerns. The comparison of women and horses and the women's reaction to a woman being branded motivates the entire plot. Here, the classical underpinnings of Howard Hughes' earlier Western *The Outlaw* (1943), in which the young Rio McDonald (Jane Russell) is treated and traded between men like a horse is instructive for any consideration of Eastwood's revision of the traditional Western. Bazin, in his analysis of that film in an essay entitled "The Outlaw—The best of women is not worth a good horse" sums up the matter: "It is no accident that the real scenario is the story of three jealous males. Two of them, Billy the Kid (Jacy Beutel) and Doc Holliday (Walter Huston) sleep with the same woman, but they love the same horse. On several occasions they come near to killing one another over the horse. But in the end they retain their friendship.... They constitute a Spartan group in which women have no emotional role" (65–66).[14] Similarly, *Ride Lonesome* (1959) and *Comanche Station* (1960), both directed by Budd Boetticher, also include paradigmatic scenes involving attempts to trade a woman for a horse. In *Comanche Station*, the emphatic comment is made that, before possessing a woman, a man should "check the brand to make sure you aren't driving another man's stock"—as Ben (Claude Akins) says to Cody (Randolph Scott). Neither of these films discuss women being equated with horses.[15] In *Unforgiven*, however, the women themselves discuss the topos of the women-horses exchange.

An important depiction of a strong woman associated with horses appears in Richard Brooks' *The Professionals* (1966). *The Professionals*, based on the novel *A Mule for the Marquesa* by Frank O'Rourke, takes place in 1917 on the Mexican border, when rancher J.W. Grant (Ralph Bellamy) hires four mercenaries to rescue his wife Maria (Claudia Cardinale). She was abducted by Jesus Raza (Jack Palance) while riding near the border—an archetypical *Iliad* situation: important and courageous men crossing borders to rescue an abducted woman. The four mercenaries are Henry "Rico" Fardan (Lee Marvin), a munitions expert; Bill Dolworth (Burt Lancaster), a dynamiter; Hans Ehrengard (Robert Ryan), a sensitive horse wrangler; and Jacob Sharp (Woody Strode), a tracker and longbow expert. The film was praised not only for avoiding the common pitfall of treating the revolutionary Raza as the stereotypical one-dimensional Mexican bandit but also for its "political insights, intricate motivations, applied philosophy and some literary grace in [its] dialogue" (Daniel 168). Another of the film's merits is its characterization of Maria, who appears when the professionals have reached Mexico. After taking her from Raza's ranch, the mercenaries realize that the husband's story sounds false. Maria explains that, before her father's death, he gave her to Grant in marriage and sold him his ranch as well. Later she adds that she had voluntarily left Grant, who had stolen millions from the Mexicans. Moreover, she and Raza, who had been working for her father, had been lovers. In an argument with Fardan, who calls Raza a thief and Maria a whore for cheating on her husband, Maria reveals herself to be a strong, politically-aware character, claiming that, if necessary, she would prostitute herself or steal because of her loyalty to the revolutionary cause, and that Fardan and Raza are not that different, for both fight for their ideals.

Maria's strength and political convictions are reinforced by her association with the horse. When Grant gets together with the mercenaries to give them instructions regarding the expedition, horses are part of their equipment. Ehrengard comments that they are excellent animals. Grant moves close to one of them and slowly, affectionately caresses it, saying: "This one is Mrs. Grant's favorite. Bred for speed." Later, when Maria discovers that Raza and his men are pursuing the group, she suddenly seizes a horse and heads off in Raza's direction. The only thing that stops her is an explosion in the canyon ahead of her, at which point Fardan and Sharp catch up with her and take her back with them. From this moment on, she rides alongside the men in the most arduous of conditions.[16] Towards the end of the journey, when her horse is hurt and must be put down, Maria is treated with sympathy by Ehrengard, who understands how she must feel about losing her four-legged companion. He even offers to spare her from having to shoot her horse. Sharp now treats her gently as well. Shortly after that it is Dolworth's turn to show a change of opinion regarding Maria, commenting "You know, Rico, there is a lot of woman there: beautiful, classy, guts." He compares her to another Maria, Fardan's wife, a Mexican who was tortured and killed by the *colorados*, a militia fighting against the revolutionaries. In the final scenes of the film, when Dolworth arrives with a wounded Raza and meets up with his companions who had gotten to the border before him, Grant sees Maria attending to Raza's wounds. He asks one of his assistants to kill Raza. The four mercenaries, however, protect Raza and come to a clear understanding that there was never an abduction. Fardan helps Maria rise from the ground after Grant's violent treatment, and the men place her and Raza in a buckboard so that they may return to Mexico. The film ends with Maria, reins in hand, driving a cart pulled by two horses and followed by the four professionals. Throughout, Maria has been portrayed variously as a lady, a whore, and a high-ridin' woman. Her equestrian skills are a fundamental element of her strong and independent nature.

In Maggie Greenwald's *The Ballad of Little Jo* (1993), a feminist view of the old West refashions the story of Josephine Monaghan (Suzy Amis), a young woman from the East who is thrown out of her home after giving birth to an illegitimate child. She heads westward, but as a woman on her own realizes that her chances for a life of dignity are slim. At this point, she decides to start dressing and living as a man, introducing herself to others as Jo. Overcoming many daunting challenges, she is able to obtain her own ranch, where she lives out her days.[17] There are two scenes that are particularly important in regard to her association with the horse throughout the film. The first occurs when Jo gets to Ruby City, dressed as a man; the second happens after her death. Here, a comparison with another film, *The Ballad of Josie* (Andrew McLaglen, 1967) is useful. *The Ballad of Josie* is a Western comedy starring Doris Day, who had also played the protagonist in *Calamity Jane* (David Butler, 1953). Like Greenwald's Josephine, Josie is forced to leave her son with his paternal grandfather after she is accused of having caused—albeit accidentally—her abusive husband's death. Absolved but alone, she decides to have her own ranch. She dresses like a man. Shocking her neighbors as she exchanges her dress for a blue shirt and pants, she gets on a horse and reappears in the city, driving a flock of sheep. In a land of cattle ranchers, her decision can only bring trouble, since sheepmen and cattlemen are rivals for the land. At one point a cowboy compares Josie to Helen of Troy, referring to the amount of conflict she was able to stir up. The scenes in which she is shown on horseback or using weapons are highly caricatured and serve to restore social order: the men agree that Josie can have a ranch, but she must raise cattle and not sheep. In the final scenes, Josie puts on an exuberant pink dress and falls into the arms of her long-time admirer Jason (Peter Graves). She is parading in a buckboard with her son and new husband, who is also candidate to the U.S. Senate.

Normative action resulting in women's use of male clothing when riding horses is also found in *Forty Guns*, *The Furies*, and *The Ballad of Josie*. In these movies, although women are portrayed as strong characters who are capable of marking out their territory in a male-dominated world, they abandon their masculine dress to don women's clothing. In *The Ballad of Little Jo*, only the spectator who knows that the male garb, hat, and even a scar made to mask the delicacy of Josephine Monaghan's face are a disguise. For a while she shares her secret with Tinman Wong (David Chung), a Chinese she saved from being lynched and to whom she provides a job on her ranch. Like Josie, Jo, too, has to struggle physically and politically to keep her ranch against the pressures of a powerful cattle company. Besides the traditional conflict between cattle and sheep ranchers, *The Ballad of Little Jo*, like *Unforgiven*, also has a prostitute whose face has been disfigured by a client, Percy (Ian McKellen), after she refused to perform oral sex on him; this is a situation that has an important impact on Jo's relationship to Percy, who is her friend.

When Jo first arrives at Ruby City on horseback, only she and the viewer know about her self-transformation—her hair cut, her change from feminine to masculine attire, and the scarring of her face—into which flashbacks to her life in the East are inserted. After Jo cuts the left side of her face, an act which is followed by her cry of pain, Greenwald cuts to the back of a horse as it moves slowly between trees. When the horse reaches a trail and a number of people become visible, its rider is now visible as well, also shown from behind. He stops and asks two people if the town in the distance is Ruby City. After answering affirmatively, the two men enunciate their admiration for the large scar on the rider's face. Jo gets off the horse and looks at the two men from an angle that enables spectators to see her face—and her new persona.

At the end, several years have passed and Jo is living alone on the ranch. She is ill, and her friend Frank (Bo Hopkins) tries to get her into town for care, but she dies on route to the doctor. Preparing her corpse for the funeral, the mortician discovers that Jo was actually a woman and runs off to the bar to tell Frank. After their initial shock, they get her ready for a picture, putting her back on her horse in male attire. Her limp body must be tied onto the animal; curiously, the picture is taken by a female photographer. The last image in the film shows a page from a newspaper: there are two images, one of the dead Jo tied atop her horse. In the other she is dressed as a lady on the day of her sister's wedding. The latter was the first photo ever taken of her, shot by the photographer who seduced her and fathered her son. Josephine may have had control over her gender and her body, given the adverse circumstances of her life, while alive, but, in the final scene, her body returns to being a sort of property, in accordance with male codes of morality, sexuality and heroism.

Be they positive or negative, the relationships between horses and women in *Forty Guns*, *The Furies*, *Unforgiven*, *The Professionals*, and *The Ballad of Little Jo* do not exhaust analytical possibilities for further studies in this area of the Western.[18] As films from different periods and in different styles, they invite further investigations into the long and complex evolution of the genre. My analysis of these films attempts to flesh out values associated with horses and women within American culture at specific places and times while demonstrating how the association of horses and women reflect our engagement with a larger cultural tradition, one whose origin is within the archetypes of Greek epic literature.[19]

Notes

1. This preface is also included in Bazin, André, *What Is Cinema: Volume II*, trans. Hugh Gray (Berkeley: University of California Press, 2004), 140–149.

2. Ibid., 147.

3. Ibid. compares Achilles and Billy the Kid. For some detailed analyses see especially

Myrsiades, Kostas, "Reading *The Gunfighter* as Homeric epic" in Kostas Myrsiades, ed., *Reading Homer: Film and Text* (Madison: Fairleigh Dickinson University Press, 2009), and the following articles by Martin M. Winkler: "Homer's *Iliad* and John Ford's *The Searchers*" in *The Searchers: Essays and Reflections on John Ford's Classic Western*, ed. Arthur Eckstein and Peter Lehman (Detroit: Wayne State University Press, 2004), 145–170; "Homeric *Kleos* and the Western Film," *Syllecta Classica* 7 (1996): 43–54; and "Classical Mythology and the Western Film," *Comparative Literature Studies* 22.4 (1985): 516–540.

4. See *Odyssey* 4.271–289 and 8.499–520 and, on the value of fighting for horses, the episode of Diomedes and Sthenalus in *Iliad* 5.267–273. In Greek mythology Helen is portrayed as a complex figure and, as Burkert argues, "a kind of Trojan horse herself." Cf. Burkert, Walter, *Structure and History in Greek Mythology and Ritual* (Berkeley: University of California Press, 1979), 74. One of the Westerns in which a woman's presence functions as a "Trojan Horse" for the group that receives it is *Ambush at Cimarron Pass* (Jodie Copelan, 1958). It is the story of arduous journey on foot by the survivors of an Army patrol and a group of ex-Confederates after the Apaches steal the troop's horses. And the way the theft occurs is thought-provoking. Two Indians on horseback, leading an attractive woman by a rope around her neck catch the attention of the whites. They leave the woman, who has passed out, near the white soldiers' camp. Sargeant Matt Blake (Scotty Brady), who sees her as a "gift from the gods," goes to the rescue along with two other men. The first word she pronounces is "horses." That very moment they realize that they have fallen into a trap: while they went out to save the woman, the Indians made off with their horses.

5. See, for instance, Stella Hockenhull's "Horse Power: Equine Alliances in the Western," in Matheson, Sue, ed., *Love in Western Film and Television: Lonely Hearts and Happy Trails* (New York: Palgrave Macmillan, 2013), 19–34. For another perspective see Mitchum, Petrine, *Hollywood Hoofbeats* (Irvine: i–5, 2014).

6. This interview is partially reproduced in the booklet that accompanies the DVD *The Furies* (Criterion Collection, 2008).

7. Stanwyck played the role of strong female protagonists in other Westerns such as *Cattle Queen of Montana* (1954) and *The Maverick Queen* (1956) and had been well known since 1935 as the title character of *Annie Oakley*. See Nelson, Andrew, "Only a Woman After All? Gender Dynamics of the Western of Barbara Stanwyck," in Matheson, Sue, ed., 161–178.

8. During the period in which *The Furies* and *Forty Guns* were made, there was another film that is also worth citing here, *Johnny Guitar* (Nicholas Ray, 1954), even though its protagonist, Vienna (Joan Crawford), cannot be seen as a "high-ridin' woman" in the literal sense. Although it is only through Fuller's film that the term has become well-known, it is not inappropriate to apply it retrospectively to several characters in films that came out before 1957. Altar Keane (Marlene Dietrich) in *Rancho Notorious* (Fritz Lang, 1952) is a comparably strong woman, driving her buckboard pulled by a handsome white horse. Vienna also has her buckboard, but will appear on horseback when she is being taken to be hanged, and curiously she is wearing a white dress rather than her habitual male attire. Her antagonist, Emma Small (Mercedes McCambridge), on the contrary, rides and uses a gun just as the men with whom she is associated.

9. For an acute interpretation of this film style, see Dombrowski, Lisa, *The Films of Samuel Fuller: If You Die, I'll Kill You!* (Middletown: Wesleyan University Press, 2008), especially 117–116. It is worth remembering here *The Lonely Man* (Henry Levin, 1957), in which the breaking of a wild Mustang by Riley (Anthony Perkins) is followed by a passionate kiss with the woman belonging to his father (Jack Palance).

10. The very name of the Jefford's ranch, The Furies, is revealing and was the name of the novel on which the film was based. In an interview with Paul Mayersberg for BBC, in 1967, Mann stated that you can take any of the great dramas, in particularly Greek plays, and set them in the West. See *The Furies*, DVD.

11. Planning to leave the ranch, T.C. tells Vance and Rip he is heading for Catalina Island, at which point his daughter, with a twinkle in her eyes, asks if he is going there because of a "wild little filly."

12. This comment may be found in his interview on the DVD of *The Furies*.

13. On this film "rewriting that famous Ur-Western, the *Iliad*," see Blundell, Mary

Whitlock, and Kirk Ormand's "*Western Values, or the Peoples* Homer: *Unforgiven* as a Reading of the *Iliad*," *Poetics Today* 18.4 (1997): 543–569, 535.

14. Bazin. Here the comments of Chris (Chris Pin Martin) in *Stagecoach* (John Ford, 1939), comparing his wife to a horse, are instructive as are Sam's (John Wayne) in *North to Alaska* (Henry Hathaway, 1960): "I've never met one [a woman] yet that was half as reliable as a horse."

15. Here it is worth remembering *El Dorado* (Howard Hawks, 1966), when Alan (James Caan) asks a rebellious girl, Joey (Michele Carey), who dresses like a man and uses a gun: "Why do you wear your hair like some wild Mustang?"

16. The other woman with a salient role in the film is Chiquita (Marie Gomez), an officer under Raza's command who is also quite a fighter and a skilled horsewoman.

17. For detailed analysis see Pitturo, Vicent, "Reverse Transvestism and the Classic Hero: *The Ballad of Little Jo* and the Archetypal Western (Fe)male" in Matheson, Sue, ed., 111–124, and Modleski, Tania, "A Woman's Gotta Do ... What a Man's Gotta Do? Cross-Dressing in the Western," *Signs* 2, no. 3 (1997): 519–544.

18. A sociological analysis of women's empowerment through horses can help us with comparative reflections on the presence of these archetypes. See Miriam Adelman's "Riding for Our Lives: Women, Leisure and Equestrian Practice in Brazil Today," *Mondes du turisme: Cheval, tourisme & sociétés* (June 2015): 48–61.

19. I am very grateful to Professor Miriam Adelman, a researcher of equestrian cultures and practices, for her support and careful translation from Portuguese, and to Professor Sue Matheson, for her meticulous editing of my first draft. I owe a special debt of gratitude to Professor Martin M. Winkler, an inspiring scholar and generous colleague, who shared his considerable knowledge on the Western and encouraged me to write this text.

Filmography

The Ballad of Josie (1967). Dir. Andrew McLaglen. Universal Mod, 2014. DVD.
The Ballad of Little Jo (1993). Maggie Greenwald. Sony Pictures, 1995. DVD.
Calamity Jane (1953). Dir. David Butler. Warner Home Video, 2002. DVD.
Cattle Queen of Montana (1954). Dir. Allan Dwan. Vci Video, 2002. DVD.
Comanche Station (1960). Dir. Budd Boetticher. Sidonis Calysta, n.d. DVD.
El Dorado (1966). Dir. Howard Hawks. Warner Bros. Home Video, 2013. DVD.
Forty Guns (1957). Dir. Samuel Fuller. 20th Century Fox Home Entertainment, 2005. DVD.
The Furies (1950). Dir. Anthony Mann. Criterion Collection, 2008. DVD.
Johnny Guitar (1954). Dir. Nicholas Ray. Team Marketing, 2015. DVD.
The Lonely Man (1957). Dir. Henry Levin. Paramount, 2003. DVD.
The Maverick Queen (1956). Dir. Joseph Kane. Republic (Universal), 2001. VHS.
North to Alaska (1960). Dir. Henry Hathaway. 20th Century Fox Home Entertainment, 2013. DVD.
The Outlaw (1943). Dir. Howard Hughes. Alpha Video, 2003. DVD.
The Professionals (1966). Dir. Richard Brooks. Sony Pictures Home Entertainment, 2005. DVD.
Rancho Notorious (1952). Dir. Fritz Lang. Warner Archives, 2009. DVD.
Ride Lonesome (1959). Dir. Budd Boetticher. In the Budd Boetticher Collection. Sony Pictures, 2008. DVD.
Stagecoach (1939). Dir. John Ford. Criterion Collection, 2010. DVD.
Unforgiven (1992). Dir. Clint Eastwood. Warner Home Video, 1997. DVD.

Bibliography

Adelman, Miriam. "Riding for our lives: women, leisure and equestrian practice in Brazil today." *Mondes du turisme: Cheval, tourisme & sociétés* (June 2015): 48–61.
Bazin, André. "Preface." *Le Western: Ou le cinéma américain par excellence*. Author Jean-Louis Rieupeyrout. Paris: Édition Du Cerf, 1953: 1–10.
_____. *What Is Cinema: Volume II*. Trans. Hugh Gray. Berkeley: University of California Press, 2004.

Blundell, Mary Whitlock, and Kirk Ormand. "Western Values, or the Peoples' Homer: Unforgiven." *Poetics Today* 18:4 (1997): 533–69.
Burkert, Walter. *Structure and History in Greek Mythology and Ritual.* Berkeley: University of California Press, 1979.
Daniel, Douglass K. *Tough as Nails—The Life and Films of Richard Brooks.* Madison: The University of Wisconsin Press, 2011.
Dombrowski, Lisa. *The Films of Samuel Fuller: If You Die, I'll Kill You!* Middletown: Wesleyan University Press, 2008.
Hockenhull, Stella, "Horse Power. Equine Alliances in the Western." *Love in Western Film and Television: Lonely Hearts and Happy Trails.* Ed. Sue Matheson. New York: Palgrave Macmillan, 2013: 19–34.
Homer. *Iliad.* Trans. R. Lattimore, Chicago: Chicago University Press, 1951.
Homer. *Odyssey.* Trans. R. Lattimore. New York: Harper and Row, 1965.
Mann, Anthony. Interview by Charles Bitsch and Claude Chabrol, in *Cahiers du Cinéma*, March 1957. Trans. Alison Dundy. Booklet of DVD *The Furies.* Criterion Collection, 2008 : 17–33.
Mitchum, Petrine. *Hollywood Hoofbeats.* Irvine, CA: i-5 Publishing, 2014.
Myrsiades, Kostas. "Reading *The Gunfighter* as Homeric epic." *Reading Homer: Film and Text.* Ed. Kostas Myrsiades. Madison/Teaneck: Fairleigh Dickinson University Press, 2009: 229–52.
Nelson, Andrew. "Only a Woman after all? Gender dynamics of the Western of Barbara Stanwyck. " *Love in Western Film and Television: Lonely Hearts and Happy Trails.* Ed. Sue Matheson. New York: Palgrave Macmillan, 2013: 161–178.
Pitturo, Vicent. "Reverse Transvestism and the Classic Hero. *The Ballad of Little Jo* and the archetypal western (Fe)male." *Love in Western Film and Television: Lonely Hearts and Happy Trails.* Ed. Sue Matheson. New York: Palgrave Macmillan, 2013: 111–124.
Modleski, Tania. "A Woman's Gotta Do… What a Man's Gotta Do? Cross-Dressing in the Western." *Signs.* 2.3 (1997): 519–544.
O'Rourke, Frank. *A Mule for the Marquesa.* New York: Morrow, 1964.
Winkler, Martin M. "Classical mythology and the Western film" *Comparative Literature Studies*, 22.4 (1985): 516–540.
_____. "Homer's *Iliad* and John Ford's *The Searchers.*" *The Searchers—Essays and Reflections on John Ford's Classic Western.* Ed. Arthur Eckstein and Peter Lehman. Detroit: Wayne State University Press, 2004: 145–170.
_____. "Homeric *kleos* and the Western Film" *Syllecta Classica* 7 (1996): 43–54.

The Sexual Signification of the Gun in Western Film

FRAN PHEASANT-KELLY

Conventionally, the gun in film is a marker of masculinity and its recognition as a phallic symbol abounds across all genres. A typical example occurs in the closing scenes of *Casino Royale* (Campbell, 2006) when a low angle shot of James Bond (Daniel Craig), who has previously been incapacitated, displays him pointing a large automatic rifle upward, unambiguously signaling his reclaimed masculine (heterosexual) position. The equation is made more crudely explicit in *Unforgiven* (Eastwood, 1992) when local town sheriff, Little Bill Daggett (Gene Hackman) describes another character, Two-Gun Corcoran, as having "a dick so big it was longer than the barrel of his Walker Colt." John Saunders notes of the same film that "the clichéd symbol of gun as phallus gets a further twist when … Bob [a character disarmed, beaten and effectively emasculated by Bill] is turned loose, his six-gun returned to him bent in an absurdly detumescent droop" (118). The interpretation of the gun as a symbol of male power, especially in relation to the Western, arises from a range of psychological, cultural and historical factors, but is also dictated by the limitations of what can be put up on screen. As historian Jenni Calder explains, "This suggestiveness clearly facilitated the cowboy's appeal at a time when the cinema refrained from explicit sex" (113). Fundamentally, representations of the gun fetishize the male sexual organ, as suggested, for instance, by Douglas Brode in his analysis of a scene in *Shane* (Stevens 1953) when a young boy, Joey Starrett (Brandon deWilde), reaches out to touch the eponymous hero's weapon: "Here again is a moment of fetishization, implying pre-adolescent Joey's Freudian fascination with that object of male power, modeled ages earlier on the phallus, serving ever since in literature as a fitting symbol for that organ" (61). Peter Lehman also indicates such a fetishization when he comments that "the privileged signifier of the phallus most easily retains its awe and mystique when the penis is hidden. The sight of the actual organ threatens to deflate and make ludicrous the symbolic phallus" (27) while Richard Dyer contends that in images of the male body, "the clenched fists, the bulging muscles, the hardened jaws, the proliferation of phallic symbols—they are all straining after what can hardly ever be achieved, the embodiment of the phallic mystique" (137).

Historical and cultural factors are particularly relevant when analyzing imagery of the armed cowboy, and, according to Edward Buscombe, the "centrality of guns in the Western is not merely a formal convention. The gun symbolizes the individual's right to self-protection in a society where the law is unreliable or absent altogether" (132). Buscombe suggests that the appearance of guns in the Western is bound up with America's past, specifically to the history of weapons technology. He explains that this arose because of a unique set of circumstances: "The Civil War produced major leaps forward in weaponry. The frontier created a steady civilian demand for cheap, reliable hand-guns and rifles. Above all, the acute labor shortage in nineteenth-century America, coupled with the absence of the skilled artisans who hand-crafted guns in Europe, gave a powerful impetus to the machine tool industry" (132). However, David Murdoch observes some ambiguity about gun ownership in frontier life, and notes that although photographs of cowboys from the 1880s onwards inevitably displayed them wearing or holding a gun, "the 1873 Colt Arm model ... was not ubiquitous in the West by any means, [and] the range of exotic pistols ... which turn up in posed portraits suggests that a good many of these firearms were studio props" (86). In this respect, Emerson Hough states that at that time in the south west there was a "growing sentiment against wearing a gun" (in Murdoch 86), although the veracity of this claim remains unclear since Murdoch adds, "the photographs of Wyoming cowboys tend to bear him out, but not entirely" (86). Arguably, the signification of the gun as phallic symbol also relates to the way that small arms are deployed in real world situations, even though Robert Arjet suggests that there are fundamental differences between use of the real gun and its representation in films. For Arjet "the discrepancies between guns in movies and firearms in real life warrants the use of two entirely different terms for two functionally separate objects—one physically and empirically understandable, and the other constructed of imagination and fantasy" (126). Nonetheless, these two dimensions are readily conflated—as Arjet subsequently concedes, "over 90% of the people who kill with firearms are men [while] in mainstream entertainment narratives, a man with a gun is a given— a movie about a woman with a gun is remarkable" (126). Moreover, in their study of the gendered impacts of small arms and light weapons, Farr, Myrttinen and Schnabel report that "small arms have played a vital role in violence, including men's use of small arms to threaten and intimidate women into submitting to rape; using small arms themselves to penetrate women's bodies; and using small arms to kill or injure women either before, during or after raping them" (9).

The resultant image of the gun as phallic substitute is so embedded in cinema and is such an implicitly acknowledged icon of the Western that it is rarely the subject of extensive scholarly discussion, one of few exceptions being Calder's analysis in which she claims that "with most Western heroes of the screen the gun is a symbol of at least masculinity, if not explicit sexuality" (114). For Calder, this (hetero) sexuality is tied not only to killing but also to virility in that "the frontier must not only be tamed but also populated" (114). Yet, according to John Cawelti, the potency of the gun does not solely rest on its phallic possibilities, but rather the way in which the cowboy hero uses it (40). In this regard, Cawelti describes how the cowboy undergoes "the complex and rigid ritual of the 'draw' before finally consummating the fatal deed. The most important implication of this killing procedure seems to be the qualities of reluctance, control and elegance that it associates with the hero" (40). Cawelti partly attributes these qualities to the distance involved when firing a weapon (as opposed to the closeness and aggression of hand-to-hand combat [41]). In a similar vein, Arjet contends that guns are important "as a means to channel and project the power of men across distance. If the attacker must physically cross the room and touch his victim, the essential masculine traits of singularity and hard boundaries are threatened" (134). Related to this, John White argues that the power of the gun lies in its capacity for violence rather than any implication of sexual prowess. Describing a scene in *Once Upon a Time in the West* (Leone 1968), when one character uses the barrel of his handgun to trap a fly, White contends that it "only serves to enhance the ominous threat of the denoted object that is dwelt upon in a series of close-ups" (51). R. Philip Loy too emphasizes the importance of weaponry, specifically that "Westerns unfold around the gun and they are films about violence" (100). Aside from these limited discussions of the gun, and arising from anecdotal connections between the media and real-world firearms attacks, analysis tends to focus on debates around the influences of media violence (for example, see Bushman, Jamieson and Rohmer; Sparks), or accounts of gun culture (Springwood) and the implications of gender for the use of such weaponry (Farr et al.).

Arguably, however, the diverse representation of the gun in the Western extends its meaningfulness beyond heterosexual phallic connotations. For instance, gunmanship in the Western is equally bound up with effeminacy and homoerotic possibilities, evidenced in films such as *3:10 to Yuma* (Mangold, 2007) and *Red River* (Hawks, 1948). Moreover, its articulation by women and children (as in *Forty Guns* [Fuller, 1957], *The Quick and the Dead* [Raimi, 1995], *Johnny Guitar* [Ray, 1954] and *True Grit* [Coen Brothers, 2010]) mobilizes values not wholly related to phallic power, virility and violence *per se*. Rather, its use in such films may reflect qualities of family loyalty, justice, and gender equality, although in real-world situations the participation of children and women in armed violence is reported to enable a sense of their empowerment (Farr et al. 8–9). Even as a weapon's failure to discharge may be a sign of male fallibility, and equally, penetration and wounding threaten masculinity, reticence in using a gun may also be important in indicating male vigor. Engaging theoretically with scholarship on the Western and its iconography, this essay therefore considers the signification of the gun in both recent and earlier American Westerns featuring men, women, and children, these including *Red River*, *The Outlaw Josey Wales* (Eastwood, 1976), *Johnny Guitar*, *3:10 to Yuma*, *The Quick and the Dead*, *Forty Guns* and *True Grit*.

The Gun as Phallic Symbol: Speed and Reticence

The use of the gun in *Butch Cassidy and the Sundance Kid* (Hill, 1969) typifies its expression as a signifier of power and heterosexual masculinity, in this case, being deployed as a foil for a potentially homoerotic relationship in a buddy film largely devoid of women. One example describes how "in the opening card-game scene, one of the card-players accuses Sundance of cheating. The scene ends with one of the film's characteristic close-ups of Butch and Sundance before cutting to long shot of the three men, enabling a display of Sundance's dexterity as he shoots the card-player's gun out of its holster. He then progressively maneuvers the gun along the floor by firing at it. The sequence unfolds quickly with rapid editing, indicating his reaction speed, and close-ups of the gun as it bounces over the floor, further drawing attention to his skills" (Pheasant-Kelly 156). Here, while gunmanship reflects qualities conventionally understood as masculinized (in both real-life and film), such as physical agility, speed, quick reaction time and accuracy, it also effectively involves direct assault on another man's weapon. If the gun in this case is perceived and articulated as a phallic signifier, restraint and a reticence to use it can have similar implications. As Cawelti states, "one source of the cowboy/s appeal is the way in which he resolves th[e] ambiguity [about violence pervading society] by giving a sense of moral significance and order to violence. He is a reluctant killer who shoots only when he is forced to it" (41). Such a scenario becomes evident in *3:10 to Yuma*, a film that revolves around the plight of Dan Evans (Christian Bale), an impoverished rancher who is unable to pay his debts to landowner, Glen Hollander (Lennie Loftin). Consequently, Hollander's men burn down Evans' barn and threaten to destroy his home. Evans' qualities of masculinity are, however, at first not wholly apparent and because of his reluctance to confront Hollander's men, together with his disability (he is an amputee) and his traits of vulnerability and sensitivity, his family, especially his elder son, William, hold him in low regard. An opportunity arises for Evans to reverse his fortunes (and, incidentally, the way that his family perceives him) by delivering Ben Wade (Russell Crowe), a notorious outlaw, to a train bound for Yuma Prison. The film opens with an attack on Evans' barn but, although Evans is awake and has his rifle at the ready, he is physically unable to respond quickly enough to the attack because of his amputated leg. Indeed, the opening scenes repeatedly draw attention to his disability as he struggles to stand up, and, rather than bolstering his masculinity by conventional means, his upended rifle serves as a crutch, the tapping of the rifle on the floor highlighting his physical incapacity (it sounds like a wooden leg). Evans struggles out to the barn, the camera unsteadily tracking behind him, further emphasizing his erratic gait. Once outside, he staggers as he is struck from behind with a rifle. The camera cuts to a low-level close-up of his face as he falls to the floor, before a second close-up reveals his amputated limb. "You have a week Evans, before we burn the house," warns Tucker (Kevin Durand), one of his attackers. Tucker sits astride his horse looking down at the fallen Evans, the framing providing an example of one of the film's many visual strategies for representing what initially seems to be Evans' emasculated position. Evans pulls his boot over the wooden stump of his leg, an action again seen in close-up to emphasize his compromised physicality, while the camera then frames William in a low-angle, long shot. As William runs towards the burning barn, the camera maintains him in long shot, centrally framed and physically active within the composition, thereby contrasting his agility with the stilted movements of his father. At the point when they both look back towards the barn, with the camera positioned behind them, William, (standing closer to the camera), appears much larger in the frame than his father and thus dominates the image, echoing the previous scenes where visually he seems to be the more prominent of the two. A close-up of William in the foreground and his father in the background sees William raise his rifle and take aim at the arsonists, his eye-line viewed by the spectator in an over-the-shoulder shot. Just as he is about to pull the trigger, Evans snatches the rifle from him. "I'll take care of this," Evans tells his son. "No you won't," replies William, implicitly criticizing his father's lack of decisive action and verbally reiterating the scene's visual implications. William thus also seems to be psychologically stronger than his father, but, at this stage, lacks his father's moral perspective.

Subsequently, we see Evans kneeling beside one of his dying cattle. Once more, the use of long shot diminishes him in the frame while William appears at the edge of the image on horseback and in an elevated position, thus dominating the scene. William confirms this visually mediated imbalance in their relationship when he says, "you should have let me save the feed." "Someday, William, you walk in my shoes you might understand," Evans tells him. "I ain't never walking in your shoes," retorts William, primarily articulating his disrespect for his father, but perhaps also alluding to his father's symbolically castrated status, related to the loss of the leg. The scene then reverses its visual dynamics as Evans stands up, cocks his rifle and unhesitatingly shoots the starving animal. A sharp focus on the gun's nozzle as he takes aim shifts swiftly to Evans' squinting eye as he fires, the quick change in focal points emphasizing the decisive nature of the act as one of compassion that contrasts with the film's other inhumane acts of human slaughter. The cinematography here also places him much more prominently within the frame and instead makes William appear smaller—this reversal being one of a number that implies his moral fortitude and compassionate masculinity.

In another scene, Evans declines to intervene when he comes across a stagecoach being ambushed by Wade, opting to observe from a distance. In contrast, the same sequence sees Charlie Prince (Ben Foster), Wade's effeminate sidekick, dismount his horse and walk swiftly towards the men injured during the stagecoach attack, the seamless continuity between the two actions implying his unhesitatingly ruthless persona. A rapidly edited sequence ensues, featuring an extreme close-up of his holster as he reaches for his gun, a rear shot cutting to medium close up as he shoots one man, and then a long shot as he stands over another and shoots him at close range. Prince's sadistic brutality is therefore visually signified by his excessive figure behavior, and is accentuated by fast editing. As he approaches McElroy, one of two remaining survivors, he reveals his name to him. "Name's Charlie Prince. Expect you heard of me," says Prince to McElroy. "Well I heard of a balled up whore called Charlie Princess," responds McElroy, intimating Prince's effeminate tendencies. At the end of the film, Prince, who is throughout suggested to be homosexual, shoots Evans in the back. Calder refers to a mythic code in the Western, and "according to this code, the bad man will ... shoot a man in the back. The good man will face his enemy and make sure his enemy is facing him" (105). Clearly, Prince's use of the gun defines him as a coward rather than a masculinized hero.

The gun is accorded a different significance in relation to the character of Ben Wade. In a comparison of the 2007 film with the original 1957 version, Peter Falconer notes that the iconography of the Western is highlighted in the remake with a "self-conscious emphasis" (62). Indeed, along with his horse and hat, Wade's gun is "marked as special and unique" (Falconer 62)— viewed in close-up, it is "black and decorated with a crucifix, is called 'The Hand of God' [and] ... is cursed" (Falconer 63), inferring a spiritual or supernatural quality, but lacking the sexual element accorded it in other Westerns.

In sum, the gun in *3:10 to Yuma* has various significations: in the case of Prince, its immoral use implicates him as a "bad man" who has effeminate traits rather than the virility that Calder describes. Correspondingly, Evans' reticence in using a weapon represents the moral and discriminate propriety indicated by Cawelti (41), while Wade's distinctive pistol relates to his infamous identity as leader of a band of outlaws.

Similar to the character of Dan Evans, the protagonist of *Forty Guns*, Griff Bonnell (Barry Sullivan) refrains from using his gun indiscriminately and, despite his notorious reputation as a killer, he is now a reformed character who works for the Attorney General. A typical example of such restraint occurs in the early stages of the film, which charts how rancher Jessica Drummond (Barbara Stanwyck) leads a posse of 40 men to dominate Cochise County, Arizona. One of the men, her brother, Brockie Drummond (John Ericson), embarks on a drunken shooting spree in the town of Tombstone, and shoots a partially sighted marshal. Following Cawelti's argument, which contends that "the hero's special skill at gun fighting ... indicates that his violence is disciplined and pure" (41), the gun, in this instance, highlights Brockie's weakness and lack of control. Since Cawelti suggests that the "controlled and aesthetic mode of killing is particularly important as the supreme mark of differentiation between the hero and the savage" (40), one might argue that Brockie conforms to the latter category. Bonnell attempts to thwart the shooting spree and, with his gun tucked into his waistband, strides down the road to confront Brockie. The camera focuses first on the relentless pace of Bonnell's feet, then slowly pans upwards before cutting to frame Brockie centrally in long shot. The effect of this intercutting is to render Bonnell prominent in the frame in comparison to Brockie, who appears smaller, further implying a lack of male vigor. Moreover, as Bonnell draws closer to Brockie, the latter merely stands stationary, the associations of physical action with masculinity therefore made apparent. The sequence continues to intercut between the two men in compositions that progressively frame them more intensely before shifting between close-ups of Brockie's gun, and extreme close-ups of Bonnell's eyes. The camera then zooms in to an extreme close-up of Brockie's gun, with the weapon positioned centrally in the frame and his one leg and crotch visible to the edge of the image, subtly suggesting a link between weaponry and the male sexual organ. A sudden extreme close-up of Bonnell, viewed from a low angle (so the spectator seems positioned just below his belt line), witnesses him grasp his gun and strike Brockie across the head. In short, both men's weapons are aligned visually with their crotch areas (and implicitly, phallic sexuality), this sequence reflecting Calder's description of the onscreen cowboy, whose "gun resting on his narrow hip, is inviting an awareness of his sexuality" (113). However, in the case of Brockie, who is immobilized by fear, this phallic sexuality is suggested to be lacking.

Contrastingly, Bonnell's active, relentless motion implies a refusal to be intimidated and a powerful masculine presence. In particular, the latter's reluctance to fire his weapon, in line with Cawelti's commentary, reinforces the signification of a controlled and assured masculinity. Furthermore, Brockie's wanton and excessive use of his gun, especially in shooting a partially sighted man, is an indicator of cowardice.

A more explicit expression of the gun as a signifier of phallic sexuality occurs in two later sequences. The first of these arises when Wes Bonnell (Gene Barry), Griff"'s brother, is being measured for a tailored, made-to-fit rifle. While the blond, alluring daughter of the town's gunsmith assesses him for the new gun, he takes hold of another rifle. The camera cuts to his perspective as he observes the gunsmith's daughter who appears to be circularly framed, as if he is looking at her down the nozzle of the rifle. Maintaining this viewpoint, the camera then zooms in more closely as he comments, "yeah, this kind of rifle is worth hanging around for," before an edit to a two-shot of the couple reveals them embracing. His desire for the gunsmith's daughter is therefore explicitly connected to the rifle and is reinforced when he asks her how long it will take to make the weapon. "A long time," she responds to which he replies, "guess it is time I settled down."

The equation of the gun with sexual desire and phallic meaning becomes even more overt in a subsequent scene when Griff Bonnell calls upon Jessica Drummond to arrest one of her "forty guns" for criminal activity. The two seem immediately attracted to each other—first intimated by their reciprocated smiles and open figure behavior—but thereafter made explicit in a conversation concerning Bonnell's gun. "I'm not interested in you, Mr. Bonnell—it's your trademark [I'm interested in] … may I feel it?" she asks him, extending one hand. Obviously referring to his gun, he responds, "might go off in your face" to which she adds, "I'll take a chance." Bonnell then reaches below the table and pulls out his weapon, which Drummond twirls before examining it closely. The entire sequence is filmed as a static two-shot in medium close-up, expressing the intimacy between them, with the sexual connotations of the gun made clear.

The Gun as Homoerotic Sign

Related to the earlier interpretation of Charlie Prince in *3:10 to Yuma*, a sequence in *Red River* further illustrates the homoerotic potency of the gun. The film recounts the story of Thomas Dunson (John Wayne) and his quest to start a cattle ranch in Texas. Early in the film he adopts an orphaned boy, Matt Garth (Mickey Kuhn), who 14 years hence, helps Dunson drive the cattle from Texas to Missouri. If Wayne as Dunson conveys a conventional figure of masculinity and toughness, then the now adult Garth (Montgomery Clift) appears somewhat feminized, primarily through his youthful looks and slender stature. This feminization becomes more obvious in the following sequence during their interaction with an approaching group of ranchers, headed by Mr. Meeker (Davison Clark) and a ranch hand named Cherry Valance (John Ireland), who stake a claim on the cattle being herded by Dunson and Garth. The camera first frames the four men on horseback in medium shot as they discuss the herd before Garth tips his hat back and addresses Valance specifically. The camera moves in closer and cuts to an over the shoulder shot directed towards Valance, an angle maintained throughout their conversation. Valance leans forward slightly toward Garth, his shirt wide open and his eye-line directly aimed at Garth. Although the two are mounted on their respective horses, the angle of framing gives the impression that they are much closer. "Who *are* you?" asks Garth to which Valance responds, "some call me one thing, some another." "What do they call you the most?" asks Garth. "By my name, Cherry Valance," states Valance, his response of "one thing or another," implicitly suggesting homosexual undertones while his name also has feminine connotations. Their discussion then moves on to Valance's renowned reputation in gunmanship. Valance continues to stare at Garth even as he talks to the other men in the group as if he is fascinated with Garth, and then asks if he can join their drive. Subsequently, the two men, now dismounted, compare and admire each other's weapons. "That's a good looking gun you're about to use back there, can I see it?" Valance asks Garth as they walk adjacent. Garth then turns round to face Valance and smiles, the camera now framing them in medium close-up. As Garth hands Valance his gun, Valance also whips out his weapon and reciprocates. "Maybe you'd like to see mine?" Valance suggests to Garth. "Nice, awful nice," says Valance, handling Garth's gun. Thereafter, the camera moves in to frame the two men more closely as they discuss the merits of a good gun. "There are only two things more beautiful than a good gun," says Valance, "a Swiss watch or a woman from anywhere." Subsequently, the two men exchange firearms and alternate between taking shots at a tin-can and offering admiring looks and comments to each other. While Arjet argues that "gunfights remove the male body from the center of the narrative, and displace the homoeroticism and homosociality yet another step" (134), in this case, their gunmanship accentuates obvious (homo)sexual nuances. This is because as they fire increasingly quickly at the tin-can, they sustain its almost continuous movement, the rapidly accelerating pace of their gun interaction connoting a sexual element. When Valance is later asked why he joined the drive he replies, "Matt turned me down. Made me wanna go. Besides, I've taken a liking to that gun of his." The mutual feelings of the two men resurface in subtle ways, principally through their lack of interest in women—for instance, when they come across a wagon train of girls bound for Nevada, and which is under attack by Native Americans, both Garth and Valance show only cursory interest in the women, to the extent that when Garth removes an arrow from one of the women's shoulders, he seems completely devoid of any emotion or attraction towards her. Later, in the film's finale, having been pursued by his adoptive father after a conflict between them, Garth is forced into a potential gunfight, but when taunted by Dunson to take out his gun, he refuses, despite being renowned for his speed of draw. He merely stands there, even though Dunson fires at him and grazes his face with a bullet. At this point, a close-up of Garth's face reveals a wry smile, and, as Dunson insults him, shouting, "you're soft! Won't anything make a man out of you?" he strikes Garth with his fists and tells him that he is "yellow-bellied and chicken-livered." Garth now retaliates and punches Dunson to the ground, the two engaging in a fistfight. Whereas Arjet contends that, "if the attacker must physically cross the room and touch his victim, the essential masculine traits of singularity and hard boundaries are threatened" (134), Garth's response merely amplifies his stoicism. Moreover, following their tussle, which is broken up by female character, Tess Millay (Joanne Dru), with whom Garth is now romantically involved, Dunson tells Garth that he should marry her. Reticence in using a gun is here therefore associated with the development of a coherent heterosexual masculinity, Garth's adult status also indicated because Dunson finally accepts him as a full partner in their ranching enterprise.

A Lack of or Failure to Discharge a Weapon

While Garth's refusal to draw his gun serves as a sign of masculinity, a lack of weaponry may suggest inadequacy for, as Calder notes, "the cowboy unarmed is a cowboy desexed" (113). This fallibility becomes even greater when there is either a failure of a gun to discharge, or when ammunition runs out. In *Unforgiven*, for instance, we learn from Little Bill Daggett how "Two-Gun Corcoran" met his demise: "That Walker Colt blew up in his hand, a failing common to that model," the loss of his hand leaving him vulnerable to a fatal final bullet. However, the implications of a failure to discharge may be quite different for a child. This is precisely the case in *True Grit*, a film that recounts how 14-year-old Mattie Ross (Hailee Steinfeld) avenges her father's death. Despite engaging the services of U.S. Marshal, Rooster Cogburn (Jeff Bridges), who is joined by Texas Ranger LaBoeuf (Matt Damon), to track down Tom Chaney (Josh Brolin), her father's attacker, it is Mattie who finally kills him. The way that the first interchange between Mattie and Chaney is filmed infers the shifting power relations between them—initially

Mattie Ross (Hailee Steinfeld) points her gun at the outlaw Tom Chaney (Josh Brolin) in *True Grit* (Paramount, 2010).

a close-up of Chaney cuts to medium long shot of Mattie. Thereafter, an extreme long shot of Chaney, with Mattie now fore-grounded, causes him to appear diminished in the frame while she is positioned as a much more dominant figure. At this point, she realizes that Chaney is her father's killer, but, as he draws closer, armed with a rifle, the visual signification reverses. He now occupies more of the frame and a long shot of Mattie from his perspective sees her now diminished. Yet, as she deftly un-wraps her gun (it is sheathed in a cloth bag rather than a holster), Mattie then equivalently occupies the composition. A slightly low camera is now directed up toward her (suggesting her empowerment), with her gun positioned center-frame. The camera then cuts to a side-on long shot that discloses Mattie again dominating the frame as she threatens to shoot him. However, Chaney patronizes her by instructing her how to cock the gun, seeming confident that a young girl will not have the wherewithal to fire at him. Undeterred, she fires and wounds him, while a second attempt misfires and she is captured by two of Chaney's accomplices. Recounting events to them, she tells one of the men, "If I had killed him I would not now be in this fix," clearly regretting the misfire, to which the man responds, "It will do it. It will embarrass you every time" as if the gun is an uncontrollable appendage of the physical body. Indeed, referring to *Shane*, Calder contends that "the gun is an adjunct of the body. The description is purposefully physical, and by implication, sexual" (113). Chaney's accomplice also comments that "most girls like pretties—but you like guns?" to which Mattie responds, "I do not care a thing in the world about guns. If I did, I would have one that worked." For Mattie, the gun therefore appears to be merely a tool enabling her to complete her mission, rather than a symbol of phallic power. Meanwhile, Chaney claims that he was shot by the Marshal, seeming humiliated that he has been hit by a girl. Later in the film, however,

Mattie fatally wounds Chaney using a particularly powerful long-range weapon, the Sharps carbine. This is indicated to the spectator to be lethal because attention is drawn to the fact that LaBeouf kills someone from 400 yards with it, the importance of distance articulated by Arjet (134) and Cawelti (40) coming into play. Ironically, however, Mattie uses the weapon at extremely close range and it is so cumbersome that she struggles to cock or even lift the gun. Moreover, as she fires it, she is thrown back by its recoil, indicating the rifle's formidability, although its use in this context is not concerned with the conscious exercise of force, but with achieving retribution and justice.

Running out of ammunition triggers an equally paradoxical scenario in the closing sequence of *The Outlaw Josey Wales*. Throughout the film, which tracks Josey Wales' (Clint Eastwood) quest to seek out his family's killers, Wales depends on a gun and, unlike the judicious use of the gun by Bonnell in *Forty Guns*, he readily deploys any available arsenal on numerous occasions. The centrality of the gun is made apparent after his homestead has been razed to the ground by Union militants in an attack which kills his wife and son. Reaching into the remains of the burnt timbers, Wales retrieves a scorched holster and, from it, pulls out his gun. Framed in close-up, it is still gleaming and seems unaffected by the fire, suggesting qualities of endurance and permanence. Thereafter, Wales practices his marksmanship and becomes affiliated with a group of outlaw pro–Confederates who are later persuaded by one of their group to surrender to the Unionists. However, the Unionists massacre the surrendered men using a concealed Gatling gun, which Wales eventually appropriates and turns on their attackers. His ultimate victim is Captain Terrill (Bill McKinney), the man who perpetrated the assault on his home and family and, although Wales has run out of ammunition, he still pursues him. Coming across Terrill, and fully aware that that his pistols are empty, Wales sequentially dry fires all 24 chambers as a means to terrify an already wounded Terrill, close-ups intercutting more intensely between each man's face as Wales draws closer. Thereafter, the camera cuts between extreme close-ups, first of Terrill's, then of Wales' eyes, each of the gun's nozzles coming into the frame as Wales raises, aims and dry fires the weapons. At the same time, Wales experiences flashbacks of the attack on his family. The camera then cuts to an ultra close-up of Terrill's eye before Wales fatally wounds him with his own sword. As Arjet contends, "Where bullets deny both visibility and tangibility knives make masculine power tangible and visible, and force a visual depiction of masculine penetration that seems perhaps too graphic and explicit for the homosocial logic of the gunplay film. Like homosocial relationships themselves, the knife makes explicit and messy what the gun keeps implied and 'clean'" (134).

The Gun and Female Potency

Douglas Pye notes that "it is generally accepted that the Western's representation of women is ... massively skewed" (13), and goes on to state that "the whole history of the Western is therefore, at one level, inescapably bound up with reducing Native Americans and women to functions in a symbolic world centering on White male characters" (13). Yet, the female gunfighter as protagonist is prominent in films including *Johnny Guitar* and *The Quick and the Dead*, in which the gun assumes significance outside its phallic connotations. Even as secondary characters in films such as *The Outlaw Josey Wales*, women take up arms to defend themselves. In *Johnny Guitar*, the gun serves as a prominent mediator of sexual tensions between butch female protagonist, Vienna (Joan Crawford), and her rival, Emma Small (Mercedes McCambridge). Their conflict partly arises because Small competes for the attentions of a cowboy known as the Dancing Kid (Scott Brady), whose affections, however, are focused on Vienna. Set in Arizona, the film tells of Vienna's intentions to capitalize on the forthcoming railroad by buying land through which it will pass for building purposes. Her authoritarian traits are foregrounded from the outset when she gives out orders to various male employees in her saloon. In response to these orders, one of the men, Sam responds, "Never seen a woman who was more a man. She thinks like one, acts like one, and sometimes makes me feel like I'm not." Dressed in a black shirt, tie and trousers and high boots Vienna is initially also masculinized in her costume and Patrick McGee explains that she "wears a pistol and dresses like a man to emphasize that she has compromised her femininity in order to become autonomous and empowered through the 'masculine' ownership of property" (70). Conversely, when the eponymous Johnny Guitar (Sterling Hayden) calls at the saloon to see Vienna (he is a former lover), he is unarmed, carrying a guitar rather than a rifle. Indeed, he is described by Peter Biskind as "a feminized outlaw who now prefers a guitar to a gun and has nothing on his mind but marriage to Vienna" (303). Regardless, his masculinity remains intact, commanded partly by his tall stature and deep voice, aspects remarked upon by other men. For instance, Tom, the saloon cook, comments, "That's a lot of man you're carrying in those boots, stranger. You know there's something about a tall man that makes people sit up and take notice."

When Emma Small and her followers, together with the town's marshal, enter the saloon, Vienna quickly secures her gun holster and descends the stairs slowly, pausing partway. Confronting Vienna, Emma claims (mistakenly) that the Dancing Kid, one of Vienna's associates, is responsible for the death of her brother, at which point Vienna aims her gun at Emma and the accompanying posse. However, the camera's position makes her appear to direct it at the spectator, a position maintained throughout the entire scene.

A discussion then centers on the stagecoach ambush in which Emma's brother was killed, and Johnny Guitar informs the marshal that he had witnessed the holdup. "Why didn't you ride down and help them?" asks John McIvers (Ward Bond), one of Emma's supporters. "With what, with this?" says Johnny, strumming his guitar. "Where are your guns?" they press him, to which he replies, "I don't wear any." However, Guitar proves his masculinity in a fistfight with Bart Lonergan (Ernest Borgnine), one of the three men who subsequently arrive with the Dancing Kid. When the men leave, another of the four, a younger cowboy named Turkey (Ben Cooper) tells Vienna that he wants to stay with her. "If you stay to look after me, who will look after you?" asks Vienna. "You talk like I'm a boy! I'm a man. I'll prove to you I'm a man!" Turkey exclaims and he suddenly withdraws his gun and shoots various objects on a nearby table, easily striking each one. On hearing the gunshots Johnny Guitar seizes the nearest gun, shoots the gun out of Turkey's hand and, in a sequence similar to that described earlier in *Butch Cassidy*, propels the gun along the floor. As Turkey retrieves his gun, he examines it ruefully, his pained facial expression suggesting that his masculinity has been dented, the preceding conversation with Vienna clearly indicating the gun as symbolic of phallic sexuality. Vienna demands that Johnny Guitar hands over the gun and even though Vienna herself wears a gun, she rarely uses it, except at the end of the film when she kills Emma in self-defense.

Likewise, in *Forty Guns*, the character of Jessica Drummond, despite leading 40 men, is hardly ever seen wielding a firearm. Rather, her power rests on a tendency to strip her men of their weapons when they have been used inappropriately. Several times throughout the film, she demands that her brother, Brockie Drummond, surrender his guns, and effectively, deprives him of his phallic power. Conversely, in *The Quick and the Dead*, female gunslinger Ellen (Sharon Stone) is quickly established as a tough woman, first, when she floors an attacker with a single punch, and second, when the innkeeper's daughter comments that "I've never seen a woman carrying a gun before." The narrative unfolds in the town of Redemption, a frontier location which is dominated by a ruthless tyrant, John Herod (Gene Hackman). Herod thrives on power to the extent that he insists on an annual shooting contest. However, one of the townspeople, Cort (Russell Crowe), a reformed gunfighter who now runs a mission, refuses to engage in violence and will not enter the contest. As a result, Herod has Cort strung up in a noose and makes him stand on a chair in the town's saloon and, with each additional refusal to enter the shooting contest, shoots out a strut of the chair supporting him. Herod's gun is first viewed in close-up and then a point of view shot from his perspective is directed down its barrel before the camera pans rapidly downwards. Herod shoots at the chair, the swift descent of the camera as he takes aim anticipating Cort's falling body. Throughout the sequence, the camera also intercuts to Ellen's anxious face before shifting to an extreme close-up of the gun's barrel as Herod cocks the trigger once more. Just as the chair gives way and the noose tightens around Cort's neck, Ellen volunteers for the contest. "No rules against ladies. It's just that women can't shoot for shit," comments Herod, at which point he fires at the one remaining intact strut on the chair. Ellen swiftly draws her gun and shoots out the ceiling rafter from which Cort's noose is suspended, swivels her gun and replaces it in its holster, her gunmanship undermining Herod's statement. In this sequence, the gun's meaning is demarcated by gender rather than any dominant phallic sexuality—for Herod the gun expresses his control and power over Cort, and McGee further identifies a racial element to Herod's dominion in that "all the white people (and one black man Woody Strode as the undertaker) seem to profit in one way or another from the fascist rule of Herod while the Mexican Americans are directly exploited" (74). For Ellen, it reflects her compassion and humanity and at the end of the film, we learn that this compassion stems from an early trauma when Herod killed her own father in an almost identical ritual. On that occasion (seen in flashback), Herod advised the young Ellen that if she could shoot through the rope suspending her father, then they would both be free to go. However, Ellen, who at that time was clearly unfamiliar with handling a gun, accidentally shot her father in the forehead, causing the gun, (specifically, an inability to use it) to have particularly traumatic resonance for her.

Despite the fact that Ellen volunteers to enter the contest, Cort is nonetheless forced to participate and, when the town clock strikes the hour (the signal to draw their guns), he swiftly shoots his opponent. He then looks down at his pistol and gasps, appearing shocked that he has used it, as if he had no conscious control over the shooting. Akin to Calder's suggestion that the gun is an "adjunct of the body" (113), Cort's firing of the gun seems to be an involuntary physical response. In another pairing in the contest, Herod shoots his opponent, Ace Hanlon (Lance Henriksen), through the hand. Hanlon claims he can shoot just as well with either hand, but Herod challenges him on this point, stating that it was he that killed some of the victims allegedly killed by Hanlon. At this instant, a sudden close-up of Hanlon's facial expression registers a moment of realization and the camera subsequently pulls back rapidly to long shot, now disclosing both Hanlon and Herod drawing their guns. However, Herod is faster, and shoots off Hanlon's thumb, the injury viewed in close-up. Herod then inserts a cigar into his mouth and the camera pans down as he strikes a match on his gun with his right hand, and challenges Hanlon on his left-handed drawing ability. Slowly and deliberately Herod raises the flaming match, (viewed in ultra close-up), before the camera cuts briefly to Ellen's anxious face and back to the two men as they withdraw their pistols once more. Herod is again faster and wounds

Hanlon's other hand, demonstrating that he is shooting to exercise power over his opponent (as Hanlon claims to be dual handed). After Herod first fires at Hanlon's feet, a side on medium close-up sees him shoot Hanlon through the chest, causing his body to convulse and blood to spurt out, these effects viewed in slow motion. In the film's finale, Ellen confronts Herod with her father's Marshal's badge and they both draw their guns. Even though injured, Ellen fatally wounds him, evidenced by a shadow of a transiently still-standing Herod which discloses a bullet hole right through his chest, the illusion of perforation being augmented by the fact that sunlight shines through the hole. When she fires again, an extreme zoom appears to track the bullet's trajectory as it strikes him through the head. Unlike Herod's display of power over Hanlon, Ellen therefore shoots to kill as an act of retribution but it is an action with obvious penetrative allusion.

Conclusion

An analysis of westerns from the 1940s to the present day shows diverse significations of the gun and while generally equated with the phallus, and often directly aligned with the penis—as intimated in *Forty Guns*, and *Unforgiven*—it can carry other meanings. For example, the way that women use guns presents a scenario often concerned with justice and retribution, as evident in Emma's revenge for the murder of her father in *The Quick and the Dead*. Dyer argues that "because only men have penises, phallic symbols, even if in some sense possessed by a woman…, are always symbols of ultimately male power. The woman who wields 'phallic' power does so in the interests of men" (136). In a sense, the way that women deploy the gun corresponds with Dyer's claim, since the manner in which Emma's avenging of her father's death is represented involves penetrative symbolism. Children too take up arms as a means to express family loyalty, for instance, Mattie in *True Grit* unhesitatingly shoots her father's killer. Notwithstanding these gendered tendencies, male characters may also engage their weapons for honorable purposes—if Little Bill Daggett in *Unforgiven* and Herod in *The Quick and the Dead* are ruthless men using their guns to articulate power, then William Munny in *Unforgiven* and Rooster Cogburn in *True Grit* employ theirs on the side of justice. In sum, while there are unquestionable references to the sexual signification of the gun, it also embraces a broader range of meanings that reflect real world gun cultures. In such situations, women and children may be equally empowered by weaponry but for reasons other than mere displays of phallic authority.

Filmography

Butch Cassidy and the Sundance Kid. Dir. George Hill. Twentieth Century Fox Film Corporation, 1969.
Casino Royale. Dir. Martin Campbell. Columbia Pictures, 2006.
Forty Guns. Dir. Samuel Fuller. Twentieth Century Fox Film Corporation, 1957.
Johnny Guitar. Dir. Nicholas Ray. Republic Pictures, 1954.
Once Upon a Time in the West. Dir. Sergio Leone. Rafran Cinematograficia / Finanzia San Marco / Paramount Pictures, 1968.
The Outlaw Josey Wales. Dir. Clint Eastwood. Warner Bros., 1976.
The Quick and the Dead. Dir. Sam Raimi. Tri-Star Pictures, 1955.
Red River. Dir. Howard Hawks. Monterey Productions, 1948.
Shane. Dir. George Stevens. Paramount Pictures, 1953.
3:10 to Yuma. Dir. James Mangold. Lionsgate, 2007.
True Grit. Dir. Coen Brothers. Paramount Pictures, 2010.
Unforgiven. Dir. Clint Eastwood. Warner Bros., 1992.

Works Cited

Arjet, Robert. "'Man to Man': Power and Male Relationships in the Gunplay Film." *Open Fire: Understanding Global Gun Cultures*. Ed. Charles Springwood. Oxford: Berg, 2007. 125–137. Print.
Biskind, Peter. *Seeing is Believing*. London: Bloomsbury. 2001. Print.
Brode, Douglas. *Dream West: Politics and Religion in Cowboy Movies*. Austin: University of Texas Press, 2013. Print.
Buscombe, Edward. Ed. *The BFI Companion to the Western*. London: BFI, 1990. Print.
Bushman, Brad, Patrick Jamieson, Ilana Weitz and Daniel Romer. "Gun Violence Trends in Movies." *Pediatrics*. 132 6 (2013): 1014–1018. Print.
Calder, Jenni. *There Must be a Lone Ranger: The American West in Film and in Reality*. New York: McGraw-Hill, 1977. Print.
Cameron, Ian and Douglas Pye. (eds.) *The Movie Book of the Western*. London: Studio Vista, 1996. Print.
Cawelti, John. *The Six-Gun Mystique Sequel*. Bowling Green, OH: Bowling Green State University Popular Press, 1999. Print.
Dyer, Richard. *The Matter of Images: Essays on Representation*. New York: Routledge, 2002. Print.
Falconer, Peter. "*3:10* Again: A Remade Western and the Problem of Authenticity." *Adaptation in Contemporary Culture: Textual Infidelities*. Ed. Rachel Carroll. London: Continuum, 2009. 62–71. Print.
Farr, Vanessa, Henri Myrttinen and Albrecht Schnabel. *Sexed Pistols: The Gendered Impacts of Small Arms and Light Weapons*. Tokyo: United Nations University Press, 2009. Print.
Lehman, Peter. "Crying Over the Melodramatic Penis: Melodrama and Male Nudity in Films of the 90s." *Masculinity: Bodies, Movies, Culture*. Ed. Peter Lehman. New York: Routledge, 2001. 25–42. Print.
Loy, R. Philip. *Westerns and American Culture, 1930–1955*. Jefferson, NC: McFarland, 2001. Print.
McGee, Patrick. *From Shane to Kill Bill: Rethinking the Western*. Malden, MA: Blackwell Publishing, 2007. Print.
Murdoch, David Hamilton. *The American West: The Invention of a Myth*. Cardiff: Welsh Academic Press, 2001. Print.
Pheasant-Kelly, Frances. "Outlaws, Buddies, Lovers: The Sexual Politics of *Calamity Jane* and *Butch Cassidy and the Sundance Kid*." *Love in Film and Television Westerns*. Ed. Sue Matheson. New York: Palgrave Macmillan, 2013. 141–160. Print.
Pye, Douglas. "Criticism and the Western." *The Movie Book of the Western*. Eds. Ian Cameron and Douglas Pye. London: Studio Vista, 1996. 9–21. Print.

Saunders, John. *The Western Genre: From Lordsburg to Big Whiskey*. New York: Wallflower Press, 2001. Print.
Sparks, Richard. "Masculinity and Heroism in the Hollywood 'Blockbuster.'" *British Journal of Criminology*. 36 3 (1996): 348–360. Print.
Springwood, Charles. Ed. *Open Fire: Understanding Global Gun Cultures*. New York: Berg, 2007. Print.
White, John. *Westerns*. New York: Routledge, 2011. Print.

Rifles and Things in *Winchester '73*

KATHERINE A. JOHNSON

Edward Buscombe's "The Idea of Genre in the American Cinema," originally published in 1970, discusses the relationship between form and content in defining genre. He states that discussion about a visual medium should concentrate on those things the audience sees on screen. In the Western genre, for instance, landscape, clothes, tools, and horses "operate as formal elements. That is to say, the films are not 'about' them any more than a sonnet is about 14 lines in a certain meter. For example, *Winchester 73* (Anthony Mann, 1950) is not about the gun, which is a mere connecting device to hold the story together. The film, like all films, is about people" (Buscombe 16). Buscombe's emphasis on the centrality of people as subject matter within the film is understandable, but to say the gun in *Winchester '73* is "a mere connecting device" obscures the importance of this particular formal object within the film, the Western genre, and American culture. The film, in fact, highlights the important role that weapons, in this case a famous rifle, have often held as things that constitute American relationships and the American identity. Jeanine Basinger's wonderfully detailed book, *Anthony Mann*, provides another view regarding the role the rifle plays. She recognizes the image of the rifle as a "motivational force" throughout the film: "All conflicts, all love, all motivation, are developed through the rifle" (81). For her the weapon is symbolic. As a "motivational force" it represents a reaction and is denied the existence of a physical thing that articulates, or connects, people in conflict or in love (Basinger 81).

Both Basinger and Buscombe fail to fully recognize the power given to the rifle from the film's very beginning: "This is the story of the Winchester Rifle Model 1873, 'the gun that won the West.' To cowman, outlaw, peace officer or soldier, the Winchester '73 was a treasured possession. An Indian would sell his soul to own one." As its first few minutes make clear this film is about a man *and* a gun. It is about the powerful obsession Americans, and "others"—as the classic Western would label the Indian—have for this weapon. This particular obsession over weapons will be discussed in the following pages; but first it is necessary to consider the ways in which certain objects have been positioned in American popular culture. For one, thing theory has often provided avenues to understand the objects in our lives as things containing a certain "thingness." Bill Brown says this "thingness" becomes visible when objects break down, stop working in expected ways, and/or are misused. They lose their culturally coded context and regain the essence of what they were originally meant to be. In this way they can be recoded as something outside the typical use.[1] Because of this redefinition of the inanimate object, the perceived reality surrounding it is remade. According to Brown, thing theory focuses on "thoughts about how inanimate objects constitute human subjects, how they move them, how they threaten them, how they facilitate or threaten their relation to other subjects" ("Thing Theory" 7). Reality is remade through the reconstitution of people's relationships to the things and the people around them.

In *West of Everything* Jane Tompkins provides a very thorough and valuable discussion of a number of Western icons (landscape, horses, and cattle). She argues these things are symbolic of the genre and its portrayal of a certain kind of masculinity. The study of iconography, however, does not end with the formal and symbolic qualities of the genre. Often more than signposts for easy recognition, those formal objects, or icons, have importance outside their genre. They can also be understood as things that provide information about the worlds and times into which Western films are released. Thus when one considers Brown's method of examining the "history *in*" a thing, as opposed to a simple retelling of the "history *of*" it ("How to Do Things" 935), the Winchester '73 of Mann's film tells a story of America's past in which rifles, and weapons like it, play important roles. The style that I identify as filmic it-narrative presents the viewer with an image of the gun that is more than iconic and/or formal. It helps to direct the hero's journey. Because the film explicitly presents the weapon as a central figure within the narrative, sharing the storyline with James Stewart's hero Lin McAdam, filmic it-narrative provides a cohesive structure to the storyline, following both the circulation of the rifle and McAdam's parallel journey of revenge. It is important to note here that filmic it-narrative visually emphasizes what the literary style of the it-narrative, or object narrative, of eighteenth-century literature does. Specifically, it illustrates the centrality of an inanimate object in the relationships between people, or subjects, particularly in relationships articulated by the object's physical circulation.[2] Thus, through narrative, composition, and camera movement, the rifle acts as more than a "mere connecting device" or "motivational force": it is a thing that very clearly holds the power to animate the film's characters, to encourage them to kill, steal, and cheat in order to possess it. In a filmic it-narrative style, as with the literary style, the line between subject and object is blurred as thing and man become co-constitutive of their relationship and the relationships between people. Ultimately, the Winchester '73's power to articulate and rearticulate the ways in which individuals present themselves and their relationships speaks to a history of such instances. Examinations of the film's treatment of the rifle, the history of its emergence as "One of One Thousand," and the significance of this gun in post–World War II America shed light on this pattern.

Winchester '73's first 15 minutes set up a pattern of treatment that then repeats throughout the film's entirety. Throughout both camera and characters treat the rifle as something other than the tool it was originally made to be. It becomes a thing that encourages people to act in certain ways and see themselves in relation to others in certain ways. Just as importantly, it is admired not so much for what it can do, but what it is and who else owns that specific model. The film's epigraph presented above plays over the opening image of two figures in the distance riding horses atop rolling hills. Then a fade to a close-up of an engraving reads:

> The First Prize
> Centennial Rifle Shoot
> Won by
> ―――――――――
> Dodge City Kansas
> July 4th 1876

The camera pulls back from this tight close-up, to a shot of the rifle on display, the voice of a young boy exclaiming his wonder at what the audience can only imagine is the gun. The film cuts to a slightly different shot of the display, allowing the audience to see the boy. Another youth adds to the exclamations of admiration: "What I'd give to have that gun." A sign details the gun on display, "First Prize Winchester Model 1873 "One of One Thousand." The camera tilts up slightly to reveal a row of older men behind the boys, all pressed up against the glass of the display window. The older men say: "One of a thousand? First one I ever seen; but mister that's a real gun." "Heard it took over a year to make it." "Yeah, they gave the first to President Grant." "I'll sure be in good company when I win that one." With no cut ending this interaction, and still in the same take, the camera pans over to two men on horseback. Newly arrived in Dodge City, the audience gets its first detailed shot of the men from the film's opening image, McAdam (Stewart) and his friend, High Spade (Millard Mitchell). The two ponder the possibility of whether or not the man they've been searching for will be in town. McAdam confidently proclaims, "He'll be here … that gun'll bring him."

Everyone in the West wants this rifle in *Winchester '73* (Universal, 1950).

After just under three minutes, the rifle's centrality has been established through dialogue and camerawork. The film presents the audience with a visual representation of the very relationship established by the characters' declarations. The environment is constituted around the weapon, its details becoming apparent as the camera moves from the rifle to the scenery and the people surrounding it. This visual treatment becomes a reoccurring pattern throughout the film as the rifle passes from character to character. Each segment of its journey beginning with the camera establishing the relationship between man and thing in the same, or a very similar, manner.[3]

Not long after this introduction, the Centennial Rifle Shoot takes place. McAdam, the hero, and Dutch Henry Brown (Stephen McNally), the villain *and* McAdam's brother, are both contestants. This segment may initially seem (at least according to narrative) to emphasize the rifle as treasure, and so a fetishized commodity, but dialogue, composition, and camera movement work together to emphasize its centrality outside the realm of economics. The competition begins with the image of a large crowd of townspeople, all seen in impressive deep focus. Near the bottom right corner of the frame is McAdam, lost in the crowd as well as the frame. Positioned in the center of the people, in the only clear open space of the frame is the town's marshal,

Wyatt Earp (Will Geer), holding the rifle. Earp praises the weapon, "the finest gun in the world," for which the contestants will shoot. It is significant here that the hero is lost in the crowd, and instead the rifle is the object of visual as well as narrative focus.[4]

The marshal passes the rifle to the contestants so they can inspect the thing for which they are competing. The camera follows it down the line, starting with McAdam and losing him again as the rifle (and the camera with it) moves from contestant to contestant. Earp tells the history of the object as the rifle travels down the line. He says, "one gun out of every ten ... twenty thousand, it comes out just perfect. Well naturally, it ain't for sale ... money won't buy it. It wouldn't be right to sell it. So the Winchester people they have given it a name. They call it 'One of a Thousand.'" He places it in the family of the perfect specimens owned by the likes of President Grant and Buffalo Bill Cody. The marshal tells the crowd, the contestants and the film's audience, with fictional flair and less detail of course, the history of the real-life Winchester Model 1873 "One of One Thousand" (more on this later). With that, the competition begins and along the line of shooters the camera moves again. Each man is framed similarly with his rifle jutting into the foreground of the image, demanding the space of the frame as each shoots.[5] McAdam, the film's hero, eventually wins the competition and the weapon, but the centrality of the rifle, specifically the Winchester Model 1873 "One of One Thousand," has already been made clear. The positioning of the Winchester and other rifles within the frame, and even more so the famous weapon's movement, determines both composition and camera movement. Both, motivated by the weapon, constitute the space and the connections between people. The power that this thing holds over the camera is a foreshadowing of the power it will hold over the film's narrative and the structure of the hero's journey. As the camera follows the Winchester 73's movement, the film and its presentation of McAdam's hunt for his father's murderer (Dutch Henry Brown) will follow the circulation of the rifle between seemingly unrelated characters.

The film's attention to the rifle demonstrates how people come to be connected through contact with the Winchester 73.[6] The rifle is no longer the tool of accuracy in hunting and warfare. In fact, the two times it is used as a weapon the man shooting it is instead killed by McAdam—first an Indian chief (Rock Hudson) dies and then McAdam's brother. Never, in fact, does the audience see the rifle used by the hero. It is, instead, a thing to be passed from person to person simply because it is "One of One Thousand." In this way, a tool meant to be used for skill in hunting, warfare, and sharpshooting becomes special only for its being the object that it is, one gun out of a set of a thousand tested during manufacturing and *said* to be more accurate than the rest. It is a thing that creates and rearticulates connections between individuals.

This fascination with things was not unusual for America, both in the late nineteenth century and the 1950s. When considering the Winchester 73 "One of One Thousand" and the rifle in general, it becomes clear that the rifle was a particular kind of gun that contributed significantly to American history. The Winchester Model 1873 "One of One Thousand" was a real weapon. In fact, numerous 1873 and 1876 "One of One Thousand" rifles were produced.[7] In 1875 the Winchester Repeating Arms Company began actively promoting these guns as weapons selected for their exceptional accuracy. Supposedly made with a barrel crafted better than all the others in any batch of one thousand, a "One of One Thousand" Winchester 1873 was recognized for its exceptional performance (Lewis 12–15). Eventually, this model came to be recognized for its rarity more so than its accuracy—although as its name suggests rarity was always meant to act as some part of the weapon's appeal.

As Merritt Roe Smith suggests, the rifle in general was in many ways a part of the American social, cultural, and economic way of life long before 1950. Smith and Edmund E. Lewis both describe Col. William F. "Buffalo Bill" Cody's 1875 endorsement for the Winchester Model 1873 lever-action rifle for hunting and fighting Indians (353–54; 10). Smith goes on to list the "sportsman-president Theodore Roosevelt" and the famous painter of American Western landscapes Frederic Remington as other historical figures that contributed to the iconicity of the Winchester rifle on the American frontier. Smith, however, describes another important role that the rifle played during the late 1800s. It was a role that spoke of an economic power, more than one of utility or cultural significance.

In the nineteenth century, the rifle was an important tool for military and hunting purposes and many Americans used them (soldiers, hunters, settlers, ranchers, and sharpshooters for instance). This role as tool for military or social survival soon morphed into one of economic importance. Smith's piece, titled "Manufacturing Technology," describes weapon manufacturing after the Civil War (of which the Winchester Company took part) as a precursor to an emerging industrial technique. He provides a brief history of the role rifles, handguns, and other weapons came to play in the economic realm of American society beginning at the end of the Civil War. According to Smith, the process by which these products were manufactured was similar to Henry Ford's assembly-line methods later used in the production of his Model Ts.[8] To use an idea well-established by Raymond Williams, the Winchester Model 1873 was a significant object of an emergent culture near the end of the nineteenth century. It did not belong to one individual societal realm (cultural) or another (economic), but was instead situated somewhere in the middle in a complex process of rearticulating the ways in which Americans related to one another and others.

The idea that the Winchester 73, in particular, was "the gun that won the West" is therefore indicative of the seizing of the frontier land identified as the "West," but also suggests that necessity required a vast amount of these weapons to be manufactured.[9] The symbolic "hero" of the Westward expansion and the object of technological manufacturing merge; the Winchester 73 was clearly both an object of and a tool for change. It is given agency in this cultural refrain, and man as a subject of action, who would have wielded the weapon, appears unimportant. This focus on objects (often violent) of and for drastic change reflects a world not unlike 1950s America where obsession over material objects and their accumulation was the norm, and where one of the most animating objects of the twentieth century—the atom bomb—gained real power.

In post–World War II America the role of the rifle as a thing special in and of itself is clear. One can see this fascination with the iconic object in both the promotional program surrounding *Winchester '73*'s release and in the broader American cultural milieu of the time. According to Lewis, in 1950, Universal, the studio's publicity firm, and the Winchester Company joined together to put on a promotional search for any still existing Model 1873 "One of One Thousand" rifles.[10] One of the program's posters claims that out of "720,610 of these lever action repeating rifles ... only 124 were of the super-accurate variety." It then asks that people contact the studio with news of any of these rifles, and that they write a previous owner history if possible. The promotional poster concludes, "We don't want your 'One of One Thousand' Model 73. We are only trying to find out how many of them are still in existence."[11] To the first 20 people to report, Universal gave a new Model 1894 Winchester rifle. This promotional program ultimately supported feelings of curiosity and fascination with the rarity of the item rather than its ability to actually be "super-accurate." As Lewis claims, both the film and the promotional search "stimulated the field of gun collecting and brought it to the attention of collectors and the public at large" (142). Gun collecting, it is important to repeat, was not new in the postwar period, but was "stimulated" as a result of this joint effort between Universal and the Winchester Company. What Brown says of the American postwar period, that it was "an era both overwhelmed by the proliferation of things and singularly attentive to them," seems to have been a period ripe for the gun collector (Brown, "Thing Theory," 14).

Gary Hoppenstand recognizes that an American "love affair with guns" began with the Western genre and established the iconic relationship between the hero and his tool for heroics (152).[12] This "love affair," however, as has been discussed, was not new to Americans in the twentieth century. People had long connected the American "West" and the American identity to weapons that could "win" land and wars for them. In the postwar period, rifles in particular were still important to the American identity, but they had become more clearly symbolic of American masculinity. Many a Western film and television show continued to rely on the iconic relationship between the American hero and his weapon[13]; and toys like the popular Red Ryder BB gun, modeled after the Winchester rifle, also encouraged the cultural tradition of father and son bonding. Mann's film, however, even more clearly positions the Winchester 73 "One of One Thousand" outside the class of gun meant solely for hunting and fighting. Both it (and the creation of a kind of collectors' network) and the promotional search surrounding its release reinforce the idea that the gun received praise not for economic or functional reasons, but for the purpose of celebrating rarity.

Attraction to the rarity, as well as the danger, of weapons was also not unusual for postwar America. At the time of *Winchester '73*'s release, America (and the world at large) was on the forefront of a decades-long obsession with the new atomic weapon. In this postwar period people had come to rearticulate their American-ness with the addition of a new weapon that could "win" wars on a much larger scale. Allan M. Winkler calls it the "atomic age" in which thoughts of the "new atomic future" circulated—for instance, in the scientific community and in the average American's everyday life (Winkler 4). It was a period when amassing weapons could mean both the security of the nation—by keeping one step ahead of the Russians—and a continuous threat to it and its people. As the common adage went, Americans during this period "learned to live" with and to love the bomb; similar to "the gun that won the West," the atom bomb was a weapon that posed both a promise and a threat to Americans in its combination of captivating and devastating power.

In 1950s America, the power that weapons (whether rifle, handgun, or atomic bomb) had in constituting relationships between Americans and others was commonly illustrated.[14] In the case of Mann's film the iconic Winchester '73's centrality is clearly defined. Its filmic it-narrative style emphasizes the weapon's power, as a thing influential in its "thingness." Postwar America was a place in which "many people were already beginning to question the purpose of their lives and whether that purpose had indeed become, almost involuntarily, too much about material things" (Halberstam ix). A film about the control a weapon has on the trajectory of a man's life could therefore have resonated on more than just a formally influential level.

Mann's film tells a particular story about the American fascination with guns (specifically rifles), and it is heavily dependent upon an icon of the Western genre. Reflecting on the story of the Winchester Model 1873 in the late nineteenth century as well as in the mid-twentieth century, it becomes clear that the appeal that guns hold as mediators of the relationships Americans form with others is nothing new. However it has changed, this captivation certainly did not emerge with the postwar obsession with material objects, and arguably it has not left us. The Winchester rifle, in particular, has long been an object and a thing to which Americans cling and by which they constitute their American identity. The fascination with this weapon as icon and thing should not be ignored; but is it enough simply to recognize that a certain iconography exists? Or that it exists at any one particular time? By exploring the history of an icon like the Winchester '73 rifle outside the visual or formal limits of the Western genre one can learn a lot about the culture to which it belongs. One can start asking questions such as what these icons, and the things that make them up, say about the people and the history that use, celebrate, and just as importantly, are shaped by them.

NOTES

1. See Brown, "Thing Theory," and "How to Do Things with Things (*A Toy Story*)."
2. The scholarly work surrounding it-narratives often describes its field as a spin-off of sorts from the larger field of thing theory. According to Mark Blackwell it was meant to examine the possibility of thing theory in eighteenth century English literature. Blackwell and fellow scholar Liz Bellamy in particular discuss certain characteristics of this style. Typically object narratives focus on an inanimate object that acts as a main character, and around which the story is told. These stories are often structured around the circulation of the thing, which as Blackwell describes it, can become the "narrative hub." For more on it-narratives, see Blackwell and Bellamy. I should make it clear that I am neither trying to oppose the defining characteristics deemed integral to the literary style of object narratives, nor am I trying to disregard the specific social and cultural contexts interwoven with the eighteenth century literary style of storytelling. I simply wish to point out similarities consistent with the it-narrative style that help to establish the relationships between the film's rifle and the people with which it comes in contact.
3. Throughout the rifle's circulation close-ups and compositions in which it is positioned in the center of the frame also reinforce the weapon's centrality. Sometimes it even sits in the frame with its barrel pointed out at the audience, the length made strange by the three-dimensional space flattened by the two-dimensional screen.
4. At one point in this scene, the camera cuts to a shot over the shoulders of three boys in the crowd. The film's audience, viewing the event as if they were behind the three, seems to be positioned as a part of the crowd of admirers.
5. Basinger identifies the domination of compositional space as a formal technique common in Mann's work, both by the hero of his Westerns and by inanimate objects (typically in his films noir)—the first, a visual representation of the hero's journey and the second, a visual technique for affecting the audience, suggesting the ability of the inanimate object to "dominate and overtake the human images behind them" (Basinger 34).
6. One very interesting example is the relationship between McAdam and Dutch Henry Brown. The audience does not know for a fact that the two are related until the very end of the film. It takes the rifle traveling from character to character and tying their narratives together to bring the two brothers together again, literally on screen and figuratively as brothers.
7. See Edmund E. Lewis' book *The Story of the Winchester One of One Thousand and One of One Hundred* for a detailed description of these rifles and their cultural roles both in the nineteenth and twentieth centuries.
8. See Smith for a detailed and insightful study of the history of weapons manufacturing in the late nineteenth century.
9. The history of this phrase is both interesting and murky. It would appear that the Winchester Repeating Arms Company has a registered trademark on the phrase "The Gun that Won the West"—see their website's page for their Model 1873 Short Rifle. But according to Smith and others (such as the Colt's Manufacturing Company) the Colt "Peacemaker" of 1873 is often also referred to as the gun that "won the West" (Smith 354). The fact that there is no proof that either of these weapons were the ones to literally "win" the West only strength-

ens the idea that the iconicity of these guns has more to do with their being the thing they are than for the purpose for which they were originally manufactured.
  10. For more on the film and the promotional search, see Lewis 138–145.
  11. For an image of the "Wanted! Poster" from which this was taken, see Lewis 140.
  12. Hoppenstand traces this "love affair" from the Western to the more modern urban vigilante genre.
  13. *Springfield Rifle* (1952) and *The Rifleman* (1958–1963) are only two very obvious examples. Films like *The Good, The Bad, and the Ugly* (1966) later emphasized the continued significance rifles play in the visual representation of the "American West."
  14. John H. Lenihan points to a certain pattern in the postwar attitude surrounding weapons. He identifies two other Westerns of the early fifties as examples of this attitude. Both *Colt .45* (also released in 1950) and *Springfield Rifle* (1952) told tales of the relationships Americans made with others, where weapons—particularly "superweapons"—were involved. These films, and others of the early fifties, expressed "the urgency of securing new weapons from irresponsible use." He describes promotional material for both films as highlighting the similarity between the white American-Indian/bandit relationship of the American West and the American/Russian relationship of the Cold War (Lenihan 167).

Filmography

Winchester '73 (1950). Dir. Anthony Mann. Universal, 2008. DVD.

Works Cited

Basinger, Jeanine. *Anthony Mann: New and Expanded Edition*. Middletown: Wesleyan University Press, 2007. Print.
Bellamy, Liz. "It-Narrators and Circulation: Defining a Subgenre." *The Secret Life of Things: Animals, Objects, and It-Narratives in Eighteenth-Century England*. Ed. Mark Blackwell. Lewisburg: Bucknell University Press, 2014. 117–146. Print.
Blackwell, Mark. "Introduction: The It-Narrative and Eighteenth-Century Thing Theory." *The Secret Life of Things: Animals, Objects, and It-Narratives in Eighteenth-Century England*. Ed. Mark Blackwell. Lewisburg: Bucknell University Press, 2014. 9–14. Print.
Brown, Bill. "How to Do Things with Things (A Toy Story)." *Critical Inquiry* 24.4 (1998): 935–964. JSTOR. Web. 9 Jul 2014. Cited parenthetically as *A Toy Story*.
_____. "Thing Theory." *Things*. Ed. Bill Brown. Chicago: The University of Chicago Press, 2004. 1–22. Print.
Buscombe, Edward. "The Idea of Genre in the American Cinema." *Film Genre Reader IV*. Ed. Barry Keith Grant. Austin: University of Texas Press, 2012. 12–26. Print.
Halberstam, David. *The Fifties*. New York: The Random House Publishing Group, 1993. Print.
Hoppenstand, Gary. "Lethal Weapons: The Gun as Icon in the Popular Urban Vigilante Film." *Beyond the Stars III: The Material World in American Popular Film*. Ed. Paul Loukides and Linda K. Fuller. Bowling Green: Bowling Green State University Popular Press, 1993. 149–163. Print.
Lenihan, John H. "Superweapons from the Past." *Beyond the Stars III: The Material World in American Popular Film*. Ed. Paul Loukides and Linda K. Fuller. Bowling Green: Bowling Green State University Popular Press, 1993. 164–174. Print.
Lewis, Edmund E. *The Story of the Winchester One of One Thousand and One of One Hundred*. Woonsocket: Andrew Mowbray Incorporated, 2009. Print.
Smith, Merritt Roe. "Manufacturing Technology." *A New Literary History of America*. Ed. Greil Marcus and Werner Sollors. Cambridge: The Belknap Press of Harvard University Press, 2009. 353–358. Print.
Tompkins, Jane. *West of Everything: The Inner Life of Westerns*. Oxford: Oxford University Press, 1992.
Williams, Raymond. "Dominant, Residual, and Emergent." *Marxism and Literature*. Oxford: Oxford University Press, 1977. 121–127. Print.
Winkler, Allan M. *Life Under A Cloud: American Anxiety About the Atom*. Urbana University of Illinois Press, 1999. Print.

The Cowboy Brew
Coffee and Conflict in the Westerns of Budd Boetticher, Jr.

CHRISTOPHER MINZ

Drinking has always been a factor in the Western. The prominence of saloons and dusty barrooms has become part and parcel of the overarching mise-en-scène of the genre. It is in these spaces that one often observes the tensions of plot and character, and thrills as the romances play out, particularly the doomed romances: Imagine the young protégé of the wizened elder cowboy, fresh and full of piss and vinegar, ready to take on the entire cadre of black-hatted villains all by his lonesome, falls in love with the sultry barmaid. Historically she's unavailable for myriad possibility of reasons, not least of which, as Robert Warshow observes in early critical discourse on the Western, she is most clearly a prostitute, and thus not a suitable woman for the proper hero of the West (108). In these often garishly decorated saloons, the preferred drink is whiskey, strong and fiery; traditionally a drink not only to intoxicate, but to show the stalwart and manly nature of the characters, proving their worth by the tightness of their jaw as they tip back their tumbler of high proof whiskey. However, whiskey in this context can also be used to diminish the stature of the character. While drinking whiskey is masculine and powerful, being seen drunk can have quite the opposite effect. Consider the saloon sequences that introduce the viewer to Dude (Dean Martin) in *Rio Bravo* (Hawks, 1959). Dude's drunkenness is shown to its limits by his humiliation and ultimate willingness to fish a silver dollar from a filthy spittoon to pay for his drink. It is used to expose the darker possibilities of the hailed masculine potency of whiskey. (It would not be difficult, under another focus, to utilize this aspect as a signal of the fragility of masculinity in the Western itself—something to which Howard Hawks would likely object). Considering the Hawksian project however, it is no surprise that this scene will be reversed later in that film, as Dude is redeemed, but as before, the humiliation is all concerned with drinking. The space of these saloons and shots of whiskey become as hostile, or even more hostile, than the wide open ranges, where roam the traditional enemies of the Western hero: cattle rustlers, Indians, and the various savage wildlife (coyotes, rattlesnakes, and stampeding cattle) ready to deprive the Westerner of his life. However, in these interior spaces, the enemy is internalized, and at times rather existential. Yet is this not the true conflict of the Westerner? The problem of how conflict is held at personal levels? How one holds his liquor becomes symbolic of his proper masculine place in the world.

But what happens when the drink is not alcohol? While alcohol will be most prominent in most Westerns, in the films of Budd Boetticher, Jr., it is far less prevalent. The drink that seems to command notice in his Western films is coffee. Peter Wollen (writing as Lee Russell) has said that Boetticher's films "may seem very unsophisticated" (Russell 196), but what lies beneath, and in these seemingly prosaic exchanges, is an entirely complex and intricate interplay of suggestion and innuendo, a simmering violence, both of the physical sort, and of the general fabric of the Western social netting. Contrary to the seemingly unsophisticated nature of them, André Bazin argues that Boetticher's films utilize an "ingenious mise en scène and above all a constant inventiveness in relation to details capable of renewing the interest of situations" (170). My intent here is to explore how Boetticher uses the exchange of coffee as a means of signaling and bridging conflict, both internal and external, and how the place of ritual coffee exchange, as well as the exchange of conflict becomes, in general, domestic spaces. This will be in keeping with an ultimate suggestion that Boetticher's films carry with them the basic thematic elements of Melodrama as outlined by Peter Brooks and others. These elements of Melodrama (a desire for moral certitude, depictions and threats to innocence, etc.) inflect the generic conventions of the Western that Boetticher boils down to basic elements. Boetticher's films function starkly, more as near skeletons of Western tropes than the full-blooded Westerns of Ford or Mann, and thus their melodramatic underpinnings show through. In these moments the notion of social mise-en-scène, a concept that features heavily in Melodrama's insistence of civil domestic order, comes into play, plays with and disrupts the viewer's understanding of etiquette and domestic protocol in the Western—especially in the masterful *Seven Men from Now* (1956), in which Boetticher focuses on domestic protocol and the exchange of coffee and challenges the social etiquette of these moments.

The placement of coffee in general within the Western genre and the West itself, despite the general focus on alcoholic beverages, is not unknown. In fact, the recipe for cowboy brew is still quite available and can be found online with a quick Google search. One of the key elements is that, prior to boiling, the water added to the coffee grounds should be cold, and often the grounds remain in the drink, much like in Turkish coffee. When one thinks on it, the importance of coffee in the cowboy life, especially if one thinks of cattle drivers and ranch hands, whose work is often begun at the absolute break of dawn, is rather obvious. Indeed, coffee enters into the Western literary narrative early on. In Owen Wister's seminal Western novel, *The Virginian*, the unnamed narrator relates one of the first nights he spends with the Virginian: "We had strange coffee and condensed milk" (24).[1] While whiskey may be, in the fictional tropes, more visible, it seems that, from a functional capacity, coffee would occupy the fore.

Margaret Visser, in her work on cultural dining rituals, sets aside sporadic, but important, moments to discuss the use of coffee in the general scheme of dinner. It is a drink that has been a dividing beverage, and one most usually aligned with women. In *The Rituals of Dinner* Visser explains that while men continue to discuss politics and other such heavy topics at the dinner table (often a ruse for unladylike bawdiness), "women are served coffee, cigarettes, and liqueurs in the library or drawing room" (281). Even outside this formalized ritual of dinner, we use coffee as an everyday ritual for a variety of reasons. If we look at the above comparison between coffee and alcohol, as it is used in Westerns, we can see a mythological contrast at work. While alcohol provides the rowdiness, and perhaps rugged masculine aggression, coffee is supposed to move one toward beginning his or her day without trouble. As Visser points out, "coffee in North America is, mythically speaking, the opposite of alcohol: it is supposed to engender sobriety" (289). In Boetticher's Westerns, it is important from this perspective that the heroes rarely seem to drink alcohol, like the heroes of most Westerns, but are quite at home with cups of coffee. If the Westerner is seen to be doing his job in any of these films (wrangling cattle, acting as sheriff, or even pursuing vengeance as a profession of sorts) then the coffee becomes part of his everyday life, primarily when a woman is present. Visser even suggests that coffee is a ubiquitous aspect of our lives, saying that "unless we have decided to treat coffee as an unhealthy and unworthy crutch which competent adults ought to do without, we drink it all day long in the office as well" (289). The only difference here is that the Westerner's office is the wide-open frontier, and his coffee breakroom those rare domestic spaces.

So with the historical placement of coffee situated, how then does Boetticher use this key factor in the Westerner's everyday life? These ordinary moments, when coffee is shared in Boetticher's films often act as pivots in the action of the film, places in which pertinent information or palpable emotion is drawn out over the drink. The coffee itself becomes a marker for conflict. Throughout his films the very staging of the scenes is wrought with the melodramatic. That this melodrama plays out in sporadic, but key domestic spaces where coffee is poured and sipped, with the menace and tension lying just beneath the surface of customary decorum, is fitting. Here is something rather ordinary, a standard ritual of dining, there should be nothing unsavory about it, yet each time coffee is shared, it signals trouble. In fact, again, this is melodrama's strength, which often lies in its ability to undercut the ordinary. Peter Brooks, discussing the films of Douglas Sirk in the 1950s, which were contemporary with Boetticher's Westerns, says that they "offer a stylish refusal of the dailiness of everyday ... it insists that the ordinary may be the place for the instauration of significance" (ix). Hence the very usualness of imbibing coffee can become, in the right director's hand, a site of the uncanny and powerful. In these cases, bordering on, or pointing toward, violence.

In his foundational work on the Family Melodrama, Thomas Elsaesser argues that Melodrama has "a particular mise-en-scène, characterized by a dynamic use of spatial and musical categories, as opposed to intellectual or literary ones" (Elsaesser 51). This description of melodramatic mise-en-scène again fits with descriptions of Boetticher's films, as far back in critical discourse as Bazin, who claimed that *Seven Men from Now* was "one of the most intelligent Westerns I know, but also the least intellectual" (Bazin 171). While stylish and smartly staged, *Seven Men from Now* resists psychologizing its characters, letting their forms work in the specific spatial mise-en-scène comparable to what Elsaesser describes. This harkens back to the contested space of the traditional Western, the rift between civilization and savagery, here eloquently staged by Boetticher across tables or in intimate wagons, and crossed by nothing but cups of coffee.

Seven Men from Now, the film that André Bazin called "an exemplary Western" (169), opens with an exchange of coffee, which is promptly followed by an exchange of gunfire. Throughout the title song and opening credits, the camera has been static, showing us a forlorn and stormy landscape, the rain beating down torrentially. As the song ends and the credits fade, Randolph Scott's character Ben Stride, a former lawman, steps into the frame, his back coming to the center. He stares at a flickering light in the far back of the frame, what we can discern is a campfire, sheltered from the rain by a rocky overhang, but clearly still open to the elements. He walks toward the fire, and Boetticher allows the camera to remain static, letting Stride almost melt into the wet, dim landscape. It is an appropriate image for him. There is a cut to a medium shot, still of Stride's back as he pulls some brush out of the way, exposing the rock outcropping that serves as a shelter for two nervous men. They drink coffee from tin cups. After being invited in, Stride speaks a line which will be repeated more than once in the film: "I'd be obliged for a cup of that coffee." While we don't know it yet, this line will serve as a point of underlying menace, a politeness covering a deep animus. Andrew Sarris says that Boetticher's films, which he files under "esoterica," function "partly as floating poker games where every character took turns at bluffing about his hand until the final showdown" (Sarris 124). Here, however, the poker is played with the dented tin cups of coffee, rather than with cards.

Before guns fire, we know that something is amiss; there is an atmospheric tension that permeates the entire scene. Both of the men who had occupied the sheltering rocks are positioned lower than the seat Stride takes, and while the camera maintains a wide three-shot, Stride, implored to help himself to the coffee, is forced to reach across the frame to get it. The nerves of the two men are accentuated in their exhausted, yet still nervous tone of voice. As the reasons for Stride being there begin to unravel—he is chasing down the men who murdered his wife, these two men among them—the men realize they are trapped. They are trapped by the structures of etiquette as surely as they are trapped by the simple knowledge that Stride is there to kill them and the fact that their backs are against the rock wall. This etiquette is unspoken, but for them to simply gun down Stride right there, while he sips his coffee deliberately would be a violation of a code in the West: one does not kill a man over dinner. Although often broken, there is a sense of honor (amongst men) that permeates the Western as surely as the dust from the trail. As the scene builds toward its climax, one of the men fills his cup again, and there is a cut to a shot of Stride, letting his tin cup droop in his hand, signaling that it is empty. The time for pleasantry has passed. As the man drinks his coffee, he asks, looking over it at Stride, if they ever caught the men who did the killing (of Stride's wife, though we do not know this yet). Stride calmly replies, "Two of 'em." The camera cuts quickly to the man throwing his cup down and reaching for his gun, then a quick shot outside the sheltering rocks as two gunshots ring out. As the coffee has finished, so too has the life of the men. And in the first five minutes of the film, two of the seven men Ben Stride seeks are dead.

How does this progress from what should seemingly be a nicety, to a violent rupture of a frontier, but one that is still domestic space? First, we must establish that this is indeed, at least in some sense, a domestic space. Perhaps the bounds of domesticity are stretched in this instance, however this scene, in some manner, parallels others in the film with more traditional domestic territory. It is a domestic space outside of the purely domestic. It functions in what I have called elsewhere, an "interior-exterior."[2] What we see in the space in this sequence is a place of eating and food preparation. While it takes place outdoors, for these men, the Western men, both hero and villain, this is domestic. It is their home. These campfires and lean-tos are the spaces where we see men cook, clean their clothes, and do all manner of chores that we could see very well in other contexts being managed in the family kitchen by women. This is rugged domesticity, but domesticity nonetheless.

The second exchange of coffee occurs in a more traditional domestic space, a dining room/kitchen in an abandoned station. The scene begins around 24 minutes into the film (a hefty way in considering the 78-minute run time), and creates a visual divide, the camera beginning in an exterior swoop, coming to rest on a lit window. Between the crossed frames of the pane, the camera frames Annie Greer (Gail Russell) moving back and forth. There is a quick cut to the interior of the station, showing an expertly staged dining room table sequence. Masters (Lee Marvin), the foil to Ben Stride, sits in the foreground, John Greer (Walter Reed), Annie's husband, and Clete (Don Barry), Masters' grubby sidekick, sit staggered on the left. Annie moves between them, serving food she has cooked. Masters compliments, with the typical venom dripping from his tongue, as only Lee Marvin can bring forth, Annie's food, and then chastises Clete when the lesser man fails to show the same faux courtesy. He "excuses" Clete to Annie, telling her that he's "a bit short on manners." Ironically, Masters is a villain rather lacking in manners himself. The domesticity here, and all the etiquette that attends it, begins to show itself to be a façade, a contested realm, especially since Annie approaches the scene with utmost sincerity. In the domestic space, her place is well established and she follows decorum as it should be, controlling her paces and pours, in spite of Masters' attempts to derail them.

It is after Masters' imploring, but patently false, appeal to manners, that Annie turns around with the coffee pot, signaling a change in the mood. She attempts, it seems, to grasp control of the situation and restore the flow of the moment. She asks if Masters would like more coffee, to which he promptly agrees, tossing out the cold remnants of his old tin cup. As we cut to a medium two-shot, Annie stands over the seated Masters, pouring his coffee. Yet, despite her superior position, the power here belongs to Masters. He leers up at her, asserting his lascivious desire to control her, what Jim Kitses calls "his stylish lust" (178). This space might be gendered as hers, but he is in control of it. Even as she turns around after pouring his cup, his gaze follows her, as though assuring his dominance, before dropping only slightly as he sips his freshened coffee. There is a palpable discomfort here, not simply because of the ogling Masters, whose unwholesome sexuality is on full display (even the way he sits, legs open, resting easy reclined in his chair, signals his potency), but also because this space, is contested in general.

As Annie turns from Masters, she asks her husband if he wants more coffee. Her question may seem a typical gesture, one which is clearly the next step in the order of pouring and basic etiquette, but Annie, in turning next to John is offering him the chance to rise to equal footing with Masters. The camera cuts to John Greer, he is situated center, but low in the frame, forlorn. He seems not to hear her. The camera cuts out to a full shot of the ensemble again, in center are now Annie and the seated Clete, who holds up his cup,

158 A Fistful of Icons

waiting with intent. Annie asks John if he wants more coffee again, and he refuses as Clete bangs his tin cup against the coffee pot in Annie's hand. She pours for Clete, and now with everyone, except for pathetic, diminished John, bearing full cups of coffee, the space of the dining room begins to open itself to small talk and onto exposition provided by Masters. This information, the chatter that follows the pour of coffee will serve to create conflict. After a short incursion into Masters' origins, Annie quickly moves the conversation to Ben Stride, with whom she is clearly infatuated on an archetypal level. Stride embodies all the Western hero traits that John Greer does not: he is rugged, masculine, and self-sufficient.

Masters' explanation of Stride's situation could easily be seen as something innocuous, but in the hands of Boetticher, the exchange of information that takes place as Masters sips his coffee is poisonous, because it is not sanctioned by Stride himself. The individual agency that Boetticher prefers his Western heroes to have has been undermined. This is, of course, exactly what Masters hopes for. He speaks in vague terms: "those that done it" for the men who murdered Stride's wife ("too bad it had to be her"), because he knows that Annie will have no choice but to ask for more information, which she does and gets the story the spectator has been also waiting to hear. Stride's wife has been murdered by bandits who robbed the Wells Fargo. The story prompts not only Annie's sympathy, but also foreshadows more information that will later be revealed, as the camera cuts to John Greer who suddenly takes an interest in the conversation and stands up to ask more. It will be explained later that he is transporting the Wells Fargo strongbox unwittingly for the thieves. The scene ends with Masters explicitly telling the Greers that the bandits killed Stride's wife, as he returns to his coffee and sips.

There is a cut to an exterior evening shot, and we see Annie leaving her space, exiting into the night where Ben Stride sits on watch. He is, as Boetticher heroes tend to be, isolated and purposely separated from the rest. This scene functions as a coda to the scene directly preceding it. Annie offers Stride coffee, which he takes, and she quickly explains what Masters told her inside. This revelation stiffens Stride, who clearly finds the openness of Masters' conversation distasteful. He quickly shuts down Annie's attempts at assuaging his guilt over the death of his wife, whom he felt he should have been able to protect. Annie flees back into the house, but is replaced by Masters who exits and passes her as she enters the building again. Masters converses briefly with Stride and lays bare his intentions to procure the stolen Wells Fargo strongbox, insinuating that if he has to go over Stride to get it, he will.

There is a short follow-up scene the next morning, which occurs after Annie's failed attempt at consoling Stride, and Masters' veiled threat. The group prepares to leave together, despite Stride's clear discomfort at having

Masters and Clete along. Once more coffee is served by Annie, who seems to be attempting to maintain decorum and manners. Stride declines, busy with his horse, but Clete quickly steps up, followed by the deliberately licentious Masters, who doffs his hat in a slow sweep, and leers down at Annie. Last she comes to John who also declines. The poles of the masculine spectrum, rugged individualism and effeminate reliance on the strength of others, have become crude mirrors of each other: the stoic Stride and the cowardly Greer. Annie walks away, the camera pulling out in front of her as she moves to put the coffee pot and extra cups away, but she suddenly looks off-screen in horror and drops them. A small band of Indians has ridden up and caught them in a potential ambush without notice. After some quick thinking, Stride releases one of the horses, which bolts off, the Indians following to claim their offering. The tension eases, and the brief coffee exchange has again coincided with danger, in this case, however, from outside influences.

This brief scene also explores the difference in the two men who declined the coffee this time: John Greer admits to being frightened by the event, to which Stride tersely replies "we all were scared." What is fascinating is that it is Greer who immediately rushes to the wagon for his rifle after hearing Annie scream at the sight of the Indians. Stride stops him and slowly and deliberately moves to release the spare horse. While it would be easy to see Greer's movement toward the gun as the masculine thing to do, fighting for his woman, Stride shows that true masculine power is in reading a situation and acting out of choice rather than impulse. Boetticher sets Greer's actions as cowardly. This even coincides with Masters' claim after the Indians have left that "that was using your head Stride, think would could'a handled 'em though." This little exchange ties Greer and Masters together in their impulsive tendencies, and they will be visually connected in the next scene of coffee exchange.

By this point in the film, it is apparent that when coffee gets poured, something tense is about to occur, as it has done so without fail. Audience expectation has been constructed by Boetticher to equate coffee with some manner of violence, or the threat thereof. Jim Kitses sees Boetticher as a sort of master gamesman, who abides by a strict set of rules and formal conventions, "developing with an elegant mathematical precision the action pyramids, growing peaks of tautness alternating with a leisurely lyricism" (189–190). The spectator has been lured and ultimately caught, coffee being the bait in the trap.

The final scene of coffee exchange in *Seven Men from Now* is a tour de force, and one of the most masterfully composed sequences and constructions of space in all of Boetticher's (if not in the Westerns at large) films. The opening shot diagrams the entire interior of the wagon in which the Greers' are traveling to California (and unwittingly carrying the Fargo strongbox). Masters enters, as the other three, Stride and the Greers, sit drinking coffee. John Greer sits up frame from Stride and Annie, who occupy the fore. Annie almost immediately offers Masters coffee, apologizing for it not being hot, to which Masters replies, "so long as it's black." Here again, as has been seen, the exchange of coffee signals the advent of tension about to erupt. The camera splits the plane along the center, cutting back and forth between two-shots, uniting Masters and John on one end, and Stride and Annie on the other. This cutting effectively elongates the wagon, making the space between the married couple appear nearly insurmountable. The interior of the wagon has become a space as vast as the frontier they are crossing.

However, much as in the opening scene, the wagon's tension filled interior is also a domestic space, as it is, for the time being, the home of Annie and John. There is meant to be ritual here, that of the home with all the attendant politeness and etiquette, even though this home is transient, and Masters subverts it with his perverse toying. His manner maintains the surface of etiquette, he thanks Annie for the coffee, but lurking beneath the surface is the menacing and disruptive threat of violence. This points to what Margaret Visser suggests, saying in *The Rituals of Dinner* that "table manners are social agreements; they are devised precisely because violence could so easily erupt at dinner" (xii). In the Westerns of Budd Boetticher, that violence often erupts in spite of a pretense of manners.

The ritual aspects of these moments, and of the interchange of the Western as a whole genre have been noticed by others. Jim Kitses points out that "on many occasions we can sense that these settings function as a stage. Characters are always passing each other cups of coffee or guns, a measure of how abstracted the action is from social norms, but also a source of paradox and irony (as well as movement within the frame). Villains throw the hero a gun, but show little respect for the ritual of the meal" (Kitses 186–7). As the scene in the wagon progresses, Masters begins to tell a story about a cowboy and a young married woman, who just happens to have looked like Stride and Annie, who run off together. Masters continues his verbal provocation, sipping and swirling his coffee, complimenting Annie's making of the coffee, in low, pernicious tones. Masters' tale of infidelity and eloping is the breaking point in the film, and in terms of etiquette makes one think of taboo topics that are not meant to be shared in polite company. The remaining sense of community between the fellow travelers, already rather precarious, breaks down in this domestic space as the etiquette disintegrates. This breakdown will become complete as Stride follows Masters out of the wagon after his story, and belts him down into the mud, demanding he leave.

There is another conflict being exposed over this coffee exchange. The menace that emanates from Masters seems to be directed towards Stride, whom we know is a roadblock to his taking the Wells Fargo box. This conflict is clear, in fact it has been stated earlier in the film, but as the scene progresses, it becomes clear that the disdain from Masters is being aimed at the cowardly John Greer. As Masters drinks his coffee, and delivers his allegorical, and quite likely untrue, tale, Greer stops drinking, becoming more forlorn as the conversation continues. There is even a refill of Masters' coffee cup amidst the story, as he reaches directly over Greer, asserting his superiority, and hands his cup to Annie. Masters has referred to John Greer as "half a man" already, but here his actions solidify his feelings. While Stride may be his enemy, John Greer is something far worse: a coward who cannot take care of his wife. There is a marked difference in demeanor toward Greer as opposed to Stride coming from Masters. Stride is treated with a certain dignity and respect, even if it is laced with venom. Greer is simply reached over, pushed aside and made small in his own domestic abode. This cowardice is something that Boetticher approaches and portrays with a vicious glee. He despises it, and in that, so do his characters, both hero and villain. This is partially why villains in Boetticher films, nor his primary focus characters are ever cowardly or callow, as they often are in the films of John Ford. In the final interview Boetticher ever gave in 2001 prior to his death in November of that year, he was asked by Wheeler Winston Dixon how he differed from Ford. His reply was to laugh and explain that "Well, I don't think John Ford and I had the same sentimentality" (66).

What has occurred in this scene however, is the pivot around which John Greer will turn and become a man in the sense that Boetticher finds proper. Stride and Masters, though tarnished, are both already properly masculine, so their journey is not one of discovery or progress. "The self-transforming choices that are the dramatic highlights of the Ranown narratives are not typically undertaken by his protagonist or antagonists, but rather secondary characters who either accompany the hero or wind up involved in the villain's greedy machinations" (Bandy and Stoehr 221). Hence, after this belittling moment, character progression becomes John Greer's purview alone, especially as both Masters and Stride remain fixed in their moral positions (Bandy and Stoehr 221).

These scenes of domesticity function along the lines of a genre blend. While the action is clearly situated in the Western generic conventions, in these little domestic scenes, the tropes and characters play out their tensions in a miniaturized version of the contested spaces of the frontier. There is a melodramatic sensibility which blurs the lines between domesticity and the frontier narratives so intrinsic to the Western. This blurring of generic and modal boundaries is not the broad industry conception of genre blending that Rick Altman describes in *Film/Genre* (Altman ch. 8). There is no tagline suggesting a generic mix along the lines of "*Red River* meets *Mildred Pierce*." Rather this set of permeable generic boundaries is a less overt mixture of tropes and styles, which suggests an inherent combination of narrative and stylistic elements that could be seen as being constitutive of the Western itself, when stripped bare to its basics, something for which Boetticher is known. Though the domestic spaces where these exchanges of coffee take place are decorated in the trappings of the Western, they are pregnant with the pathos of melodramatic institutions. Coffee itself becomes an object to introduce the melodramatic and domestic into the general space of the Western. Coffee becomes a nexus point that focuses all the tension and energy of the melodramatic that is occurring between Western figures in these ritualized domestic spaces. While the Western is not known particularly for its portrayal of the domestic sphere, when it does portray it, the home is the space of the woman. The role of women in film is not something Boetticher was particularly progressive about, saying that "what counts is what the heroine provokes.... In herself, the woman has not the slightest importance" (Russell 199–200). However, in these films, regardless of Boetticher's intention, Melodrama occurs, and historically Melodrama is most often thought of as "women's film" and thus as these moments carry such weight in the films, showing the rare image of feminine agency (it is Annie's doling out of the coffee that she has made that will compel the narrative forward) and it becomes prudent to explore how these scenes operate.

Melodrama exists, according to Peter Brooks, "in large measure ... to locate and articulate the moral occult" (5). This search for moral occult, or moral certitude, derives from the loss of religious authority in the wake of the major secular political revolutions at the close of the eighteenth century, most pointedly in France. Melodrama grows as a theatrical movement in the wake of these revolutions, and its lasting appeal speaks to, perhaps, the irrevocable absence of dominant (moral) authoritarian structures. As a result, the Melodramatic mode of expression itself becomes a way of exploring, testing ground, and searching for an innocence that could very well be forever lost. Melodrama searches for an ideal, looks for "the way" in the face of an increasingly uncertain modernizing world. This search for an ideal seems to be precisely the description of the Western, especially those late Westerns that were released before the increasingly fractured morality of the "revisionist" films of the late 1960s took hold. What are Boetticher's films but this search for a "moral occult?" Divorced from the grand historical themes of John Ford, the Western becomes Melodrama; its search concerned with merely the morality of the individual or individuals in a world which Boetticher depicts as being increasingly that of the collective?

There is a melancholy to this task however, as the sweep of change exists despite Boetticher's desires. As is clear from these late 1950s Westerns, there is little to be done about the oncoming modern world. Brooks explains that "Melodrama represents both the urge towards resacralization and the impossibility of conceiving sacralization other than in personal terms" (16). This personalized sacralizing is the Boetticher hero's quest and ultimate failure. Because he can only see the sacredness of individualism, call it American Exceptionalism, through the lens of pure individuality. Boetticher states that the only stories he finds compelling are those in which the hero is doing what he specifically wants. Boetticher is quoted in Russell as saying, "I prefer my films to be based on heroes who want to do what they are doing, despite the danger and risk of death" (197). For Boetticher the only option is his heroes finding the sacred on their personal level. However, in Boetticher's eyes, this personal sacredness is a lost notion in the collectivized modern world. While this is a melodramatic tinting over the portrait of the Western, coloring it with pathos, it is a melodrama sans resolution. Without a return to the ideal, the Westerns of Boetticher collapse the melodramatic without giving in to that genre's insistence on closure. It should be noted, as the *BFI Encyclopedia of the Western* points out, there is more of a sense of resolution in *Seven Men from Now* than there will be in the later Boetticher films (Buscombe 297).

Following Thomas Elsaesser's "particular mise-en-scène, characterized by a dynamic use of spatial and musical categories, as opposed to intellectual or literary ones" mentioned at the outset of this essay in regards to melodrama, I argue that it is possible to find a placement for this particular mise-en-scène, in this case coffee and its place within the routines of daily lives, in what Adrian Martin refers to as "social mise-en-scène." The general idea in this concept is that mise-en-scène is not wholly what is constructed in front of the camera, but also derives from "the simple but powerful idea that cinema works with a particular type of loose but definite material: the codes and rules of society" (Martin 131). All of the little ritualistic exchanges of coffee in the film gather their placement in the mise-en-scène from the general social codes of the world at large, and this imbues them with certain interpretations and expectations. Hence when Clete in the coffee scene in the kitchen doesn't compliment Annie Greer, Masters apologizes for his lack of manners. Yet at the same moment, we are cued to a certain blemish in the social mise-en-scène, as Masters has his foot on the table. The spectator knows, because of the general understanding of social codes, that his appeal to etiquette is superficial. As Jean-Louis Comolli argues that "it is naïve to locate *mise en scène* solely on the side of the camera: it is just as much, and even before the camera intervenes, everywhere where the social regulations order the place" (Comolli 139). Thus without our particular social understanding of the etiquette involved in these domestic scenes observed in Boetticher's film, the impact of the subverted social sensibility is inevitably lost. Social mise-en-scène offers a context for the otherwise formal element of the scenes. Working in concert, the social understanding of etiquette and the formal elements of the films, makes the uneasy tension between the subversion of etiquette and what should be there becomes more palpable.

In short, *Seven Men from Now* builds its momentum off the caffeinated exchange of coffee. As has been shown, much of the tension that will eventually break expresses itself in these moments that should be instances of domestic nicety but instead are subverted in this film. *Seven Men* repeatedly uses coffee to signal danger or threat, but it is not alone in Boetticher's *oeuvre* in placing coffee at points of contention. Coffee is a part of the daily ritual of human beings the world over, and thus for Boetticher to subvert the standard drinking practices of this beverage, to find in the serving and drinking of coffee such tension, or rather to use a prosaic habit to such mean effect is at once a warping of the genre, and also a sly critique on social practice in general. While whiskey is the drink for the traditional Westerner, for Boetticher's brand of Western hero, black coffee is the iconic drink of choice.

Notes

1. One of the useful aspects of the B&N Classics reprinting is that they offer clarifying footnotes. In this case a description of the coffee: "strong coffee made over an open fire, in the West called 'cowboy brew.' 'Cowboy coffee' was whiskey served neat" (24).

2. In an essay forthcoming from Edinburgh University Press (2016) concerning the uses of space in Boetticher's Westerns, I make the claim that Boetticher constructs certain exterior shots as though they were interiors, often trapping characters within them. This creates a closed off mise-en-scène, that functions as though they were inside.

Filmography

Rio Bravo (1959). Dir. Howard Hawks. Warner Home Video, 2010. DVD.
Seven Men from Now (1956). Dir. Budd Boetticher. Paramount, 2005. DVD.

Works Cited

Altman, Rick. *Film/Genre*. London: Palgrave Macmillan, 1999.
Bandy, Mary Lea and Kevin Stoehr. *Ride, Boldly Ride: The Evolution of the American Western*. Berkeley: University of California Press, 2012.
Bazin, André. "An Exemplary Western." *Cahiers du Cinema: The 1950s*. Ed. Jim Hiller. Cambridge: Harvard University Press, 1985: 169–172.
Brooks, Peter. *The Melodramatic Imagination: Balzac, Henry James, Melodrama, and the Mode of Excess*. New Haven: Yale University Press, 1976.
Buscombe, Edward, ed. *The BFI Companion to the Western*. New York: Da Capo Press, 1988.
Dixon, Winston Wheeler. "Budd Boetticher: The Last Interview." *Film Criticism* (2002): 52–72.
Comolli, Jean-Louis. "Machines of the Visible." *The Cinematic Apparatus*. Ed. Teresa De Laurentiis and Stephen Heath. New York: St. Martin's Press, 1980. 121–143.
Elsaesser, Thomas. "Tales of Sound and Fury: Observations on the Family Melodrama." *Home Is Where the Heart Is: Studies in Melodrama and the Women's Film*. Ed. Christine Gledhill. London: BFI, 1987: 43–69.
Kitses, Jim. *Horizons West: Directing the Western from John Ford to Clint Eastwood (New Edition)*. London: BFI, 2004.
Martin, Adrian. *Mise-En-Scène and Film Style: From Classical Hollywood to New Media Art*. London: Palgrave Macmillan, 2014.
Russell, Lee. "Budd Boetticher." *The Western Reader*. Ed. Jim Kitses and Gregg Rickman. New York: Limelight Editions, 1998: 195–200.

Sarris, Andrew. *The American Cinema*. New York: Dutton, 1968.
Visser, Margaret. *The Rituals of Dinner: The Origins, Evolution, Eccentricities, and Meaning of Table Manners*. New York: Grove Weidenfeld, 1991.
Warshow, Robert. *The Immediate Experience: Movies, Comics, Theatre, and Other Aspects of Popular Culture*. Enlarged Edition. Cambridge: Harvard University Press, 1954/2001.
Wister, Owen. *The Virginian*. New York: Barnes and Noble Classics, 1902/2005 (B&N edition).

Cowboy Accommodations
Plotting the Hotel in Western Film and Television

MONICA MONTELONGO FLORES

Wyatt Earp (Kurt Russell): "What's your idea of heaven?"
Josephine (Dana Delany): "Room service" (*Tombstone*, 1993)

Audiences imagine the tired traveling cowboy's anticipation of riding into a town with a hotel, where he can take off his boots, his hat, and re-join the "civilized." So often, the Western hotel is a multifarious location in the genre's many cycles throughout its cinematic history. Yet, the hotel and its associated sites have been conventionalized as a major feature of the genre and made into a curator of the West, conjuring meanings and ambivalent feelings about the West as region and as myth. The performative functions of the hotel are often characterized in binary fashions and loaded with connotations, including those of domesticity, capitalism, criminality, sexuality, civilization, and progress associated with Westward expansion (Flores 306). In this way, the site has been treated as adaptable and as a necessity in the matrix of Western iconography. This essay demonstrates multiple ways in which hotels and their associated accommodations are established and reconfigured in the landscape of Western cinema and television,[1] and tracks examples of hotels in periods, plotting the trends in their treatments as they relate to the shifts in the national and cultural imagining of the West. Films and television programs discussed in the period between 1939 and 1969 produced images of the hotel that often became the icons of the Western, setting notions of domesticity, cultural contact, and urbanization of the West into the mainstream. The films and television programs discussed from 1969 to 1995 remark on the ways the hotel icon is dually asserted and challenged by an increase in representations of American counter-culture, a retreat from original Western narratives, a reliance on the successes of previous Westerns, and postmodern approaches entering the mainstream. Finally, the examples from cinema and television studied from 1996 to the present join the hotel iconography with themes concerning race, crime, violence, and sexuality. In this period, there is a re-establishing of the icon and a new reliance on the mutability of the hotel as a symbol.

First Come, First Serve: Making the Hotel into an Icon (1939–1969)

John Ford's *Stagecoach* (1939) cements the role of the hotel in the landscape of the Western within the first minutes of the film in which establishing shots of the "Tonto Hotel" are seen on the town's main street. Audiences are expected to recognize the hotel's name as a reference to the *Lone Ranger* series, which was begun in 1933 as a radio program. The film displays the hotel as a referential site viewers should track and locate as part of the Western landscape. While linking *Stagecoach* to the nationally recognized *Lone Ranger* series, "Tonto," the Lone Ranger's Indian sidekick, is also a reminder of the usurping of Indian land during the process of creating the U.S. In the Western, the hotel's symbolic function juxtaposes civilization and nature on the frontier. Due to this juxtaposition of symbols, the hotel in Western cinema and television has been treated in varied but measured ways as a "contact zone." Mary Louise Pratt describes contact zones as "social spaces where cultures meet, clash, and grapple with each other, often in contexts of highly asymmetrical relations of power, such as colonialism, slavery, or their aftermaths as they are lived out in many parts of the world today" (Pratt 33). In *Stagecoach*, the hotel is a weighty symbol of the complex negotiations of identity and space in the building of nationhood.

Another Ford film, *My Darling Clementine* (1946), offers the hotel as an urbanizing and civilizing space. In the film, the hotel is used as a watch post for the new town Marshal, Wyatt Earp. The image of Wyatt Earp (Henry Fonda) sitting on a chair, foot propped against a post, leaning back, becomes the most important and recognizable image of the film as it situates Wyatt at once in a position of authority and civility. By placing Earp on the porch of the hotel to perform his duties as marshal, the film connects urbanization with the policing of the West. At the hotel, the marshal decides who enters, exits, and stays in the city. When an unwelcome criminal attempts to stay in town, Earp is quick to turn him away, ordering him to get back on the stagecoach. Here, Earp's actions turn the hotel, often a criminally associated site, into a lawful entry point.

In *Stagecoach* and *My Darling Clementine*, the hotel is often cast as a site of segregation and social maintenance. In *High Noon* (1952), Helen Ramirez (Katy Jurado) has been relegated to the town's hotel, in part because of her racial and sexual inscriptions. Yet, from her hotel room, Helen attempts to subvert the town's racism by negotiating business meetings and ownership of property, and by saving the film's hero, Marshal Will Kane (Gary Cooper). Intervening in Kane's wife's ideologies, Helen's character uses the hotel to transform the West into a site in which she can engage in limited, but critical, agency.[2] In this way, *High Noon* comments on the coding of the hotel as a space of segregation in Western cinema.

In *The Rifleman* (1958–1963), the hotel is also a space in which segregation is evident. Katy Jurado from *High Noon* guest stars in the episode entitled "The Boarding House" (1959), written and directed by Sam Peckinpah. Jurado plays a young woman named Ana who was forced into a gambling ring as a teenage girl. Upon her arrival at North Fork, the show's hero, Lucas McCain (Chuck Connors), pays her a visit and tells her they don't want "her kind" in the town. Ana chastises Lucas for being judgmental and tells him with honesty and authority that she has changed her immoral ways and escaped the gambling ring. Lucas apologizes for his offense and the town supports Ana when the gang returns to try to ruin her now reputable boarding house. Most notably, *The Rifleman* revises the trope of the hotel seen in *High Noon* into a boarding house, a site historically deemed more acceptable for women and children traveling in the West. For viewers familiar with *High Noon*, the sexuality associated with Helen Ramirez in her hotel room is dissolved in the portrayal of Ana's ownership of a respectable boarding house, while the boarding house also separates Ana from the criminality that is often assigned to the hotel.

With this in mind, the hotel is represented in Western cinema and television as a microcosm of society, in which the problems of the outside world are not only represented by but also condensed into the building's spatial structure. Molly Berger frames the hotel site and subject as a "city within a city," explaining "the social relationships inside the hotel were extensions of prevailing patterns of urban life, replicating the anxieties, prejudices, and dangers found outside its walls" (133). The narrative functions of this microcosm vary from hotel to hotel in Westerns. These varied shiftings, recyclings, or reinventings of the hotel trope more closely construct an image of American relationships to the West.

For example, criminality and violence associated with the hotel are made apparent in an episode of *Bonanza* (1959–1973) entitled "A Good Night's Rest" (1965). When Ben Cartwright's (Lorne Greene) sons make it difficult for him to get to sleep, he decides to head into town to stay at the hotel. On his way to the hotel, Cartwright gets involved in a gunfight between two gamblers, Frank and Larry. Feeling that he should be given the opportunity to win his money back, Frank attacks Larry in the street, after Larry refuses to play any longer. When Larry is injured, he retreats to the hotel to be doctored and asks Ben to hold his winnings in case Frank returns and in the event of his death to give the winnings to his family. Eventually, Frank comes to the hotel to kill Larry and reclaim his money, but fails when Ben intervenes. The ease of access to a hotel room facilitates the criminal intentions of the gambler and the Eastern hotel manager who allows Frank to wait in Larry's room to attack him acts as an accessory to Frank's crime. The manager's lack of ethics is further made apparent when he attempts to blackmail Ben. The episode generates an image of the hotel as a societal microcosm, in which the corrupt control the entry and exit of people.

While the hotel in this episode of *Bonanza* is a criminal site, its association with sexuality is comic. In the episode, Mrs. Jenny Jenkins (Jean Willes), a local widow who has begun living in the hotel after the death of her husband, attempts to engage Ben in flirtation. Ben, exhausted, respectfully distances himself from Mrs. Jenkins throughout her flirtations. Besides Mrs. Jenkin's flirtations, a young married couple argues over the validity of their marriage ceremony, keeping Ben awake, and involving him as mediator. The episode is able to balance the meanings associated with the hotel, and because sexually implied occurrences happen at the hotel, Ben's station and morality is not questioned. Adopting this formula also fractures the weight of the site as a cultural contact zone into something less severe. The comic treatment of the hotel offers the television of the period a way to include sexual content in a measured and limited fashion.

McLintock! (1963), like *Bonanza*, combines the domestic and sexual connotations of the hotel for comedic purposes, appropriating the hotel as a site for domestic comedy. McLintock (John Wayne) deals with a heated divorce situation after his estranged wife, Cathy (Maureen O'Hara) leaves him because she suspects infidelity. The hotel codes Cathy as an inept domestic, who believes herself socially above the domesticity required in her marriage to McLintock. The film's conclusion amplifies the comedic and domestic themes as McClintock attempts to "domesticate" Cathy, tame her, and even humiliate her into submission, after he chases her out of her hotel room, into the town, and proceeds to spank her. A prescriptive for its era's management of marriage and divorce, *McLintock!* suggests that it is the woman's role to preserve her marriage. Because of negative associations with sexuality and the lack of the need for a female domestic, the hotel, as the site of Cathy's estrangement from her husband, leads the viewer to presume that she is responsible (and punishable) for her marriage's failure.

In an episode of *Rawhide* (1959–1966) entitled "The Gray Rock Hotel" (1965), the realities of domestic violence in marriages are thematically linked to the hotel. In the episode, many of the drovers fall ill with fever and look for shelter at an abandoned hotel in a ghost town. A fugitive woman, Lottie (Lola Albright), has been using the hotel as a hideout after she is accused of the murder of her husband. Lottie confesses to plotting against the men, causing them to become more ill, but also explains she has been abused by men her entire life. At the end of the episode, Lottie runs out into gunfire, unable to escape the traumas of her past, even after Lottie's victimization is revealed as the cause of her transgressions. Like *McClintock!*, the episode holds Lottie accountable for her domestic failures, represented by the empty domestic space—the abandoned hotel—as well as her death at the end.

A different sort of domestic tragedy drives the narrative in *True Grit* (1969). Fourteen-year-old Mattie Ross (Kim Darby) looks to hire a lawman to hunt down her father's killer. Once Mattie arrives in town, she lives in the boarding house which housed her father who was shot. In what is considered to be a reputable boarding house, Mattie's discomfort, brought on by poor food, lack of sleeping space, and inquiries by LaBoeuf (Glen Campbell), shows that the space suggests the symbolic fracturing of Mattie's own family as a result of her father's murder. *True Grit* adopts the domestic theme seen in the treatment of hotels in earlier Westerns in order to remind viewers of Mattie's reasons for violence are the loss of her father and a search for justice.

From Hotels to Motels: Transitions in the Western Landscape (1969–1995)

In the same year *True Grit* (1969) was released, *Easy Rider* (1969) was exhibited across the U.S. and received a largely favorable reception. *Easy Rider* reconfigures the Western to tell the story of two young drifters named Wyatt (Peter Fonda) and Billy (Dennis Hopper), approaching the West through the politics and style of 1960s counter-culture. As an acid Western, *Easy Rider* marks a turning point in the iconography of the hotel, where its legacy is questioned. In the film, Wyatt and Billy are refused service at a motel because of their "hippie" appearances and engagement in motorcycle culture. Through their referential names, the popular Western icons of Wyatt Earp and Billy the Kid are cast outside "civilized" spaces, a departure from Ford's Wyatt Earp on the hotel porch in *My Darling Clementine*. Except for this scene, the film excludes motels and the characters sleep mostly outdoors, which leads to Jack Nicholson's character, George Hanson, being murdered in the open. Nonetheless, *Easy Rider* begins to shift notions of the hotel trope. In the following year, *The Cheyenne Social Club* (1970), a comedy with a risqué twist, stories the iconography of the boarding house in the sex trade business. John O'Hanlan (Jimmy Stewart) wants to turn his recently inherited brothel into a reputable boarding house. However, due to a preexisting arrangement, the land and brothel can only remain in the ownership of O'Hanlan if the women working in the brothel are allowed to stay. Here, the brothel/boarding house is used comically, as a way to satirize the evolution of the hotel in the West. The treatment of the boarding house in the film questions the reputable hotels seen throughout the genre, via the sexually implied arrangements often represented in Western films dealing with the urbanization of the region.

The popular television series *Little House on the Prairie* (1974–1983) reminds the viewer of the dangers of urbanization and greed when the Ingalls move from their homestead to the city (Season 5, Episodes 1–4, 1978). Charles (Michael Landon) and Caroline Ingalls (Karen Grassle) are hired to work as the manager and cook at the Dakota hotel. The hotel and its owner, Mr. Standish, serve as antitheses of the Ingalls' respectable morals and principles established earlier in the series. Charles is consistently belittled by Standish, is refused advances in pay for his daughter's birthday present, and is refused the privilege of celebrating Independence Day because of to Standish's greed. Caroline is also belittled by the advances of Standish's saloon workers who come to eat in the hotel, where she cooks and serves the patrons. The episodes balance the "evils" of the hotel and hotel owner by having Standish's neighboring business, a saloon, burned down by his own son who carelessly lit a firework inside. The Ingalls only live and work in the hotel for four episodes before returning to their home in Walnut Grove.

The period following *Little House on the Prairie* capitalizes on audiences' familiarity with the Western through sequels, reunions, and remakes. Most often, this occurs in made-for-television films, such as *High Noon, Part II: The Return of Will Kane* and *Bonanza: The Next Generation* (1988). In particular, the treatment of the Tonto hotel in the 1986 made-for-television remake of *Stagecoach* displays the hotel as unsafe, suggesting that immorality has become normalized and that Lucy has no secure space for herself and her unborn child. In the 1936 original, Lucy Mallory (Louise Platt), the pregnant wife of a Calvary officer, sits with another reputable woman in front of the hotel, away from the saloon; Dallas, the prostitute exiled from the city; and the drunkard doctor. The hotel is a space that marks Lucy as exceptional and separates her from the bunch on the stagecoach. In the 1986 remake, Lucy (Mary Crosby) sits fanning herself in the hotel on a bench alone, with gambling and drinking occurring a few feet away. The remake suggests women are vulnerable in the Western hotel and, more so, that the hotel is less civilized than previously indicated in earlier films. Though not a particularly progressive film, *Stagecoach* (1986) revises the genre's previously protective treatment of women in its portrayal of the hotel.

While often not categorized as a Western, *Twin Peaks* unites film noir and Western conventions (a combination established by *High Noon*) into a format for serial television. Co-creators David Lynch and Mark Frost relocate the typified Western location and landscape to the Northwestern U.S.-Canada border, reuse the conventionalized tropes of the sheriff and Indian tracker, and merge urban and rural settings in the series. The hotel is reimagined as a high-end resort, and its lodge-style architecture brings the natural setting indoors. What is critical in *Twin Peaks'* recasting of the hotel is that the site signifies a supernatural doorway, fusing the Western's gateway to civilization with the horror genre's place for paranormal activities. This postmodern approach encourages viewers to compare the site's treatment within and without the Western genre. The series also codes the space as being sexual via its references to Marlon Brando's *One-Eyed Jacks*, the name given to the brothel owned by the hotel's proprietor, Ben Horne (Richard Beymer).[3]

Reflecting the 1990s desire for revisionist Westerns as well as the Neo-Western genre of the 2000s, *Twin Peaks* provides a new and formative transmission of Western images and narratives to audiences. *Tombstone* (1993), on the other hand, looks at the Western again with hopeful eyes, conventional characters, and clearly aligns the hotel's iconography with civility. When Wyatt Earp (Kurt Russell), his brothers, and their wives enter Tombstone looking for a room at the hotel, they are quickly offered three cottages. The Earps are recognized as proper members of society, whereas the hotel residents are improper and marginal. Notably, Doc Holliday (Val Kilmer) and his immigrant prostitute girlfriend live in the hotel, as they were not deemed fit for cottages. Similarly, *Maverick* (1994), a remake of the popular 1950s–1960s television series, simplifies the living space of the hotel by combining it with the saloon. When gambler/con-artist Bret Maverick (Mel Gibson) arrives into town, his station immediately is understood as criminal via his rooming at the saloon/hotel. Both *Maverick* and *Tombstone* narrate a simplified West through these strict social prescriptions assigned to the hotel, recalling the earliest Western conventions. Ultimately, this sort of treatment of the hotel and the West avoids the social commentary that the following era constructs in regards to race and revision.

Race-ing West: Old and New Themes Revisited (1996–Present)

In the mid–1990s, the rhetoric of multiculturalism refocuses the Western. Robert Rodriguez's *From Dusk Till Dawn* (1996) is a Western driven into new territories, crossing borders, and locating it within postmodern traditions. Written by Quentin Tarantino (who successfully brought postmodernism to a mass audience in *Pulp Fiction* [1994]), this film merges crime, horror, and Western genres, treating the motel as a criminal site. The criminals are white, the mestiza/os are monsters, and audiences identify with the outlaw, Seth (George Clooney) as a result of the hyper-sexualized and monstrous Mexicana/o characters. Yet, the film also shows that monsters exist outside the supernatural. For example, Seth and his brother Richie (Quentin Tarantino) take a woman hostage after a robbery. Seth leaves Richie to watch over the hostage and upon his return, Seth discovers the woman raped and beaten to death by Richie, who is a sexual predator. This representation of the motel as a site linked with sexual criminality is further evidenced when the brothers meet a family at another motel and kidnap them in order to use their RV to cross the border into Mexico. In the motel room, the father (Harvey Keitel) and his adopted Korean son, Scott (Ernest Liu), are wrongly perceived as being sexually involved by Seth and Richie (who assume Scott is a child prostitute) during their confrontation. When the daughter (Juliette Lewis) walks in the room, Richie immediately fantasizes about her sexually. The sexuality and criminality associated with the hotel in films such as *The Cheyenne Social Club* are treated with more severity and violence in *From Dusk Till Dawn*, characterizing the hotel as a site in which degradation escalates and intensifies.

Racial subjects and topics become more prominent during this period. *Shanghai Noon* (2000), for example, treats the hotel as a comedic prop in the teaming of Roy O'Bannon (Owen Wilson) and Chon Wang (Jackie Chan). In the film, Roy and Chon bond over a Chinese drinking game played while soaking in two adjacent bath tubs. The hotel is used as a site where the white cowboy and the Chinese imperial guard are able to create camaraderie in a comedic manner, despite their racial and cultural differences. Yet, the satirical treatment of the Western questions the hotel's impact as a "bonding space," suggesting the friendship characterized is a parody of the unlikely pairings seen in early Westerns.[4]

Homosexuality is also linked to the motel in two Westerns released in 2005. *Brokeback Mountain* (2005) and *The Three Burials of Melquiades Estrada* (2005) comment on how the motel space is sexually charged via relationships between men. While *Brokeback Mountain* offers the motel as a site for Ennis (Heath Ledger) and Jack (Jake Gyllenhaal) to hide their relationship, a trope typical in films dealing with forbidden romance, *The Three Burials of Melquiades Estrada* handles the motel's sexual connotations, homosexuality, and race in more complicated terms. Pete (Tommy Lee Jones) and Melquiades (Julio Cedillo) take two women, one working as a prostitute and the other in an unhappy marriage, to a local motel where the couples check into separate rooms. However, no sexual encounter occurs between Melquiades and Lou Ann (January Jones) as he is clearly uncomfortable with the woman, in part because he speaks only Spanish and she speaks only English. This scene in the motel leads the viewer to conclude Melquiades and Pete's relationship has a veiled romantic undertone, specifically when Pete becomes unstable after Melquiades' murder. The motel positions Melquiades to be "outed" by his lack of desire for Lou Ann. Further, Melquiades' racial difference is magnified when he is alone with Lou Ann, a white woman, in the motel. The film uses the motel as a site where the racial and sexual are combined and juxtaposed to the sexually criminal, as prostitution occurs in the room next door.

Criminality without sexual implications is a common theme in *No Country for Old Men* (2007). This film vacillates in its treatment of hotels and motels, where the characters are either hunted or hunting, reinforcing the dichotomy of symbols in the Western landscape. After Llewelyn (Josh Brolin) comes across cartel money at failed shoot out, he is forced to go on the run in order to avoid being captured by both the police and cartel. Llewelyn hides in several motels, chased by a hitman named Chigurh (Javier Bardem). Significantly, Llewelyn uses the layout of the motel to hide his money from Chigurh, relying on its adjoining rooms to escape. Llewelyn appropriates the architecture of the building to avoid capture and remain hidden.

Similarly, *Breaking Bad* (2008–2013) locates the motel outside sexual criminality by visually linking it with a hospital, claiming "illness" and criminality are equally corrupting in the narrative. Walter White (Bryan Cranston), a high school chemistry teacher, cooks meth in order to pay his hospital bills and save money for his family after his death. During a hospital stay, he sees a painting of a family waving goodbye to a man as he rows out to sea. Walter sees the same painting in a motel where he is meeting hitmen to set up the murder of several witnesses. The double usage of the image narrates the motel as a place for the "sick," commenting on the thematic treatment of the site as criminal, immoral, and even mentally unstable. The idea of mental instability reminds viewers of films which embedded the image of motels into popular culture, such as Alfred Hitchcock's *Psycho* (1960).

One television series, however, disputes the necessity of stability and place in the Western in its literal and figurative treatment of the motel. *Supernatural* (2005–) deals with the lives of two brothers, Sam (Jared Padalecki) and Dean Winchester (Jensen Ackles), who are hunters of all things supernaturally evil. Nomadic and without a home, the brothers are infused with the heroics assigned to cowboys of early Westerns. The series offers a plethora of motels to explore, however one episode stands out in its management of the iconic site.[5] In "Hammer of the Gods"(Season 5, Episode 19, 2010), Sam and Dean come across a four star hotel on a deserted highway called "The Elysian Fields," a meeting place for non–Western gods including, Kali, Mercury, Odin, and Ganesh. These gods use the hotel to lure and trap the brothers when they are caught in a heavy rain storm. Then, they use the Winchesters to lure the Judeo-Christian Lucifer to the hotel, a long-time rival of the gods and the brothers. The episode treats the hotel much differently from the previous motels, which are designed as being low-budget and tacky. The Elysian

Fields Hotel is grand, bright, and deluxe, placing the non–Western gods in a space of luxury, while at the same time assigning them to a site associated with temporary living, as well as criminal and sexual activity. More specifically, the episode recounts the earlier themes of hotel management as scheming and untrustworthy. Mercury, who plays the role of the hotel lobby clerk, betrays the other gods by contacting Lucifer. Mercury does this because he believes they might be able to "talk" instead of fight. Lucifer kills him and the other gods, with the exception of Kali, coding Mercury's hopes of a peaceful intervention as a betrayal. The treatment of the motel lobby clerk is reimagined, as Mercury is well-meaning, yet naïve about the true nature of the violence allowed to enter the hotel.

Conclusion

The examples of Western film and television discussed in this essay illustrate the major trends, breaks in conventions, and recasting of the hotel (and its associated sites) plotted throughout the periods. While a focus on the domestic and civilizing notion of the hotel dominated in the years between 1939 and 1969, varying views of sexuality and criminal intent were associated with the hotel as well, though often treated in comic ways. Western cinema and television in the period between 1969 and 1995 challenged the images of the hotel as a gatekeeping system by questioning its authority and evolution. Yet, in the later years of this period, romanticized notions of the West infiltrated the challenging of these images. The current period, beginning in 1996, demonstrated an increased awareness of multicultural rhetoric, discussions of race, sexuality, and postmodern treatments of the hotel. This treatment of the hotel site, its symbolic meanings, and the influence of the hotel's iconography in Western cinema and television reveal attempts over decades to recast the hotel's figurative conventions in order to produce more complex narratives, images, and associations in the landscape of the Western.

Notes

1. This includes boarding houses and motels.
2. For a more detailed reading of the hotel in *High Noon,* please refer to my article, "Helen's Hotel Room: The West, the Hotel, and the Mexican Female Body as Decolonial Sites in *High Noon*" in *Quarterly Review of Film and Video.*
3. Marlon Brando's *One-Eyed Jacks* (1961) comments on the usage of the hotel in Western cinema as well. The conventionalized hotel is nearly absent from the film. Instead, Brando's character, Rio, and his gang hold up in a beach front Chinese-owned lodging facility. The film recasts the typical hotel and main street imagery by emphasizing the location, "West," through the ocean and beach, and comments on the role of Chinese immigrants in the landscapes of the West. The film presses the iconography of the West so far that they end up in the "East."
4. The Lone Ranger and Tonto would be an example of such a pairing.

5. The motel rooms are so popular in the series that entire fansites are dedicated specifically to the motel settings, categorizing and documenting the themes in each episode.

Filmography

Bonanza. NBC, 1959–1973.
Bonanza: The Next Generation. Dir. William F. Claxton. CBS. 23 March 1988.
Breaking Bad. AMC, 2008–2013.
Brokeback Mountain. Dir. Ang Lee. Universal Studios, 2005.
The Cheyenne Social Club. Dir. Gene Kelly. National General Pictures, 1970.
Easy Rider. Dir. Dennis Hopper. Columbia Pictures, 1969.
From Dusk Till Dawn. Dir. Robert Rodriguez. Miramax Films, 1996.
High Noon, Part II: The Return of Will Kane. Dir. Jerry Jameson. Charles Fries Productions and Orion Television, 1980.
Little House on the Prairie. NBC, 1974–1983.
Maverick. Dir. Richard Donner. Warner Bros, 1994.
McLintock! Dir. Andrew V. McLaglen. United Artists, 1963.
My Darling Clementine. Dir. John Ford. Twentieth Century-Fox, 1946.
No Country for Old Men. Dir. Joel Coen and Ethan Coen. Paramount Pictures, 2007.
One-Eyed Jacks. Dir. Marlon Brando. Paramount Pictures, 1961.
Psycho. Dir. Alfred Hitchcock. Paramount Pictures, 1960.
Pulp Fiction. Dir. Quentin Tarantino. Miramax Films, 1994.
Rawhide. CBS, 1959–1966.
The Rifleman. ABC, 1958–1963.
Shanghai Noon. Dir. Tom Dey. Touchstone Pictures, 2000.
Stagecoach. Dir. John Ford. United Artists, 1939.
Stagecoach. Dir. Ted Post. Heritage Entertainment Inc., Plantation Productions, Raymond Katz Production, 1986.
Supernatural. CW, 2005–.
The Three Burials of Melquiades Estrada. Dir. Tommy Lee Jones. Sony Pictures Classics, 2005.
Tombstone. Dir. George P. Cosmatos. Hollywood Pictures, 1993.
True Grit. Dir. Henry Hathaway. Paramount Pictures, 1969.
Twin Peaks. ABC, 1990–1991.

Works Cited

Berger, Molly W. *Hotel Dreams: Luxury, Technology, and Urban Ambition in America, 1829–1929*. Baltimore: Johns Hopkins University Press, 2011.
Flores, Monica Montelongo. "Helen's Hotel Room: The West, the Hotel, and the Mexican Female Body as Decolonial Sites in *High Noon*" *Quarterly Review of Film and Video*. January 2015 (Vol. 32, No. 4), 301–313.
Pratt, Mary Louise. "Arts of the Contact Zone." *Profession 91* (1991): 33–40.

When Worlds Collide
Town and Country, Mise-en-Scène in Have Gun, Will Travel

ROBERT E. MEYER

Among the more complex examples of its genre, *Have Gun, Will Travel* ran from 1957 to 1963, a time when the Western ruled American television. From its disturbing pre-credit sequence, through the scenes at the Hotel Carlton in San Francisco, to the closing shot of the lone rider moving off into a hostile environment, the show found much of its meaning in the visual representation of the two worlds in which Paladin (Richard Boone), the show's hired-gun hero, functioned so effectively. The result was, as Gaylyn Studlar has put it, "one of the most morally ambiguous, tonally complex, and sexually sophisticated adult Westerns of the era" (14). The mise-en-scène of this program—the costumes, the locations, the interiors, even the physical characteristics of its star—all contribute to a rich texture expressive of the intricacies of Paladin's position in the multi-faceted world of the Old West. The characterization of Paladin and the worlds that he inhabits, even sculpts, convey a depth of meaning that is at the heart of the show's value and lasting significance.

To begin, Paladin is unlike most Western heroes in the variety of his wardrobe. The Lone Ranger changed clothes, but always to a disguise, assuming a temporary identity to help him outwit the bad guys. A more apt comparison to Paladin can be found in *Zorro*, the Disney-produced Western set in Spanish California, loosely based on the novels of Johnston McCulley. In these stories, the hero has a dual identity. By day, he is mild-mannered Don Diego de la Vega (Guy Williams), a timid fop who avoids violence to such a degree that his father thinks him dishonorable. Don Diego wears the costume of privilege: short jacket with elaborate brocade, tight pants, floppy bow tie. In fact, he probably reminded viewers of a stylish matador, but without the courage. By night Don Diego becomes Zorro, who dresses—like Paladin—all in black, a color that marks both characters as suspect in the eyes of many. The difference, of course, is that the purpose of Zorro's costume—besides making it difficult to see him in the dark—is to disguise his "true" identity, enabling him to engage in subversive activities that Don Diego (the privileged aristocrat) would neither pursue nor sanction. His mask allows him to play a role completely at odds with the one linked to his everyday (that is, fancy) clothes. The two sides of his character are meant to be kept completely separate.

For Paladin, the change in costume primarily represents a change in milieu—only his focus is altered, never his identity. When in San Francisco, Paladin dresses like a gentleman—even a dandy—whose tastes run to the luxurious, and who is rarely engaged in earning the money that makes his exorbitant lifestyle possible. His most formal outfit is a tuxedo with ruffled shirt, bow tie, top hat, black cape with silk lining and, to complete the ensemble, a cane—probably gold-tipped, but in black and white it's impossible to tell for sure. In this get-up, Paladin may call to mind Spencer Tracy in the 1941 version of *Dr. Jekyll and Mr. Hyde,* perhaps an unintended but strangely appropriate resemblance. In any event, when dressed in his tux, Paladin is usually on his way home from the opera, or on the way there, although in the latter case he rarely makes it out of the lobby before Hey Boy (Kam Tong)—a member of the hotel staff whose duties are apparently limited to attending to Paladin's needs—brings him a telegram with a job offer. On more casual occasions, Paladin appears in one of a variety of suits that dial down the formality. A knee-length frock coat (usually with pinstripes and a black velvet collar in the first few seasons), a ruffled shirt with obstreperous cuffs, and a satin bow tie constitute a sort of everyday costume. Thus attired, he may be found in the lobby of the Hotel Carlton, peering intently at a chessboard, or composing a note at the little writing desk provided by the hotel management for its guests' convenience. Paladin's stylish appearance in his everyday suit invariably catches the eyes of the elegant women passing through the hotel lobby, and more than one episode begins with a brief vignette of sexual frustration, as our hero makes eye contact with a lovely lady only to be derailed by Hey Boy before things can develop. A more intense variation on this trope has Paladin enthusiastically occupied with a lady whose palpable delight with him is short-circuited by the inevitable interruption. In one such incident (Season 4, Episode 29 "The Long Weekend") Paladin and his potential consort are ensconced on a loveseat in the lobby of the Carlton, enjoying the use of a stereoscope (an early form of a device better known to later generations by the brand-name "Viewmaster"). The hilarity of their response to this visual gimmick stands in contrast to the dour faces of the two representatives of a silver-mining town who are waiting for the right moment to attempt to engage Paladin's services.

The Paladin of the Hotel Carlton is essentially a man of leisure with expensive tastes. In fact, he comes across as "a hero with a suspicious amount charm and education, fastidiousness and verbal finesse" (Studlar 39). Paladin is not the strong, silent type. His lifestyle includes ample time for relaxation and his clothes reflect this. In his room, he is often seen in an elegant satin dressing gown—usually accompanied by the ubiquitous ruffled shirt but now with the neck open and the bow tie dispensed with, an outfit that bears more than a passing resemblance to the one displayed in many contexts by Hugh Hefner, the founder of *Playboy* magazine who was engaged in "the cultural construction of a new masculine model" (Mock 93), complete with erotic overtones. Paladin, this knight without armor, occasionally even strips down to his shirtsleeves, as in an episode (Season 5, Episode 1 "The Vigil") that opens with a shot of Paladin in the Carlton's multi-purpose parlor—*sans* jacket but *avec* satin vest and watch-chain—kissing a dark-haired beauty whose long black gloves and off-the-shoulder gown give her the air of the temptress. The striking image of her playfully accepting the cigar Paladin places between her teeth is the last we see of her. Thus Paladin brings to life the fantasies promulgated by *Playboy*, which debuted in 1953, whose readers imagine a world in which they have the opportunity "to meet, and be done with, a new woman monthly" (Mock 99).

The opening of "A Knight to Remember" (Season 5, Episode 13) is a rare scene in which Paladin appears in San Francisco dressed in black—albeit not in his familiar range outfit. Here he wears a black turtleneck, black pants and leather gauntlets as he finishes a fencing duel with a faceless man who quickly exits after admitting defeat (*"Touché!"*). The lone spectator to this action—a woman in a fashionable dress seated at a ringside table for a better view—lures Paladin by asking, "Now that you've won me, Paladin, what do you intend to do with me?" Paladin's response ("Well, I have been giving that some medieval thought") is one of many sexually suggestive lines of dialog in the series. When Paladin makes his move, their kiss is interrupted by Hey Boy's insistence that Paladin read a telegram—the latest offer of employment. An interesting parallel may be drawn here—and elsewhere—between Paladin and James Bond, the playboy hero of the long-running series of steamy espionage films (based on novels that were popular in the 50s and 60s). Like Paladin, Bond's wardrobe is varied and elegant (sometimes including a black turtleneck) and—again, like Paladin—his sexual encounters are frequently interrupted by duty or danger. On the other hand, Bond is always played by a handsome actor, such as Roger Moore, who, coincidentally played one of the gambling eponymous brothers on *Maverick*.

Of course the most recognizable outfit in Paladin's wardrobe is his all-black range suit, in which he appears—most often in silhouette—in the pre-credit sequence of each episode. In the first two episodes (and a few others from Season 1) Paladin's "on-the-job" attire is remarkable for its hint of formality: his black shirt is buttoned to the Adam's apple, and a white satin necktie hangs to mid-chest. His hair also seems a bit too well tended for the character as he would develop—a nattily-coiffed Paladin was soon deemed incongruous with the rough-and-ready demands of his gunfighter persona. After the first few episodes, the necktie would disappear, the collar would be left open (in later seasons the button-down black shirt was replaced by an open-neck pullover shirt, still black, of course), and the hair would be stylishly unkempt beneath the black hat. In 1959, Richard Boone appeared on the game show *What's My Line* as a "mystery challenger" in this version of his range outfit (plugging not his television program but rather his appearance on Broadway as Abraham Lincoln in *The Rivalry*). The sight of Boone, in character as Paladin, striding across the stage of the New York studio where the program was taped must have caused a ripple of nervous excitement in the audience. He appeared on the show again in 1963, after *Have Gun, Will Travel* had ended its run, this time in a conventional 1960s business suit, plugging *The Richard Boone Show*, sporting no facial hair (and referring to his role as Paladin as a "black-shirt lead").

In two episodes of *Have Gun, Will Travel*, characters other than Paladin misappropriate his trademark black duds, albeit temporarily and, ultimately to their cost. In one (Season 2, Episode 28 "Maggie O'Bannion") he is bushwhacked and deprived of his clothes, which are later are seen on one of the bushwhackers who unwisely flaunts his bounty. In that episode, Paladin appears of necessity dressed as a ranch-hand, wearing what seems to be a remarkably well-tailored denim jacket and jeans ensemble, and subsequently dazzles Maggie O'Bannion (Marion Marshall), the owner of the ranch, to the point that she initiates a passionate kiss (shown in close-up with a fade to black, suggestive of a sexual interlude). In "Cage at McNaab" (Season 6, Episode 23) a more perilous exchange occurs when Paladin, due to a convincing ruse by a desperate wife (Jaqueline Scott), is tricked into a prison cell when the real criminal—the woman's husband (Christopher Dark)—steals his clothes and leaves Paladin to face the hangman. For much of the rest of the episode—including a shot in which Paladin is shown dressed in prison rags, shaking the bars of his prison door and roaring in righteous outrage—Paladin is deprived not only of his trademark togs but of the power they presumably endow.

After the fact, it seems obvious that Richard Boone was born—or made—to play Paladin. No pretty boy (especially when compared to other western heroes like James Garner or Steve McQueen), not particularly handsome, not even in the rugged sense (think Hugh O'Brian or James Arness), Boone exuded an appeal that transcended beauty. Here was a man whose appearance reflected a singularly dominant personality: cleft chin, sparkling white teeth, deeply lined and pock-marked face, over-sized nose over a rakish moustache and a physique that seemed both brutal (Richard Boone was at one time a boxer) and graceful (he also studied dance with Martha Graham). The brutal side of Boone's physique was emphasized in Paladin's "out-of-my-way" walk—leaning slightly forward, powerful shoulders hunched, long but measured strides, each step an emphatic statement of purpose. Never was this aspect of Paladin's persona more fully emphasized than in "The Black Bull" (Season 6, Episode 31, directed by William Conrad, the voice of Matt Dillon when *Gunsmoke* was a radio program). In the climax of this episode, which takes place in Mexico, Paladin faces off in mortal combat with Baron Nino Ybarra (Carlos Romero)—a retired matador driven mad by jealousy over his wife's (Faith Domergue) past relationship with Paladin—set in a bull-ring with Paladin cast in the role of the bull. Here Paladin is dressed in an ornate variation on his usual black working kit, a high-necked black shirt with puffy sleeves and a jewel-encrusted belt. Once in the ring, he lunges furiously at his mounted tormentor, crashing into the *burladero* (eventually reducing this protective wall to splinters), and is repeatedly pounded to the ground before finally succeeding, not through his wits but through sheer force of will and brute strength, in disarming the Baron and killing him.

And then, of course, there's the moustache. Unlike most Western heroes of the 50s and 60s, Paladin sported some facial hair. And not just any facial hair—a neatly trimmed moustache that lilted up at the ends in a stylish display of masculine bravado. Josh Randle (Steve McQueen), Rowdy Yates (Clint Eastwood), Matt Dillon (James Arness), Wyatt Earp (Hugh O'Brian)—all were clean-shaven. There was a moustache on *Gunsmoke* of course, but it was on the face of Doc (Milburn Stone), and, flecked with gray, it showed the wearer's age rather than his power as a man of action. There was facial hair on *Wagon Train* too, but again Ward Bond's moustache gave him a grandfatherly air, in contrast to the sexy younger man in the cast, the clean-shaven Robert Horton as Flint McCullogh.

Paladin's moustache contributed to the multi-faceted nature of his character. On more than one occasion, a character remarks on his resemblance to a fanciful image of Satan. In the last episode of Season 2 ("Brimstone"), Paladin steps up to an open-air bar in a rough mining town only to see that among the libations available is a bottle of Diablo Tequila, the label of which is adorned with a pencil-sketch image of a man sporting horns and a moustache—the type who would drink, or perhaps serve this brand of tequila—shown in extreme close-up and bearing a striking resemblance to Paladin himself. The payoff of this little joke occurs in the episode's climax when Paladin (employing his knowledge of chemistry) throws a sulfur bomb over his shoulder releasing a cloud of smoke—hence the brimstone connection—behind which he mysteriously disappears. In the aforementioned episode

"The Vigil," the client—a woman named Adella Forsyth (played by Mary Fickett, known to fans of the long-running soap opera *All My Children* for her role as Ruth Martin)—pulls out Paladin's business card with a scathing remark: "I've seen it [the card] tacked in my brother's study—a reminder of Satan's physical presence among us." Paladin, drunk after a night of card playing and debauchery, blinks in bemused incomprehension. Boone's resemblance to (someone's idea of) Satan was used to advantage in other contexts, such as the 1967 film *Hombre* in which Boone's character responds to the timid approach of a young woman (Margaret Blye) with a rough embrace and a lusty full-mouth kiss. When she flees, chastened and dismayed, he laughs uproariously, head back, teeth flashing, reveling in his wickedness.

With regard to set design, the aesthetic intentions of *Have Gun, Will Travel* are apparent from the opening post-credit shot of Episode 1 ("Three Bells to Perdido"), which begins with a close-up of a street sign informing us that we are on "Pacific St." The presence of a street sign suggests an urban setting while the name of the street places us in the far West—or beyond. The camera pulls back and down to reveal a shop-window adorned with a message touting "Fresh Sea Food" and "Bar." This refers to something that is rarely present in Westerns (seafood) and something that is almost never absent (saloons, called "bars" in the city). As the shot continues its downward arc, a helmeted police officer (who would seem more at home in London or New York) comes briefly into view before a pair of horses (a Western image) hitched to a stately carriage passes by, driven by a liveried cabman. Paladin's world is a place where East meets West in multiple senses.

From then on, the mantle of citified refinement is carried largely by—or in—the Hotel Carlton. Most episodes—though by no means all—open with one of two stock exterior shots of the Hotel—one facing San Francisco Bay (sometimes lit for day, sometimes for night) and one facing the hills of the city (again, one daytime scene and one at night, although on at least one occasion there is the suggestion of dawn). This initial shot then dissolves to a setting within the hotel where action serving as a diversion from—or a springboard to—the main plot of the episode occurs. Most frequently these prologue sequences take place on the hotel's first floor, the layout of which is revealed to viewers bit by bit over the course of the series.

The architecture of the lobby establishes the elegance of the Carlton. Paladin—and other characters and countless extras—enter by passing a carved-wood grandfather clock in the hallway that leads to a short, wide flight of carpeted stairs, providing access to the lobby. The reception desk—to the right of these stairs, as seen by viewers—boasts marble paneling under a solid wood counter, behind which the bored clerk stands guard over a honeycomb of cubby holes—no doubt used to store the guests' keys and to collect their correspondence. A set of dual staircases with banisters supported by marble paneling leads to the upper floors and the guest rooms. A recessed landing where the two staircases meet houses a bronze statue of a—partially nude—female figure, and the stairs display bronze carpet-rods, which occasionally appear in extreme close-up if the opening includes the classic shot of walking feet belonging to an as-yet-unknown character making an entrance. Lush ferns or other plants are sometimes seen atop the pedestals at the landing, completing the effect of a well-tended oasis of civilization.

The main area of the lobby is furnished with several seating areas and the small wooden writing desk, where Paladin is often found working on his correspondence or, more likely, reading one of the many newspapers from all over the West that bring him news of opportunities for profitable exploits. A wide double door permits access to the parlor, in which Paladin does some of his entertaining. It is here, for example (Season 2, Episode 36 "The Fifth Man") that Paladin, dressed in his smart everyday suit, demonstrates his knowledge of whiskey in a blind taste-test by correctly identifying four separate brands, in one case down to the address of the distillery ("26th and Breckinridge" in Louisville). The Carlton's elegantly furnished dining room is just off the lobby, accessed by a pair of French doors with half curtains that afford some measure of privacy for the diners. Service is provided by waiters in black tie and tails—and on one occasion by Hey Boy in his finest black vest, satin smock and trousers—who carry wine in crystal decanters on silver platters to be placed gently on white tablecloths.

Paladin's suite at the Carlton, the details of which are also presented piecemeal over many episodes—is a remarkable bit of set design. Curtains are everywhere: covering windows, framing doorways, embrasures and the bookcases that are full of the literature and philosophy that provide Paladin with his profound and amusing quotations. A bust of Shakespeare has pride of place upon a pedestal next to a bookcase and betokens its owner's sophistication and erudition, qualities that are on display in other ways in almost every episode. A surprisingly large miniature cannon (Paladin's is a world of contradictions) adorns the mantel beneath what appears to be a reproduction of "Man with a Golden Helmet," a painting long attributed to Rembrandt but now believed to be the work of an unknown artist. No doubt Paladin could tell us the true provenance of both the original and his reproduction. An expansive carved-oak desk sits in front of the large windows that presumably allow a view of the street. A small rotating world globe is positioned on the ledge of the bay window. The suite is Paladin's sanctum sanctorum, where he entertains women and where men who enter with rude intent are usually quickly reduced to sputtering impotence—or unconsciousness.

However, Paladin would not be Paladin if he never sallied forth from San Francisco. The main action in most episodes takes place in the wild part of the West, depicted with a combination of rich variety and banal repetition.

Long shots of magnificent vistas—often created on location in northern California or Oregon—serve to establish the setting of many episodes. Some dispense with the San Francisco prologue, showing our hero from the outset as an archetypal figure, the lone horseman facing the menacing isolation of the mythic western environment: Paladin pausing on an exposed ridgeline, snow-capped mountains in the background; Paladin riding up to offer assistance to a woman grieving over a dead mule on the desert floor; Paladin entering town on horseback, leaning forward against a torrential downpour. The isolation of the world of the West is further emphasized by the remote cabins, farmhouses and ranches visited by Paladin.

And then of course, there are the towns. The same (surprisingly wide) main street is used in multiple episodes, sometimes teeming with western activity, sometimes dressed as a ghost town with the requisite tumbleweed, boarded up doorways and signs hanging askew. Once, the main street of a town is the scene of a baseball game (Season 4, Episode 4 "Out at the Old Ball Park"). Paladin serves as the umpire—his all-black outfit taking on new significance—positioning himself behind the pitcher (as was the custom in nineteenth-century baseball) to make his rulings. The game is a confusion of violent hijinks with Paladin bellowing "safe," "out" or "take your base" surrounded by protesting players and onlookers and sometimes crawling among the tangle of arms and legs around home plate as he tries to determine the correct call. The most amusing play—this is, after all one of the humorous episodes that occasionally crop up in the *Have Gun, Will Travel* oeuvre—occurs when a batter hits a long drive which a fielder catches while smashing through the display window of "Peggy's Shoppe" to the protestations of portly Peggy (a milliner, no doubt, played by Peggy Rea who appears in other episodes as Maggie the Irish charlady at the Carlton) and to the delight of the spectating "saloon girls" who applaud their approval from the steps of the "Last Chance" saloon.

Most of the time, however, the towns of the Old West are depicted in economical—that is to say, repetitive—images. Each town has a saloon, with a swinging half-door on one side, the bar on the other, manned by a bartender in gartered long sleeves. In some of these saloons, hunting trophies—deerheads, antlers, bearskins—adorn the walls as a sign of a more remote setting. Most towns have a hotel—where Paladin finds accommodations—with a predictable floor plan: reception desk to the right, staircase to the rear. The upper floor hallway is usually the same set as that used for the Hotel Carlton, suitably dressed down.

In these western towns are found offices—sometimes that of the sheriff, lawyer, or doctor, and occasionally that of the stagecoach line—where the furnishings constitute a weak echo of the lavish sophistication of Paladin's life in San Francisco. The ubiquitous Franklin stove, the oil lamps with simple reflectors, the dusty file cabinets beneath rifle racks, the occasional bucolic scene depicted in a roughly framed painting—all make repeated appearances in the rooms in which Paladin must negotiate his uncompromising terms.

Paladin's encounters with women are an important part of his development as a character, and as with most aspects of the series, women are shown in a variety of guises. The genteel women that are the object of Paladin's attentions in San Francisco are always elegantly attired. Low-cut gowns, button-up collars with lace trim, puffed sleeves, elbow-length gloves, pendant earrings, bejeweled necklaces, feathered *chapeaux*—all these and more are on display in the lobby of the Hotel Carlton (and occasionally in Paladin's suite).

One of the most interesting women characters to appear in *Have Gun, Will Travel*—at least to Paladin—is Dr. Phyllis Thackeray, played by June Lockhart (soon to be of *Lassie* fame). The casting of this quintessential domestic figure of the 50s and 60s, who is both motherly and girlish in appearance, as the only female character to capture Paladin's heart, is notable, as is her attire, which is generally at odds with her status as physician. When we first meet her, Dr. Thackeray is dressed in a smart cowgirl outfit: poodle skirt (she's astride a horse on her way to treat a sick child), vest and blouse with leather gauntlets and a cowboy hat complete with chinstrap. Later she appears in a fetching faux-pinafore with buttons down the front and a cute little bow tie—a surprisingly girlish outfit for such a strong professional woman in a man's world. At the end of the episode, Paladin asks Dr. Thackeray to join him on his journey back to San Francisco. In an acknowledgment of the incompatibility of the rugged life of the uncivilized West and Paladin's refined existence at home, she refuses, citing "too many velvet settees there." Apparently only Paladin is comfortable in both worlds.

The saloon girl figures prominently in the portrait of the West offered by *Have Gun, Will Travel*, usually in a strapless, off-the-shoulder low-cut satin dress, necklace (sometimes in the form of a collar), spit curls, and occasionally a feather in the hair. These women can often be dismissed as caricatures, or cheap copies of Marlene Dietrich (or Amanda Blake), but occasionally the writers and directors build interesting episodes around them. One example is "Odds for Big Red" (Season 5, Episode 4, directed by Richard Donner and written by Betty Andrews), in which the title character is the proprietress of a rough saloon who has been accidentally shot (not by Paladin of course, but by his opponent in a "fair fight"). Big Red (Hope Holliday) must undergo surgery, performed by a gambler (Richard Ney) pressed into service by Paladin, who serves as a combination nurse and anesthesiologist during the operation. A low-angle shot shows the "doctor" grimacing under the strain of the situation, with Paladin nearby, whiskey bottle in hand, his black hat tilted back to show a brow furrowed with confident concern.

The Madonna and the whore motif is played out in "Be Not Forgetful of Strangers" (Season 6, Episode 15, directed by Richard Boone, one of 28 episodes he directed). In this episode, Paladin enlists saloon girl "Annie" (Pat Newby) to help when a young woman traveling with her husband goes into labor on Christmas Eve. Annie and Paladin act as a pair of guardian angels who help bring new life into the hard-scrabble world of the West. Paladin guards the door while Annie acts as midwife in a successful delivery which culminates in a tableau with the recumbent new mother receiving the good wishes and humble gifts of the saloonkeeper and drunken revelers, as Paladin looks on approvingly, a black-clad figure dominating the scene from the background.

For all its rugged masculinity—or perhaps because of it—*Have Gun, Will Travel* appeals to a sense of fantasy in its viewers, a fantasy born of a desire to combine all admirable qualities in a single individual. Paladin has impeccable manners whether in San Francisco or on the job. He dresses well—again, as appropriate to the context—and he demonstrates deep knowledge in almost every conceivable domain. Whiskey, wine, the veterinary sciences, oil wells, mining, commerce, the law—no matter the topic, Paladin holds his own against the experts and regularly bests them. His knowledge of languages stretches credulity—a sample of episodes reveals him speaking Hindi, French, Chinese, Armenian, Apache—even Australian (he says "fair dinkum" in one episode to convince an Aussie miner that he's a straight shooter). His knowledge of Spanish is well beyond that of the ordinary Western hero whose ability is usually limited to "vaya con dios" and a few other formulaic expressions. His less-than-handsome face only enhances this effect; we may understand that he has come by his advantages without the benefit of being good looking.

Thus Paladin is able to enact scenarios that gratify viewers on multiple levels. Many episodes include moments of visual artistry in which the mise-en-scène emphasizes Paladin's role as the man for any occasion. An example of how the ordinary can be transformed in the hands of a skilled director is found in "The Man Who Lost" (Season 2, Episode 31). In a windstorm, Paladin tracks and captures Ben Coey (Mort Mills), a fugitive accused of raping a woman and murdering her husband. With no jail available, Paladin ties him to a bed at a local inn, and when Coey taunts the woman (Barbara Hayden) who has been brought in to identify him as the man who "attacked" her, director Ida Lupino positions the camera behind the bed's elaborate headboard, effectively shooting through the wall that had been there in earlier conventional shots. This allows viewers to see the woman as she enters the room framed by part of the headboard, and provides a frightening perspective of Paladin's anger when he grips the headboard to support himself as he slaps the (now clearly guilty) rapist with the back of his hand. Of course, Paladin later kills one of the woman's brothers (Jack Elam) and wounds another (Ed

Nelson) to prevent them from exacting rough justice on the villain before Paladin can take him in for trial.

These, and countless other instances throughout *Have Gun, Will Travel*'s six-year run, show Paladin as a man of both fine judgments and decisive—sometimes brutal—action. Unlike other complicated Western heroes—such as Ethan Edwards (John Wayne) in *The Searchers*, who, even in victory, is obliged to turn his back on the open door of civilization—Paladin has his feet firmly planted in both the civilized and the savage parts of the West. In fact, he functions as a sort of itinerant purveyor of civilization, giving the lie to those who view his mere presence—he is, after all, a black-clad hired gun—as a threat to the stability that is so elusive in the West. His moral rectitude is such that, by the end of each episode, those involved come to realize that civilization stands a better chance because of Paladin's intervention. This comes as no surprise to viewers who have seen him in San Francisco, where his refinement—both sartorial and otherwise—suggests a level of cultivation unsurpassed in the annals of the Western. They meet, in Paladin, a character whose necessarily brutal tendencies are offset by his commitment to the rule of law and the gentle pursuits that are possible in a provisionally civilized world.

Filmography

"Be Not Forgetful of Strangers." *Have Gun Will Travel*. Dir. Richard Boone. Date aired 22 December 1962.
"The Black Bull." *Have Gun Will Travel*. Dir. William Conrad. Date aired 13 April 1963.
"Cage at McNaab." *Have Gun Will Travel*. Dir. Gary Nelson. Date aired 16 February 1963.
Dr. Jekyll and Mr. Hyde. Dir. Victor Fleming. Metro-Goldwyn-Meyer, 1941.
"The Fifth Man." *Have Gun Will Travel*. Dir. Richard Whorf. Date aired 30 May 1959.
"Gold and Brimstone." *Have Gun Will Travel*. Dir. Richard Whorf. Date aired 20 June 1959.
Hombre. Dir. Martin Ritt. Twentieth Century Fox Film Corporation, 1967.
"A Knight to Remember." *Have Gun Will Travel*. Dir. Andrew V. McLaglen. Date aired 9 December 1961.
"The Long Weekend." *Have Gun Will Travel*. Dir. Byron Paul. CBS. Date aired 8 April 1961.
"Maggie O'Bannion." *Have Gun Will Travel*. Dir. Andrew V. McLaglen. Date aired 4 April 1959.
"The Man Who Lost." *Have Gun Will Travel*. Dir. Ida Lupino. CBS. Date aired 25 April 1959.
"Odds for Big Red." *Have Gun Will Travel*. Dir. Richard Donner. Date aired 7 October 1961.
"Out at the Old Ball Park." *Have Gun Will Travel*. Dir. Richard Boone. Date aired 1 October 1960.
"Three Bells to Perdido." *Have Gun Will Travel*. Dir. Andrew V. McLaglen. CBS. Date aired 14 September 1957.
"The Vigil." *Have Gun Will Travel*. Dir. Andrew V. McLaglen. CBS. Date aired 16 September 1961.

Works Cited

Mock, Erin Lee. "Paladin Plays the Field: 1950s Television, Masculinity, and the New Episodic Sexualization of the Private Sphere." *Love in Western Film and Television—Lonely Hearts and Happy Trails*. Ed. Sue Matheson. New York: Palgrave Macmillan, 2013. 91–109. Print.
Studlar, Gaylyn. *Have Gun—Will Travel*. Detroit: Wayne State University Press, 2015. Print.

Executioner, Judge and Priest
The Desert Sublime in Westerns

HELEN M. LEWIS

In her *Mountain Gloom and Mountain Glory*, a classic work on the formation of the theory of the Sublime, or "the Aesthetics of the Infinite," Marjorie Hope Nicolson analyzes the prerequisites for and the function of the Sublime in European literature. The truly Sublime landscape involves in Nature a ruggedness, a wildness, an asymmetry, a vastness, an awesomeness, at the power of Nature, and even a sense of terror. Because of the European and the British landscapes, mountains, rushing streams, thunderstorms, and waterfalls—elements of Nature that demonstrate power and that often contain an element of danger—became the typical sources of the Sublime in contrast to the merely beautiful and contained or controlled elements of Nature. When defining the Sublime, seventeenth-century British philosopher Henry More described a transferring of awe—terror mingled with exultation—"once reserved for God"—to an "expanded cosmos, then from the macrocosm to the greatest objects in the geocosm—mountains, ocean, and desert" (Nicolson 143). For More, viewing expanses in Nature implied contemplating God as the Creator of those vast spaces. By the eighteenth century, Joseph Addison, in his poem *Pleasure of the Imagination* (1704), also included "'a vast uncultured desert'" as one of the sources of the Sublime, in the list of "'huge heaps of mountains, high rocks and precipices, [and] a wide expanse of waters'" where one sees not so much the beauty or the prettiness of the scene, but rather becomes struck by its "'magnificence'" (Nicolson 313). In the twentieth century, the desert landscape often serves as a natural and logical setting for many Westerns, its magnificence enhanced by expansive panoramic presentations that expose the vastness of space generally recognized as being such an important part of the West. The desert's vastness in its Sublime implications has inspired directors to apply desert landscapes to inform character in Western movies.

When selecting desert locations as points in which to develop character, some Western film directors have translated to the screen the concept of the Sublime in its moral and ethical sense. John Ford in *The Searchers* (1956) and Sergio Leone in *The Good, the Bad, and the Ugly* (1966), for example, both emphasize the desert as the place in which character transformation can occur over a relatively long period of time. In other Westerns, directors have capitalized upon the desert in the sense of Sublime with a briefer exposure to the power of the wilderness to reform characters; these include Monte Hellman's *The Shooting* (1966), King Vidor's *Duel in the Sun* (1946), John Ford's *Three Godfathers* (1948), and Ray Milland's *A Man Alone* (1955). In these films, the desert landscapes assume the roles of executioner to destroy, of judge to offer a trial by endurance, and of priest to encourage atonement in characters willfully or unknowingly touched by the deepest implications of the desert setting.

As executioner, the desert serves as a fine way for the human killer to destroy his victim without wasting ammunition or even soiling his own hands. In his brutal short story "Gun-Devil of Red God Desert" (1943), Tom Roan has several men wrap in wet cowhide a man with whom they have feuded for years. They leave the "enemy" to die a gruesome death. Their sadism proves similar to that exhibited by gunman Billy Spear in Monte Hellman's *The Shooting* (1966), when Spear leaves men to die in the desert. Notably, Hellman's treatment of the desertscape recalls journalist Richard Hinton's evaluation of the desert in *The Handbook to Arizona 1877*. Hinton compares the "utter desolation of this region" to the deserts found in the Judeo-Christian tradition, writing that "the valley of the lower Jordan and the shores of the Dead Sea are not more barren. For many miles not a shrub or even a blade of grass is seen—only a howling wilderness of rock and drifting sand" (23). In Hellman's vast emptiness, gunman Billy Spear insists that young Coley Boyard wait on the trail until the "pursuit" party completes its mysterious mission in the desert.[1] Believing Coley has a better chance alone in the desert than in close contact with gunslinger Spear, Willett Gashade— the hired tracker and partner of Coley—tells the boy to stay behind, leaving Coley water and offering the futile admonition, "Find some shade." Billy Spear lags behind Willett Gashade and the Woman with No Name in order to steal Coley's water. He confesses to the cold-blooded murder of another of Coley's partners and then warns the boy, "Go sit down over there. And think on this: far as your voice gon' carry, ain't too far for me to turn right 'round and hit you right in the eye.... Your brain's gonna fry out here, you know that." A proving ground for character, the desert seems to have dried any drop of humanity that Billy Spear might have had before this mission.

But the desert does not just bring out the worst in humanity, like in Billy Spear and the Woman with No Name, who seem ruthlessly determined to

190   A Fistful of Icons

do a job that prevents them from responding to humanity's true helplessness before the Sublime manifested in the Desert. Both Coley Boyard and Willett Gashade, though not in the desert deliberately to seek God and defeat demons, find themselves facing demons represented by the humans with whom they travel, beings more savage than the natural forces of the waterless terrain. Coley does offer kindness to a man with a broken leg whom the man's friend, the Woman with No Name, had abandoned and does risk his life to warn Gashade of Spear's guilt, a guilt that Gashade has suspected. Coley might not consciously weigh his act, but he does "lay down his life for his friend"—the highest sacrifice one can make for another.

For one reason only, to prevent more violence by the cruel Billy Spear, Willett Gashade continues to track an unknown fugitive fleeing from the Woman with No Name. As Gashade declares, "There ain't gonna be no kill." With no water and their horses collapsed, the party finally corner their quarry in some high rocks. During a fist fight in which Gashade succeeds in disarming and knocking out Billy Spear, Gashade comes the closest to facing his own dark inner self. Gashade picks up a rock to smash Spear's head; he raises his hand for the momentum, his eyes shift away to the side, and he smashes hard, six times. When the camera pans back, the viewers realize that Gashade has not fallen to the level of a Billy Spear. Willett Gashade, a man of principles, has mastered his lust for revenge by destroying Spear's gun hand rather than killing the man who murdered Gashade's partners. The suffering in the desert seems to have purified Gashade while evaporating, to the same degree, whatever humanity Spear might have had.

In an ending which leaves many unresolved questions, the Woman with No Name begins dueling with the fugitive whom Gashade had wanted to protect, perhaps to bring back to town for a fair trial. As Gashade approaches, the viewers see that the fugitive could pass as Gashade's twin, Coigne, possibly the unknown fugitive hastening out of town for running down a "man and a little person—maybe a child." As Gashade leaps towards the Woman with No Name who simultaneously with Coigne aims and fires, Gashade falls to the ground next to her, looks up, and says, "Coigne." The film ends here— without the viewer's knowing whether Gashade or the Woman with No Name or Coigne is shot or mortally wounded. Director Hellman leaves the audience wondering whether Gashade succeeded in deflecting the Woman's aim and, therefore, saved the fugitive, possibly his brother. However, whether he saved his brother's life proves secondary to the fact that Gashade had prepared to die for a total stranger when he leaped to deflect the Woman with No Name's aiming at a man not known until that moment. Only after the leap does Gashade see the face and know for certain the identity of the fugitive tracked by the Woman with No Name. Hellman leaves unanswered the question of whether the Woman with No Name caught Coigne's bullet or whether

Gashade caught the bullet, thus, sacrificing himself for the second time in the film.

The barren wilderness serves not only as a perfect backdrop for the barren, loveless characters of the Woman with No Name and Billy Spear, but it also provides a stage from which characters can devolve to their most brutal and demonic selves (like the Woman with No Name and Billy Spear) or evolve to their most selfless nobility (like Coley Boyard and Willett Gashade). Without water and horses to take these characters out of the desert, the results of the duel seem inconsequential until one puts them in the context of the Sublime in the Judeo-Christian tradition of placing spirituality in the wilderness. Coley Boyard and Willett Gashade seem to have become complete men, each having passed the moral test of the desert, while the Woman with No Name and Billy Spear do not pass that test. James Cowan says of the trials of a man, like Antony's in the desert, that "[t]he demonic st[ands] not merely for all that [is] hostile to man: the demons [sum] up all that [is] anomalous and incomplete in man" (18). In this sense, the physical act of living or dying proves of little import in the moral contest; only the individual's resistance to the demons matters in his or her encounter with the Sublime in the desert.

Another climactic and telling gun duel between a woman and a man occurs in Gore Vidal's *Duel in the Sun*. Here, as in John Ford's *The Searchers*, the desert landscape provides a constant reminder of human vulnerability. The social stigma and human corruption in *Duel in the Sun* and racial territorial conflicts in *The Searchers* provide the demons in these films. In both films, the directors use large pan shots to contrast the smallness of the ranches with the vast, open, desolate countryside that seems good for feeding a few cattle but not for nourishing people. To illustrate that vastness, Vidor employs the silhouette shots of Senator McCanles on a hill at sunset to give outlaw son Lewt escape money and of the Senator in his wheelchair at the edge of the prairie when his family seriously, visibly begins disintegrating after his wife's death.

Surprisingly, in *Duel in the Sun*, Pearl Chavez, the Mexican-French daughter of Mrs. McCanles' girlhood suitor, becomes more vulnerable indoors than outside, where one would expect her to weaken before the forces of man and nature. Pearl, wanting to be a "good girl," resists Lewt's seductions outdoors, even spending an entire day up to her neck in a waterhole rather than let the lurking Lewt see her naked. This virtue, however, becomes tarnished by Lewt's insinuations that night at home. Eventually, cornered in her room where she has intently scrubbed the floor during a thunderstorm, Pearl succumbs to Lewt. Although she appears to Lewt's brother, Jesse, to kiss back, when Jesse whom Pearl loves, discovers Pearl and Lewt together later that night, Vidal shows Pearl afterwards in a chair crying as a result of Lewt's rape. Unwilling to marry her, but wanting to possess her—she wears his brand, says Lewt—Lewt later attempts to kill his brother Jesse in cold blood when Jesse tries to rescue Pearl from Lewt. Earlier that week, Pearl had declared, "Jesse, I wish I could die for you." "Let's hope you never have to do that, Pearl," he responded, failing to realize that he has killed her in a sense by becoming engaged to another woman, a pure woman, although he had earlier spoken of love for Pearl after her seduction by Lewt. Knowing Lewt will return to kill the Jesse he has only wounded, Pearl, truly a "good girl" in the broadest moral sense, now determines to travel two days and two nights alone in the desert to find and stop Lewt.

Because she cannot restore life, the Woman with No Name in *The Shooting* admits that "there is no point" to her relentless pursuit of the man who ran down "a man and a little person—maybe a child," but Pearl has purpose in her pursuit of Lewt into the desert. Pearl knows what she must do to save and secure Jesse's life. Not thinking of the consequences to herself, Pearl has decided to kill Lewt in order to save Jesse for another woman. Undergoing the trials by fire presented by the heat of the desert and the gunfire exchanged with Lewt, Pearl proves herself a woman of price greater than Jesse realized. Indeed, Jesse had quickly abandoned her to the swine Lewt when he discovered Lewt had violated Pearl. Pearl who had lost herself indoors now gains freedom and redemption outside in the wilderness by laying down her life for another. Actually, Pearl sacrifices herself for a whole generation, since Jesse will wed the railroad baron's daughter, will likely have sons, and will quite probably become the governor of Texas. Once again, the desertscape becomes a location in which the individual faces and conquers his or her demons, even if proving one's moral worth comes at the cost of one's life.

Like Hellman and Vidor, John Ford emphasizes the desert Sublime in *Three Godfathers* (1948), but in this film the protagonists, three young bank robbers, Bob Hightower, Pedro, and the Abilene Kid, quite literally become involved with the biblical story of Jesus' birth and triumphant march into Jerusalem on Palm Sunday. Critics have stressed the obvious Christmas/Nativity symbolism of the film, but placing the desertscape against the ministry of the adult Jesus shifts focus to the inseparable unit of Christmas, Passover, and Easter redemption in the Christian tradition. Unlike the sadistic Billy Spear in *The Shooting* and the unthinking Lewt in *Duel in the Sun*, Bob Hightower and his partner Pedro take care of their pal the Abilene Kid, or William Kearney, wounded early in *The Three Godfathers* during the bank robbery that resulted in their fleeing to the desert. The injured Kid even says "please" when he asks for water after a sandstorm that could spell their physical salvation in escaping the sheriff—if they only had access to water.

Although caring for the Abilene Kid endangers Bob Hightower and Pedro, neither man considers abandoning their wounded partner. *The Shooting* and *Duel in the Sun* emphasize the sterility of the desert because the characters themselves know they face a final self-confrontation against an enemy, unnamed or named; thus, searching for waterholes does not become their pre-occupation. In contrast, in *Three Godfathers*, the lack of water provides the pivotal point for the later sacrifice, for in seeking an alternate water supply after the sheriff has put guards on the nearby water tanks, the trio discover the pregnant woman abandoned in a wagon in a sandstorm.

Through a long "[b]ut that wouldn't a been so bad if..." running gag, Ford reveals that the woman's tenderfoot husband has foolishly dynamited the waterhole at Terrapin Tanks in order to make the water flow faster. As Bob Hightower says, "Fool Tenderfoot's dead, I guess, but he's gonna keep right on killing people just the same, that'll come here banking on water." Hightower may be a bank robber, but he is no killer. When one considers the stages of dying of thirst—the thirst, the delirium, the point past pain—one realizes that unwittingly the Tenderfoot will cause as much suffering in the desert as Billy Spear deliberately intended for Coley Boyard and Willet Gashade in *The Shooting*.

While the young bank robbers know they must keep moving to escape the sheriff and to find water, they delay two days to help the woman deliver her child, to squeeze barrel cactus for water for her and the baby, and to tend to the newborn's first needs. Before she dies, the mother exacts a promise from the three godfathers to protect the infant, a promise that that they know demands of them a life sacrifice through capture and jail for the delay, if not outright death in the desert. The obvious Nativity story parallels eventually lead to the salt flat that the robbers must cross in order to bring Robert William Pedro, the baby, to the nearest town. The men know their risks, yet they take them. While the Kid dies in prayer after trying to refuse water for the sake of his godson, Pedro commits suicide when a broken leg prevents his journeying: for Hightower to make a splint and then carry Pedro on a travois would have taken time away from the baby's chances for survival. Ford, however, lets the audience see Pedro pray before hearing the shot, so even the suicide seems free of sin or guilt; it becomes an act to save a new life.

In contrast to the Kid and Pedro, Bob Hightower experiences the greatest struggle because he does not have the religious principles of his partners to carry him through the desert. Still, his sheer commitment to the little life, when he could just have abandoned the baby to save his own, reveals a spiritual transformation, completed without benefit of clergy. In fact, the Desert Fathers themselves lived in isolation from the Church, seeking pure one-on-one communion with God like their models in Scripture, both Old and New Testaments. St. Jerome wrote in praise of the desert, "'O solitude where those stones are born of which in the Apocalypse is built the city of the Great King'" (Gannon and Traub 18); surely the stones signify the bank robbers here building a New Jerusalem for themselves via their complete self-sacrifice. For some experiencing its trials, the desert itself becomes the priest showing the way to atonement. Thomas M. Gannon and George W. Traub in *The Desert and the City* associate spirituality with a "yearning for self-surrender" (18) in every man; "[i]t has led some men, in spite of themselves, in a moment of heroic decision, to give their lives for others" (18). Unlike Willet Gashade's seemingly instinctive response in *The Shooting* and Pearl's quick, deliberate action to protect Jesse and perhaps avenge herself upon Lewt in *Duel in the Sun*, Hightower has several days in which to consider carefully his desperate situation, yet each day he resumes his selfless commitment to his unexpected godson.

Once Hightower stumbles into town with the baby protected in his arms, he undergoes a trial for robbing the bank and a trial for custody of the baby. He wins the baby from its blood kin, Aunt and Uncle Buck Sweet, the sheriff, by offering to raise the boy properly; Hightower will "teach him good horse sense, and respect, and say 'yessir' when he's spoke to," fine values, but Hightower makes no mention of Bible or church. Although offered liberty in exchange for the child, he would not sell the child for his own freedom. Instead, Hightower gains custody of the child and rides off to his one-year minimal jail sentence. The good women of the town sing Hightower off to prison to the hymn "Bringing in the Sheaves"; surely in their stereotyped judgmental eyes, risking one's life to save a stranger's baby provides positive proof of redemption. Once again, men who have encountered the Sublime in the desert have faced their inner selves, overcome their own immorality, and have glimpsed a higher order—at least in values.

Of the many desert Westerns, one of the most intriguing in terms of use of the desert as both a place and an instrument of atonement remains *A Man Alone*, directed by Ray Milland. In this Western, which opens with an unidentified but well-dressed lone rider in the desert, the encounter with the Sublime occurs when the desert comes to the men, not the men to the desert. Isolated in a small town, in fact in the cellar of the sheriff delirious with yellow fever, Wes Steele has taken shelter during a sandstorm which prevented the town mob from spotting him after he had shot a deputy in self-defense. Unfortunately, the sandstorm that saved him from lynching has also blocked the roads leading out of town so that Steele cannot escape even after digging himself out of the two feet of sand covering the cellar door. Through an unusual meeting with the sheriff's inquisitive daughter Nadine, Steele, a gunman, comes to terms with himself.

According to Fathers Gannon and Traub in *The Desert and the City*, the solitary "is one who is aware of a basic aloneness within himself which, in reality, unites him to all other men…. Hence, his isolation is the foundation of a deep and gentle sympathy with other men; even more, it is the doorway by which he enters into the mystery of God and brings others into that mystery by the power of his love and his humility" (27). When Steele slowly reveals the forces and reputation that made him a gunman but not a murderer of women and children as accused, the viewers and Nadine through her probing questions sense that he has felt a desire to change, to reform. As he tells Nadine, "You don't always have much choice. Fellas come along trying to prove that you're not as good as they are. Pretty soon it gets out of hand and you find that you gotta shoot to live." This confession of sorts has credibility because Steele reveals to Nadine that he did attend church in former days, and he even exposes his true identity in church where the real killer holds a hypocritical solitary wake for the dead man. But Steele has never admitted to himself these feelings until, in a town blockaded by the desert sands, Nadine's clipped questions challenge him to quit gunfighting. Like a retreat master, Nadine forces Steele to examine his "inner consciousness," while the sandstorm provides the location of his spiritual retreat. With no escape from the sandstorm, Steele has the time and the solitude to evaluate his past and his future, under Nadine's moral prodding. Thus, the desert acts upon Steele throughout the film, even in the indoors scenes in the town.

Hiding in the basement, both Nadine and Steele share their inner conflicts. Steele's own sense of solitariness as a fugitive makes him sensitive to Nadine's secret hope chest concealed in the basement from a possessive father. Steele understands the loss of freedom when one lives in reaction to others; thus, the desert storm has allowed Steele, in the tradition of the Desert Solitary, to bring the concept of reform (redemption) to Nadine, trapped by obligations to her father. She now envisions a life with Steele. Although a lynch mob and the desert's storm have trapped Steele in town, the moral reflection which results proves the same as if he had willingly made a religious retreat. He begins putting the needs of others before his own safety, similar to Bob Hightower in *The Three Godfathers*. By deciding to delay his own escape to help Nadine nurse her father, his double enemy as sheriff and as jealous father, Steele places himself before the lynch mob. Confronting his own corruption that led indirectly to the massacres blamed on Steele, Sheriff Gil Corrigan helps Steele escape. Ironically, the sheriff had begun as an honest man, but he became corrupt only after the desert's harshness broke him as a rancher! But just as the mob—a fickle crowd wanting to hang somebody, anybody—ropes the sheriff, Steele returns, willing to surrender his life for his enemy's. The mob now under duress, and Steele's gun, releases the sheriff to attack the truly guilty man, the banker Stanley. Steele wonders, "Who knows if this place is any worse than the next one I'd hit. But from the way things look now, it's got a good chance of being better. I'm stayin.'" Sheriff Corrigan replies, "Let's go home!" Thus, Steele, through the desert's intervention, finds atonement, and redemption for his past; through his free choice to leave the gunman's life, he finds a home.

In *A Man Alone*, the desert embodies the Sublime as a place where men and women confront and succumb to their moral trials or discover themselves to be capable of surrendering for others, willing to die so that others might live. Not all characters identify this sacrifice with the Judeo-Christian tradition, but the viewer can both enjoy the awesome expanse of the desert Sublime and admire those characters who, in facing the desert, achieve a type of reformation or redemption by experiencing and withstanding the trials of the wilderness. The Western desert offers a Sublime wherein one realizes one's inner capacity for evil or good, as well as one's moral strength and the ability to redeem oneself.

Taking on the roles of an executioner to destroy, a judge to offer a trial by endurance, and a priest to encourage atonement in characters willfully or unknowingly touched by its deepest implications, the Western desert, whether the place found in Monte Hellman's *The Shooting* (1966), King Vidor's *Duel in the Sun* (1946), John Ford's *Three Godfathers* (1948), or Ray Milland's *A Man Alone* (1955), proves to be about much more than vast tracts of panoramic landscape. Its Sublime aesthetic includes a spiritual/moral element, for viewing the vastness of its scenery involves actions on the part of the soul and/or imagination and to recognize as William Wordsworth did, "the spirit that rolls through all things."[2] As a way to the Deity, the desert in the Judeo-Christian culture has traditionally served as a moral proving ground. From the call of Abraham to travel the wilderness to a land God would show him to the 40 years' wandering of the Israelites under Moses, from the cries of Hosea, Jeremiah, and Isaiah to the voice of John the Baptist in the wilderness, the desert's arid landscape has served as a space in which humanity comes face-to-face with God. Peter Ansor in his *The Call of the Desert* (1973) declares that since Moses encountered God at Mount Horeb, "the belief became common that God dwelt in the desert and that to find him, it was necessary to go out into the wilderness." In the Old Testament, the ancient Hebrews saw the true nature of the Sublime. Under the influence of the New Testament narratives of the Temptations of Jesus in the desert and His frequent retreats into the wilderness to pray, the Desert Fathers, early Christian monks of the fourth century, began retiring, as did Jesus, to an isolated, forbidding place, in which they would not only encounter God, but also face and, they hoped, defeat the demons through an ascetic lifestyle.[3] In the Western, the desert, carrying in itself echoes of the Sublime, endures as a place which invites the viewer (with the protagonist) to encounter the Divine in a continual reenactment of a morality play. In the Western desert, a man—or a woman—can come to terms with himself—or herself—as well as with a higher source of values of whatever name one chooses to give it.

Notes

1. The Woman with No Name hires Billy Spear, Willett Gashade, and Coley Boyard to track an unknown man who ran down two people in town, one possibly a child. Viewers never know but might surmise whether the two victims were her family. The hired men do not know the woman's personal motives nor do they know the fugitive; partners Gashade and Boyard first seem to go along in case the pursued man is Gashade's brother.

2. Wordsworth's "Lines Composed a Few Miles above Tintern Abbey" (1798) consists of a reflection about the poet's return to a favorite childhood place in the country. With an Eastern philosophical approach, Wordsworth intuits an immanent spiritual presence in Nature, not the transcendent Western deity:

> And I have felt
> A presence that disturbs me with the joy
> Of elevated thoughts; a sense sublime
> Of something far more deeply interfused,
> Whose dwelling is the light of setting suns,
> And the round ocean and the living air,
> And the blue sky, and in the mind of man;
> A motion and a spirit, that impels
> All thinking things, all objects of all thought,
> And rolls through all things [ll. 95–104].

3. One of the earliest of the monks in the fourth century to venture into the desert, Antony of the Desert, deliberately went out to the "tombs" to have a show-down with the demons. In Antony's biography, Athanasius describes one such duel during which the demons called out, "'Get away from what belongs to us! What are you doing in the desert?'" (Vivian and Athanassakis 89). Antony stayed, eventually encouraging more steadfast souls to seek spiritual communion with God in the solitude once possessed by the demons. Translated into modern terms, of course, Antony encountered the demons of his own self-centered desires, a contest between what proved noblest and what proved basest in his character.

Filmography

Duel in the Sun (1946). Dir. King Vidor. MGM, 2004. DVD.
A Man Alone (1955). Dir. Ray Milland. YouTube, n.d. Web. 12 Aug. 2015.
The Shooting (1966). Dir. Monte Hellman. Criterion Collection, 2014. DVD.
Three Godfathers (1948). Dir. John Ford. Warner Home Video, 2007. DVD.

Works Cited

Anson, Peter F. *The Call of the Desert: The Solitary Life in the Christian Church*. 1964. London: William Clowes & Sons, Ltd., 1973. Print.
Cowan, James. *Desert Father: A Journey in the Wilderness with Saint Anthony*. Boston: New Seeds Books, 2006. Print.
Gannon, Thomas M., S.J., and George W. Traub, S.J. *The Desert and the City: An Interpretation of the History of Christian Spirituality*. Chicago: Loyola University Press, 1969. Print.
Hinton, Richard J. *Handbook to Arizona 1877*. 1877. Glorieta, NM: Rio Grande Press, 1970. Print.
Nicolson, Marjorie Hope. *Mountain Gloom and Mountain Glory: The Development of the Aesthetics of the Infinite*. New York: W.W. Norton & Co., 1959. Print.
Vivian, Tim, and Apostolos N. Athanassakis, trans. *The Life of Antony by Athanasius of Alexandria*. Kalamazoo, MI: Cistercian Pubs, 2003. Print.
Wordsworth, William. "Lines Composed a Few Miles Above Tintern Abbey, on Revisiting the Banks of the Wye During a Tour, July 13, 1798." *Poets.Org*. Academy of American Poets, n.d. Web. 5 May 2015.

Machines in the Garden
Technology and the Western in the 1960s and 1970s

Martin Holtz

In "The Idea of Genre in American Cinema," Edward Buscombe describes iconography as the decisive component that generates the story patterns we come to expect of genre films. Icons provide the visual identity that triggers thematic and narrative associations and expectations. In the case of the Western, these icons conventionally include the rural outdoor setting, the wide-brimmed hats and other cowboy clothing, horses, but also the "tools of the trade," six-guns and the like, and "miscellaneous physical objects" such as trains (Buscombe 15–16). Citing the opening scene from *Ride the High Country* (1962), Buscombe argues that while icons, in this case a man wearing Western gear on horseback riding into a small Western town, provide familiarity, the genre thrives on the inclusion of contrastive "novelty" elements, in this case a policeman, a car, and a camel, in order to generate original meaning.[1] Conventionally, the iconography of the Western is of a distinctly pre-industrial nature, which is why the appearance of a car in Peckinpah's film is so startling. In fact, as Jane Tompkins argues, a most common explanation for the emergence of the Western in late nineteenth century America is that it provides a fictional "escape from the conditions of life in modern industrial society: from a mechanized existence, economic dead ends, social entanglements, unhappy personal relations, political injustice" (4). While there is certainly truth to that observation, the Western has always had a more complex relation to industrial America than simple escapism. In true Derridaean fashion, the Western has always contained the traces of industrialism that it defines itself against.

Befitting its chronotopical identity, the Western is about a historical moment of transition (cf. Cawelti 22–23), a state in flux most famously expressed in the idea of the frontier, the mythical dividing line between the wilderness and a civilization in the process of westward expansion on the continent where Frederick Jackson Turner saw the potential for the "perennial rebirth" of a uniquely American character in the interaction of individual and nature (4). Jim Kitses' influential description of genre dynamics as a "shifting ideological play" of a "series of antimonies" (59) perhaps best captures this process of becoming that is at the center of the Western. The genre is as much about "the wilderness" as about "civilization," as much about "nature" as about "culture," as much about "the West" as about "the East," about "agrarianism" as "industrialism," about "the past" as "the future" (59). This is why machines in one form or another are part of the iconographic inventory of the Western as indicators of industrial progress.

Leo Marx has illustrated the ways in which the literature of the 19th and early 20th centuries dealt with the transition from an agrarian to an industrial America in the form of the overriding metaphor of the "machine in the garden." As a representative of industrial development, the machine, be it in the form of the railroad or the mill wheel, veers between being portrayed as a disturbance of the pastoral ideal (15–16) and as a benevolent contributor to turning the wilderness into a "middle landscape" (150), as violent, exploitative, and setting off frighteningly uncontrollable energy (346–350, 355–356) and as an "instrument of power," "at once a testament to the will of man rising over natural obstacles, and, yet, confined by its iron rails to a predetermined path" (191). This tension between distance and integration can also be observed in the classical Western. Richard Slotkin distinguishes between "progressive" Westerns like *The Iron Horse* (1924), *Union Pacific* (1939), and *Dodge City* (1939), in which the railroad is embraced as a symbol of progress, and "populist" Westerns like *Jesse James* (1939) and similar social bandit films, in which the railroad serves as the symbol for industrial corruption and exploitation, both forms ultimately following a similar ideological agenda of either celebrating industrial capitalism or fashioning mythical remedies for its discontents (22–23, see also Buscombe 208).

As machines have taken on the iconographic role of representing historical progress, their portrayal in Westerns at a time when the genre itself was starting to interrogate its own validity calls for attention. In the 1960s and 70s, Westerns were increasingly regarded as an incongruence, their association with an ideological project of celebrating a frontier spirit of westward expansion appearing out of touch with a modern technologized society riddled by countercultural turmoil and anti–Vietnam War protests. Looking at their portrayal of the harbingers of progress, focusing on cars, trains, and steam engines, this essay argues that by employing these icons the Western maintained its own relevance as a critical commentator on modernity at the same time as it critically inspected its own outmodedness.

Trains, Planes and Automobiles

As far as means of transportation go, the horse is of course the preeminent icon of free movement and individualism, the epitome of nature tamed to serve human needs without losing any of its "dignity, grace, and power" (Buscombe 23; cf. Tompkins 93; cf. Cawelti 38). The car appears as the most prominent machine in Westerns of the 1960s and 1970s,[2] often serving as the iconic intrusive foreign body that symbolizes the end of the horse and the arrival of mechanized modernity (cf. Buscombe 81). *How the West Was Won* (1962) ends on a celebratory note with a montage of urban America, prominently featuring a top-down shot of an L.A. freeway labyrinth teeming with cars, presumably to showcase the achievements of modern civilization as the crowning end point to winning the West. This imagery to illustrate an unabashedly progressive ideology has been derided as unintentionally satirical and inapt (French 83; Lenihan 154), and it stands appropriately alone among the decidedly negative portrayals of cars in contemporaneous Westerns, which fall into two broad categories. One tendency is to emphasize their destructive potential, the other to demonstrate their ineptitude. These two tendencies correspond to two different approaches to the genre, the one bemoaning its own demise, the other reasserting its authority, while being critical of modernity.

French emphasizes the "progressively lethal use of the car by Sam Peckinpah" (82). In *Ride the High Country* the disturbance seems gentle enough. The car appears suddenly behind the unsuspecting rider and honks its horn while rushing past. A short wince of horse and rider and a look of disbelief at the disrespectful impatience of the machine are enough to emanate a considerable metaphorical resonance. Echoing Leo Marx's observation of "the blast of the train whistle interrupting Nathaniel Hawthorne's pastoral idyll at Sleepy Hollow" (Lenihan 156), the machine is first and foremost a sudden disturbance, something unexpected that confounds both character and viewer. Adding discomfort is the fact that the rider is in the way of the car and made to clear it, an image that reappears with similar overtones in *The Shootist* (1976), only that John Wayne is decidedly more unimpressed by the angry driver. "Get out of the way, old man," the policeman yells at Joel McCrea's Steve Judd, signaling that the values the classic Western hero stands for are obsolete and in the way of "progress." The remainder of the film develops, celebrates and finally mourns the passing of said values, which can be summarized as the self-respect of knowing and doing the right thing regardless of superficial personal benefits, and it is precisely this respect for moral obligations that is undermined by the indiscriminate impatience of the machine.

Peckinpah develops this theme further in *The Wild Bunch* (1969). Here

General Mapache (Emilio Fernández) stops his car to talk to Pike (William Holden) in *The Wild Bunch* (Warner Bros., 1969).

the car appears as suddenly and unexpectedly as in the prior film, this time driving straight towards the camera, but, due to the telephoto lens, hardly seeming to make any headway. Even more so than in *Ride the High Country*, the staging thus emphasizes the confrontational character of the car while hinting at its limitations. The crosscutting between the car that parades around the compound and the bewildered reaction of the bunch, their standing up an unsure wavering between mock salute and incredulity, adds a comic note. Clearly, the car, particularly in its association with the self-proclaimed general Mapache, signals an establishment of hierarchical decorum that is mocked for its grotesque incongruity (cf. Seydor 185). The confrontational hierarchy that is introduced by the car is further amplified by its association with death and destruction when Pike Bishop, the leader of the bunch, mentions the use of planes ("one of those things that can fly") in the upcoming war (the film is set 1913). The inhumanity of the mechanistic slaughter that World War I unleashed finds a symbolic equivalent in the scene where Angel, the one member of the bunch that, like Steve Judd in *Ride the High Country*, refuses financial benefits and instead represents a compassionate defiance of despotism, is tied to the car and dragged through the dust. The comedy of the car's introduction gives way to shock at its potential for casual violence (cf. Seydor 186). What is significant about the way the car is used as an instrument for torture is the distinct carelessness of the procedure. The passengers indulge in mindless merriment indifferent to the human being that is dragged along, metaphorically illustrating the celebratory air of technological progress beneath which true human needs are cruelly disregarded. Fittingly, the car goes around in circles, belying its progressive promises.

Also in *The Ballad of Cable Hogue* (1970) the car is introduced in a combination of festive behavior and multidimensional carelessness. It arrives at Cable's water hole at the moment when he is about to exact revenge on the person that left him to die in the desert several years before. The victim's cries for help are unheeded by the merry party in the car, the water hole ignored. The symbol of progress just passes by, oblivious to human suffering and small business operations. Just a short while later, Cable's erstwhile lover Hildy returns from San Francisco in a fancy dress and a fancy car with a fancy chauffeur. The comedy of the incongruous sophistication does not diminish the implication of hierarchy and arrogance. Yet Hildy, as a messenger of civilization about to take Cable with her, is at all times a loving, free-spirited and highly sympathetic character, which is why the accident that happens is all the more tragic, even if it is presented in a highly laconic way. Cable accidentally unfastens the brakes of the car when loading in a suitcase and, unable to stop the machine, is overrun. What this scene communicates is the allure of progress (Hildy's attractiveness), its self-perpetuating inevitability (the impossibility to stop the car once it is in motion), its unintentional destructiveness (killing the small business owner who is simply in the way), and Cable's unwitting complicity in setting it in motion (as a small business owner he participates in the kind of capitalist enterprise that gave rise to the efficiency and commercial appeal of machines). If the film shares the sentiments of *The Wild Bunch*, its tone is distinctly more matter-of-fact than angrily desperate. Progress simply happens, violent and unforgiving in its unexpected consequences, but ultimately too unstoppable (and attractive) to find the time for lamentation (cf. Seydor 228, 245–246, 250; Kitses 227; Durgnat/Simmon 78).

The association of machines with the corporatization of the West is further developed in Peckinpah's post-western *Junior Bonner* (1972). In that film, family homesteads are erased by giant bulldozers to make way for air-conditioned mobile homes dreamt up and celebrated by real estate entrepreneur "Curly" Bonner as the future "home on the range" emerged in "total electric living." The film pokes fun at the commercialization of a consumer-friendly pastiche image of the West at the same time as it bemoans its disrespect for a more authentic lifestyle that is embodied by Curly's brother "Junior" and his father and ex-rodeo champion "Ace." The "Frontier Days" rodeo becomes the contested site in which a mechanized commercialism, embodied by giant rodeo stock trucks and a circus-like parade of tractors and other supposedly "frontier" agricultural machinery driving around in circles in grotesque celebration, competes with the exhilarating feats of the rodeo riders themselves in their primal contest with nature's force of wild bulls and wild horses, a competition that is accentuated by the pervasive use of split-screen cinematography that juxtaposes mechanical time-taking with mesmerizing slow-motion shots of rodeo acrobatics. The participation of Junior and Ace in what is ultimately a commercial trivialization of a frontier spirit signals the triumph of machine over man. An escape from such a life seems only possible in two ways. One is a departure from the land of the closed frontier altogether: Junior buys his father a one-way ticket to Australia with his prize money, the only place where an authentic frontier is still believed to exist.[3] The other possibility is the redefinition of the car as a provider for some sort of free existence. The final image of Junior driving into the sunset with his horse locked in the trailer carries a distinct ambivalence. On the one hand, the car takes Junior away from the circus-like rodeo in town and into the majestic landscape of the West, on the other, it still confines him to the road, which is sure to lead him to another garish rodeo. Nonetheless, the film indicates what Peckinpah was to develop further in *Convoy* (1978) where truck drivers are portrayed as the descendants of the cowboys and the road emanates a frontier spirit.

The earlier post–Westerns, *The Misfits* (1961), *Lonely Are the Brave* (1962), and *Hud* (1963), have a more definite and at times blatantly negative attitude towards the car. In *The Misfits*, cars are repeatedly associated with broken relationships. Roslyn gets a busted car as a divorce present, Gay's wife had sex with another man in a car, and Gay himself falls off a car when he drunkenly cries for his children, who abandoned him. Numerous shots of the title characters crammed in a pick-up truck suggest the containment of mechanized transportation (cf. Gallafent 246). This containment becomes especially pronounced when Gay and Guido go mustang-hunting in the highlands. The giant flat desert serves as the foil to the imprisonment of the characters in the pick-up.[4] The capture of wild horses had served in the past as the kind of primal expression of a man vs. nature competition just as the rodeo in *Junior Bonner* or in *The Misfits* itself. Taming the horses meant settling the West, but times have changed. Now the horses are sold to glue factories where they are turned into product. Capturing them means killing them. Because of their activity, Gay and Guido evince a cruelty that is inherent in the commercialization of the West and so participate in the destruction of the kind of freedom that they used to thrive on. When the horses are slowed down with tires attached to the lassos around their necks, the connection between them and the cowboys becomes even more obvious. The car culture has taken away a freedom of movement and becomes a harbinger of doom. Gay's desperate justification of his actions in that he is doing "the same thing I always done, they just changed it around" puts as much blame on the cowboy's inability to recognize and accept responsibility for his own complicity in destroying the values he used to stand for as it riles against the cultural conditions that have corrupted the cowboy's way of life. If Gay's carelessness of existence used to be an expression of defiant individuality ("I just live"), mechanized commercial culture has turned it into indifference towards life. In the end he tries to have it both ways, wrestling down a horse single-handedly only to cut the rope that ties it to the car and release it into freedom.

As in *Junior Bonner*, this defiance can only go so far, as he and Roslyn drive away in a car when they leave Guido behind (cf. Gallafent 249).

In *Lonely Are the Brave*, cars and other machinery are staged as barriers to free movement and communication, creating in numerous shots a visual "dividing line that breaks up or interrupts a world of infinitely extensive space" (Gallafent 242). The road is a dangerous border to cross for horse and rider. *Mise-en-scène*, editing, and sound design emphasize the threat and the confinement of cars by finding charged compositions (the rear-view mirror framing the horse) and accentuating the unpredictability of their sudden appearance. The film is essentially about the attempt of a "bureaucratic, machine-run, rule-bound modern world" personified by the police force to circumscribe the "spontaneity, beauty, freedom from rules and routines" (Tompkins 102) personified by the carefree drifter Jack Burns and his horse. Jack manages to elude the police for the better part of the film thanks to his cunning and adaptation to the rugged landscape in which the police's wobbly jeep, the impersonal communications system, the stifling bureaucracy of procedure, and the arrogance of a helicopter crew contribute to all and out failure. The helicopter goes down with a shot tail rotor under the eyes of the incredulous police captain who cannot help but recognize and decry the imbecility of the institution he represents and who ultimately feels a thinly veiled sympathy for the cowboy (cf. Gallafent 244). If Jack's successful escape showcases the incompetence of machinery, his accident when crossing a road at night illustrates their unforgiving destructive volatility. A truck carrying lavatories, which is introduced at the beginning of the film and whose journey is inserted sporadically into the narrative as if to stress both inevitability and pure chance, accidentally hits the horse, which has to be shot when authorities arrive at the scene. The random and disgraceful nature of death by machines is accentuated by the flurry of lights and noises, the apologies of the driver, and the sad realization that the horse had to die because civilization arrived in the form of toilets (cf. Lusted 227).

In *Hud*, finally, the car becomes a symbol for the cowboy's own destructive carelessness, who runs over a flower bed in his shiny Cadillac just as casually as he provokes crashes that lead to the death of his brother and father (the latter being thrown from his horse). Hud is the representative of a mechanistic commercialism in which the individual's responsibility for others (be it in the breeding of cattle or in interpersonal relationships) is replaced by a hedonistic search for cheap and transient pleasures.[5] The forceful killing of the father's cattle herd infected by foot-and-mouth disease, whose grave is dug up by giant bulldozers, is the symptomatic scene that illustrates the unceremonious swiftness with which the annihilation of an entire lifestyle is brought about by machines. The funeral of the father is aptly framed by a line of cars surrounding the church.

The scenario of *Rancho Deluxe* (1975) offers a peculiar blend of elements from *Lonely Are the Brave* and *Hud*, but it replaces their dismal outlook with irreverent comedy. Here the two cowboy protagonists drive around in their pick-up truck (described by the Native American father of one of them as a "sickness" that drives people apart) and go about their hedonistic pleasures, which, however, significantly involves a healthy amount of subversive energy when they rustle the cattle of a local rancher who has a helicopter at his disposal. Machinery is omnipresent in the film, variously providing dull pleasure, authoritarian control, regulated assembly line work, or showing harrowing ineptitude. Ultimately, the rustling is stopped incongruently by Slim Pickens on horseback who manages to intimidate the driver in a giant truck by prancing in front of him. The two misfits are sent to the eponymous free range prison, and ironically enjoy their lives on horseback much more than in the machine-infested civilization.

The incompetence associated with machinery that is hinted at in *Lonely Are the Brave* and *Rancho Deluxe*, particularly in their portrayal of helicopters, is more fully explored in Westerns that reassert the validity of old-fashioned frontier justice in an age of "make love, not war" sentiments. These films often feature aging classic Western stars like John Wayne and Robert Mitchum, who are eager to demonstrate their persistent/continuing capabilities by battling arrogant youngsters, who stand in for a wayward 60s generation. In *The Good Guys and the Bad Guys* (1969), cars are a feature of an overly sophisticated, effeminate, and ultimately weak society, which ignores the threats of an outlaw gang rather than strengthening the police force so as not to scare away potential investors. Against the caricature of a corrupt, greedy, and perpetually horny liberal mayor, Robert Mitchum and George Kennedy play characters who bring down the cruel outlaws with old-fashioned law and order in a climactic chase involving horses and a railroad, while the rest of the town arrives at the scene too late in a slapstick car pursuit complete with shrill honking and one car obliterated by the train. Clearly, cars do not get the job done, and they tend to accentuate the physical incapacitation of their passengers whose concern for a refined appearance stands in the way of pragmatic action.

Similarly, in *Tell Them Willie Boy Is Here* (1969) and *The Last Hard Men* (1976) the lawmen need to abandon their cars and dude outfits in order to man up and pursue the outlaws in rugged, rocky terrain, thereby establishing (with reluctant efficiency in *Willie Boy* and with gleeful sadism in *Last Hard Men*) that law and order require drastic action. Perhaps the most sustained expression of this ideology can be found in *Big Jake* (1971). In that film the eponymous hero, played by John Wayne, refuses to join the posse led by his sons (played by Wayne's actual sons Patrick and Ethan) on "velocipedes" and motorcycle in order to rescue his grandson Little Jake from a band of brutal outlaws. Here again the "middle generation" is portrayed as partly arrogant in their technological savvy and partly irredeemably rotten and vicious. In a telling shot the convoy of automobiles passes by Wayne's one man on a horse outfit on a bridge while the rider takes the rough route through the water. The suggestion is clear, the seeming superiority of the machines in terms of speed and visual positioning is undercut by the steady flexibility of the more natural form of progression. In the ensuing scene, the noise of the cars alerts the outlaw band to the posse's presence, which is promptly ambushed. Quickly, tires are blown, engines explode, and vehicles uncontrollably veer across cliffs and shatter into pieces. Only the motorcycle can create some havoc until it, too, sends its rider into the dust. With the vehicles gone, the survivors join the elder horseman, learn to respect his ways and collaboratively under his leadership manage to rescue the grandchild.

While cars may be the most prominent machine in Westerns of the 1960s and 70s, the most commonly featured machine in the genre as such is the railroad. Its importance for the classical manifestation of the progressive and the populist Western has already been highlighted. In the 1960s the tendencies of the populist Western to emphasize the railroad as the representative of capitalist expansion and greed become even more pronounced. *Once Upon a Time in the West* (1968) is among the most sophisticated films to explore both the populist and progressive implications of the railroad. Here the railroad magnate dreams of reaching the sea with his machine but chooses the wrong methods to achieve his goal. Instead of collaborating with the settlers in towns, farms, and water points along the way, he coerces them into giving up their land with the help of his henchman Frank. The train compartment with its lush, garishly decorated interior from which he conducts his business is an apt symbol for his inability to socially interact with others and preferring the isolating bubble of civilized refinement. This prison created by individualist big business enterprise proves so crippling, both physically and emotionally, that it will eventually become his death trap when it ends up stranded in the desert,[6] his dream of seeing the ocean dwindling to the size of a puddle. In the final scene, however, the train is redefined as a machine controlled by human cooperation, when it carries the railroad workers standing on the engine in a progressive vision of industry as communal effort.

The Wild Bunch complicates the ideology of the populist Western. In line with convention, the railroad company is portrayed as "the antithesis of both family and Bunch values, a faceless corporation, the mercenary spirit incarnate, the symbol of all that is wrong with modern civilization" (Slotkin 605). Its pursuit of the bunch is so unashamedly base in its economic prerogatives that it does not shy away from slaughtering civilians in a planned ambush, hiring sadistic yet incompetent gunmen, and torturing a member into betraying his former partners.[7] Yet, the bunch itself, despite its open war with the railroad is not so easily separable from its methods. In the opening scene they arrive in town riding their horses along and within the railroad tracks. On the one hand, this can be read as a subtle indication of the trap that is awaiting the bunch, on the other hand, it illustrates the limitations of the bunch in increasingly evincing the same kind of volatile greed that characterizes the railroad. In terms of progressive corruption of erstwhile ideals (whether populist or progressive), their paths indeed run parallel.

The centerpiece of the film is the elaborate train robbery that shows the bunch at the peak of their game, smoothly harmonizing to master the awesome force of the machine. The robbery shrewdly exploits the fearsome self-perpetuating energy that the engine harbors. After they have made their escape, they put the engine in reverse so that it crashes with tremendous force into the unhitched wagons in which the guarding soldiers keep their horses. The machine thus destroys itself and (almost) its protectors. This scene is symptomatic for the portrayal of trains in Westerns of that time that continually address the frightening destructive potential of machines.[8] If the machine can harbor and perpetuate such impressive energy to create dynamic motion on its own, it is at all times in danger of going out of human control. The bunch directs this destructive potential back at the machine, simultaneously exposing and neutralizing it.[9]

Various Westerns provide thematic inflections of such self-destructive machine portrayals. In the climactic chase scene from *The Good Guys and the Bad Guys* the train simply crashes when it is made to pass its destined stop where the outlaws await its arrival. Its ruins provide the backdrop for a classic shootout. In *Joe Kidd* (1972) the train brings the duded-up mercenary killers to town in order to hunt down Native settlers whose land claims are a thorn in the flesh of the railroad bosses. The title character surprises the posse when he crashes the train into a saloon, thereby turning around the "progressive" thrust of the railroad and exposing it as an instrument of destruction harmful to civilization. In *Rio Lobo* (1970) the Southern Guerilla fighters bring down a Northern train by means of nature: grease on the tracks, bees in the caboose, and ropes tied between trees to arrest the power of the engine. They turn the tightly armored compartment into a trap for its passengers.[10] In *Butch Cassidy and the Sundance Kid*, finally, the fortification of the train is so strong that the dynamite to blast it open completely demolishes the entire car.

Routinely, the train is portrayed as a bringer of mostly negative representatives of civilization: the mercenary killers in *Joe Kidd*, the superposse in *Butch Cassidy and the Sundance Kid*; the Pinkertons in *The Great Northfield Minnesota Raid* (1972), who arrive too late for action. However, the railroad can also bring more positive figures of civilization, adding to the ambivalence of progress. In *Once Upon a Time in the West* Jill McBain arrives on the train, hopeful and radiant. Admittedly, she needs to undergo a transformation, in terms of dress and attitude, in order to become the symbol for an earthy sustaining spirit that will form the basis of a burgeoning civilization. Just like Jill and Hildy in *Cable Hogue*, Constanze Miller in *McCabe and Mrs. Miller* (1971) arrives as a finely dressed prostitute in Presbyterian Church, combining the allure of progress with its hankering for commercial calculation. Her arrival on a primitive steam engine signals a new step in the development of the settlement. She is (literally and figuratively) hungry for personal gain, and her independence and professional competence turn bumbling entrepreneur McCabe's local brothel into a community center and moneymaker. Yet it is precisely her competence as a business woman that attracts corporate interest, and McCabe finds himself battling for his life against a posse of hired killers when he refuses to sell out his teeming business. The machine with which Miller arrives reappears during this final confrontation. While McCabe battles the killers alone, the steam engine is used to quench the fire that has broken out in the church. The rescue of the hollow symbol that nobody has visited, let alone shown any appreciation for throughout the film, manages to unite the community in a combined and successful effort while McCabe is unknowingly left to die in the snow and Miller seeks oblivion in an opium den. The machine has thus won, both in terms of big business taking over small business and a hypocrisy of values triumphing over compassion, and once again the individuals destroyed by the machine are those who are complicit in introducing it.

Perhaps the most unique comment on such complicity can be found in *The Great Northfield Minnesota Raid*. In the film Cole Younger, the intelligent strategist of the James-Younger gang, shows a wide-eyed fascination for the "marvel of mechanics." On the train to Northfield he is enthralled by a salesman's presentation of miniature boxers and (foreshadowing the ending) a singing bird in a cage. The commercial spirit pervades the presentation of machines in the film, but Cole seems to be more fascinated with their inherent "wonderment." Mostly to attract customers, a calliope, a steam-powered organ, is presented in front of the bank that the gang is planning to rob. However, the instrument initially produces lots of steam but little music, indicating the bumpy road that leads to progress. Only after Cole fixes the gauge right before the robbery is it workable. During the robbery a raving vagabond is shot and lands on the calliope, which produces a shrill, unnerving sound that alarms the population, again a machine spinning out of human control. With the timelock on the safe frustrating any attempts at loot, the gang is apprehended empty-handed, and Cole ends up being paraded around the town in a cage while the calliope plays a melodious tune. The subversive outlaw spirit that Cole represents has been tamed by civilization and is transformed into a myth of the past, safely integrated into a conservative ideology of populism set to catchy music. The irony of Cole assisting the marvel of mechanics in capturing the gang is transformed into a smile on his lips when he joyfully recognizes that the calliope finally works.

Conclusion

Technology in the Westerns of the 1960s and 70s, unsurprisingly, harbors overwhelmingly negative qualities. Developing the tendencies further that Marx observed in the course of nineteenth-century American literature, machines are not only a disturbance of the pastoral ideal, they are multidimensional killers, routinely associated with death and violence, cold-hearted corporate capitalism, pseudo-sophisticated hierarchy, mindless hedonism, rule-bound confinement and limited movement, dynamos of self-perpetuating energy that spin out of control and cause random destruction, or they are harrowingly and comically inept to live up to a frontier spirit of ruggedness and persistence. This negative portrayal is complicated by the occasional allure that machines have for characters, their air of civilized progress, particularly when they are associated with women. The heroes whose traditional lifestyle and values are destroyed by machines are either stylized as the saviors from the corruptions of modernity or unwittingly are complicit in assisting in their ascent. In this way, Westerns criticize both the progressive and populist incarnations of the genre and their ideologies of industrial progress and mythical salvation from its evils respectively. The reasons for this subversive turn can be connected to the general critical self-inspection that the genre undertook in the wake of 1960s social turmoil, questioning the cultural tenets that had traditionally supported the ideology of American exceptionalism and progressiveness. With its self-critical attitude, the Western not only maintained its cultural relevance, it also offered itself as a particularly appropriate vehicle of cultural criticism, suggesting a society in the making that exposes its own flaws at the moment of making the step into the age of machines. In this way, the negative portrayal of machines has become an iconographic mainstay of the Western, which has assumed the role of being a critic of the aberrations of modernity while maintaining a self-reflexive distance towards its own mythological underpinnings.

The science fiction film *Westworld* (1973) serves as a fitting metaphor for the development of the genre in this respect. In the film, the West is depicted as a mechanically fabricated fantasy world designed to cater to middle class male ideas of relaxation, echoing the emergence of the genre in the age of industrialization. Its cyborg gunfighter, however, malfunctions and starts attacking the representatives of middle class normality, killing them for real. Thus, the Western world, meant to celebrate industrialization's ascendancy by way of providing divertive pleasures and a frontier spirit of progressivism, comes back to haunt and attack the very values which gave birth to it. Ironically, the disturbing machine in the fictional West's garden of conservative complacency is the black-hatted gunfighter, the American frontier's most recognizable villain.

NOTES

1. This is how Buscombe describes the scene: "[k]nowing the period and location, we expect to find at the beginning a familiar western town. In fact, the first few minutes of the film brilliantly disturb expectations. As the camera moves around the town, we discover a policeman in uniform, a car, a camel, and Randolph Scott, dressed up as Buffalo Bill. Each of these images performs a function. The figure of the policeman conveys that the law has become institutionalized; the rough and ready frontier days are over. The car suggests [...] that the west is no longer isolated from modern technology and its implications. Significantly, the camel is racing against a horse; such a grotesque juxtaposition is painful. A horse in a western is not just an animal but a symbol of dignity, grace and power. These qualities are mocked by it competing with a camel; and to add insult to injury, the camel wins" (23).

2. Cars and other modern vehicles also appear with regularity in early B-Westerns, particularly during the 1930s (cf. Fenin/Everson 13; Buscombe 31; Slotkin 273–276). *Overland Stage Riders* (1938) featuring John Wayne is particularly illustrative of the B-Western's tendency to confuse "temporal references that had the effect of expanding the mythic space of the Western, making it a kind of cinematic fourth dimension in which heroes from an earlier epoch battled the evils of the present time" (Slotkin 273). In that film, Wayne and his Mesquiteers assist the operators of an airplane transport service against the sabotage activities of a rivalling bus line, helping along technological progress by means of horseback riding and climactic shootouts.

3. Such a reference to Australia can also be found in *Butch Cassidy and the Sundance Kid* (1969) and *Support Your Local Sheriff* (1969).

4. Guido joins the hunt for horses in a plane, which carries the same destructive connotations as in *The Wild Bunch*. Guido was a bomber pilot in World War II and repeatedly tells with pride about his efficiency as a killer.

5. A place to look for cheap pleasures are the bars that Hud frequents, in which "debased Country and Western music [...] issues from juke-boxes" (French 82). The jukebox is another machine that makes a regular appearance in the post-Westerns, bespeaking the loss of an authentic culture and its replacement with its commercial aberration. The musical commercialization of the cowboy cult is brought to its satiric culmination in Robert Altman's *Nashville* (1975), in which Ronee Blakley sings a hymn to the proud modern cowboy: "He's got a tapedeck in his tractor and he listens to the local news/He finds out where the 'vestor's bidding while he's ploughing through the country blues/He was a cowboy and he knew I loved him well." In *Rancho Deluxe* (1975), jukeboxes are joined by arcade games, whose monitors frame the cowboys' faces in an illusion of activity.

6. *The Train Robbers* (1973) features an even eerier image of a train wreck half-swallowed by desert dunes.

7. Deke Thornton is coerced into "giving his word" to the railroad to hunt down the bunch. "That's not what counts. It's who you give it to," Ernest Borgnine's Dutch argues. His attempts to tell the bunch apart from the others (the good guys from the bad guys) are more stubbornness than conviction.

8. This stance echoes the fears of incalculable forces set off by the machine age addressed by Henry Adams at the turn of the 20th century in his influential essays "The Dynamo and the Virgin" and "The Law of Acceleration" (379–390, 489–498; cf. Marx 345–350).

9. The train is not the only machine in *The Wild Bunch* that develops an out of control destructive energy. Peckinpah's film very prominently features a machine gun. The machine gun had entered the genre on a big scale in Italian Westerns like *Fistful of Dollars* (1964) and *Django* (1966). It also makes an appearance in *The Professionals* (1966), *The War Wagon*

(1967) and *100 Rifles* (1968). Weapons of course belong to the "tools of the trade" of the Western, and as Buscombe says, "there is a special irony in the combination within the Western of a traditional ideology of self-reliant individualism which is, paradoxically, dependent on the gun, a piece of technology which was one of the earliest flowers of the industrialized collectivism of the machine age" (132). Where in the classical Western, the six-gun functions as an indicator of the personal skill of the fast draw, the sophisticated weaponry used in Westerns of the 1960s and 70s (besides the machine gun this includes scoped rifles and semi-automatic weapons in *Joe Kidd*, *The Missouri Breaks*, *Billy Two Hats*, *Big Jake*) introduces an element of unfairness. Now it is the one who can afford the best weapons who wins the gunfight, not necessarily the most skilled gunman. In *The Wild Bunch* it is initially General Mapache who wields the machine gun, which not only stresses the hierarchical dimension of modern weaponry but also the distinctly militaristic nature of mechanized killing (cf. Lenihan 51). The introduction of the machine gun is undoubtedly comic, with Mapache giddily grasping it like a child playing with a new toy, barely being able to control it, barely missing his own men, and finally being thrown down by its force only to immediately get up and try again. The comedy, however, does not diminish the frightening qualities of uncontrollable destructiveness and the obvious exhilaration felt by the shooter at the awesome power that he unleashes (cf. Seydor 186–187). These qualities are presented at their most frightening in the final shootout when one member of the bunch after another takes the helm at the gun and joyfully slaughters the onrushing mass of soldiers while often being thrown around by bullet hits himself so that the direction of the gunfire seems positively random at times. True to Adams' "law of acceleration" (and the spirit of the contemporaneous Vietnam War) the destruction progressively escalates, especially after Pike hits boxes of dynamite that explode in all directions. The dance of death that the bullet-riddled bodies perform is the visual correspondence to the triumph of machine over man: it is the machine that animates the twitching bodies in grotesque movements after human agency has ceased, and the gun keeps firing after Pike receives his mortal wound.

10. In *The War Wagon* the eponymous vehicle similarly entraps the heavily armed guards. The machine-gun equipped but horse-drawn transport vehicle for dirty railroad money becomes a metal tomb when it speeds across a cliff after it is demolished by a tree trunk.

Filmography

The Ballad of Cable Hogue. Dir. Sam Peckinpah. Warner Bros., 1970.
Big Jake. Dir. George Sherman. Cinema Center Films / Batjac Productions, 1971.
Billy Two Hats. Dir. Ted Kotcheff. Algonquin, 1974.
Butch Cassidy and the Sundance Kid. Dir. George Roy Hill. Twentieth Century Fox Film Corporation, 1969.
Convoy. Dir. Sam Peckinpah. United Artists, 1978.
Django. Dir. Sergio Corbucci. B.R.C. Produzione S.r.l. / Tecisa, 1966.
Dodge City. Dir. Michael Curtiz. Warner Bros., 1939.
Fistful of Dollars. Dir. Sergio Leone. Jolly Film, 1964.
The Good Guys and the Bad Guys. Dir. Burt Kennedy. Robert Goldstein Productions, 1969.
The Great Northfield Minnesota Raid. Dir. Philip Kaufman. Universal Pictures, 1972.
How the West Was Won. Dir. John Ford / Henry Hathaway / George Marshall / MGM, 1962.
Hud. Dir. Martin Ritt. Paramount Pictures, 1963.
The Iron Horse. Dir. John Ford. Fox Film Corporation, 1924.
Jesse James. Dir. Henry King. Twentieth Century Fox Film Corporation, 1939.
Joe Kidd. Dir. John Sturges. Universal Pictures, 1972.
Junior Bonner. Dir. Sam Peckinpah. American Broadcasting Company, 1972.
The Last Hard Men. Dir. Andrew V. McLaglen. Twentieth Century Fox Film Corporation, 1976.
Lonely Are the Brave. Dir. David Miller. Joel Productions, 1962.
McCabe and Mrs. Miller. Dir. Robert Altman. Warner Bros., 1971.
The Misfits. Dir. John Huston. Seven Arts Pictures, 1961.

The Missouri Breaks. Dir. Arthur Penn. Devon / Persky-Bright, 1976.
Nashville. Dir. Robert Altman. Paramount Pictures, 1975.
Once Upon a Time in the West. Dir. Sergio Leone. Rafan Cinematografica / Finanzia San Marco / Paramount, 1968.
100 Rifles. Dir. Tom Gries. Twentieth Century Fox Film Corporation, 1969.
Overland Stage Riders. Dir. George Sherman. Republic Pictures, 1938.
The Professionals. Dir. Richard Brooks. Columbia Pictures, 1966.
Rancho Deluxe. Dir. Frank Perry. Elliott Kastner Productions, 1975.
Ride the High Country. Dir. Sam Peckinpah. MGM, 1962.
Rio Lobo. Dir. Howard Hawkes. Cinema Center Films / Batjac Productions, 1970.
The Shootist. Dir. Don Siegel. Paramount Pictures, 1976.
Support Your Local Sheriff! Dir. Burt Kennedy. United Artists, 1969.
Tell Them Willie Boy Is Here. Dir. Abraham Polonsky. Universal Pictures, 1969.
Union Pacific. Dir. Cecile B. DeMille. Paramount Pictures, 1939.
The War Wagon. Dir. Burt Kennedy. Universal Pictures, 1967.
Westworld. Dir. Michael Crichton. MGM, 1973.
The Wild Bunch. Dir. Sam Peckinpah. Warner Bros., 1969.

Works Cited

Adams, Henry. *The Education of Henry Adams.* Ernest Samuels (ed.). Boston: Houghton Mifflin, 1973.
Buscombe, Edward. *The BFI Companion to the Western.* London: BFI, 1988.
_____. "The Idea of Genre in the American Cinema." *Film Genre Reader IV.* Barry Keith Grant (ed.). Austin: Texas University Press, 2012. 12–26.
Cawelti, John. *The Six-Gun Mystique Sequel.* Bowling Green State University Press, 1999.
Durgnat, Raymond, and Scott Simmon. "Six Creeds That Won the Western." *The Western Reader.* Jim Kitses, Gregg Rickman (eds.). New York: Limelight, 1998. 59–83.
Fenin, George N., and William K. Everson. *The Western: From the Silents to the Seventies.* New York: Grossman, 1973.
French, Philip. *Westerns: Aspects of a Movie Genre and Westerns Revisited.* Manchester: Carcanet, 2005.
Gallafent, Edward. "Not with a Bang: The End of the West in *Lonely Are the Brave, The Misfits* and *Hud*." *The Movie Book of the Western.* Ian Cameron, Douglas Pye (eds.). London: Studio Vista, 1996. 241–254.
Kitses, Jim. "Authorship and Genre: Notes on the Western." *The Western Reader.* Jim Kitses, Gregg Rickman (eds.). New York: Limelight, 1998. 57–68.
_____. *Horizons West: Directing the Western from John Ford to Clint Eastwood.* new ed. London: BFI, 2004.
Lenihan, John H. *Showdown: Confronting Modern America in the Western Film.* Urbana: Illinois University Press, 1980.
Lusted, David. *The Western.* Harlow, England: Pearson/Longman, 2003.
Marx, Leo. *The Machine in the Garden: Technology and the Pastoral Ideal in America.* New York: Oxford University Press, 1973.
Seydor, Paul. *Peckinpah: The Western Films: A Reconsideration.* Urbana: Illinois University Press, 1999.
Slotkin, Richard. *Gunfighter Nation: The Myth of the Frontier in Twentieth-Century America.* New York: HarperPerennial, 1992.
Tompkins, Jane. *West of Everything: The Inner Life of Westerns.* New York: Oxford University Press, 1992.
Turner, Frederick Jackson. *The Frontier in American History.* New York: Dover, 1996.

"Dynamite blows two ways"[1]
Dynamite in Western Films

GILLES CHAMEROIS

George Roy Hill's *Butch Cassidy and the Sundance Kid* (1969) begins with the Kid visiting the new bank in town, and scrutinizing with a worried look the increasingly sophisticated apparatus of locks and safes he has to outsmart if he is to continue his outlaw activities. The second time he and Butch Cassidy try to open one of these new safes, in a train they have just raided, they blow up the whole car, sending all the banknotes flying into the air. The Kid exclaims, "Think you used enough dynamite there, Butch?" The use of dynamite in the Western is readily associated with such spectacular pyrotechnics, and with second-degree 1960s Westerns pushing the codes of the genre past the limits of verisimilitude, whether they were produced in Italy or just under the influence. Indeed, in "Big Bang Hypothesis," Robert MacLean intimates that dynamite is an apt metaphor for the whole of 1960s cinema's breaking away from traditional codes, and he mentions quite a few Westerns, from *Johnny Guitar* (1954) to *Duck, You Sucker!* (1972). Dynamite, however, has been bound up with the Western film from its inception. *The Great Train Robbery* (1903), generally considered to have inaugurated the genre, took as its basis the very same historical events as *Butch Cassidy and the Sundance Kid*,[2] at a time when the gang was still active. The gangsters open a strongbox using dynamite and, in the colorized versions of the film, the explosion is one of the few elements to be hand-colored, along with the gunshots and the lady's gowns at the ball (Yojimbe 68). The film's explosion thus aestheticized and turned into spectacle the event virtually at the same time as it happened. Delineating the history of the relationship between dynamite and Western films hence means going back to the origins. It involves the study of the relation of film and of dynamite to other technologies—that of the train, for example, in the case of Porter's film as in many others. Film was invented at the very moment when the American frontier had been pushed out by the inexorable advance of the technological developments of the East, and all the new technology could record was the disappearance of the West, and its recreation in "imagination, or better in hyper-reality. It was envisaged as the place where the positive values of the nation could find refuge" (Leutrat 20).[3] The most famous last shot in *The Great Train Robbery* stages each time anew the death of the spectator, as the leader of the gang fires directly toward the camera. In the same way, Westerns from the beginning have repeatedly staged the destruction of the West, and the ineluctable character of the dynamite explosion has been used more and more insistently as a symbol of this destruction, especially from the 1960s onward.

We will follow a chronological line, make no attempt at exhaustiveness, and rather follow a meditation that could have been different had different films been chosen for emphasis, a meditation that in its conclusion will aim to approach the paradoxical links between dynamite and the materiality of film. The greatest classical Westerns are haunted with the genre's "original melancholia" with a universe at once "immediately close and irremediably lost," "that has just disappeared" (Cohen 55). However, we will first show that during the Golden Age the use of dynamite, which often occurs in lesser films—with the notable exception of *Rio Bravo*, arguably classicism's blaze of glory—at first eschews the contradictions of such a backward gaze. We will also show, however, that this occultation itself is revelatory. In contrast, as we will see, the new Westerns appearing from the end of the fifties, and then mainly the spaghetti Westerns of the sixties, use dynamite in their efforts at exposing this occultation, and at shattering the traditional codes of the genre, thus saving it from repetition and degeneration. We will then turn our attention to the legacy of the spaghetti Western in the Mexico Westerns of the 1960s and early 1970s, which feature dynamite extensively in their efforts at re-inventing and re-adapting the genre's codes to a newfound frontier. Finally, we will study the increasing use of dynamite in more recent Westerns, concentrating our attention to those that stage the end of the genre in spectacular explosions, the better to renew it.

Classical Westerns

Stephen R. Bown, in his history of dynamite, insists on the importance of the invention for the second half of the nineteenth century: "All the great hallmarks of nineteenth-century industrial and technical know-how, the famous monumental projects that defined the era were conceived and completed, with great loss of life, terrible suffering and injury, and in some cases incalculable and irreparable environmental damage, only because of the frightening power of dynamite and its variations" (84–85). A great many of the examples Bown analyzes are linked to the westward expansion of the United States after the Civil War, as dynamite was invented in 1867, and the Western films cover a good part of the wide array of uses Bown mentions, as a small sample from the beginning of the fifties can show: in *The Homesteaders* (1953), dynamite is used to clear rocks and stumps to make a farm; in *Blowing Wild* (1953), set in South America, it is associated with oil wells; it is used to blast a tunnel in *Carson City* (1952), and to build a road in *Dynamite Pass* (1950); in *The Arizona Cowboy* (1950), it is linked to an irrigation project. The most common elements linked to dynamite, however, are the railroad, as in *A Ticket to Tomahawk* (1950), and mines, as in *The Duel at Silver Creek* (1952). Dynamite is a perfect embodiment of the ambiguous view of technology in the Western, first because, like any technology, and especially any technological weapon, it can be used for good or bad, and second because, like any technology, it marks the relentless progress of the Frontier and the doomed future of the West. As an initial example, we will approach the different, contradictory uses it can be put to in *Rainbow Valley* (1935), a "Poverty Row" Western with John Wayne. In the film, John Wayne plays John Martin, an engineer and undercover agent who helps defeat gangsters who frighten prospectors so as to get their claims, and who keep sabotaging the road which is to link the "lost valley" of the title to civilization, law and order. Dynamite is used first by an old-timer who defeats half of the gang single-handedly by throwing dynamite as he drives his car, the only one in the valley. Finally, the gangsters steal dynamite from the roadworks but, tricked by John Martin and his superior engineering skills, the gangster setting off the final explosion, which he believes will wreck the road, instead creates a final pass for it to go through and kills all the rest of his gang.[4]

A number of elements can be recognized here as the standard elements in the use of dynamite in classical Westerns. Dynamite is first used by the forces of progress and civilization to blast away blocking elements, these material elements being symbolically linked to the villains blocking communication and the free play of competition. It is often linked to other technological elements, here the car. What is more, dynamite allows one single individual, or a small group, to vanquish a bigger or stronger group, as is evident in the figure of the old-timer, who will often be associated with dynamite. But dynamite blows two ways: more often than not, it is also used by the villains to hinder progress. Because of its power it can also become the weapon of the coward[5] or of the maniac.

A deeper paradox is involuntarily implicit in one of the last images of the film, a shot of the pass created by the final explosion, worthy of William Henry Jackson's lunar photographs of the havoc caused by the construction of Western railroad lines. *Rainbow Valley* has been linked to the East, but the valley does not seem worthy of its name any longer, and this original destruction heralds the arrival of more automobiles. Dynamite made the conquest of the West possible, but in so doing it turned the West into something else than the West. It is a paradox that is largely eschewed in the classical Western's use of dynamite. Two examples will suffice, *Canadian Pacific* (1949), a hymn to the railroad, and *The Big Trees* (1952), with Kirk Douglas. In *Canadian Pacific*, dynamite is used by both sides. The old-timer dynamite specialist, named Dynamite, manages at one point to escape the Native Americans whom the villains have tricked into helping them in their sabotage by proposing dynamite sticks for them to smoke.[6] On the other side, as is explained by the leader of the gangster fur traders, intent on stopping the railroad to keep his monopoly over the trade, "it only takes a couple of sticks" to stop progress. Bown notes the importance of dynamite for the historical laying out of the line, and adds that "hundreds, if not thousands, of ill-treated Chinese coolies perished in the blasting accidents during the construction" (93). No images of Chinese coolies, ill-treated or otherwise, will be found in the film. What is also occulted, in sharp contrast to the opening images of 1940s trains underlying the importance of the line, is the change to the landscape brought about by the train, and by dynamite in making way for the train. The first images of *Canadian Pacific* show its hero, a surveyor by trade, walking in beautiful sceneries actually shot in National Parks (Gaberscek and Stier 263), thus in areas that in reality had to be forcefully preserved from the transformations brought about by the train. After using dynamite in the right way, and defeating its improper use by the traders and by Native Americans,[7] the surveyor can look at the same beautiful landscape, accompanied by his wife-to-be, in the final images of the film. Making way for the transcontinental train seemingly has had no effect on the land, and the final images intimate that no effect is implied in the future.

The Big Trees (Felix E. Feist, 1952) at first sight seems to deal with the environmental effects of the conquest of the West. The ruggedly individualistic timber baron played by Kirk Douglas, after trying to rob Quakers out of their claims, finally gives in to love and decides to side with them in their efforts to save their sequoias, which are sacred to them. He convinces them to fight his evil competitor and to blow the dam he uses to prevent them from selling their sustainably-grown timber, instead of relying on their customary non-violence: "You can't pray this dam out of the way!" You can't, but dynamite used by a God-fearing community and by a redeemed man can restore the river to its natural flow. Indeed, more generally, the explosive finales of classical Westerns mark a return to the natural flow of things, to a natural order that had been hindered by evil individuals. The most memorable of these explosive finales, and the model for many which would follow, is Howard Hawks' *Rio Bravo* (1959). As Hawks has remarked, the idea of the film came from two elements, his daughter's idea for the final scene and his dislike of *High Noon*'s contrived, liberal plot (McBride 163). So the restored order at the end of the film is also a vindication of—and a nostalgia for—what the Western should have remained. The importance of dynamite in the plot is prepared from the start, as a wagon full of the explosive arrives at the corral where the final shootout will take place. And as Jean-Louis Leutrat and Suzanne Liandrat-Guigues note, "the idea of the dynamite sticks is a screenwriting trick which allows to explode the narrowness and formal abstraction [of the film] so as to open up a new, pluridimensional space" (96). The paradoxes of dynamite are integrated into Hawks' insistence on the value of professionalism. Far from dynamite being the weapon of the coward, or worst of the people, the final scene exalts the coordinated teamwork of a few committed individuals, and mixes its use of dynamite with the most professional of skills, gun skills, as the dynamite sticks, conveniently, have not been provided with fuses and have to be shot at to explode.

The explosive finale would play a role in a number of later Wayne vehicles:

> Dynamite explosions are used in the Hawks of *Rio Bravo*, *El Dorado* [1966], and *Rio Lobo* [1970] in ways paradoxically constructive. The number of Wayne's films which conclude with explosions of evil and old disorder is impressive. Besides the Hawks trilogy, so do *The Comancheros* [1961], *The Sons of Katie Elder* [1965], *War Wagon* [1967], *Hellfighters*, *The Train Robbers*, [1973] and *Rooster Cogburn* [1975].
>
> The power and desire to blow things up with dynamite or nitroglycerin, to burn and rebuild, are so frequent and so dominating they suggest symbolic force as much as narrative device, they are expression of infantile, primal urges to destroy opposition, force surrender, and reshape reality. This power ... is always a dramatic way to clear out the old, to make space for new starts [McGhee 127].[8]

In other, less enthusiastic words, these are just so many examples of the myth of regeneration through violence exposed by Richard Slotkin.[9] The explosive finale expresses faith in violence, faith that it can bring about a return to a blank slate, thus eschewing the paradoxes we have delineated by offering a new beginning, after the closure of the film.

Spaghetti Westerns

In 1968, when an interviewer observed "Westerns are different today," John Wayne answered, "Not mine" (Eyman 450).[10] But of course something radically different had been happening in other films at the end of the 50s and in the 60s, films in which explosions no longer reflected the classic dream of closure and return to a pre-existing order, but rather the uncertainty of the very settings the plots are based on.[11] Robert MacLean takes the example of the opening of *Johnny Guitar* (1954): "The explosions that begin *Johnny Guitar* ... signal that things are falling apart, the center has not held, and inaugurate a hell through which the chief characters must pass" (6). Nicholas Ray's film opens with the dynamite blasts which mark the inexorable advance of the railway. As Johnny remarks to Vienna, "They're closing the pass," and the railway men are thus altering both the geography of the landscape and the possible future available to the characters, narrowing rather than expanding its possibilities. The train, so often associated to dynamite, has changed polarities as compared to *Canadian Pacific*. From a force of westward expansion it has turned into the force than comes to destroy what was once the West. Likewise in Ray's *The True Story of Jesse James* (1957), the railway is the driving force for the monopolistic forces of the East, and of the North, which come to disrupt the homesteaders' simple lives, by blowing their setting to pieces as the Pinkertons blow up the James' house. It is only after this original disruption that dynamite can become a weapon for the James, a weapon that perfectly represents the impossibility of their quest for a return to the normalcy of home, as, unlike what happens in *The Big Trees*, a dynamite blow cannot possibly undo the effect of a preceding blow, but only worsen it.[12]

The biggest attack on the settings and codes of the traditional Western would obviously come from the spaghetti Western, with much help from dynamite. This is evident as early as Leone's first Western, *A Fistful of Dollars* (1964). Towards the end of the film, The Man with No Name, left nearly dead by one of the two evil gangs that fight over the town, is given dynamite by an old undertaker, his only ally. There is of course an unwritten rule in any Western, spaghetti or otherwise, and it is that a stick of dynamite that appears at some stage has to be put to use. But, although he has to fight an entire gang on his own, The Man With No Name will only use the dynamite to stage his return to the town, first with the sound of the explosion, then by emerging from the smoke. The regenerative explosion has become mere spectacle, a play of smoke over dust.

The Good, the Bad and the Ugly[13] stages the encounter of two technologies that will be systematically associated in later films, the machine gun and dynamite, or rather here its ancestor in the form of gunpowder wrapped in paper. The Man with No Name and his momentary ally use the sticks to destroy a bridge that is the object of a bloody, useless battle between the Union and Confederate armies. Robert MacLean analyses the role dynamite can play in uncovering the essential link between setting and plot, and it is of paramount importance here: the explosion destroys the setting that is the occasion for the battle, and thus shows the inanity of the plot on which war is based. And as we will see when we come to study the use of dynamite in Mexico Westerns, in his final Western, *Duck, You Sucker!*, Leone uses dynamite throughout to explode the settings and the codes both of the Western and of the spaghetti Western, closing the period of the Golden Age of the spaghetti Western, which he had opened with *A Fistful of Dollars*. This Golden Age saw dynamite used in numerous variations. The clichés of the Western and, increasingly, of the spaghetti Western itself, were constantly undercut, for example through denying expectations. A stick of dynamite reveals itself to be a candle in *I Am Sartana, Trade Your Guns for a Coffin* (1970). In Clint Eastwood's *High Plain Drifter* (1973), heavily influenced by the spaghetti Western, the Drifter throws dummy sticks which do not explode. In Monte Hellman's *China 9 Liberty 37* (1978), the sticks finally blow after an incredibly long time—incredibly, that is, in a Western's action scene. Ridiculous variations on clichés are offered: the sergeant in *Those Dirty Dogs* (1973) throws dynamite with a sling, and the hero in Sergio Sollima's *Run, Man, Run* (1968) has a lit dynamite stick put into his mouth by his captors.

The classical Western's insistence on skill is debunked in two opposite ways. Skills are advantageously replaced with technology: in Sergio Corbucci's *Django* (1966), a stick of dynamite and a rigged machine gun can create havoc in a whole gang without any human intervention after Django has left. On the contrary, skills can be exaggerated much beyond verisimilitude, which is the case throughout *My Name Is Nobody* (1973), directed by Tonino Valerii. Sergio Leone gave the original idea, produced the film and directed some scenes (Giré 278), including the showdown with the Wild Bunch towards the end of the film, during which a single man defeats the 150 men of the bunch by exploding their saddle bags, which are full of dynamite. Neil Campbell insists on Leone's use of intertextual references, including self-references, in this and other films, and remarks that in 1968 Barthes presented the literary text's incessant play of references as an explosion (132, 147).[14] In spaghetti Westerns, the explosion is also literal, and not only do references and codes get to be blown up to bits, but equally characters and whole settings. A potent image is given in an otherwise poor film, Antonio Margheriti's *Dynamite Joe* (1968). As his name indicates, Dynamite Joe is unbelievably skillful with dynamite, but what is more interesting is the obvious use of models in the special effects accompanying the pyrotechnics of the explosion of a whole mine. Here the filiation between the spaghetti Western and the peplum is most evident, as is and the comical force of the explosion to expose the fact that the setting is nothing more than a setting (Simsolo 83). Up until the spaghetti Western, from *The Great Train Robbery* onwards, dynamite in Westerns had always been used to exhibit real explosions and real destruction, even if only material, to give weight to its display of obviously faked deaths.

Mexico Westerns

The most visible legacy of the spaghetti Western, which we now propose to study, might be the link between dynamite and revolution. In Leone's words, "Plastic is the first weapon of the revolutionary. Not the machine gun! Not the gun! No, the God of Revolution is the explosive" (Simsolo 151).[15] Dynamite had sometimes been a weapon of choice for the revolutionary in American Westerns preceding the sixties, a striking example being *Viva Zapata!* (1952), where it could turn women into warriors, getting killed as they managed to blow up a gate with egg baskets full of dynamite.[16] But it becomes widely used as American filmmakers turn to Mexico to find back the flavors of the Old West, much like the mercenaries of *The Magnificent Seven* who cross the border to find occasion to use their gunslinging skills. The original film (1960), which Richard Slotkin presents as "nearly an allegory of American policy in Vietnam" (485), precedes spaghetti Westerns and does not feature dynamite, but is for Slotkin exemplary of "a mythic narrative whose structure insistently drives toward resolution in an all-encompassing, satisfying, purifying, spiritually regenerative act of violence" (486). Later films in the series use dynamite as a recurrent vector of this all-encompassiveness, whether it is used by the peasants, as in *Return of the Seven* (1966), or by a specialist among the mercenaries, as in *Guns of the Magnificent Seven* (1969). The use of dynamite in the two films exacerbates more than questions the myth of "selective targeting" which Slotkin sees as "the besetting fantasy of combat operations" (484) common to *The Magnificent Seven* and to the conduct of the Vietnam War—and, may we add, of later wars as well. Even the less simplistic *100 Rifles*, which like other Westerns of the period shows growing anxiety over the Vietnam War and presents "spectacular and literal displays of *excessive* violence by both sides" (575)[17] indulges in the same explosive finale, with all the major heroes throwing dynamite, with no collateral damage. In this respect at least, it is does not question the myth of regenerative violence any more than a John Wayne movie.

In contrast, three important films of the period, *The Professionals*, *The Wild Bunch* and *Duck, You Sucker!*, tried in different ways to expose this myth. The way Richard Brook's *The Professionals* (1966) achieves this is first by moving the explosive finale to the middle of the film, thus questioning its aftermath, and in fact completely transforming its reading. The professionals change allegiance at the very end of the film, and decide to hand back Maria (Claudia Cardinale) to her revolutionary lover instead of handing her to her husband, the railway tycoon who paid them to retrieve her. By the same token, all the casualties they have inflicted to the revolutionaries become at the very least collateral damage. Bill Dolworth (Burt Lancaster) is the professional specialized in dynamite, "for whom sex and violence are different aspects of the same action. Both involve 'explosions,' and both (he says) create life" (Slotkin 569). He is of course quite instrumental in the victory of four men over an army of revolutionaries in the battle scene. In a line reminiscent of the words of the hero of *The Big Trees*, "You can't pray this dam out of the way," he says as he is rigging a mountain pass to cover the escape of the group, "You light this fuse and dynamite, not faith, will move that mountain." The line can be taken as a perfect expression of materialistic nihilism, but a redeeming reversal comes at the end of the film, after Bill and the revolutionary bandit, seemingly maimed to death in the mountains, discuss their disillusion as to the revolution. Perhaps is it only when there is nothing left to believe in, at the point of utmost vulnerability, that faith becomes newly possible. In the Mexican Westerns we are going to consider from now on, and indeed also in the more recent Westerns, the role of dynamite always hovers between two different definitions of materialism, one that equates it with nihilistic annihilation and one that puts faith into matter and insists that something is left after the redemptive shattering of illusions brought about by dynamite.[18]

A few months after the release of *100 Rifles*, Sam Peckinpah's *The Wild Bunch* staged violence in such a way that it shattered the myth of its regenerative value. Although most collateral damage in the film is the work of guns in the opening sequence and the machine gun in the rest of the film, dynamite plays a significant role in underlining the sexual and suicidal dimensions of the fascination with violence. As Marsha Kinder has stated, "In the *Wild Bunch* the excessive violence is orgasmic rather than cathartic" (66). If dynamite is not used in the butchering of innocent by-standers that opens the film, it is used later to prepare for the final explosion of violence. Early in the film, as the Bunch light the fuse that is going to blow a bridge to cover their escape into Mexico, their cart gets stuck, and a long sequence intercuts between the fuse and their attempt at freeing the cart. The sequence plays on a rhythmical building of tension followed by release and explosion as the bridge explodes just after the Bunch has cleared it. As Hitchcock has shown, the emotional and almost physical response to such an impending explosion "is more powerful than the feelings of sympathy or dislike for the characters involved" (Truffaut 5). In other words, a hackneyed suspense scene here embodies all the paradoxes of our reaction to violence on screen, which will be exposed in the final scene. On another occasion, a member of the Bunch jokingly throws a stick of dynamite with just enough fuse in front of the old-timer of the bunch just as he is about to defecate, again linking dynamite to tension and release, this time in a comic mode, but whose senselessness shatters to pieces any pretension at a regenerative role. And on another occasion dynamite is used by the Bunch to rig their crates of rifles, threatening suicide by explosion as insurance against being robbed by the Mexican general who is supposed to buy the weapons, in a gambit whose winner is the one who has no reason to live. These uses of dynamite prepare for the final outburst of violence, and an explosion of dynamite comes at its climax.

Sam Peckinpah was at first meant to direct the last Mexico Western we are going to consider, *Duck, You Sucker!* with which Leone wanted to "put to death the traditional Western and the Western [he] had invented" (Simsolo 152). The Irish revolutionary Sean Mallory is a dynamite and nitroglycerin expert who cons Mexican bandit Juan Miranda into attacking the Mesa Verde National Bank, which holds political prisoners instead of gold. Dynamite is used throughout the film, starting with Sean's grandiloquent entrance as he shows the inside of his overcoat, full of vials and sticks: "You pull that trigger and shoot me, I fall. And if I fall ... they'll have to alter all the maps." The line is exemplary of the wish to destroy the setting, as were the intended opening credits, showing a peasant working in a Mexican landscape: "There is a series of shattering explosions. The smoke envelops the cactus and the mountains, and when it clears, we see a completely flattened horizon. Then the peone comes out from behind a pyramid of stones, looks around in a stupefied way, shrugs, and starts again to move some earth with a plough as if nothing had happened" (McLean 5). If in *Canadian Pacific* or *The Big Trees*, social order could be restored as the monopolistic forces were defeated, and the setting could stay intact, or indeed be restored to its virginity, in *Duck, You Sucker!* the opposite holds true: the whole setting is blown up, but no change in the setting, no matter how dramatic, can change anything to the injustice of the social order. However the destructive power of dynamite is not utterly vain, as it can also shatter any illusion to pieces. Writes Christopher Frayling: "Sean ... repeatedly detonates the contexts upon which Juan depends for his sense of identity—moves him from analog to digital, from the continuous to the discrete—as Leone does the myths and stock gestures which are his materials, acceptance of or identification with which constitutes an uncritical failure to duck" (152). These "myths and stock gestures" include those of the Western, of the spaghetti Western, and of the revolutionary sixties. Sean, who has known one revolution, says, "When I started using dynamite, I believed in many things, all of it! Now, I believe only in dynamite." The line echoes Burt Lancaster's belittlement of faith in *The Professionals*. It seems to take its disillusionment one step further, and the film ends with the explosion of a train full of dynamite, and with severely wounded Sean committing suicide with a dynamite-filled cigarette. Sean at one stage, realizing thanks to his peasant friend Juan that the revolution was but an illusion, had thrown in the mud a book by Bakunin he had been reading. Likewise Leone shatters his film to pieces to invite us to step outside, disillusioned at last and believing, not in books or in films anymore, but in friendship, dynamite, and mud, which is more than nothing, as materialism need not be nihilistic. From now on the Western, if it is to continue to exist, or rather if it is to be born again, will have to reconstruct its codes, and insist on their constructed and counterfactual character while at the same time offering a way out of the purely gratuitous effects of flaunted superficiality.

More Recent Westerns

Since *Duck, You Sucker!*, at least three important Westerns, *Heaven's Gate* (1980), *Pale Rider* (1985), and *Django Unchained* (2012), have included massive explosions of dynamite, each staging in its own way, like *Duck, You Sucker!*, the end of the Western.[19] In their final battle against the henchmen of the cattle barons in Michael Cimino's *Heaven's Gate*, the immigrants mix dynamite, the poor people's weapon of choice, with Roman art of war in the form of protective chariots, the idea for which Jim Averill, the marshal leading the posse of immigrants, got from his studies at Harvard. During the Johnson County War that serves as a model for the film, these "arks of safety" were actually built so as to get close enough to throw dynamite on the henchmen, in a final showdown that nearly took place, but didn't, as the Army moved on to save the henchmen before they do in the film (McDermott 31).[20] Cimino's move is directly opposite to that of John Wayne's choice to finish Alamo with the explosion of the gunpowder reserve that nearly took place historically, but didn't (Edmondson 371). In Wayne's film, the final regenerative violence was a way to build the myth of the nation anew, in Cimino's, it is used to debunk it, and especially to debunk the version of the Johnson County War proposed by *Shane* (1953). Shane's final words as he left the county he had pacified with his guns were "there aren't any more guns in the valley." Cimino answers that the struggle can obviously know no end, as the order restored by the powers that be is corrupted and has to be fought again. All that cinema can do is to stage a counterfactual near-final explosion, and insist that it is not final.

In staging this final showdown, Cimino also notoriously staged the end of New Hollywood, of his studio, and nearly of his career. The film premiered two weeks after Reagan's election and, considered as much of a class traitor as his leading character Jim Averill, Cimino was assassinated by the critics. But if the film was a box office bomb, we should remember that the name "blockbuster" comes from the name of a World War II bomb (Odello 13). To *Heaven's Gate* could be applied the unconventional definition of the word given by Hervé Aubron about Hitchcock's *Marnie*: "a film which does not represent mass but which rushes toward it, which does not merely suggest it but runs the risk of mass, a film which deliberately heads for disaster" (62).

In comparison, Clint Eastwood's *Pale Rider*, which is heavily influenced by *Shane*, at first seems to be a return to the tenets of classicism. Preacher, played by Clint Eastwood, comes from nowhere to rescue a group of tin-panners from the evil deeds of industrial miners "raping the land" with hydraulic mining. Dynamite is used twice in the film. First, in their efforts at intimidating the tin-panners, the industrialists use it to dam the creek. The tin-panners had actually thought about using dynamite to find gold but, considering the risks for the creek, had decided against it, "choosing instead to sustain nature so it can sustain them" (Heumann and Murray). The use of dynamite by the industrialists thus underlines their lack of respect for the environment, and echoes the attack on nature of their industrial mine. However, the second time dynamite is used, it is by Preacher and the leader of the tin-panners, who nonchalantly throw a dozen sticks and destroy the whole hydraulic mine. Thus, what dynamite and other technologies have done to the environment, dynamite can undo. The film begins with images of pristine nature, from which emerge first the gang of intimidators then, once a young girl has prayed for a miracle, Preacher, accompanied by a roll of thunder. The final images are of the same pristine nature, with Preacher going away, accompanied by the echoing words of love and thankfulness from the young girl. He can go back to where he came from, having restored proper relations with nature and within society, with the help of a little dynamite, properly used. But if the implied dream is the same in *Pale Rider* as in *Canadian Pacific* or *The Big Trees*, it is clearly shown to be the dream of a ghost, in the subjective and objective construction of the phrase: dreaming of a ghost who can come and save us from the effects of time equates dreaming like a ghost, and in a way being a ghost. Staging the impossible return of nature to its virginity in the form of a dynamite explosion, brought about by a ghost, is a way to acknowledge the impossibility of a return to mythical time, and "*Pale Rider* acknowledges history's undeniable influence on the mythic action." (Prats, 115). The effects of dynamite, like those of history, are irreversible. But the Western genre has always been concerned chiefly with the mythical staging of the irreversibility of history, most obviously in the ineluctable disappearance of the Frontier.

Quentin Tarantino's *Django Unchained* also stages a counterfactual explosion, which this time does not restore nature to its virginity, but on the contrary empowers one single slave to bring about the spectacular end of a plantation in an act of righteousness that is both implausible and anachronistic—the film takes place in 1858, nearly ten years before the invention of dynamite—act of righteousness. The ending of the film also stages its own expenditure, as it turns carnage into fireworks in the final explosion. Earlier on, Django had blown up one of its captors, played by Tarantino, who virtually evaporated from the screen before being replaced by Django, emerging in dissolve from the cloud of smoke, a clear nod to *A Fistful of Dollars*. This self-cancellation and the final explosion in some way resemble the surface effects of the extravagant explosions in Gore Verbinski's *Lone Ranger* (2013), reflecting on the constructed nature of the tale just told.[21] But they also intimate that what is left when all has disappeared is the material world, where no such grandiose act of justice took place, and the film, which is not pure surface,[22] but matter, and part of the material world. The counterfactual explosion is but the continuation of the explosion that started at the end of *Inglorious Basterds*, where rolls of nitrate film caused a whole cinema to explode, killing Hitler in the process: "I found the idea of nitrate film very rich. On the one side it is an apt metaphor for the power of cinema, on the other side it is not a metaphor, it is quite literal: you don't need dynamite when you've got nitrate film. Literal and metaphorical: that's great" (Tarantino 10–15).

In *Django Unchained*, Emmanuel Burdeau comments, "Tarantino has so well assimilated this materialism of the image that he no longer feels the need to flaunt it" (148).

* * *

Perhaps a fitting image for the power shared by dynamite and by the materiality of film is the time when the film stops and begins to consume itself, exposing the white screen behind the shadows its images had created, and, in the times of nitrate film, menacing fire and explosion. In his study of the materiality of film, Garrett Stewart states that in the moment film stops, or pretends to stop in the freeze frame, "the photogrammatic moment, even against the grain of narrative recuperation, may sometimes dynamite and anatomize a film's illusion of movement," thus recalling the "death-dealing discreteness" of photography which underlies cinema (38, 254). But Stewart insists on the fact that the relation is two-directional: "All photography is a kind of death; all instantaneous annihilation on film owes a debt to photography" (254). This indeed is also the conclusion of Robert MacLean's study of explosions in 1960s cinema, as he shifts his attention from film to the relation between photography and film: "Like the photograph, the explosion is a violent rupture of context and continuity, imposes decomposition, makes things dead, and is thus a potential tool of liberation" (6). In the case of Westerns, what is photographed and re-photographed over and over again is the end of the Frontier, and the force of the photograph stands in belying the illusion of re-creation brought about by the movement of the film. Some of the films we have mentioned make the connection. Nicholas Ray, for example, who emphasizes the role of dynamite in his version of the Jesse James story, also accumulates references to photographic apparatuses: onlookers steal two photographs as keepsakes at the scene of Jesse's death, and the explosion of a photographic flash punctuates the shootout when the James gang have been framed—pun intended. Monte Hellman also includes the startling explosion of a photographic flash in *China 9 Liberty 37*. *The Wild Bunch*'s opening images, as well as segments of the opening credits, are highly contrasted freeze frames of the protagonists riding their horses over railway tracks, nearly all white and a few dashes of black, as if indeed the film was about to turn to pure white and burn itself up, bringing to the image itself the cruel holocaust of scorpions by children at the beginning of the film, and the explosion that closes the final massacre. And, of course, *Butch Cassidy and the Sundance Kid* includes a long sequence of old-style stills of the heroes' escapades in New York and Europe, and ends on a freeze frame as Butch and the Kid run to their certain death as they face dozens of Bolivian soldiers. The silent film in the opening credits is a spoof of *The Great Train Robbery*, but already placed under the shadow of mourning, as its opening credits assert that, unlike Porter's film, it was filmed once the members of the gang were already "all dead." This mourning for the Frontier has been occulted in the classical Western's use of dynamite, before being turned into a cruel joke by the spaghetti Western. Dynamite has thus been used both to stage and to expose the myth of regenerative violence. Perhaps there is some regeneration to be found in the explosive power of each individual image. Perhaps, in each of the jumps between the shaky black and white photograms of the beginning of *Butch Cassidy and the Sundance Kid*, can we imagine, as in watching *The Great Train Robbery*, a painter delicately holding the nitrate film to paint each frame of the explosion, and taking literally Pasolini's remark that "making cinema is like writing on burning paper" (216).

Notes

1. The title of this essay is borrowed from a 1958 episode of the Western TV series *Bat Masterson*.

2. Karen R. Jones and John Wills, *The American West: Competing Visions* (Edinburgh: Edinburgh University Press, 2009), 232. It is to be noted that the historical Cassidy's attacks on occasions involved the excessive charges of dynamite depicted in George Roy Hill's film, for example the June 2, 1899, attack near Wilcox, Wyoming.

3. The translations of references given in French are mine.

4. A similar reversal occurs at the end of another of Wayne's B Westerns, *Riders of Destiny* (1933), as the dumb acolytes of the villain controlling the town's water supply blow up a well in order to block access to water and instead free up a whole river.

5. See for example its use by the villainous gunsmith in *The Sons of Katie Elder* (1965), who will eventually die in the explosion of the gunpowder in his own shop.

6. The trick is echoed in *The War Wagon* (1967), with John Wayne and Kirk Douglas, where the Native Americans are made to drink nitroglycerin. Dynamite is a weapon of choice in the victory of higher technology and knowledge over the Native Americans, as in *The Paleface* (1948), *Only the Valiant* (1951), *Last of the Comanches* (1953), *Massacre Canyon* (1954), or *Apache Ambush* (1955). It is rare indeed for the Native Americans to retaliate in kind, as in *Kit Carson* (1940).

7. And surviving the explosion of several cases of dynamite at close range...

8. Among these films, only *Hellfighters* is not a Western. *El Dorado* does not include explosions, in fact when asked to write a scene involving an exchange of prisoners and copying that of *Rio Bravo*, the scriptwriter, Leigh Brackett, "refused to write this unless Hawks promised not to use dynamite again" (Todd McCarthy, *Howard Hawks: The Grey Fox of Hollywood*

[New York: Grove Press, 2000], 618). Some explosions are more spectacular than others. *The Comancheros* (1961) includes only two minor explosions, and *Rio Lobo* builds up expectations of a *Rio Bravo* finale only to deflate them with a single, poorly aimed stick of dynamite. All the remaining films give a major role to dynamite or nitroglycerin in the finale, and often build up towards it throughout the film.

9. See in particular, for what concerns us, *Gunfighter Nation: The Myth of the Frontier in Twentieth-Century America* (New York: HarperPerennial, 1993).

10. John Wayne in "John Wayne, the Iron Duke, Sets 2–4 Pics for Next Year," interview with Frank Barron, *The Hollywood Reporter*, 28 May 1968: 28–68, is quoted in Scott Eyman, *John Wayne: The Life and Legend*.

11. Robert MacLean remarks, "Small wonder, then, that the explosion has become such a fundamental element of film vocabulary; explosions destroy settings" in "The Big-Bang Hypothesis: Blowing Up the Image." *Film Quarterly* 32.2 (Winter 1978–1979): 2–7, 3.

12. The railway agent throws a hand grenade, and not dynamite, in the version that really formalized the elements of the tale, Henry King's 1939 *Jesse James*, analyzed by Richard Slotkin, 295–301. Ray emphasizes the role of dynamite, but keeps the hand grenade. Dynamite as such does not really belong to the universe of such classical filmmakers as Henry King and John Ford, with minor exceptions in Ford's case, as far as I am aware *The Ace of the Saddle*, a 1919 silent film. The explosion at the end of *Drums Along the Mohawk* (1939) is obviously gunpowder.

13. Dynamite is also used in *For a Few Dollars More* (1965).

14. See similar remarks in Robert MacLean, 132–133.

15. See also El Chuncho's words to a beggar he gives his money to at the end of Damiano Damiani's *A Bullet for the General* (1966): "Don't buy bread with that money, hombre! Buy dynamite, dynamite!"

16. Explosives are also much used by the Juarista peasants in Robert Aldrich's *Vera Cruz*, but they do not include dynamite, as the film is set one year before its invention. Such anachronism did not bother Don Siegel in *Two Mules for Sister Sara* (1970), set at the same period.

17. Along with the presence of violence on both sides, one can note that the evil German adviser, a cliché of the Mexico Westerns' representation of the evil streak in technology, manages to escape unhurt, and the equally evil but syrupy representative of the U.S. train company tries apparently successfully to corrupt the new revolutionary victor.

18. I develop elements similar to those found here on *The Professionals*, *Duck, You Sucker!* and *Pale Rider* in "Pynchon, Leone and Dynamite" found in *Thomas Pynchon and the (De)vices of Global (Post)modernity*, ed. Zofia Kolbuszewska (Lublin: Wydawnictwo KUL, 2012), 54–68.

19. In the same period, a number of remakes added dynamite to spice up the originals, as *Dawn Rider* (2012) or *3: 10 to Yuma* (2007), in which Chinese coolies do work on the construction of the railroad, and other remakes increased the role of dynamite, as *Lone Ranger* (2013) or *American Outlaws* (2001), a Jesse James version that ends well.

20. Here John D. McDermott is quoting Asa S. Mercer, *Banditti of the Plains, or The Cattlemen's Invasion of Wyoming in 1892* (Cheyenne: A.S. Mercer, 1894).

21. The most spectacular explosion in *Lone Ranger*, that of the bridge, is actually counterfactual in the tale itself, as it is added as an afterthought by Tonto in his improvised tale to the young boy who hears the story.

22. Or even worse pure digits, if we recall Tarantino's dislike of digital cinema.

Filmography

The Ace of the Saddle. Dir. John Ford. Universal Film Manufacturing Company, 1919.
American Outlaws (2001). Dir. Les Mayfield. Warner Home Video, 2001. DVD.
Apache Ambush (1955). Dir. Fred F. Sears. Columbia Pictures Corporation 1955. DVD.
The Arizona Cowboy. Dir. Robert G. Springsteen. MPO Productions, 1950.
The Big Trees (1952). Dir. Felix Feist. Alpha Video, 2002. DVD.
Blowing Wild (1953). Dir. Hugo Fregnose. Team Marketing, 2015. DVD.

A Bullet for the General (1966). Dir. Damiano Damiani. Blue Underground, 2012. DVD.
Butch Cassidy and the Sundance Kid (1969). Dir. George Roy. 20th Century Fox Home Entertainment, 2000. DVD.
Canadian Pacific. Dir. Edwin L. Marin. 20th Century Fox, 1949.
Carson City (1952). Dir. Andre De Toth. Warner Archives, 2009. DVD.
China 9 Liberty 37 (1978). Dir. Monte Hellman. Alpha Video, 2010. DVD.
The Comancheros (1961). Dir. Michael Curtiz. 20th Century Fox Home Entertainment, 2003. DVD.
Dawn Rider (2012). Dir. Terry Miles. Nasser Group North, 2012. DVD.
Django (1966). Dir. Sergio Corbucci. Blue Underground, 2007. DVD.
Django Unchained (2012). Dir. Quentin Tarantino. The Weinstein Company, 2013. DVD.
Drums Along the Mohawk (1939). Dir. John Ford. 20th Century Fox Home Entertainment, 2005. DVD.
Duck, You Sucker! (1972). Dir. Sergio Leone. MGM (Video & DVD), 2007. DVD.
The Duel at Silver Creek (1952). Dir. Don Siegel. Universal Studios Home Entertainment, 2013. DVD.
Dynamite Joe (1968). Dir. Antonio Margheriti. Artus Films, 2013. DVD.
Dynamite Pass. Dir. Lew Landers. RKO Radio Pictures, 1950.
El Dorado (1966). Dir. Howard Hawks. Warners Bros Home Video, 2013. DVD.
A Fistful of Dollars (1964). Dir. Sergio Leone. MGM (Video & DVD), 2011. DVD.
For a Few Dollars More (1965). Dir. Sergio Leone. MGM Canada, 2006. DVD.
The Good, the Bad and the Ugly (1966). Dir. Sergio Leone. MGM, 2004. DVD.
The Great Train Robbery. Dir. Edwin W. Porter. Black Maria Studios, 1903.
Guns of the Magnificent Seven (1969). Dir. Paul Wendkos. Fox Video (Canada) Limited, 2004. DVD.
Heaven's Gate (1980). Dir. Michael Cimino. Criterion Collection, 2012. DVD.
Hellfighters (1968). Dir. Andrew V. McLaglen. Universal Studios Home Entertainment, 2015. DVD.
High Noon (1952). Dir. Fred Zinnemann. Team Marketing, 2015. DVD.
High Plains Drifter (1973). Dir. Clint Eastwood. Universal Studios Home Entertainment, 2010. DVD.
The Homesteaders (1953). Dir. Lewis Collins. Warner Archive, n.d. DVD.
I Am Sartana, Trade Your Guns for a Coffin (1970). Dir. Guiliano Carnimeo. Echo Bridge, 2015. DVD.
Inglorious Basterds (2009). Dir. Quentin Tarantino. The Weinstein Company, 2009. DVD.
Johnny Guitar (1954). Dir. Nicholas Ray. Team Marketing, 2015. DVD.
Kit Carson (1940). Dir. George B. Seitz. eOne Films Distribution, 2013. DVD.
Last of the Comanches (1953). Dir. Andre De Toth. Columbia Pictures Corporation 1953. DVD.
Lone Ranger (2013). Dir. Gore Verbinski. Walt Disney Studio Home Entertainment, 2015. DVD.
Massacre Canyon (1954). Dir. Fred F. Sears. Columbia Pictures Corporation 1954. DVD.
100 Rifles (1969). Dir. Tom Gries. Twentieth Century Fox, 1998. DVD.
Only the Valiant (1951). Dir. Gordon Douglas. Team Marketing, 2015. DVD.
Pale Rider (1985). Dir. Clint Eastwood. Warner Home Video, 2010. DVD.
The Paleface (1948). Dir. Norman Z. McLeod. Universal Home Studios Entertainment, 2006. DVD.
The Professionals (1966). Dir. Richard Brooks. Sony Pictures Home Entertainment, 2005. DVD.
Rainbow Valley (1935). Dir. Robert N. Bradbury. American Pop Classic, 2012. DVD.
Return of the Seven (1966). Dir. Burt Kennedy. Fox Video (Canada) Limited, 2001. DVD.
Riders of Destiny (1933). Dir. Robert N. Bradbury. American Pop Classic, 2012. DVD.
Rio Bravo (1959). Dir. Howard Hawks. Warner Home Video, 2010. DVD.
Rio Lobo (1970). Dir. Howard Hawks. 20th Century Fox Home Entertainment, 2003. DVD.
Rooster Cogburn ... and the Lady (1975). Dir. Stuart Millar. Universal Home Studios Entertainment, 2010. DVD.

Run, Man, Run (1968). Dir. Sergio Sollima. Blue Underground, 2004. DVD.
The Sons of Katie Elder (1965). Henry Hathaway. Warner Bros, 2013. DVD.
Those Dirty Dogs (1973). Dir. Giuseppe Rosati. Wild East Productions, 2014. DVD.
A Ticket to Tomahawk. Dir. Richard Sale. Twentieth Century Fox Film Corporation, 1950.
The Train Robbers (1973). Dir. Burt Kennedy. Warner Bros. Home Video, 2007. DVD.
The True Story of Jesse James (1957). Dir. Nicholas Ray. 20th Century Fox, 2007. DVD.
Two Mules for Sister Sara (1970). Dir. Don Siegel. Universal Studios Home Entertainment, 2014. DVD.
The War Wagon (1967). Dir. Burt Kennedy. Universal Studios Home Entertainment, 2013. DVD.
The Wild Bunch (1969). Dir. Sam Peckinpah. Warner Bros. Home Video, 1997. DVD.

WORKS CITED

Aubron, Hervé. "Titanic et autres paquebots : rêveries et dérives d'une industrie lourde." *Blockbuster: philosophie et cinéma*. Ed. Laura Odello. Paris: Les Prairies ordinaires, 2013: 45–64.
Brown, Stephen R. *A Most Damnable Invention: Dynamite, Nitrates, and the Making of the Modern World*. New York: Thomas Dunne, 2005.
Burdeau, Emmanuel. "Vers sa destinée : *Django Unchained*." *Quentin Tarantino, un cinéma déchaîné*. Nantes/Paris: Capricci/Les Prairies ordinaires, 2013: 135–154.
Campbell, Neil. *The Rhizomatic West: Representing the American West in a Transnational, Global, Media Age*. Lincoln: University of Nebraska Press, 2008.
Chamerois, Gilles. "Pynchon, Leone and Dynamite." *Thomas Pynchon and the (De)vices of Global (Post)modernity*. Ed. Zofia Kolbuszewska. Lublin: Wydawnictwo KUL, 2012: 54–68.
Cohen, Clélia. *Le Western*. Paris: Cahiers du Cinéma/CNDP, 2005.
Edmondson, J.R. *The Alamo Story: From Early History to Current Conflicts*. Plano: Republic of Texas Press, 2000.
Eyman, Scott. *John Wayne: The Life and Legend*. New York: Simon & Schuster, 2014.
Frayling, Christopher. *Sergio Leone: Something to Do with Death*. London: Faber and Faber, 2000.
Gaberscek, Carlo & Kenny Stier. *In Search of Western Movie Sites*. Victorville, CA: CP Entertainment, 2014.
Giré, Jean-François. *Il était une fois ... le Western européen*. Paris: Dreamland, 2002.
Heumann, Joseph K., & Robin L. Murray. "*Pale Rider*: Environmental politics, Eastwood style." *Jump Cut* 47 (2004).
Jones, Karen R., & John Wills. *The American West: Competing Visions*. Edinburgh: Edinburgh University Press, 2009.
Kinder, Marsha. "Violence American Style: The Narrative Orchestration of Violent Attractions." *Violence and American Cinema*. Ed. J. David Slocum. New York: Routledge, 2001: 63–100.
Leutrat, Jean-Louis. *Le cinéma en perspective : une histoire*. Paris: Armand Colin, 2005 [1992].
Leutrat, Jean-Louis, & Suzanne Liandrat-Guigues. *Rio Bravo de Howard Hawks*. Paris: L'Harmattan, 2013.
MacBride, Joseph. *Hawks on Hawks*. Lexington: University Press of Kentucky, 2013 [1982].
McCarthy, Todd. *Howard Hawks: The Grey Fox of Hollywood*. New York: Grove Press, 2000.
McDermott, John D. "Writers in Judgment: Historiography of the Johnson County War." *Wyoming Annals* 65.4 (Winter 1993–1994): 20–35.
McGhee, Richard D. *John Wayne: Actor, Artist, Hero*. Jefferson, NC: McFarland, 1990.
MacLean, Robert. "The Big-Bang Hypothesis: Blowing up the Image." *Film Quarterly* 32.2 (Winter 1978–1979): 2–7.
Mercer, Asa S. *Banditti of the Plains, or The Cattlemen's Invasion of Wyoming in 1892*. Cheyenne, WY: A.S. Mercer, 1894.
Odello, Laura. "Exploser les images, saboter l'écran." *Blockbuster : Philosophie & Cinéma*. Ed. Laura Odello. Paris: Les Prairies ordinaires, 2013: 5–25.

Pasolini, Pier Paolo. "Être est-il naturel ?" [1967]. *L'Expérience hérétique : langue et cinéma*. Trans. A. Rocchi Pullberg. Paris: Payot, 1976: 216–219.
Prats, Armando J. "Back from the Sunset: The Western, the Eastwood Hero, and *Unforgiven*." *The Western*. Spec. issue of *Journal of Film and Video* 47.1/3 (Spring-Fall 1995): 106–123.
Simsolo, Noël. *Conversation avec Sergio Leone*. Paris: Cahiers du Cinéma, 1999.
Slotkin, Richard. *Gunfighter Nation: The Myth of the Frontier in Twentieth-Century America*. New York: Harper Perennial, 1993.
Stewart, Garrett. *Between Film and Screen: Modernism's Photo Synthesis*. Chicago: The University of Chicago Press, 1999.
Tarantino, Quentin. Interview with Charlotte Garson and Thierry Méranger. Trans. [into French] Charlotte Garson. *Cahiers du Cinéma* 646 (June 2009): 10–15.
Truffaut, François, with the collaboration of Helen G. Scott. *Alfred Hitchcock*. New York: Simon & Schuster, 1985.
Wayne, John. "John Wayne, The Iron Duke, Sets 2–4 Pics for Next Year." Interview with Frank Barron. *The Hollywood Reporter* 28 May 1968: 28–68.
Yumibe, Joshua. *Moving Color: Early Film, Mass Culture, Modernism*. New Brunswick, NJ: Rutgers University Press, 2012.

Trippy Pictures
Iconicizing the American Acid Western

ALEXANDER DAVIS

The Acid Western is, like many of the terms we use to classify film genres, a retroactive categorization. First described by Jonathan Rosenbaum in a 1996 review of Jim Jarmusch's *Dead Man*, and later used again in the 2000 BFI Film Classics monograph on the same title, Rosenbaum posits that "'acid Westerns' are revisionist Westerns in which American history is reinterpreted to make room for peyote visions and related hallucinogenic experiences, LSD trips in particular" (51). While some of the most memorable Acid Westerns certainly conform to this rather limited qualification—most notably the surreal *Greaser's Palace* (1972), and *Walker* (1986)—Rosenbaum's nevertheless invaluable characterization is too constricting to fully appreciate the diversity within the subgenre as well as the wide-ranging developments that were a part of the Acid Western's "overall strategy of 'making strange'" (61) during one of the most tumultuous periods of American history. Reducing the Acid Western to a mere semantic construct ignores much of what differentiates Rosenbaum's own subcategorizations of "acid Westerns" from "pot Westerns" (51); certainly far more is at stake than the drug-specific influence behind *Zachariah* (1971) or *Pat Garrett and Billy the Kid* (1973). Thus this essay seeks to expand and elaborate the definition of the Acid Western through an exploration of its variegated and diverse influences and iconography in the context of its turbulent incipience: the late 1960s and early 1970s.

Throughout this period the majority of Acid Westerns can be viewed in relation to ongoing developments in the Vietnam War and domestic culture clashes. As the increasingly negative opinion on the Vietnam War poisoned the victorious post–World War II environment the Western became a site to renegotiate Americans' rapidly changing relationship with their national identity. In terms of the Acid Western, a unique subgenre rooted in the general revisionist impulses of the genre as a whole, yet sprouted from countercultural aesthetics mixed with New Hollywood conditions, three symbols are reflective of these developments: the Western landscape, representations of Native Americans or "Others" in general, and the changing figure of the cowboy. Throughout the long sixties (roughly 1959–1975), Acid Westerns critically investigated these symbols with Brechtian strategies of, as Rosenbaum says, "making strange," with the purposes of effectively reversing the above dictum by infusing historical legends with contemporary imagery.

Tuning In and Dropping Out: Approaches to the Acid Western

As noted above, in his definition of the Acid Western, Jonathan Rosenbaum briefly suggested a splintering of the subgenre into two distinct categories: "pot Westerns" and "acid Westerns." Rosenbaum's separation is surely useful, given that for such a relatively small and short-lived subgenre, the Acid Western has managed to cover a wide spectrum of emotions and narratives, moving from the slow-paced and melancholic of Monte Hellman's *The Shooting* to the surrealistically wild *Greaser's Palace* by American cinema's enfant terrible Robert Downey, Sr. Each of these subcategories rely on drug-related experiences to communicate their message, yet do so in significantly different ways. For example, pot Westerns which include such films as *The Shooting*, *Ride in the Whirlwind*, *McCabe & Mrs. Miller*, and *Pat Garrett & Billy the Kid*, take a heavily melancholic, paranoid, or elegiac tone in their approach to the genre. On the other hand, Acid Westerns, like *Zachariah* or *Greaser's Palace* are far more energetic, and feel freer to dip into more playful twists of the genre.

Although the influence of marijuana on films like *Pat Garrett & Billy the Kid* is certainly undeniable, I nevertheless find Rosenbaum's distinction cumbersome and restricting when considering the subtleties between films in the subgenre as a whole. How, for instance, is one to categorize Dennis Hopper's *The Last Movie* within Rosenbaum's schema? Certainly not as vibrantly rambunctious as *Greaser's Palace*, nor as driftingly paced as *Ride in the Whirlwind*. It becomes difficult to do anything other than claim it as an Acid Western left in a third, "miscellaneous" category. Similarly, *Butch Cassidy and the Sundance Kid* is far too upbeat and flamboyant to claim "pot Western" status, but lacks any of the surreal or fully anachronistic injections to be on par with an "acid Western" like *Zachariah*. To avoid such sloppy generic distinctions (or, at least, further sloppily distinctions, given the inherent problematics of generic categorization), I hope to use this essay to propose subgenres of "bad trip" Acid Westerns and "good trip" Acid Westerns through deep readings of films emblematic of both.

This seemingly minute elaboration has two key implications for understanding the films about to be discussed. The first allows for a broader framework in which to understand them—one categorized by emotional pitch rather than a loosely defined concept of which drug "seems" to permeate them the most. Secondly, the term "*Acid* Western" is important in and of itself, signaling that these films were, importantly, reframing the "film-as-dream" discourse so popular at the time of their making into a "film-as-hallucination" one. As Timothy Leary passionately argued, "LSD allowed individuals to test their realities. LSD allowed individuals to explore the inner workings of their minds. LSD-induced visions developed people's spiritual capacities.... LSD, in other words, through its reality-bending properties, challenged people to rethink social norms and life patterns" (Farber 23). These films were not (for the large part) mere entertainments, but were rather envisioned as counteracting prevailing concepts of "the Western" and the ideological implications therein. For these artists, the revolutionary capabilities of LSD experiences "naturally threaten every branch of the Establishment," and this notion should be kept at the heart of any consideration of the subgenre (Leary & Alpert 34).

Further into the West: A Brief History of Countercultural Imagery

Key to understanding the more gradual development of the Acid Western is an understanding of the concurrent development of the psychedelic and anarchic spirit of the counterculture. The counterculture did not land with an immediate and explosive thud along with the many mortarboards of seniors in the mid-sixties, or rise, phoenix-like, from the ashes of Bonnie and Clyde in 1967. This section provides a brief overview of the rambunctious [H]appenings of the early 1960s, particularly those which paved the path that such countercultural cowboys as Butch Cassidy and the Sundance Kid would later traverse. Three particular movements from this era are particularly relevant for this study: the group of performance artists gathered under the name Fluxus, the literal movements of Ken Kesey and his Merry Pranksters as they crossed the country in 1964, and the guerrilla theater groups exemplified by the Diggers, but rooted in R.G. Davis' San Francisco Mime Troupe.

"Purge the world of bourgeois sickness, 'intellectual,' professional & commercialized culture, PURGE the world of dead art, imitation artificial art, abstract art, illusionistic art, mathematical art,—PURGE THE WORLD OF 'EUROPANISM'!" Thus exclaimed Fluxus founder George Maciunas in his

1963 manifesto for the group, announcing one of the most radically important movements in art history (Oren 13). Fluxus, a group of performance artists which included such diverse artists as Nam June Paik, Jonas Mekas, La Monte Young, Joseph Beuys, John Cage, and Yoko Ono,[1] sought "to deflate artistic pretensions" by entirely blurring the line between life and art through the creation of "events," which were "pivoted on a limited number of actions which were so simple, and so closely related to everyday life, that they could easily escape notice" (Joselit 117–121).

Over the course of its somewhat indeterminable period of existence, Fluxus made revolutionary contributions to everything from painting, music, design, film, architecture, sculpture, and performance art, as well as pioneering developments in "innovative media such as artist's books, correspondence art, minimal music, structural cinema, conceptual music" and more (Friedman 94). Alternating between registers of the playful (as in Yoko Ono's *Self-Portrait*, in which the viewer extracts a mirror from an envelope) to the shocking (Nam June Paik's infamous *Etude for Pianoforte* from October 1960, in which Paik leapt from the stage and cut off the tie of his much revered idol John Cage), Fluxus embraced a wholly anarchic spirit. The group's flaunting of an egregious disregard for rules in art and art institutions (as when Maciunas and other picketed the Museum of Modern art in early 1963, baring signs exclaiming, "DEMOLISH SERIOUS CULTURE! DESTROY ART!" [Oren 10]) would go on to have an immense impact for later sixties protest groups.

Drawing from the rambunctious, but good-hearted, spirit of Fluxus, as well as the development of guerrilla theater groups during the period, but with situated within a more politically radical context, were Abbie Hoffman and the founders of the Youth International Party (Yippies) in 1968. With the Yippies, Hoffman took the political motivations of the Mime Troupe and The Diggers and drove it into far more absurdist and anarchic artistic areas. Through a series of wildly outrageous demonstrations, disrupting the New York Stock Exchange by showering the floor with dollar bills, levitating the Pentagon to rid it of evil spirits, and nominating Pigasus, a 145-pound pig, for president at the Chicago Democratic National Convention, Hoffman attempted to shock the American public into noncompliance with government policies.[2] As Julie Stephens has noted, of utmost importance to Hoffman were "incongruity, incoherence, and contradiction," for "'confusion is mightier than the sword" (Stephens 31). The horrors of Vietnam were such that they required a new form of protest and disagreement—they represented "a different kind of enemy previously ignored by the Left in America: the confines of language and a particular form of rationality" that prohibited the understanding sought by the new generation. The anarchic methods of these sixties groups sought to show that the rules by which the world had been abiding did not need to simply be challenged, but needed to be discarded with entirely.

Largely independent of these politically artistic groups, yet arguably more central to the development of the counterculture's aesthetic, were Ken Kesey and the Merry Pranksters, who travelled cross-country during the summer of '64 in their psychedelically-designed bus, "Furthur." As chronicled by Tom Wolfe in his infamous *The Electric Kool-Aid Acid Test*, for Kesey and the Pranksters, "the original fantasy ... had been that Kesey and four or five others would ... drive to New York for the New York World's Fair. On the way they could shoot some film, make some tape, freak out on the Fair and see what happened" (Wolfe 67). While the trip was certainly one filled with its fair share of raucousness and vivacity, it was ultimately one geared toward deep inner exploration in the service of a larger group harmony. Their Eastward journey "is a story of individuals keenly sensitive to the fact that they live in a new world and delighted by the prospect of exploring it ... and [to] draw new energies into themselves" (Bredahl 68). Or, as Kesey eloquently laid out in the trip's artistic statement: "None of us are going to deny what other people are doing.... Everybody is going to be what they are, and whatever they are, there's not going to be anything to apologize about" (Wolfe 73). Aided with an amount of hallucinogens sure to make Hunter S. Thompson raise an eyebrow, the Pranksters drove to find new levels of acceptance and expression by reversing the trajectory of American development.

Wolfe's book, which created an immediate and immense sensation upon its publication in 1968, was but one of a number of highly important literary experiments published in the late 60s that influenced the counterculture, three particularly relevant to the Acid Western were Rudy Wurlitzer's *Nog* (1968), Ishmael Reed's *Yellow Back Radio Broke-Down* (1969), and Richard Fariña's *Been Down So Long It Looks Like Up to Me* (1966). Wurlitzer, acclaimed screenwriter of such significant countercultural films as *Pat Garrett and Billy the Kid* and *Walker* (not to mention the original draft of Jarmusch's *Dead Man*), tells the story of a man who may be named Nog, or may have simply encountered a man named Nog in the past as he drifts through a series of hallucinatory westward-moving episodes. Written in a highly stream-of-consciousness style, *Nog* attempts to replicate in prose the experience of an extended acid trip, emphasizing the narrator's sensory experiences of the story over any conventional description. *Yellow Back Radio Broke-Down*, however, is the deeply satirical story of the Loop Garoo Kid, a black member of a circus group who finds himself amongst a series of increasingly violent and bizarrely behaving characters. Opening with an epigraph from William S. Hart, Reed borrows a technique from some of the modernist writers of Hart's era, writing in short paragraphs, separated by breaks, without any distinctions between quotations and narration, thereby refusing the reader any direct access to the novel's increasingly chaotic and bizarre episodes. Fariña's *Been Down So Long It Looks Like Up to Me*, by far the more formally conventionally told story of the three, nevertheless spoke deeply to the countercultural members with its story of the anarchically spirited Gnossos Pappadopoulis as he makes his psychedelic, lovesick journey across the U.S., to Cuba, and back again.

While many of the films discussed below never touch on these artworks or movements directly, they share important characteristics, or can be viewed as spiritual brethren. Hellman, for instance, after making *The Shooting* and *Ride in the Whirlwind*, became so enamored with Wurlitzer's *Nog* that he hired him to write the screenplay for *Two-Lane Blacktop* (Jones 179). Similarly, despite lacking direct citation, Robert Downey, Sr.'s *Greaser's Palace* attempts to send up the conventions of the Western in such highly outrageous ways it immediately calls to mind the sort of hijinks a cinematic Abbie Hoffman would perform. As important as these contextual discussions are, it is to the films that we now turn.

"A fabulous melancholy": Bad-Trip Acid Westerns

A profile of a horse quickly turns his head, looking behind him as eerily anxious music picks up on the soundtrack. The opening shots of Monte Hellman's *The Shooting* (1966), generally agreed to be the retroactive spearhead of the Acid Western genre, are immediately laden with feelings of deep paranoia. The edits of the opening credits provide us with no information besides the knowledge that one unnamed character is being followed by another unseen one—an unknown, but heavily felt threat leers over the narrative's beginning.

Two men look out across a desolate landscape, with nothing but a menacing wind covering the soundtrack. Nodding silently to each other, they begin a descent down a rocky slope before wordlessly preparing for an assault on a passing stagecoach. Dark, foreboding music again fills the screen as the credits roll, introducing us to Hellman's follow-up, *Ride in the Whirlwind* (1966). These two films, despite made with many of the same crew members within months of each other, are nonetheless wildly different in everything but their tone of constant, pervading paranoia.

In his landmark book *Sixguns & Society: A Structural Study of the Western*, Will Wright outlines what he has found to be the four most common narratives of popular westerns from the 30s to the 70s. For Wright, these break down into the "classical plot," where a solitary cowboy "rides into a troubled town and cleans it up, winning the respect of the townsfolk and the love of the schoolmarm," the "vengeance variation," whereby a protagonist leaves a group in order to punish criminals the group was itself unable to punish, the "transition theme," in which the group (or society, as Wright frequently terms) begins to reject the hero, who is no longer able to stand against it, and finally the "professional plot," in which a talented and valuable hero, or heroes, is only willing to aid a society that pays him (Wright 32–85). Throughout his analyses, Wright further identifies four key oppositional binaries that Western myths negotiate: "inside society/outside society, good/bad, strong/weak, [and] wilderness/civilization" (75).

What is especially remarkable about Hellman's films, *The Shooting* in particular, is the degree to which they directly subvert Wright's structural analyses.[3] While, arguably, both can be loosely categorized according to the "vengeance variation," they avoid participating in his binary schemas. *The Shooting*, by limiting the vast majority of the film to no one other than the four main characters, sidesteps inside/outside society and wilderness/civilization dynamics—these characters exist *only* outside society and *only* in the wilderness. In fact, the Acid Western subgenre as a whole is preoccupied with outlaws, be they part of a bad or good trip. Evident in the subgenre are outlaws in the typical sense, on the run from the law as in *Butch Cassidy and the Sundance Kid* or *Ride in the Whirlwind* (in the latter case, "law"), as well as outlaw in the literal sense, existing outside the law or society entirely, fulfilling the "drop out" idealism of many hippie communes, like the group of brothers in Warhol's *Lonesome Cowboys*, or, in a less utopic sense, our lead characters of *The Shooting*.

In another move concurrent with larger trends of the Acid Western, Hellman further corrupts notions of good/bad and strong/weak within *The Shooting*. For a large part of the film, no character holds superiority. Willett Gashade (Warren Oates) is a hired hand to the unnamed Woman (Millie Perkins), by whom Willett's own hired hand, Coley (Will Hutchins), is increasingly seduced. The first half of the film focuses on the tenuous power struggle between the Woman and Gashade, he being a necessary employee in service of her goal, she refusing to relinquish any control outside decisions of navigation (going so far as to let free a supply mule that she had adamantly protested being used at the start. Trailing the three is hired gun Billy Spears (Jack Nicholson), a menacing figure who serves to maintain the checks and balances between the Woman and Gashade.

The inherent morality of these characters' journey, whether it's good or bad, is constantly at question. The Woman's purpose for "going to Kingsley," as she puts it in the film's opening, remains entirely unclear until the final moments, wherein we learn it is to kill Coley and Gashade's partner, Coigne, the same man who drunkenly killed her child. This revelation is no help in mediating spectators' feelings toward the narrative; the horrors of killing a child being certainly irredeemable, is complicated by the perpetrator being a dear friend to the protagonists to whom the audience has been aligned, and who have now become participants in his execution.

The notion of justice and the distinction between good and bad has been a hallmark of the Western since its incipience—as Robert Warshow famously stated, the genre is so popular and longstanding because it "offers a serious orientation to the problem of violence such as can be found almost nowhere else in our culture" (46). Yet throughout the Acid Western, and the Vietnam-era Western as a whole, the idea that anyone who employs violence can be either good *or* bad, and not some complex mixture in between, becomes the new norm. A fuzzy Acid Western if there ever was one, *The Professionals*, exhibits this the best. By and large a standard Western aside from its complicated politics, *The Professionals* is a story that, as Michael Coyne succinctly states, takes the form of "boys are hired to rescue girl form bandit, boys discover girl loves bandit, boys give girl back to bandit" (Coyne 132). By revealing the professionals' motivations as not only false—the girl's husband having lied about her being kidnapped—but antithetical to their nature as "heroes" in the first place—the girl never wanted to be saved. Throughout the 60s and 70s, the Acid Western was one where justice was either an entirely unclear or muddled concept, as in *The Shooting*, or one where it is constantly shifting or oscillating across sides, as in *Pat Garrett and Billy the Kid*.

"In every respect, Western topography helps dramatize more intensely the clash of characters and the thematic conflicts of the story," wrote John G. Cawelti in his *The Six-Gun Mystique* (24), and the Acid Western is certainly no exception. The bad trip Western, in particular, seems to particularly exploit the potency of landscape. What were once the momentous mountains and plains of John Ford or Howard Hawks, become, in the bad trip Westerns, thoroughly uninhabitable, threatening, and devastatingly desolate deserts.

Given that *The Shooting* and *Ride in the Whirlwind* were shot back-to-back, their landscapes appear similarly sinister, however, as previously discussed, the narrative of *The Shooting* presents an environment infinitely more malevolent than majestic. It is the waterless, arid desert the eventually brings down the "pro"tagonists—the Woman's fierce determination to avenge the death of her son leading to her own downfall, the vacuous desert becoming a symbol for the soullessness of its characters. Kent Jones, in his excellent essay on the films of Monte Hellman, argues for something similar within *Ride in the Whirlwind*, writing that the film's mood "is tired and a little sad … the cowboys … are insignificant men who seem to be receding into the landscape" (Jones 176). For this later film, the function of the environment is similar, with the landscape becoming a desolate abyss that envelops lost, misguided characters, rather than one that destroys overly determined, violent ones.

The landscape is equally important in the other bad trip Acid Westerns of the period.[4] Andy Warhol, in his "fuzzy" avant-garde/Acid Western, disposes of it completely, filming almost the entirety of his *Lonesome Cowboys* in close-up or midshot. In Warhol's West, the space of America has, itself, no space to exist. Warhol challenges Jim Kitses' notion that "the plains and mountains of western landscape can be an inspiring and civilizing environment, a moral universe productive of the western hero, a man with a code," by showing how the landscape is fundamentally incompatible with the open [homo]sexuality that so pervades the film (Kitses 58). It thus becomes even more ironic that federal agents charged Warhol with transporting pornography when trying to move his film across state borders.

Kitses also comments on the incredible significance of the landscape to Sam Peckinpah's *Pat Garrett and Bill the Kid*, through a discussion of a shot that has Billy the Kid visible only in his inverted reflection in a pond. For Kitses, this invisible "real" Billy, but visible "dark reflection" is emblematic of an "America in the dark and dead in the water." This use of the landscape invites spectators "to contemplate the past as a mirror to our own era, the complexity of the relationships with both heroes and genre, the love for what the Western was and the necessity of seeing it anew, of turning it all upside down … everything is there, crystallized in a post-modern emblem for the genre" (241). Perhaps it is this image more than any other that encapsulates what the Acid Western is all about—the ability to convey such deeply felt emotions sensationally, phenomenologically, rather than narratively or mythically.

"Leave your teardrops behind": Good Trip Acid Westerns

Although the discussion has henceforth centered around the mildly depressing bad trip Westerns, it has largely been so as to set the stage for the wildly difficult to describe experiences that are what I term good trip Acid Westerns. These films, with the exception of the hugely popular *Butch Cassidy and the Sundance Kid*, tend to be lesser known, and even lesser seen, including, as mentioned, Robert Downey, Sr.'s arguable magnum opus, *Greaser's Palace*, the deeply pacifistic *Zachariah*, and the complex, *Easy Rider* follow-up *The Last Movie*.

While bad trip Acid Westerns are characterized primarily by a tone and mood derived from their imagery—the overbearing desert and ominously pursued outlaws combining to create a deep sense of paranoia and foreboding, the good trip Acid Western relies almost uniquely on the employment of anachronisms within its *diegesis*. Good trip Acid Westerns imbue their settings with things that do not belong in order to defamiliarize the genre and force us to consciously relate the historically set narrative to contemporary social conditions. In their discussion of *Zachariah* Murphy and Harder argue that although "these anachronisms are clearly aimed at humor ... [the] crazy quilt of nineteenth- and twentieth-century patches may also be read as a statement about the fundamental connections between the populism of that time and the counterculture of [the 60s]" (not paginated).

If the landscapes of bad trip Acid Westerns are characterized as an America no longer suitable for its inhabitants, the landscapes of good trip Acid Westerns represent an America that simply no longer makes sense. That is not to say that they are no less malevolent—the multiple spaces of *Greaser's Palace* are incredibly violent, populated by a malevolent white-sheet-ghost who kills at will—but merely that they are additionally imbibed with the anarchic spirit of confusion advanced by Fluxus artists and the Yippies. Despite Murphy and Harder's convincing case that these anachronisms are done to draw political similarities, they ignore the aspect of anachronisms that comment on the absurdity of the contemporary condition. For many counterculture artists of the late 60s and early 70s, the ongoing developments of Vietnam and domestic politics were as equally absurd as, say, a character parachuting into a nineteenth-century narrative—it is important to recall that all Acid Westerns under discussion in this section were produced and released after the Tet Offensive and the revelations of the My Lai Massacre. Thus, the trenchant argument for pacifism advanced by *Zachariah* is not merely a comedic pro-dove message, but one that simultaneously, and implicitly comments on the very insanity that the world had devolved into by that point in time.

This is perhaps best exemplified by a warning fable the hero (Jesse) of *Greaser's Palace* tells the citizens of Seaweedhead Greaser's town about a monster named "Bingo Gas Station Motel Cheeseburger with a Side of Aircraft Noise and You'll Be Gary, Indiana," who "*loves* to hurt people." Jesse is able to prevent the monster from killing the members of the town by stating that he believes the townspeople can "make this a better world to live in." This Frankenstein of square-ideals has obvious connotations that need little elaboration: the counterculture is at risk of being dismembered and devoured by a powerful straight-world entity. The fact that this message is conveyed through such an outlandish story underscores the filmmakers' belief in the very preposterousness of such a situation existing in the real world.

As noted earlier, heroes in good trip Acid Westerns are also qualitatively different from those in the bad trip category, and largely contribute to my terming this grouping as "good" trips. There heroes of *Butch Cassidy and the Sundance Kid* are significantly more affable and enjoyable than those of bad trip Westerns, and more jovial in personality. Compared to Billy the Kid in Peckinpah's film, who, as Dylan sings has "guns across the river aimin' at" him, Butch and Sundance aren't long "from happiness step[ping] up to greet" them. The literal "trips" of these films are also, in and of themselves, generally more pleasant. Jesse of *Greaser's Palace* is on his "way to Jerusalem to be an actor-singer," awaited by "the agent Morris," his story drastically more upbeat than the revenge tale of *The Shooting*. And while *Pat Garrett and Billy the Kid* carries on until the Kid's final death, its "double-murder/suicide" (Kitses 227), *Butch Cassidy and the Sundance Kid* freeze frames on the heroes' final living moment—a move that manages to both further the film's irreverent spirit via a reference to Truffaut's *The 400 Blows*, as well as make sure the film is one of endless optimism; as spectators we never have to see them die.

To return to Jesse, the successes of good trip heroes occur because these filmmakers believe in them, believe that they can make this a better world to live in. In a reflective exchange with one of his crewmembers, Seaweedhead Greaser laments that he cannot wrap his arms around each and every one of his townspeople, and let them know that everything will be okay. "Why not?" questions his partner. "I'm not bizarre enough," he replies. These heroes of good trip Acid Westerns, however, *are* bizarre enough, are icons of the Beautiful People Ken Kesey and the Merry Pranksters were reaching toward becoming. Good trip Acid Westerns, again taking cues from earlier 60s art movements, embraced paradox to express their utter dissatisfaction with the world they lived in and their complete hope in the people who inhabited it. While bad trip Acid Westerns examined the deterioration of people and country, good trip Acid Westerns proposed a late-era rally for the countercultural spirit, searching for the freeze frame that would preserve their idealism in the face of a Gas Station Motel Cheeseburger future.

Notes

1. A well-defined group of Fluxus participants—the Fluxcore, as Maciunas frequently called them—is often quite difficult to discern given its status as a "voluntary" movement—as one member of the movement described, "[Maciunas] could tell the world what Fluxus was, and anyone who wanted to do that kind of thing was Fluxus" (Joselit 123). For more, see Friedman and Frank.

2. These, and other of Hoffman's exploits are described in Doyle (86–7 for the NYSE), Stephens (37–9 for the Pentagon), Hoberman (213 for Pigasus).

3. It should be noted, however, that Wright strictly limits himself to discussing the most popular—as defined by box office success—Westerns of the period (Wright 29). Despite Hellman's attempt to make "classic," A-Westerns on B-budgets (Jones 173), this was certainly not the case, with his films languishing in obscurity for many years.

4. For lack of space, and with great reluctance, I've left one of the great Acid Westerns out of this discussion, Robert Altman's *McCabe & Mrs. Miller*, given the sublime and thorough treatment of it provided by Robert T. Self in his *Robert Altman's* McCabe & Mrs. Miller: *Reframing the American West*. For specific discussion of this film's landscape, please see 61–62.

Filmography

Dead Man. Dir. Jim Jarmusch. Pandora Filmproduktion, 1995.
Easy Rider. Dir. Dennis Hopper. Pando Company Inc., 1969.
The 400 Blows. Dir. François Truffaut. Les Filmes du Carrosse, 1959.
Greaser's Palace. Dir. Robert Downey Sr. Greaser's Palace Ltd., 1972.

The Last Movie. Dir. Dennis Hopper. Alta-Light, 1971.
Lonesome Cowboys. Dir. Andy Warhol. Andy Warhol Films, 1968.
McCabe and Mrs. Miller. Dir. Robert Altman.Warner Bros., 1971.
Pat Garrett and Billy the Kid. Dir. Sam Peckinpah. MGM, 1973.
Ride in the Whirlwind. Dir. Monte Hellman. Proteus Films, 1966.
The Shooting. Dir. Monte Hellman. Proteus Films, 1966.
Two-Lane Blacktop. Dir. Monte Hellman. Universal Pictures, 1971.
Walker. Dir. Alex Cox. In-Cine Compañia Industrial Cinematográfica, 1986.
Zachariah. Dir. George Englund. ABC Pictures, 1971.

Works Cited

Bredahl, A. Carl. "An Exploration of Power: Tom Wolfe's Acid Test." *Critique: Studies in Contemporary Fiction* 23.2 (1981): 67–84.
Cawelti, John G. *The Six-Gun Mystique Sequel.* Bowling Green, OH: Bowling Green State University Popular Press, 1999.
Coyne, Michael. *The Crowded Prairie: American National Identity in the Hollywood Western.* New York: I.B. Tauris, 1997.
Doyle, Michael William. "Staging the Revolution: Guerrilla Theater as a Countercultural Practice, 1965-68." *Imagine Nation: The American Counterculture of the 1960s and '70s.* Eds. Peter Braunstein and Michael William Doyle. New York: Routledge, 2002. 71–97.
Farber, David. "The Intoxicated State/Illegal Nation: Drugs in the Sixties Counterculture." *Imagine Nation: The American Counterculture of the 1960s and '70s.* Eds. Peter Braunstein and Michael William Doyle. New York: Routledge, 2002. 17–40.
Fariña, Richard. *Been Down So Long It Looks Like Up to Me.* New York: Random House, 1966.
Friedman, Ken. "The Literature of Fluxus." *Visible Language* 40.1 (2006): 90–112.
Friedman, Ken, and Peter Frank. "Fluxus: A Post-Definitive History: Art Where Response Is the Heart of the Matter." *High Performance* 7.3 (1984): 56–62.
Hoberman, J. *The Dream Life: Movies, Media, and the Mythology of the Sixties.* New York: The New Press, 2003.
Hockett, Jeremy. "Guerilla Theater." *American Countercultures: An Encyclopedia of Nonconformists, Alternative Lifestyles, and Radical Ideas in U.S. History.* Ed. Gina Misiroglu. New York: Routledge, 2009. 345–346.
Jones, Kent. "'The Cylinders Were Whispering My Name': The Films of Monte Hellman." *The Last Great American Picture Show: New Hollywood Cinema in the 1970s.* Eds. Thomas Elsaesser, Alexander Horwath, and Noel King. Amsterdam: Amsterdam University Press, 2004. 165–194.
Joselit, David. *American Art Since 1945.* London: Thames & Hudson, 2003.
Kitses, Jim. "Authorship and Genre: Notes on the Western." *The Western Reader.* Eds. Jim Kitses and Gregg Rickman. New York: Limelight Editions, 1998. 57–69.
_____. "Peckinpah Re-visited: *Pat Garrett and Billy the Kid*." *The Western Reader.* Eds. Jim Kitses and Gregg Rickman. New York: Limelight Editions, 1998. 223–243.
Leary, Timothy, and Richard Alpert "The Politics of Consciousness Expansion." *The Harvard Review* 1.4 (1963): 33–37.
Murphy, Bren Ortega, and Jeffery Scott Harder. "1960s Counterculture and the Legacy of American Myth: A Study of Three Films." *Canadian Review of American Studies* 23.2 (1993): not paginated.
Oren, Michel. "Anti-Art as the End of Cultural History." *Performing Arts Journal* 15.2 (1993): 1–30.
Reed, Ishmael. *Yellow Back Radio Broke-Down.* New York: Doubleday, 1969.
Rosenbaum, Jonathan. *Dead Man.* London: BFI, 2000.
Self, Robert T. *Robert Altman's McCabe & Mrs. Miller: Reframing the American West.* Lawrence: University of Kansas Press, 2007.
Stephens, Julie. *Anti-Disciplinary Protest: Sixties Radicalism and Postmodernism.* New York: Cambridge University Press, 1998.

Warshow, Robert. "Movie Chronicle: The Westerner." *The Western Reader*. Eds. Jim Kitses and Gregg Rickman. New York: Limelight Editions, 1998: 35–47.
Wolfe, Tom. *The Electric Kool-Aid Acid Test*. New York: Picador, 1968.
Wright, Will. *Sixguns & Society: A Structural Study of the Western*. Berkeley: University of California Press, 1977.
Wurlitzer, Rudolph. *Nog*. New York: Random House, 1968.

"Reach for the Sky!"
Western Iconography, the American Frontier and the Story of Pixar in Toy Story

Ashley Sufflé Robinson

In 1984, John Lasseter—a young CalArts grad who would later become the chief creative officer of both Pixar and Disney Animation Studios—hit rock bottom. His pitch for a computer-animated version of *The Brave Little Toaster* (1987) was panned, and Lasseter was fired from Disney after the meeting's conclusion. When Ed Catmull (later the president of Walt Disney and Pixar Animation Studios) discovered that Lasseter and Disney had parted ways, he brought Lasseter onto his team at LucasFilm Creative Graphics (Price 53). Both men believed they could marry technology and art, so they set about producing a two-minute short titled *André and Wally B.* (1984) to prove their hypothesis. Seeing the potential of *André and Wally B.*, Steve Jobs bought into Lasseter and Catmull's vision. The three founded Pixar, Inc., in 1986, and by 1995, Lasseter and his team released *Toy Story* (1995), the world's first full-length computer animated film.

No one at Pixar—including Lasseter, who co-wrote and directed the film—could have imagined *Toy Story*'s success. While the novelty of computer animation generated buzz for the movie, its story captured both critics' and audiences' hearts.[1] What is it about *Toy Story* that continues to make it so compelling? Digital animation is only part of the movie's draw—*Toy Story*'s true appeal comes from the film's engagement with the American West. As Lasseter explains, "at Pixar ... [w]e like to show the audience something that on one level they're familiar with, but then we show it to them in a way that they've never seen before" ("Storytelling"). In the case of *Toy Story*, this "familiarity" rests on Pixar's deliberate use of iconography from the nineteenth-century American frontier and American Western films. In *Toy Story*, Pixar plucks classic images, tropes, and themes directly from the Western and reimagines them for a new generation. In doing so, Pixar does more than just revitalize the "dead" genre of the American Western; it also reconnects contemporary America with one of its foundational myths and its archetypical identity.

Lasseter and the Pixar team reinterpret the idea of both the frontier and frontierism in *Toy Story*. As historian David Hamilton Murdoch argues, the nation's commitment to progress has been a double-edged sword (21). In the nineteenth century, to progress meant to journey westward, conquering the wilderness and spreading civilization. Unfortunately, as Fredrick Jackson Turner pointed out in his frontier thesis, the march of civilization necessitated the demise of the western frontier. As the country advanced into the twentieth century, the "spirit of the frontier" that advocated opportunity, potential, and freedom for all seemed increasingly obsolete (Murdoch 79). Pixar, however, rejects contemporary disenfranchisement of the American myth. Instead, *Toy Story* embraces the idealism of the frontier, advocating for a return to the values of nineteenth-century American identity. *Toy Story* combines the scientific futurism inherent in computer animation with the values of the American West, and in doing so argues for the continued relevance of the frontier's ideologies. Ultimately, Pixar uses the iconography of the classic Western throughout *Toy Story* to re-popularize both the American Western and the American myth.

The Western and the Digital Frontier

Lasseter himself reinforces the connections between *Toy Story* and the West. In a junket interview promoting the movie, an interviewer asked, "So how pioneering would you say the film is since it's the first [computer animated movie]?" Lasseter responded, "You know, being the first one ... it's revolutionary" (ScreenSlam). This brief exchange is telling, especially when considering *Toy Story* against the backdrop of the American Western. First, the interviewer's use of the term "pioneering" rhetorically connects Pixar's foray into digital animation with those men and women who embraced Manifest Destiny and headed West to chase frontier opportunities. While the frontier remained open, American pioneers were also hailed as American myth-makers; they displayed the heroic qualities "of integrity, morality, chivalry, honor, courage, and self-reliance" that are recognized as part of American national identity (Agnew 12–13). Linking *Toy Story* to America's core values solidifies the connection between Lasseter's film and the mythological narratives of the American West.

Lasseter's response echoes and affirms the subtext of the interviewer's question. Lasseter not only stresses that *Toy Story* is the "first" of its kind, but he also pushes the film's connection to the American West further by claiming *Toy Story* as "revolutionary" and invoking the transformative potential of the American frontier. During the nineteenth century, the acquisition of the United States' western territories reshaped the nation geographically, and it also created a space where, as Richard Aquila states, people became "the masters of their own destinies" (2). By nature of its wilderness, the nineteenth-century West was "brimming with opportunities," and consequently, the region became inextricably linked with the ideals of freedom and progress (West 272). The West became a space that reconceptualized social, political, and economic structures. In referring to *Toy Story* as "revolutionary," then, Lasseter reinforces the film's connection with the ideology of America's historical frontier, and he foreshadows *Toy Story*'s engagement with the American myth through the images and iconography of the West and Western film.

Considering Pixar's history and the movie's pioneering nature, it is no surprise that Lasseter builds on the imagery and mythology of the American West in *Toy Story*. Throughout the film, Lasseter's use of Western iconography provides audiences with familiar footing through which to engage with a new method of storytelling. By capitalizing on the well-known storylines, tropes, and themes of the West, Pixar created a narrative that would immediately resonate with viewers. But overcoming the novelty of computer animation was not the only hurdle in the way of Pixar's success. To prevent investors from pulling their funding, *Toy Story* also needed to turn a profit both domestically and abroad (Bettinger). This solidified Lasseter's decision to build on the American Western. Despite its recent wane in popularity, the genre had historically married the American myth and film with incredible success.

It is worth pausing to briefly discuss the international appeal of the American West, especially in terms of Western films. Interestingly, the global appeal of the West began with the opening of the frontier itself. The globalization of the West and its mythology began in the late nineteenth century through the Wild West show, travel narratives, and dime novels, but the popularity of the frontier exploded with the advent of modern cinema. Westerns drew in audiences from all over the world, and the genre counted the likes of Joseph Stalin, Jorge Luis Borges, and Simone de Beauvoir among its fans (Mitchell 15). As Lee Clark Mitchell explains, "The Western's ability to maintain its hold as the most popular of genres may have been partly due to the starkness of its materials—of familiar characters, settings, and situations that allow contested agendas to be defined simply yet suggestively" (17). By the height of the golden age of the Western in the 1950s and 1960s, the American cowboy was more than just a national hero: he had become a global icon.

But by the time Lasseter had begun conceptualizing *Toy Story*, the Western film had faded from the popular consciousness. While the icons of the

West continued to be recycled in popular culture, the Western's popularity waned as its core audience aged out of the key Hollywood demographic (Agresta). For Pixar, the genre's presented a unique opportunity to revitalize the Western and its idealism for mainstream moviegoers. *Toy Story* introduces the Western—now stripped down to its golden age roots—to a new generation of viewers.

Toy Story: *Reimagining the American Western*

As Perry Nodelman points out, "In popular culture nowadays, cowboys only occasionally ride the range, primarily in texts that put twists on the old stories," specifically citing "the cowboy as toy in the Toy Story movies" as evidence of the shift (144). In *Toy Story*, Lasseter's use of Western iconography, especially variations of the cowboy, embrace the values of the nineteenth-century American West. The imagery of the West permeates *Toy Story* from the first second of the film. As the Pixar logo fades to the now-iconic blue sky wallpaper, the camera pans down to reveal an Old West town recreated in cardboard and Crayola. Glimpses of "big sky" country along with the saloon, hotel, "skool," and the "wanted" poster for One-Eyed Bart immediately evoke the American frontier found in dime novels and, later, classic Western film. As historian Will Wright explains, the classical Western is "the prototype of all Westerns, [it is] the one people think of when they say, 'All Westerns are alike'" (32).

Borrowing the Western's powerful iconography, Lasseter offers viewers everything they need to understand the movie's unfolding narrative in its first 15 seconds: a villain (One-Eyed Bart) will threaten the town and a heroic cowboy will save the day. True to trope, One-Eyed Bart robs the town's bank, terrorizes a damsel in distress, and lashes innocent sheep to the train tracks to ensure the town's citizens compliance. With all hope seemingly lost, Bo Peep cries out for "somebody" to "do something," and Sheriff Woody enters on cue accompanied by a heroic soundtrack reminiscent of those composed by Aaron Copland. He tells Bart to "reach for the sky," and after defeating Bart's attack dog, Woody throws the villain in jail. Conflict neatly resolved, Andy declares, "You saved the day again, Woody!" and the opening credits roll.

This opening, which draws heavily on the dime novel, combines nostalgia and imagination in order to, in Nodelman's words, "twist" the Western's framework. *Toy Story* embraces the constructions of heroism and virtue forged on the American frontier. Woody, Bart, and Bo Peep participate in what Wright defines as "the story of the lone stranger who rides into a troubled town and cleans it up, winning the respect of the townsfolk and the love of the schoolmarm" (32). As Wright would agree, the dichotomy between hero and villain, the triumph of good over evil, and the hero's protection of civilization serve as Western touchstones. Andy's imaginative play establishes the structural trajectory of the rest of the film. More important, this scene encourages audiences to draw parallels between *Toy Story* and the classic Western.

As a Western hero, Woody embodies the values of bravery, ingenuity, intelligence, and hard work that Jeremy Agnew argues are intrinsic to American cowboy heroism as he risks himself to save the town and brings Bart to justice. But Woody is more than a free-range cowboy: he is a sheriff, which also makes him representative of the law and socially codified morality. In the classical Western plot, the "opposition of good versus bad" creates an explicit separation of values "between the social, progressive values of the members of society versus the selfish, money values of the villains" (Wright 52). In *Toy Story*'s opening scene, Lasseter emphasizes the tension between good and evil, exploring its ideological resonances via the visual iconography associated with Woody and One-Eyed Bart. Woody's position as the hero validates all of the ideals and values associated with his cowboy heroism, which is supported by both the aesthetics and technical composition of the scene. Lasseter uses a tight shot to focus on the visual markers of Woody's lawman status, namely his hat and badge. Furthermore, when Woody alone occupies the screen, he is bathed in golden light, visually symbolizing his innate goodness. In contrast, Bart's comically oversized gun suggests his violent nature (Woody's holster is noticeably empty), and his physical deformity (his missing eye) emphasizes his moral deficiency. Lasseter connects Woody to "goodness" and morality through the Western's iconography; the visual markers represent American values in their most distilled form. As a classic cowboy figure, Woody transports the idealistic values attached to American frontier heroism from its dime novel past into *Toy Story*'s digital present.

Lasseter quickly establishes that *Toy Story* is not a traditional Western, nor will it merely rehash the Western's traditional structure in a new medium through Andy's imagination. As a child, Andy does not understand the constraints of genre; while the opening scene suggests he understands how Westerns operate, Andy tinkers with the formula. He stretches Slinky the dog between Woody and Bart, declaring him to be an "attack dog with a built-in force field," thereby destabilizing the classic Western narrative with an element borrowed from science fiction. The structure is further twisted when Woody retaliates, summoning his "dinosaur, who eats force-field dogs." The film transitions from a prototypical Western into something more unfamiliar, marking the beginning of *Toy Story*'s revision of the Western genre.

The introduction of Buzz Lightyear represents another version of the

Western myth reconstructed for a mid-twentieth-century America. Though the literal West had been closed for decades, the onset of the space race in the 1960s provided Americans with a new frontier. The idea of claiming space in the name of "the Land of the Free" dominated American popular culture in the following decades, and suddenly, the definitions of heroism originally attributed to the cowboy were transferred to the astronaut. But space was more than just a secondary territory of the Western: as Gene Roddenberry, the creator of *Star Trek*, proclaimed, it was America's "final frontier." The space race doubled America's commitment to innovation while reconnecting the country with its core values of freedom and opportunity. With this in mind, Buzz Lightyear expresses the movement of the frontier from a historical to an ideological location.

Lasseter parallels Woody's and Buzz's appearances to emphasize this transition. When Woody first meets Buzz, he clambers over the edge of the bed (formerly his special spot, as assigned by Andy). Buzz's "crashed" space ship lies against Andy's pillow. Woody peeks over the edge of the bed, only to have inadvertently snuck up on the bedroom's newest occupant. Lasseter frames the shot by placing Woody's face behind and below Buzz, signaling Woody's diminished status; he also uses a low-angle shot and the same golden light to signify Buzz's position of power and his heroism. As the camera focuses on Buzz's chiseled features and "Space Ranger" badge, viewers are reminded he is a modernized iteration of Woody's frontier lawman.

Buzz's presence also evolves the literal frontier into an imaginative one. As Woody looks on, the astronaut starts exploring Andy's room, but not quite like the audience expects. Instead of introducing himself as a toy, Buzz analyzes the landscape around him like an explorer. The camera moves to Buzz's point of view, and viewers hear the whoosh of his space suit's respirator. He pages "Star Command" to make contact with his home base, and after seeing the state of his ship, realizes he needs to recon the area. He begins recording his observations into his arm communicator: "mission log, star date 4-0-7-2. My ship has run off course en route to sector 12. I've crash-landed on a strange planet. The impact must have woken me from hypersleep. [Jumps on bed.] Terrain seems a bit unstable. [Taps arm display sticker.] No readout yet if the air is breathable. And there seems to be no sign of intelligent life anywhere." In the opening scenes, Andy—an ostensibly "real" boy—plays through a scene from a classical Western film. The audience knows the story is fabricated even though it is positioned within a historical narrative; once Woody breaks character with his first speaking lines after the opening credits, the illusion shatters. The frontier once again fades into the past, and the audience understands the reality of *Toy Story*: the toys can talk, they act like people, and they live in "our" world. The Western scene's power comes not from its connection to reality, then, but from the historic legacy of the Western frontier.

Unlike Woody, who acts more like a mayor than a cowboy when outside of Andy's imagination, in his first scene, Buzz plays the part of an *actual* frontiersman. Like Lewis and Clark, he surveys and explores the landscape like a documentarian, recording his findings to report back to Star Command. Instead of entering Andy's room as just another toy, he challenges Woody's role. He is Buzz Lightyear, "Space Ranger, [with the] Universe Protection Unit" through and through. When Hamm the piggy bank asks him where he comes from, Buzz answers, "I'm stationed up in the Gamma Quadrant of Sector Four." Then, as Buzz interacts with Woody and the other toys, the audience realizes Buzz believes he is a real space ranger. This becomes especially clear when Woody insists Buzz is a "T-O-Y. Toy!" and Buzz corrects him, saying, "I think the word you're searching for is 'Space Ranger.'" The irony inherent in Buzz's perception of reality transforms the toy room into a liminal space which functions as an imaginative frontier. Instead of just being a new toy, Buzz instead becomes a stranger in a strange land.

The narrative of outer space captures the imaginations of Andy's toys. Much to Woody's chagrin, Buzz regales Rex, Slinky, Hamm, and the rest with tales of his intergalactic adventures and his quest to defeat the evil space emperor, Zerg. As the toys crowd around Buzz, he shows off his bells and whistles, prompting Mr. Potato Head to ask, "How come you don't have a laser, Woody?" This is the first moment in *Toy Story* where Woody is marginalized, and his position becomes more tenuous as Buzz makes a case for his superior heroism. When Woody continues to try to prove Buzz is nothing more than a toy, Buzz rises to the challenge. He opens his flight wings and dives off the side of Andy's bed. But instead of crashing to the ground as one would expect, Buzz rides a car through a looping track, arcs though the air, attaches to a plane dangling from the ceiling, and acrobatically lands back on the mattress to much celebration. Whether purposefully or not, Buzz bends the reality of the toy room to his own imaginative narrative. Historically, the toys have needed Andy's imagination to escape the structures of their lives. Buzz offers them new frontiers to explore by combining the frontier myth with ideological frontier spaces.

This, of course, creates tension between Woody and Buzz—and between the competing representations of the Western. Lasseter establishes the conflict from the moment Buzz and Woody meet. He frames the shot with the two characters face-to-face. Buzz immediately trains his laser on Woody's forehead, and the two circle each other like prizefighters in the ring. Woody worries about Buzz taking what he refers to as "his spot," but his attempt to regain his position is unsupported by his fellow toys:

> WOODY: It's just a mistake.
> MR. POTATO HEAD: Well, that mistake is sitting in your spot, Woody. [Chuckles.]

REX: [Gasps.] Have you been replaced?
WOODY: What did I tell you earlier? No one is getting replaced.

The tension in the scene continues to build as Woody insists, "Yes, it is a mistake because, you see, the bed here is my spot." Woody's repetition of the word "spot" makes this exchange particularly interesting when one considers the end of the frontier in the West. When the Census of 1890 declared the West civilized, Turner lamented "And now ... the frontier has gone, and with its going has closed the first period of American history" (227). The connection between space, place, and identity marked a significant turning point in the nation's history. In *Toy Story*, this drama is recreated when Woody and Buzz meet.

As a product of the American West, Woody is deeply concerned with physical place. His identity hinges on being "Andy's favorite toy," and as such, his rightful "spot" is on the bed. Buzz is equally concerned with place. In this scene, Buzz refers to his role as a space ranger from the Gamma Quadrant of Sector Four repeatedly. Ironically, Buzz is the only character who does not realize the Gamma Quadrant is not real, yet it remains equally powerful within the context of the film and identity construction. Displacing Woody, Buzz reduces the significance of the physicality of place in general—suddenly, the geographical reality of the frontier matters *less* than the ideals it represents.

The establishment of the two parallel crises in *Toy Story*—the transition of the frontier from literal to ideological space and the conflict between nostalgic and progressive iterations of American identity—culminates in a montage of Andy's room. As Woody looks on, Andy changes the room's Western-themed décor to outer space. As the toys point out, Woody's pull string seems archaic in comparison to Buzz's laser lights, wings, and what Hamm refers to as a "quality sound system." Buzz, with all his gadgets and gizmos, represents the next iteration of the American myth and national identity. With progress, Lasseter argues, comes change, but not without consequences. Here, progress is connected to loss: the loss of identity, of selfhood, and of tradition. By the end of the scene, Woody has been relegated to the toy box, and he can only look on jealously as Andy snuggles in bed with Buzz.

The World Outside: The American Western Reconstructed

In exploring the frontier as an imaginative construct, *Toy Story* plays with the possibility that imaginary frontiers abound in contemporary America. A shift in perspective, such as moving from Andy's room to the "real" world outside, is all that is needed to experience them. Woody, in an ill-fated attempt to regain his position, accidentally knocks Buzz out of Andy's window. This accident marks the beginning of the first leg of Woody and Buzz's adventure. The two are now "lost toys," and they must figure out how to get home. Outside of the safety of Andy's room, the toys are in completely foreign territory. Here, Lasseter uses dramatic irony to establish the persistence of the frontier. While viewers recognize the trappings of modern life in this scene, the toys are adrift. The world around them has gone from civilized to completely unpredictable. In a place rife with danger and the unknown, Woody finds himself thrust into a frontier based not on physical space, but on one's *perspective* of that space. Because the audience is aware of the mundane reality of the filling station while Woody is not, representations of the world outside Andy's room function in a liminal fashion. Thus, Lasseter argues for the frontier's continued existence, relevancy, and pervasiveness.

Once Lasseter establishes the presence of the frontier in contemporary America, he reconciles the traditional values of the American myth (via Woody) with American progress (via Buzz). For Woody, escaping the wilderness means reuniting with Andy at Pizza Planet, but he must simultaneously contend with Buzz, who would rather "rendezvous with Star Command" than return to Andy's room. To try and save them both, Woody plays on Buzz's sustained belief in his intergalactic mission, convincing him that Pizza Planet is a space station. Unfortunately, at Pizza Planet, the two find themselves in the clutches of Andy's toy-destroying neighbor, Sid. Lasseter turns to Western iconography to reconcile America's past with its present in *Toy Story*. As Western historian Richard Slotkin points out, regeneration through violence found in the Western remains deeply connected to America's understanding of selfhood.

Sid's house threatens violence from the moment Woody and Buzz wake up. Audiences already know the two heroes are in trouble, and the color scripts in these scenes reinforce a general sense of foreboding. Unlike Andy's room, which is decorated in bright colors, Sid's room is dark and coded in greens and browns. It resembles what Joseph Campbell's monomyth labels "the inmost cave": the darkest, most dangerous location on a hero's journey to self-actualization. In a traditional Western, this would be the heart of the violent frontier, and Sid's room comes complete with its own set of "savages." As Woody and Buzz try to orient themselves, they encounter Sid's monstrosities: toys that have been taken apart and put back together in garish combinations. Woody and Buzz react with fear and horror, referring to them as "cannibals" and "savages."

But their fear is misplaced; Sid is the savage, not his toys. As Murdoch explains, the Western "presents the Indian as alien, implacable and irredeemable, an aspect (perhaps the most fearsome aspect) of the untamed land to be conquered by the march of progress" (9). Sid serves as a new iteration of the Western "savage," and Lasseter plays on stereotype to deepen the film's connection to both the Western genre and emphasize to audiences the real danger of Woody and Buzz's situation. The combination of visual symbolism and the misfit toys make the potential violence in Sid's room palpable, so it is unsurprising when Woody and Buzz find themselves on the wrong end of Sid's temper.

Woody suffers trauma at Sid's hands multiple times during this section of *Toy Story*, but the most notable instance occurs when Sid "plays pretend" by accusing Woody of being a spy. Sid paces around the room while Woody lays crumpled on the floor, and the audience prepares for the worst when Sid declares, "Well, we have ways of making you talk." He grabs a magnifying glass and focuses it on Woody's forehead until it smokes. Buzz reinforces Woody's heroic nature afterward, telling him that "a lesser man would've talked under such torture." His endurance of violence regenerates Woody's heroic nature, which has been compromised by his interactions with Buzz.

Buzz also undergoes his own regeneration through violence, but his trauma is psychological. When Buzz first arrives in Sid's room, he is still determined to return to Star Command. The physical abuse he suffers—being shot by suction darts (another nod to the film's Western roots)—does not deter him. However, as he searches for a way out of Sid's house, he sees a commercial for Buzz Lightyear action figures playing on television. The shattering impact of this moment of self-recognition is expressed when his final attempt to prove that he is a Space Ranger fails. He tries to fly, only to crash and have his arm pop off: Buzz mentally and physically falls apart.

In an emotional scene, Woody pleads with Buzz to snap out of his existential crisis. Woody tells Buzz he is just confused, which prompts Buzz's passionate response: "No, Woody. For the first time, I am thinking clearly. You were right all along. I'm not a Space Ranger. I'm just a toy, a stupid, insignificant toy." Unlike Woody, who knows he belongs in Andy's room, Buzz cannot return to Star Command. But like Buzz, Woody also suffers from displacement. Beyond his worries about being cannon fodder for Sid's experiment, he has been ousted by Buzz, who was not interested in being a "good" toy. Buzz and Woody's perspectives create a middle ground for Lasseter's melding of America's past and present identities. This moment of clarity commits Woody and Buzz to a shared vision. By joining forces to reunite with Andy, they establish a middle ground for America's Western past and its present in the space age.

Thus, in the closing scenes of the movie, Woody and Buzz capitalize on each other's strengths to follow the moving truck to Andy's new home. While Buzz is still strapped to a rocket, Woody uses his old-fashioned know-how to transform Buzz's helmet a magnifying glass to light the rocket's fuse, and he and Buzz hold on as they take off in pursuit of Andy's car. Woody fears they will blow up before they can reach safety, but Buzz opens his wings just in time. Buzz may outpace the cowboy in terms of technology, but it is experiential wisdom that allows them to succeed. As the pair glides to earth, Woody—not Buzz—exclaims, "To infinity and beyond!" In the final scenes of *Toy Story*, tradition and progress have come into harmony with one another: Andy's room is decorated in equal parts Western and space décor, and Woody and Buzz both have their own pillows on Andy's bed. In the film's closing moments, Lasseter reconciles what seem to be two competing ideologies, arguing they are both important to American identity.

The American Myth and the Pixar Story

Lasseter's decision to take the Western and "show it to [audiences] in a way that they've never seen before" launch *Toy Story* to critical acclaim and serves as the cornerstone for Pixar's enduring success. After all, computer animation had the potential to be a flash-in-the-pan moment in cinema history. Instead, thanks to Lasseter's strong storytelling and emphasis on audience connection, Pixar has had 20 years of successive box office hits. Despite the diverse intellectual properties that make up the Pixar catalog—among them, *The Incredibles* (2004), *Cars* (2006), and *Monsters, Inc.* (2001)—Pixar continues to return to the Western heroes who started it all.[2] Each subsequent movie in the *Toy Story* trilogy has been more successful than the last, and Pixar is not done yet: Lasseter has recently announced production on *Toy Story 4* (Truitt). Woody, Buzz, and the gang are set to reassemble for a new adventure, even though audiences thought they had ridden into the sunset.

It is difficult to overstate the importance of the Western and the American myth not only to the *Toy Story* films, but also to Pixar's continued success as a company. The pull-yourself-up-by-your-bootstraps, achieve-your-wildest-dreams narrative of the frontier myth has been a foundational narrative for Pixar from its earliest days; what began as "a group of men and women in a garage pursuing a dream" has now become the "crown jewel of the Walt Disney Co" (Price 266). As a company, Pixar has fully embraced the American dream and forged ahead into a technological frontier. Perhaps even more importantly, Pixar has given new life to the Western itself. While the genre might look slightly different, its underlying narrative structures and iconography remain recognizable and powerful. From the existence of frontiers to regeneration through violence, *Toy Story* demonstrates the Western's continued resonance with America and American audiences.

Notes

1. It is hard to understate the commercial and critical success of *Toy Story*. It became the "highest-grossing film of 1995" (Price 128) and would go on to earn over $360 million worldwide that year ("Toy Story"). This was largely due to its overwhelmingly positive critical reception. For example, Owen Gleiberman from *Entertainment Weekly*, *Toy Story* was "far from just a technological breakthrough.... [This] hellzapoppin fairy tale, about a roomful of gleaming suburban toys who come to life when humans aren't around ... has the purity, the ecstatic freedom of imagination, that's the hallmark of the greatest children's films." Film reviewers from across the nation echoed his opinion, including Roger Ebert, who dubbed *Toy Story* "a visionary roller-coaster ride of a movie" that would define the trajectory of the animation industry for decades to come.

2. Although Pixar's diverse film catalog has earned over $4.5 billion and seven Academy Awards for Best Animated Feature, the *Toy Story* movies remain its cornerstone ("Franchises: Pixar"). After the unexpected success of *Toy Story*, Pixar followed up on the original film with the release of *Toy Story 2* (1999). The sequel proved lightning could strike twice: not only did *Toy Story 2* smash *Toy Story*'s box office records, it was a "rare sequel that seemed as original as the original" (Price 128). Once *Toy Story 2* wrapped, Lasseter immediately turned to his co-director, Lee Unkrich, and said, "Let's do it right now. Let's make it three [*Toy Story* films]" (Alexander). Unfortunately, despite having a concept for the next installment in the trilogy, development would grind to a halt due to ongoing friction between Pixar and its one-time parent company, Disney (Alexander). Consequently, it took eleven long years for *Toy Story 3* (2010) to make it to the big screen; once it did, however, it would become the highest grossing movie of 2010 and, until the release of *Frozen* (2013), the highest-earning animated feature of all time (Reed).

Filmography

Toy Story. Dir. John Lasseter. Pixar Animation Studios, 1995.

Works Cited

Agnew, Jeremy. *The Creation of the Cowboy Hero: Fiction, Film and Fact*. Jefferson, NC: McFarland, 2015. Print.
Agresta, Michael. "How the Western Was Lost (and Why It Matters)." *The Atlantic*. The Atlantic Monthly Group, 24 July 2014. Web. 3 Mar. 2015.
Alexander, Bryan. "Why Pixar Took So Dang Long for 'Toy Story 3'" *NBC 5 Dallas–Fort Worth*. NBCUniversal Media, LLC, 18 June 2010. Web. 15 Apr. 2015.
Aquila, Richard. "Introduction: The Pop Culture West." *Wanted Dead or Alive: The American West in Pop Culture*. Ed. Richard Aquila. Urbana: University of Illinois, 1996. 1–17. Print.
Bettinger, Brendan. "Pixar by the Numbers—From TOY STORY to BRAVE." *Collider*. Complex Media, Inc., 24 June 2012. Web. 3 Mar. 2015.
Ebert, Roger. "Toy Story." RogerEbert.com. Ebert Digital LLC, 22 Nov. 1995. Web. 15 Apr. 2015.
Gleiberman, Owen. "Toy Story." *Entertainment Weekly*. Entertainment Weekly, Inc., 24 Nov. 1995. Web. 15 Apr. 2015.
Mitchell, Lee Clark. *Westerns: Making the Man in Fiction and Film*. Chicago: University of Chicago, 1996. Print.
Murdoch, David Hamilton. *The American West: The Invention of a Myth*. Reno: University of Nevada, 2001. Print.
Nodelman, Perry. "I See by Your Outfit: B Westerns and Some Recent Texts About Cowboys." *Jeunesse: Young People, Texts, Cultures* 3.2 (2011): 141–61. Print.
Price, David A. *The Pixar Touch: The Making of a Company*. New York: Alfred A. Knopf, 2008. Print.
Reed, Ryan. "'Frozen' Becomes Highest-Grossing Animated Film Ever." *Rolling Stone*. Rolling Stone, 31 Mar. 2014. Web. 15 Apr. 2015.

ScreenSlam. "Toy Story: John Lasseter Exclusive Interview." Online Video Clip. Perf. John Lasseter. *YouTube*. Google, 31 July 2014. Web. 02 June 2015.
Storytelling Is Key to Success—Pixar's John Lasseter. Prod. Russia Today. Perf. John Lasseter. *NewsLook*. NewsLook, Inc., 2015. Web. 3 May 2015. http://www.newslook.com/videos/451708-storytelling-is-key-to-success-pixar-s-john-lasseter.
"Toy Story." *Toy Story—Box Office Mojo*. IMDB.com, Inc., n.d. Web. 15 Apr. 2015.
Truitt, Brian. "Woody, Buzz and the Gang to Return in 'Toy Story 4.'" *USA Today*. Gannett, 07 Nov. 2014. Web. 15 Apr. 2015.
Turner, Frederick Jackson. "The Significance of the Frontier in American History." *Annual Report of the American Historical Association for the Year 1893* (1893): 190–227. Archive.org. Web. 12 July 2015.
West, Elliot. "Selling the Myth: Western Images in Advertising." *Wanted Dead or Alive: The American West in Popular Culture*. Urbana: University of Illinois, 1996: 269–92. Print.
Wright, Will. *Six Guns and Society: A Structural Study of the Western*. Berkeley: University of California, 1975. Print.

Burying the Past
Cemeteries, Burial and Remembrance in the Western

ANDREW HOWE

Although the specter of death lies at the heart of the war film, the gangster film, and the film noir, burials and funeral rites are not commonplace. Only the horror film has been noted for its consistent focus upon graveyards. Cemeteries, graves, and burial rites, however, often play key roles in Westerns. These markers of death are commonly presented as sites of shared memory, occasionally presented as sites of contested memory, and always appear as a continual reminder of mortality in a genre focused upon new possibilities and frontiers. The Western's obsession with this narrative trope reminds its viewers of the price of Manifest Destiny, offers personal and communal loss as markers of masculinity, provides its revenge narratives with sites of contemplation and closure, and offers cemeteries as expressions of missed opportunity, gender and self-sufficiency, race and exclusion, and the passage of time. Cemeteries in Westerns may not be as iconic as they have become in horror films. However, they are more than a mere backdrop against which the tone of the genre is set. This chapter will explore burial sites and cemeteries in their various types and narrative functions, focusing particularly–but not exclusively–on the following: improvised burials and the Allen family cemetery in *Lonesome Dove*, the terrible carnage of the American Civil War and the Sad Hill cemetery in *The Good, the Bad and the Ugly*, and the canoe as an indigenous mode of burial in *Dead Man*.

To date, very little has been written about the critical role played by burials and cemeteries in the Western. In his 1996 work *Westerns: Making the Man in Fiction and Film*, Lee Clark Mitchell does dedicate a few pages to necrology in the genre, largely through the prism of its intersection with masculinity studies. Other than Mitchell's compelling analysis, there has not been much criticism of a general nature devoted to this topic. To date, burials and cemeteries in the Western have been examined on a case-by-case basis, which is surprising, as the act of burial and the location of buried bodies are often important aspects of plot and setting, frequently serving as moments of respite and providing clarity between hardship and loss in the past and future narrative developments of determination or revenge. At their core, quiet moments in cemeteries are ones of reflection and remembrance.

Arguable, no Western is as obsessed with burial, graves, and cemeteries as is the television miniseries *Lonesome Dove* (1989). Based upon Larry McMurtry's sprawling 1985 novel, the story follows the adventures of retired Texas Rangers Augustus McRae (Robert Duvall) and Woodrow F. Call (Tommy Lee Jones), and their compatriots, as they drive a herd of cattle from the Rio Grande in Texas to Northeastern Montana. The journey is filled with danger and numerous members of their party perish along the way, the nature of their burial dependent upon time, place, and practical need. No matter where these bodies are commemorated and left, the text indicates two universals: burial as an act of human compassion is necessarily tempered by the practicality of situation, and despite any difficulties humans are pre-occupied with physically marking a final place of rest, even if the passage of time will obliterate such a sign of respect.

In the Western, a cemetery is where an individual is buried, a tendency that reveals the utilitarian ethos of the frontier. Many Western narratives are set far from civilization or are located in a situation filled with danger or some other time imperative, making the transportation of a dead body back to a population center—and burial in a proper, communal cemetery—impractical. This "bury you where you die" approach to internment occurs not only in *Lonesome Dove* and its sequels and prequels, but also in a host of other Westerns. For such burial sites, there is no permanence, as weather and time destroy the single grave marker unless, of course, it is made of stone, and even then weeds can overgrow it. The first burial of this nature in *Lonesome Dove* involves three casualties incurred during a run-in McRae has with Blue Duck (Frederic Forrest), a half-Mexican/half-indigenous bandit based upon the historical Cherokee figure involved with Belle Star's 1880s gang. By this point in the narrative, McRae—hunting the dangerous bandit in order to recover his friend and lover, Lorena Wood (Diane Lane)—has fallen in with July Johnson (Chris Cooper), a sheriff from Fort Smith, Arkansas, and his traveling companions. Instead of following McRae's advice and protecting his own, Johnson accompanies McRae into the camp of Kiowas and white fur traders associated with Blue Duck. They manage to free Lorena, but Johnson returns to find that his son Joe, his deputy Roscoe, and a girl named Janey who had recently joined them have all been murdered by Blue Duck. The scene where McRae discovers Johnson digging in the hard dirt with a tin plate is exceptional, with both actors at their very best. With his dead son lying by his side, looking almost serene, Johnson is all confusion and emotion as he digs, unable to fully process what has happened and his role in the tragedy. In the midst of this emotional upheaval, Cooper's portrayal still manages a level of subtlety, as competing emotions flash across his face: sadness at his loss, anger at himself for not listening to McRae, confusion over the loss of masculinity in not being able to protect those reliant upon him, and desire for vengeance. He keeps repeating: "It's my fault. You told me to stay." McRae exudes sympathy, but also practicality, noting that setting out after Blue Duck will not help, noting that "giving pain for pain ain't going to bring him back." Clearly, McRae is no stranger to death and the complex emotions it elicits. The only thing one can do is to scratch shallow graves out of the unyielding ground of the Llano Estacado, a small graveyard for a beloved son, faithful deputy, and a girl about whom they know nothing other than her name. The meager rock cairns provide a reminder of the sacrifice that occurs on the frontier and serve as a permanent marker of memory for a frontier folk accustomed to a fluid existence.

The graves of several other characters in *Lonesome Dove* are similarly marked with rock cairns, including that of Joshua Deets (Danny Glover), an ex-slave and master tracker who rode with McRae and Call in the Texas Rangers. When he is killed during a misunderstanding with a band of starving Indians, Call has him buried on a hilltop overlooking the river by which he died. In addition to the cairn, the normally emotionally distant Call carves a wooden headstone: "Josh Deets. Served with me 30 years. Fought in 21 engagements with the Comanche and Kiowa. Cherful in all weathers, never sherked a task. Splendid behavior." Due to wind, rain, sunlight, and time, the wooden marker will not last long, but here it is the ritual that counts, the physical act of carving and the words said around the grave. Not all such deaths are similarly celebrated in *Lonesome Dove*, however. There is also a dark side to the "bury you where you die" approach to death, especially when the living operate within a moral vacuum and/or have no connection whatsoever to the deceased. After shooting a Kiowa warrior because the man refuses to gamble, Blue Duck notes: "By God, life is cheap up here on the Canadian. It's apt to get cheaper." The dead man's compatriots leave him where he lies and afford him no burial rites, being either more interested in gambling or afraid of being similarly served by Blue Duck. In another scene, on a pole-boat making its way up the Arkansas River, one man stabs another in a conflict over a woman. The dead man's burial rites include having his pockets hastily rifled for valuables before his body is heaved overboard unceremoniously.

In *Lonesome Dove*, the primary cemetery of importance is the family plot of Clara Allen on her farm near Ogallala, Nebraska. Clara is a horse trader who, in her youth, was very close to Augustus McRae. When we first see her, she stares sadly out a window at the three tombstones commemorating her three dead sons, and then back to her comatose husband, who will soon join them. As we discover in *Return to Lonesome Dove*, when her farm burns completely and she spends a few minutes in the family graveyard before leaving her farm for good, one of her sons died within the first year of his life. On the frontier, childbirth and the months that followed it were dangerous times for both mothers and children. Names weren't always conferred right away due to the large number of children who perished soon after their birth. Even after getting through that difficult period, life on a frontier farm was dangerous, with prairie fires, Measles and other diseases, hostile indigenous groups, farmyard accidents, and a whole host of other potential dangers. As Clara says to her foreman: "Sometimes, it seems like grave digging's all we do around here." The Allen family cemetery illustrates three important points about such places on the frontier: (1) graves and graveyards can give those living on the unstable frontier a sense of stability in memory; (2) the nature of the frontier is such that the rootedness of a graveyard may become a liability, with those attached to it forced to move away due to circumstance; and (3) due to high levels of attrition, a large, multi-generational family unit is important, as the passage of time becomes, in essence, the passage of history from one generation to the next, as children participate in the ritual of paying respect to those they may, or may not, have known.

Lonesome Dove and the other four miniseries set in that fictional universe—*Return to Lonesome Dove* (1993), *Streets of Laredo* (1995), *Dead Man's Walk* (1996), and *Comanche Moon* (2008)—feature other ways in which bodies are commemorated. McRae and Call are forced to hang their former Texas Ranger compatriot, Jake Spoon (Robert Urich), who had fallen in with a gang of horse rustlers making their way to the Kansas frontier. Before the hanging, Jake argues that he shouldn't be hung along with the leader of this gang—Danny Suggs—and Danny's two brothers, as he did not kill any of their victims himself. Displaying the mixture of knowing empathy and practical resolve that typifies his character, Gus replies: "You know how it works, Jake. You ride with an outlaw, you die with an outlaw. I'm sorry you crossed the line." Although Jake and the two younger Suggs brothers are later cut down and buried, the unrepentant Danny is left to hang with a sign reading "Man burner and horse thief" pinned to his chest, his final resting spot a noose hung from a tree.[1] This ending for the violent criminal provides narrative satisfaction for the somewhat lengthy detour from the cattle drive, as it was Danny who shot and killed, and then hung and burned, two farmers before McCrae and Call eventually found these victims and gave them a proper burial.

The end of the miniseries quite literally enumerates the cost of the cattle drive and, by extension, Manifest Destiny, although through the heroic valorization of McRae, Call. Furthermore, their cattle drive as a project of westward expansion is ultimately celebrated rather than critiqued. After McRae dies of gangrene from an arrow wound, Call accedes to his final request and takes his body south to bury it by a creek near San Antonio, the location where the former Texas Ranger had his fondest memories courting Clara. As he constructs the grave marker near San Antonio, Call gives us a rare glimpse into his emotions, crying over and even arguing with his buried friend. However, after affixing the crosspiece, the ever-practical Call pats the rock cairn and departs, visiting the small town of Lonesome Dove before returning to Montana. It is here that the cost of expansion westward is finally vocalized, but ironically in a cataloguing of dead that does not involve any indigenous. When asked by his old cook, "What about the others?" Call lists the dead first, reeling off a list of burial sites: "Jake's buried up in Kansas. Deets, Montana. Gus is in a little stand of pecan trees alongside a creek where he used to picnic with a woman." After giving due memory to the dead, the only other thing he says is that "most of the rest" reached Montana safely.[2] From start to finish, *Lonesome Dove* is obsessed with funeral rites—as sparse as they might be—and burial locations, no matter how simple or improvised. In a place of violence and death, the message is that the act of remembrance is even more important than ever.

Although it was released over 20 years earlier, *The Good, the Bad, and the Ugly* (1966) advances a more nuanced view of Manifest Destiny than *Lonesome Dove*. Much like *Lonesome Dove* a generation later, this film explores the cost of nineteenth-century nation building. However, the cost of Manifest Destiny in *The Good, the Bad, and the Ugly* is less personalized, linked specifically to American politics and the catastrophic impact it has upon the land and the people who populate it.[3] The film is set during the American Civil War and features three characters—Blondie (Clint Eastwood), Tuco (Eli Wallach), and Angel Eyes (Lee Van Cleef)—attempting to locate a stash of gold bullion, all the while avoiding getting drawn into the developing military conflict. The film focuses upon the carnage of war, with entire towns destroyed by canon fire until they, in essence, become graveyards. The violence that these three men visit upon one another in order to acquire the gold pales in comparison to the violence created by the excesses of war. As John Lenihan notes: "Leone juxtaposes these violent individuals fighting among themselves for money against the large-scale slaughter incurred by national rivalries. To kill for money is rational and less destructive than to fight a war for some idealistic cause. Eastwood and his foes spend as much energy eluding the destructive path of the war as they do getting the drop on each other."[4] Although the film resists easy identifications, Blondie is usually understood as the protagonist because he is assigned the moniker "good," because he seems to have about the only moral compass (albeit a decidedly weak one), and because he is this film's version of "The Man with No Name," a stranger-protagonist that appears in Leone's other Spaghetti Westerns—*A Fistful of Dollars* (1964), *For a Few Dollars More* (1965), and *Once Upon a Time in the West* (1968)—and in modified form in later films directed by Eastwood, such as *High Plains Drifter* (1973) and *Pale Rider* (1985).[5]

Scenes of death are everywhere in this film: the overland carriage carrying Bill Carson, who knows of the gold's location, is mysteriously attacked, with everyone in it left for dead in the desert; a prisoner is forced to carry a black coffin through the streets, much like Jesus of Nazareth being forced to carry his cross, before being shot by the Union troops escorting him, then placed in the coffin and left by the side of the road; Blondie's partner in the catch-and-release game that he and Tuco had previously played is left to hang, wondering why Blondie hasn't shot the rope and allowed him to escape. Patrick McGee notes that the "barren and colorless landscape ... epitomizes Leone's vision of the West as the landscape of death."[6] McGee advances his critique, noting that these characters are already symbolically dead, even those who aren't doomed to die by the end of the narrative: "The Man with No Name is already symbolically dead, and that's why he has no name, though he is called by various names in Leone's Westerns."[7] At one point, Tuco tells Blondie that there are those with the noose around their neck, and those "who do the cutting." This phrase foreshadows the ending of the film, when the three men meet in the Sad Hill Cemetery, which is filled with dead soldiers from an ongoing, pointless military action over a nearby bridge. The three men stride through fields of American dead before having their own apocalyptic battle amidst the grave markers. The fact that the Sad Hill Cemetery becomes a place not of memory, but of calculated and brazen theft, calls into question the very heroic nature of nation building and the cost of such a venture in which a whole generation of American men had their livelihoods, and in many cases their lives, stolen. Lee Clark Mitchell links the film's resistance to valorizing traditional views of Manifest Destiny to the symbolic death of the Western protagonist, making an argument about bodily animation that could just as easily apply to the infamous closing scene of *The Wild Bunch* (1969): "In a world with no larger vision of progress or of a coherent past, rules no longer apply, and all that distinguishes the hero from anyone else is mere emotional detachment—a style that seems like nothing so much as death itself, with the hero's body become a corpse, as motionless and stark as desert landscape. In particular, Leone's 'reign of violence' strips character down in scenes of walking-dead, where individuals only seem to come alive once they have been shot."[8] The death of the Western is as ignominious as the demise of its heroes and villains. That Angel Eyes reaches for his gun first but is a step too slow and is shot by Blondie is nothing new, but the manner in which he is shot into an open grave, seemingly animated in the process, his hat and gun following him a few seconds later due to Blondie's continued and skillful ministrations, provides a humiliating yet comic demise for this character. Tuco's ordeal in the final few moments of the film is no less humiliating, and also come about due to a subversion of the cemetery as a place of remembrance of bravery and sacrifice. For no reason other than general sadism, Blondie puts a noose around Tuco's neck and forces his former partner to perch atop a rickety wooden cross, only shooting the rope attached to the overhanging tree at the moment Tuco is about to hang. Instead of commemorating the dead of war, the cemetery is a backdrop for human greed, depravity, and sadism. The fact that the gold is found in a grave that reads "Unknown" suggests that a cemetery is more a dumping place for the human waste of war than a place of memory. Leone reminds us that lost within the mythic trappings of Manifest Destiny, the true cost of nation-building, when it comes to human lives, really is "Unknown."[9]

If the terms pessimistic, nihilistic, and apocalyptic apply to Sergio Leone and his cinematic followers, then stronger language must be found to categorize Jim Jarmusch's film *Dead Man* (1995). The film has been referred to, by various critics, as being psychedelic, surrealist, and absurdist.[10] There are those who believe that, 20 years after its release, this film is still ahead of its time, while others argue that it performs the erasure of the Western.[11] The plot of this film is quite simple: Cleveland accountant William Blake (Johnny Depp) journeys to the American Southwest in order to take a job, gets shot within 24 hours of arrival, and spends the balance of the film on a journey of revelation to the Pacific Northwest—guided by an indigenous man—as he slowly dies from the bullet lodged next to his heart. The sites witnessed by Blake and the people he meets along the way evoke a tremendously complex view of the West and its demise, culminating in a burial rite that reminds the audience that whereas the Western genre has traditionally been fascinated with rigid and corporate European forms of burial and remembrance, a great many indigenous lives were also lost during the course of continental settlement. For the colonizers, these deaths were largely out-of-sight/out-of-mind, with the only entrance into Hollywood narratives by indigenous figures being the occasional, and often reductionist, reference to "sacred burial grounds."

Jarmusch's opening is poetic, cutting between the churning pistons of a train and the passenger compartment transporting Blake west. Not only does this character share a name with the English poet, but the journey he undergoes is also one that moves from innocence to experience and charts the fine line between madness and genius. In between bouts of sleeping, Blake looks out at the landscape, noticing evidence of violence and loss. As Alexandra Keller notes, the frontier is not at all the romantic notion advertised by Manifest Destiny: "A shot of a burned-out covered wagon is followed a few shots later by one of destroyed tepees. This is a frontier of decay, not progress."[12] Physical decay is accompanied by moral decay in the next scene, as suddenly as if on cue most of the passengers on the train leap up, open windows, and begin blasting away frenetically at a buffalo herd. As the train's coalman brags to Blake, the previous year a million bison were killed in this fashion. Jarmusch withholding the reverse shot of the bison being slaughtered has the effect of demonstrating the strength of cinematic conditioning when a gun is fired, as there is a sense of lack of fulfillment in *not* seeing the dead and dying bison, an important marker of the excesses of Manifest Destiny. A few moments later, however, the results of a previous bison hunt are visible, as Blake exists the train in the town of Machine and walks to the factory where he has been promised employment. The name of the town is also symbolic, indicating the impending demise of the West with the arrival of the railroad, the privileging of the technological over the biological, making the wholesale slaughter of bison possible, and facilitating efforts by the U.S. Army to further root out or contain various indigenous groups. As Blake walks towards the factory, numerous bison skulls are attached to a large wooden wall. The eye is drawn to this macabre spectacle, but dwarfed and almost hidden in the foreground are a few human skulls, a reminder that the American Bison was not the most unfortunate biological casualty of rampant westward expansion. Rosenbaum notes that the specter of genocide undergirds the entire film, although it is never really brought to the forefront.[13] Historically, the excesses of Manifest Destiny have been almost entirely ignored in film, overwhelmed by numerous tales of heroism, bravery, and determination, with any sacrifices noted those of white victimization rather than the indigenous peoples, cultures, and languages that were destroyed.

Discovering that his job has already been given to another man, and threatened at gunpoint by John Dickinson—the crazed owner of the factory (Robert Mitchum, in one of his final performances)—Blake subsequently finds himself involved in a lover's feud after spending the night with a woman who befriends him. A spurned suitor finds the two abed, shooting the woman before being shot in turn by Blake. As it turns out, the man whom Blake shot was Dickinson's son, and he flees from the three men hired by Dickinson to kill him. Blake carries with him a bullet, lodged near his heart after it passed through the only person in Machine to show him kindness. After witnessing the buffalo hunt and wall of skulls and even after losing his job, Blake's loss of innocence is now complete, the bullet making this distinction not only meta-physical but also corporeal. He journeys northwest, keeping one step ahead of the bounty hunters. He symbolically loses his glasses, but gains a guide in the form of Nobody (Gary Farmer), a half-Blackfoot/half-Blood character. Although the philosophical underpinnings of William Blake's *Songs of Innocence and Experience* provide the bedrock for Jarmusch's tale, Joseph

Conrad's *Heart of Darkness* seems a better touchstone for the actual journey itself, with increasingly bizarre and horrific episodes preceding the final death scene. As Dennis Lim noted upon the 2011 Blu Ray release of the film, *Dead Man* represents "a journey toward death that Jarmusch juxtaposes with the violent birth pangs of a destructive society and the spiritual regeneration of a lost soul."[14] Evidence of this societal decay abounds: a village burned to the ground; a tiny fawn accidentally killed during a gun battle; an outpost where the missionary in residence hands out smallpox-infested blankets to local Indians; and, the viscera of one of the bounty hunters, murdered and cannibalized by one of his peers. Indeed, Cole Wilson (Lance Henriksen)—the cannibalistic bounty hunter—is a terrible yet terribly fascinating character. Without much screen time, he becomes the living embodiment of all of that is wrong with this society, a critique of capitalist consumption made literal, fulfilling Rosenbaum's vision of *Dead Man* as "one of the ugliest portrayals of white American capitalism to be found in American movies."[15] Cole turns on his own fellow bounty hunters, according them no dignity of burial or burial rite. Instead, he shoots one and leaves him face down in a pool of water, and then kills and eats the other. The train and the town of Machine were pungent enough as symbols of Jarmusch's critique of Manifest Destiny and its excesses. In Cole, that threat is condensed within a singular entity tasked with tracking down and destroying the protagonist.

Blake, however, is not without his resources. He develops the ability to kill in cold blood—shooting two U.S. marshals—although his primary aid is Nobody, who serves as a companion and guide. Like Blake, Nobody does not belong in this world, as his name indicates. As a child, he was captured and taken to London, which is where he was exposed to and fell in love with William Blake's poetry. Not accepted as an equal by his white captors, he was then shunned by his people upon returning home, dubbed "He Who Talks Loud Saying Nothing" for speaking of his experiences in England, which were beyond their comprehension. Although he lacks a bullet close to his heart, Nobody is also marking time until his own death. His passage through life is not just about guiding Blake on the young accountant's journey of self-discovery, but instead finding his own place in the world. He ends up giving his life for Blake, dying in a shootout with Cole (who also perishes) in order that Blake take his final step undisturbed. Moments before, Nobody had put Blake into a canoe, a burial rite of the Makah Indians.[16] He tells Blake: "It's time for you to leave now, William Blake. Time for you to go back to where you came from." Despite having largely embraced his new personae, the delirious Blake has one more moment of linkage to his old life: "You mean Cleveland?" Nobody responds: "Back to the place where all the spirits come from and where all the spirits return. This world will no longer concern you." And it doesn't, as Blake is whisked downriver and out to sea, embracing (willingly or not) this death ritual that has been conferred upon him. As Rosenbaum notes, the receding canoe is a familiar trope, a stand-in for the horse that carries Shane or The Man With No Name out of the narrative and into myth.[17] In *Dead Man*, death is not so much a physical merger with the land but rather a meta-physical one, with Blake's own death standing in for the massive, and largely unheralded, numbers of indigenous dead consumed by the colossal appetites of Manifest Destiny.

Alexandra Keller notes how *Dead Man* very carefully includes many of the icons of the Western genre, and in doing so establishes the film's *bona fides* as a Western. However, these icons are marshaled not in order to perpetuate the standard vision of the West, but instead undermine it. At its core, the film "[is] not an elegy for the West, or even for the Western, like *The Man Who Shot Liberty Valance*. The deserts, the mountains, the Conestogas, the tepees, the buffalo, the bones, the dirt, the gore: put all these symbols together with the minimal narrative, suggests *Dead Man*'s prologue, and it is still possible to see the history of the Western. The frontier Jarmusch presents looks devastated and if there is an elegiac quality to the film, it is an elegy of rage."[18] The idea of a closed frontier preceded Jarmusch's film by a full century, coming at a time when early cinematic technologies were in their infancy. In 1893, historian Frederick Jackson Turner noted the closure of the frontier and, in essence, the death of the West. The following quote, from Turner's famous essay "The Significance of the Frontier in American History," is prescient in anticipating *Dead Man*: "The wilderness masters the colonist. It finds him a European in dress, industries, tools, modes of travel, and thought. It takes him from the railroad car and puts him in the birch canoe."[19] Much as Leone used the American Civil War as the historical and political backdrop for *The Good, the Bad, and the Ugly,* Jarmusch metaphorically explores throughout Blake's journey the excesses committed against the American Indian during westward continental expansion. Normally, such a project of white privilege of perspective would be viewed as problematic, as was the case with, among other "enlightened white man" tales, *Dances with Wolves* (1990) just a few years before. However, *Dead Man* has largely avoided such a critique. Perhaps this is because Jarmusch employed indigenous actors, often in roles associated with their own tribal affiliations. Perhaps it is because of the richness and audacity of the character written for Nobody, who casually kills offending whites and refers to Blake on several occasions as "Stupid, fucking white man!" Perhaps it is because of the attention he paid to indigenous languages and cultures. Whatever the reason, Blake represents the transition from innocence to experience, from naïve optimism about the project of Manifest Destiny through disillusionment and eventual rebirth. He is a white character who in the end is taken out to sea in an indigenous burial canoe, suggesting that re-evaluating American history is possible, and that those who come after may recognize Manifest Destiny for what it truly was.[20]

Although not all graveyards are alike, many represent the Enlightenment concept of the Sublime in that they combine the terrible nature of death with the often-beautiful spectacle of funeral rites and burial markers. In the Western genre, cemeteries have the added complexity of existing upon the frontier and the liminal space it represents. Turner noted the frontier as the "meeting point between savagery and civilization,"[21] but one could also argue that burial is similar as an act often brought about because of violence or some other negative, catastrophic problem, but encapsulated in a ritual of remembrance that is very civilizing. Burial is also a barrier between finality and memory, an act that consigns what was (the immediate past) to what has been (the mythic past). As Slavoj Zizek notes: "the funeral rite exemplifies symbolization at its purest: through it, the dead are inscribed in the text of symbolic tradition, they are assured that, in spite of their death, they will 'continue to live' in the memory of the community."[22] Although in this passage Zizek is discussing society's pre-occupation with the zombie narrative, the same holds true with the Western. As Lee Clark Mitchell notes, the cemetery represents a place of stability between the twin frontiers of the land and of death, with the trappings of the funeral central to the sense of communal loss:

> This link between landscape and death, inaugurated in the tableaus that close *The Last of the Mohicans*, recurs most compellingly in the Western as a process of bodies being returned to their source, forced back into the landscape from which they emerged. This motif helps explain the ubiquity of cemeteries in the fictional West, as settings for the numerous funerals and burials that punctuate its narratives. Each town has its own Boot Hill not simply because violent times require it, when men who die with their boots on must be buried.... [T]he measuring for a rude coffin, the digging of a grave, the lowering of a body into the ground, the solemn reading of a few last words, the depiction of mourners standing speechless or singing a hymn off-key, the slow turning away at last: all are part of a ceremony as central to the Western as the shoot-out or the lynching.[23]

Although it has never been accorded iconic status as it has in the horror genre, cemeteries, burial rites, and graves are very much a key part of the Western's cinematic landscape. Moreover, such sites and the practices that attend them are key reminders of the past, of loss and sacrifice, and most importantly of the dark, violent underbelly of Manifest Destiny, where the land quite literally swallowed up many of the people who sought to tame it, or who stood in the way of that project. Above and beyond the iconography of the gun and the horse, which respectively represent violent action and the freedom of transportation, the cemetery, a complex symbol, simultaneously reminds us of the violent nature of the frontier while demonstrating the importance of kinship and memory, all the while keeping score for the excesses of Manifest Destiny so often ignored in these tales of heroism and bravery.

Notes

1. This scene evidences a mixture of time-honored ritual and utilitarian exigency. The ex-rangers are utterly practical, despite the emotional difficulty of having to hang a friend. When asked where Call is going, McCrae responds: "To pick out a tree to hang you from, son." However, there are important elements of ritual, such as when they attempt to hang the Suggs brothers in birth order, although one of the horses spooks early, hanging the youngest brother before his time. And true to tradition in hanging criminals, the Suggs are all executed without their boots. Jake is allowed to keep his, perhaps due to his former service as a Texas Ranger, or perhaps as a narrative device allowing him to recapture some of his dignity by spurring his horse, saving his old friend McCrae from having to personally execute him.

2. After enumerating the expedition's losses, one final cost is revealed when Call finds out that the local saloon owner, Xavier Wanz, was so sad that Lori decided to join the expedition that after it departed he locked himself in his saloon before burning it to the ground.

3. According to Patrick McGee: "The world of the Man with No Name is a world that comes to pass after an apocalyptic event" (McGee 168). McGee suggests that the event in question is the coming of the railroad. Given Leone's focus upon the transformative nature of the railroad, both in this film and, especially, in *Once Upon a Time in the West*, it would appear that McGee's conjecture is correct.

4. See Lenihan 169–171.

5. Charles Bronson's "Harmonica" is often left off this list, although his character and the plot of *Once Upon a Time in the West* (not to mention the fact that Leone wanted Eastwood for this role) clearly establish his *bona fides* as one of the many heads of The Man with No Name.

6. See McGee 179.

7. See McGee 168.

8. See Mitchell 171.

9. Two films made in the decade following *The Good, the Bad, and the Ugly* mine a similar, nihilistic vein, taking the criticism even a bit further. In *Cemetery Without Crosses* (1969)—a French stab at the Spaghetti Western—nearly all of the characters, morally bankrupt each and every one, end up dying. There is no large cemetery evident, the very title of the film testament to the idea that the entire West is a cemetery, a blasted, apocalyptic landscape with debris, some of it human, littering decaying ghost towns. Although not quite as bleak as *Cemetery Without Crosses*, Clint Eastwood's *High Plains Drifter* (1973) encloses a pungent critique of the excesses of capitalism within what amounts to a ghost story. In this revenge tale, an entire town is guilty in the death of its former sheriff, Jim Duncan. Fearing that he is about to bring down the corrupt mining company upon which so many of them rely for jobs, the town allows Duncan to be beaten to death. Their comeuppance appears in the form of the Stranger (Clint Eastwood), a mysterious and magical figure who agrees to protect them from the thugs who murdered Duncan, and who are about to be let out of jail. Although he ends up killing these three men, he destroys the town in the process, and it becomes clear that he is in fact the ghost of Jim Duncan, returned to wreak vengeance upon those who wronged him. At the end of the narrative, the Stranger rides of into the distance, his work done. The town has been destroyed, and those who remain have commissioned a gravestone for their ex-sheriff.

10. Mary Bandy views *Dead Man* as a cinematic inheritor of Alejandro Jodorowsky's *El Topo* (1970) (Bandy 273), and Patrick McGee notes its surreal qualities (McGee 76). Jonathan Rosenbaum denotes the film an "Acid Western," one where the movement is, instead of east-to-west, from life-to-death, with drugs (peyote), altered realities, and elements of counter-culture taking center stage (Rosenbaum 51).

11. See Rickman 382–383.

12. See Keller 256.

13. See Rosenbaum 20.
14. See Lim D6.
15. See Rosenbaum 18.
16. The specific makeup of this burial rite is where Jarmusch makes a rare misstep in his depiction of indigenous culture. Although numerous groups from the Pacific Northwest practice canoe burials, none of these involve canoes sent out to sea. According to 19th century ethnographer George Gibbs: "The common mode of disposing of the dead among the fishing tribes was in canoes. These were generally drawn into the woods at some prominent point a short distance from the village, and sometimes placed between the forks of trees or raised from the ground on posts" ("Burial in Canoes"). Gibbs goes on to list several other funeral practices involving canoes (including burial), none of which involve the canoe being put out to sea. Perhaps this anomaly can be explained away by the fact that Nobody is from the Great Plains, and is interpreting this ritual as best he knows how. It is interesting to note, however, that this funereal rite has a greater resonance with the Old World, where Vikings and other northern Germanic groups did employ burial ships. Furthermore, Old Norse is one of the origins of the last name "Blake."
17. See Rosenbaum 58–59.
18. See Keller 256–257.
19. See Turner 61.
20. Two films that use the act of burial as an opportunity for pointed social criticism involve U.S.–Mexico border politics. Although appearing in just two scenes, the Obregon family cemetery in *Giant* (1956) plays an important role in the film's critique of racism directed against Tejanos living in Texas. When we first see Angel Obregon II, he almost dies of a fever following his birth. Although he is saved, the framing of the family cemetery in the background through the open door of the Obregon hovel is a not so subtle reminder that, for the ethnic poor of that time and place, it can be a short trip from birthing bed to eternal place of rest. Eighteen years later, Angel II returns home in a coffin after having been killed in action during World War II. The ensuing funeral is purposefully uncomfortable, and at one point landowner Bick Benedict sheepishly hands Angel Obregon, Sr., a folded Texas state flag. Obregon Sr. plays along, although there is a moment of awkwardness on his end, no doubt due to the realization that he is being presented with a flag associated with a political entity that stole Texas from Mexico, an outcome that has resulted in the Benedicts living in the large ranch house and consigning the Obregons to their life of servitude. This realization compounds the steep cost that the Obregon family has paid–in the form of their son–for the maintenance of a society that largely excludes them from any sort of political or economic empowerment. The cemetery and Obregon II's burial within it will stand for his family as a reminder of that cost, but also of the progress and change that will inevitably come. *The Three Burials of Melquiades Estrada* (2005) is fascinating in that it links burial to value, negotiated by a combination of geographic location and race and class status. In his first burial, Melquiades Estrada (Julio Cedillo) is accidentally shot by Border Agent Mike Norton (Barry Pepper), who fearing sanctions leaves the undocumented worker where he lies. After the body is discovered and the crime investigated, Melquiades is accorded a simple burial in an American cemetery. However, there is no attempt to find out who this man is, his name recorded simply as "Melquiades Mexico," because those who worked with him, and who now bury him, never endeavored to learn his last name. And finally, in order that he have a respectful burial, Melquiades' only friend—Pete Perkins (Tommy Lee Jones), the foreman of a local ranch—kidnaps Norton, forcing him to dig up, transport, and rebury Melquiades in his home town, on his own land.
21. See Turner 60.
22. See Zizek 22–23.
23. See Mitchell 173–174.

Filmography

Cemetery Without Crosses (1969). Dir. Robert Hossein. Arrow Video, 2015. DVD.
Comanche Moon (2008). Dir. Simon Wincer. Sony Pictures, 2008. DVD.

Dead Man (1995). Dir. Jim Jarmusch. Miramax, 2015. DVD.
Dead Man's Walk (1996). Dir. Yves Simoneau. Vivendi Entertainment, 2010. DVD.
El Topo (1970). Dir. Alejandro Jodorowsky. Abkco Films, 2014. DVD.
A Fistful of Dollars (1964). Dir. Sergio Leone. MGM Home Entertainment, 1999. DVD.
For a Few Dollars More (1965). Dir. Sergio Leone. MGM Home Entertainment, 1998. DVD.
Giant (1956). Dir. George Stevens. Warner Home Video, 2003. DVD.
The Good, the Bad, and the Ugly (1966). Dir. Sergio Leone. MGM Home Entertainment, 2004. DVD.
High Plains Drifter (1973). Dir. Clint Eastwood. Universal Studios, 2012. DVD.
Lonesome Dove (1989). Dir. Simon Wincer. RHI Entertainment, 2008. DVD.
Once Upon a Time in the West (1968). Dir. Sergio Leone. Paramount Pictures, 2003. DVD.
Pale Rider (1985). Dir. Clint Eastwood. Warner Home Video, 2010. DVD.
Return to Lonesome Dove (1993). Dir. Mike Robe. Hallmark Home Entertainment, 2003. DVD.
Streets of Laredo (1995). Dir. Joseph Sargent. Vivendi Entertainment, 2010. DVD.
The Three Burials of Melquiades Estrada (2005). Dir. Tommy Lee Jones. Columbia Pictures, 2008. DVD.
The Wild Bunch (1969). Dir. Sam Peckinpah. Warner Brothers Entertainment, 2006. DVD.

Works Cited

Bandy, Mary Lea, and Kevin Stoehr. *Ride, Boldly Ride: The Evolution of the American Western*. Berkeley: University of California, 2012.
"Burial in Canoes." *Native American Nations*. Native American Nations, 2000. 25 July 2015.
Keller, Alexandra. "Historical Discourse and American Identity in Westerns since the Reagan Era." *Hollywood's West: The American Frontier in Film, Television, and History*. Ed. Peter C. Rollins and John E. O'Connor. Lexington: University of Kentucky, 2005. 239–260.
Kendrick, James. "A Return to the Graveyard: Notes on the Spiritual Horror Film." *American Horror Film: The Genre at the Turn of the Millennium*. Ed. Steffen Hantke. Jackson: University of Mississippi, 2010. 142–158.
Lenihan, John H. *Showdown: Confronting Modern America in the Western Film*. Urbana: University of Illinois, 1980.
Lim, Dennis. "Jim Jarmusch's cosmic western resurfaces." *Los Angeles Times*. 17 August 17 2011. D6.
McGee, Patrick. *From Shane to Kill Bill: Rethinking the Western*. Madden: Blackwell, 2007.
Mitchell, Lee Clark. *Westerns: Making the Man in Fiction and Film*. Chicago: University of Chicago, 1996.
Rickman, Gregg. "The Western Under Erasure: *Dead Man*." *The Western Reader*. Ed. Jim Kitses & Gregg Rickman. New York: Limelight, 1998. 381–404.
Rosenbaum, Jonathan. *Dead Man*. London: Palgrave MacMillan, 2000.
Turner, Frederick Jackson. *History, Frontier, and Section*. Albuquerque: University of New Mexico, 1993.
Zizek, Slavoj. *Looking Awry: An Introduction to Jacques Lacan through Popular Culture*. Cambridge: MIT, 1991.

The Four Archetypes of the Three Burials (of Melquiades Estrada)

WICKHAM CLAYTON

Forgive the spoilers, but this is the actual ending of a Western film: a 32 rides off into the sunset, with dubious prospects for the future, in no small part due to his possible insanity. A villain cries, begs for atonement from someone who he has harmed, and calls after the hero to see if he will be okay. A housewife leaves the home to head back east. A saloon girl is perfectly happy in her job and with her life, turning down an opportunity to run away with the hero.

The Three Burials of Melquiades Estrada (Tommy Lee Jones, 2005) ends, to use understatement, unconventionally. And while the final encounters with these characters seem to fly in the face of Western tradition, these are consistent with the entire characterological development within a film that relies on the understanding and expectations established by the generic tropes of the Western to achieve affect. The film centers on the killing of a Hispanic immigrant, Melquiades Estrada, on the borderlands of Texas; his initial burial in a shallow grave by the killer; his pedestrian burial by the local authorities; and the journey taken by his killer at gunpoint—by Melquiades' closest friend—to his home town in Mexico to make a final resting place. *The Three Burials of Melquiades Estrada* uses this central narrative to examine the lives of four key characters surrounding the events, all of whom initially fit into classic Western generic archetypes.

Although there has been a significant amount of work on the film over the last ten years, and understandably so as it is quite a striking text, there seems to be few points of consensus on reading and interpreting it, which suggests the complex pleasures and heavy ambiguation the narrative itself communicates. Many writers, however, acknowledge the debt the film owes, at least in foundational principle, to the classic Western. Matthew Carter looks closely at the point in the film in which the "hero" steps into his role:

> We are now in recognisable [sic] "Western territory": when the lawful representatives of civilisation [sic] are unable or, in this case, unwilling to mete out justice, the gunfighter springs into action.
> It is, of course, the borderlands that provide the geography in which Pete can live out his mythic role as the hero. Its constitution of deserts, mountains and canyons likens itself to the historical epic and immediately begs comparison with the aesthetic qualities of westerns past, the Monument Valley terrain of Ford or the apocalyptic deserts of Leone and Sam Peckinpah; perhaps also with the southwestern novels of Cormac McCarthy [174–75].

Carter, however, identifies this familiar "Western territory" as the groundwork for a film that relies heavily on metanarration and discusses this at great length in his book.

Camilla Fojas similarly identifies traditional genre tropes, utilizing a cultural and socio-political methodology, stating, "*The Three Burials of Melquiades Estrada* is closer to the tone and aesthetic of the classical Western through its main features: the cowboy, the presence of the law, the contact between cultures, and the slow pace of the small town" ("Border Media," 38). David H. Zimmerman finds characterological links to the classic Western through Melquiades Estrada himself. Zimmerman writes that this character "follows a clear tradition of cowboys whose importance is not tempered by death or the grave" (218). Furthermore, Claudia Gorbman highlights a very precise aesthetic link, in contrast to her other case study, *Dead Man* (Jim Jarmusch, 1995), to formulaic and generic conceptions of filmmaking, stating:

> *The Three Burials of Melquiades Estrada* takes a more conventional approach to its music. Like a number of post-classical westerns, and indeed like numerous American films since the 1980s, it deploys both orchestral scoring and pre-existing songs in what is commonly called a hybrid score. The scoring generally complements the emotional tone of the narrative events, and the songs, all of which are diegetic, help constitute the characters' world. The songs additionally work to comment on narrative action and indicate ethnic separations and mixing of characters [208].

Some of these commentators note that the film establishes, then subverts, or offers commentary on, Western tropes. Carter writes, "*Three Burials* both deconstructs the myth and shows, in an imitative form, the fate of the man who follows it" (176). Fojas identifies a narrative element as a metaphor of the genre, stating, "As Pete and Mike search for Melquiades' village. It becomes apparent that this mythic utopia, like its cinematic counterpart in the classical Western, does not exist" ("Border Media," 38). Zimmerman notes how the overarching methodology for reading texts within the boundaries of his chapter falls short, writing that "the limitations of such an approach become clear;

the reading strips the text of its ambiguities by assuming, affirming, and even reinforcing a shared point of view" (221). Lee Clark Mitchell similarly focuses almost entirely on the film's ambiguities. He acknowledges that the film is a commentary on the classical Western, yet states that "Jones's film seems hardly a Western at all, with neither nostalgia for a simpler past, nor investment in the triumph of law and order, nor contemplation of the redemptive power of violence, nor (most importantly) attention to appropriate forms of masculine behavior. All those aspects familiar to the genre are absent" (446). Though Mitchell does point out that, "Such questions notwithstanding, what does remain clear is that dead as the classic Western may appear to be, our own residual faith in the genre brings it alive once again" (447).

Considering these established views of *The Three Burials of Melquiades Estrada* and its relationship to traditional, classic films in the Western genre, I propose considering *The Three Burials of Melquiades Estrada* a film which adopts the tropes of a genre (the Western), more specifically the character archetypes central to that genre, as defined by Philip French, and subverts the expectation of character archetype behavior through a precise means of temporal displacement. Most specifically, *The Three Burials of Melquiades Estrada* places archetypes established and developed during the "classical" period of Hollywood production to "modern-day" Texas. The film is populated by characters with established roles, carrying specific expectations, within a culture that recontextualizes the positions and motivations of these archetypes. The film is set in the Texan borderlands in the mid–2000s, where a mobilized, regimented group—the U.S. border patrol—brings race relations and federal (as well as social) politics into clear relief. What was traditionally conceived as a lawless land is now supervised, not always successfully, by authoritarian representatives. This is a time when many people in civilization travel in cars and trucks, and watch TV at home. And within this framework, we have the Hero, Pete (Tommy Lee Jones), the Villain, Mike (Barry Pepper), the Housewife, Lou Ann (January Jones), and the modernized Saloon Girl, Rachel (Melissa Leo). These four archetypes, over the course of the film, largely become uneasy in their roles and fail to arrive at their generically mandated end.

Pete

In this film, Pete, played by director Tommy Lee Jones, is our Hero. Or, more accurately, Pete is the character that most closely resembles (and is identifiable as) the hero archetype outlined by Philip French: "the hero is the embodiment of good. He is upright, clean-living, sharp-shooting, a White Anglo-Saxon Protestant who respects the law, the flag, women and children;

he dresses smartly in white clothes and rides a white horse that is his closest companion; he uses bullets and words with equal care, is a disinterested upholder of justice and uninterested in personal gain. He always wins" (French 30). However, this description, in application to Pete, requires several asterisks. It should suffice to say that, coming long after the popularization of revisionist westerns in the 1960s and 70s, and holding firmly onto that tradition, the character, as do all archetypal characters in this film, problematizes the description quite consciously. Pete, though, is clearly recognizable as the "Hero" in a classical sense during the first half of the film, approximately—the period wherein all the archetypes are established, before a period of destabilization.[1]

Pete is, obviously, a White Anglo-Saxon, and likely Protestant if he subscribes to any theological framework. He does dress, for someone who earns a living through physical labor, smartly, in light blue denim, often shot using desaturated, washed-out cinematography in outdoor location shots, which make these clothes, if not strictly white, appear white. On a purely visual level: White Man → White Clothes = Good/Hero.

In terms of Pete's personality and values, he again aligns with French's description. At the start of the film, he is seen as a friend of the law—Pete is on a first-name basis with the sheriff—and most importantly, initially trusts the law to seek justice, by believing the authorities are searching for Melquiades' killers. Although Pete does not express any sentiments about the flag, he is clearly seen as one who respects human life. Melquiades is a young man when they meet and Pete comes to think of him like a son; Pete is knowledgeable and accepting of other cultures, as is shown through his fluency in Spanish and respectful attitude towards the people he meets in Mexico; Pete appears to treat the women around him with kindness and care as evinced through his relationship with Rachel and his (relative) consideration for the comfort of Lou Ann when he kidnaps Mike. He does shoot rarely, but accurately, and only says what he feels is necessary. When he discovers that the police are not interested in seeking justice, Pete then becomes, as he sees it, the sole upholder of justice (though not disinterested), and is, indeed, absolutely uninterested in personal gain. Whether he is, in fact, the winner at the end of the film is questionable, though he consistently wins the smaller victories, for better or worse.

Therefore, according to French's identification of the Western hero, Pete is clearly positioned, both visually and narratively, as such. As the film progresses, however, Pete's position as Hero becomes consistently undermined, although there is no apparent hero to take his place. The point of deviation for Pete is his kidnapping of Mike, the apparent western Villain. Although his treatment of Mike in this scene may seem somewhat brutal it is never fully framed as unjustified—it is, at best, ambiguous. The problem with

"Hero" characterization comes with Pete's treatment of Lou Ann. Pete knocks on the door of their trailer and catches Mike off guard at night as he is dressed in shorts, a t-shirt, and flip-flops, and Lou Ann is dressed in thin white clothes for bed. Instead of taking Mike when he is alone, Lou Ann is terrorized as well—Pete has to point his gun at her and threaten to kill her so she will stop screaming. He tells her that Mike has killed Melquiades, and takes Mike out to his truck after making him dress in his uniform. There is then a cut to Lou Ann tied to a chair with duct tape over her mouth. She is breathing and obviously panicked. While there is practical utility in these things—ensuring Mike is unarmed, preventing neighbors from alerting the authorities, and keeping Lou Ann from alerting the authorities herself– his personal mission overrides her well-being.

This is placed at odds with the final shots of them together, with Pete covering the bound and gagged Lou Ann with a blanket to keep her from getting cold, and paternally, if dazedly, stroking her cheek in an effort to soothe her as they watch TV. This is undercut by the apparent madness in his appearance and behavior. Furthermore, Pete's role as the Hero archetype is complicated by his sadistic behavior towards Mike. Pete seems to go out of his way to ensure Mike gets hurt as they travel, although in the end Pete prefers not to kill him, rather, he wants Mike to ask forgiveness of Melquiades, before leaving him alive. However, Pete's sensitivity to Mexican culture adds further complexity to this dynamic.[2] Just as it is difficult to condemn the young Mexican woman whom Mike punches in the face at the beginning of the film, which I will discuss in the next section, for grudgingly hurting Mike when he needs her help, Pete justly (though potentially problematically) pointedly calls Mike a "*gringo* son of a bitch" when confronting him with his crime of killing an (to Mike's knowledge) anonymous Mexican person. Pete rightly calls out Mike's abuse of privilege, though he, as French's "White Anglo-Saxon Protestant," is himself acting as avenger. Fojas reads this dynamic as particularly significant, saying, "*The Three Burials of Melquiades Estrada* takes the idea of the benevolent Anglo, long a trope of the border film, to its logical extreme. This deconstructionism is a unique consequence of the cross-border collaboration between (screenwriter) Arriaga and (director) Jones. Arriaga locates the Anglo benevolence as part of an Anglo male fantasy about Mexicans and Mexico" (*Border Bandits* 194; parenthesis mine). Similarly, in a different piece Fojas locates this attitude within the character of Pete, stating, "In a relationship symptomatic of interracial transborder dynamics, Melquiades is a blank slate upon which Pete projects his fantasies of Mexico and Mexicans" ("Border Media," 38).

However, Pete, as the film's protagonist and Western Hero, cannot simply be deemed an anti–Hero, or a Villain in Hero's clothing. More than any other character in the film, the character of Pete is the vessel of what Todd Berliner calls "*Characterological inconsistencies*, when characters behave in ways consistent with their previous characterizations. For example, the senatorial candidate has unbending integrity vs. the candidate does what he must to get elected (*The Candidate*, 1972)" (Berliner 27; parenthesis in original). This can manifest within Heroes particularly who behave in ways that complicate the audience's ability to "root" for them. The last half of the film continually depicts events and behaviors that alter the audience's comfort with Pete, or at the very least ambiguates his motives. Characterological inconsistencies are mainly limited to Pete, however, other characters appear to act outside of their archetypal limitations, when, in fact, their actions are consistent with their archetypes within a fictional universe with fewer limitations.

Mike

As with the Hero archetype, French identifies the Western Villain: "The villain, on the other hand, is the embodiment of evil; he dresses in black, rides a dark horse and is doomed to die. He is often a smooth talker and has lecherous designs on women; he is only concerned with advancing his own cause but beyond that has a positive commitment to destruction" (30).

From the beginning, Mike is the film's Villain. He is a border patrol officer whose dark green uniform proves a direct muddy contrast to Pete's almost white clothes. He isn't a smooth talker, but he does speak forcefully, and his designs on women are, broadly speaking, lecherous. His own cause is self-defense, and he does appear inclined toward destruction. The death he is doomed to is not a literal one, but a spiritual, figurative one—which, in turn, results in Mike arguably being the film's protagonist.

Mike is a lawman whose zeal for the job, intense bigotry, and strong interest in self-preservation results in the use of disproportionate violence in the execution of his duties. In the first scene that shows him working as a border patrol agent, he chases a young couple crossing the border illegally farther than his colleagues. Once he catches up with them, he kicks the young man in the stomach, and punches the young woman in the face, breaking her nose, yelling "Stay down, bitch!" His supervisor admonishes him, saying, "You were way overboard there, boy," to which Mike replies, "No, sir, fuck it. They were trying to get away." Mike refuses to acknowledge the severity of his violent actions even when confronted by his supervisor, while clearly and forcefully asserting his view. This is echoed later, once Mike has been kidnapped by Pete, who verbally confronts him about killing Melquiades. Mike merely responds that Melquiades shot first.

Primarily, Mike does have lecherous designs on women, of a fashion. While his physical interaction with women is limited to the time he spends with his wife, Lou Ann (which includes an instance of sexual intercourse—rape, in fact—which is ultimately cold and selfish, only focusing on his own pleasure), he is often looking at pornographic magazines, even while he is working. In fact, he is trying to find a private place to masturbate to one of his magazines when he hears a gunshot, which causes him to panic, ultimately killing Melquiades. This is also observed by Michele Aaron, who writes that Mike's "self-serving, onanistic place in the world is epitomized by the cold, one sided sex he has with his wife (ignoring her 'stop it,' his swift pleasure-taking barely interrupts her view of the television) and his repeated attempts to 'jerk off.' Indeed, his unwitting shooting of Melquiades arises directly from his getting out of his jeep to masturbate" (Aaron 195; parenthesis in original). Significantly, the film doesn't adopt a moralist position towards pornography or sex work, as I will show in the next two sections, but it appears indicative of the character's tendency towards the objectification of women, of which his sexual encounter with Lou Ann is evidence.

As I have stated, "his own cause" is self-preservation. As a law enforcement officer, his killing of Melquiades, a Hispanic man, would not only compromise himself but the Border Patrol Agency. This is even more important following his physical violence toward the young couple at the beginning of the film. Mike is silent about the incident, even with his wife, who hears about it from Pete. This is all linked to Mike's "commitment to destruction," however, this is only apparent in the first half of the film, as Pete's kidnapping of Mike shifts the power structure between the two characters, and is the catalyst for the most significant character arc of the film.

After the kidnapping, the Western Hero has complete power over the Villain. Mike is tied and taken on a journey at gunpoint, first to exhume the body of Melquiades, then across the U.S./Mexico border, and finally to find Jiménez to bury Melquiades. Throughout the journey, Mike, unsure of his fate at the hands of Pete, and due to extreme discomfort, tries to escape repeatedly. This is still indicative of his goal of self-preservation instead of seeking peace and atonement—Mike is obviously troubled about shooting Melquiades, for example when he chokes after lighting up a cigarette in the mall parking lot, resulting in silent tears, a sequence broken up by images of him panicking over the dying body of Melquiades. However, the journey forces Mike to accept responsibility for the murder, to develop familiarity if not empathy for others, as is seen when he is talking with and sharing tequila with people as Pete asks for directions to Jiménez, and to atone for his wrongdoings both physically (being beaten by the young woman whose nose he broke) and spiritually (crying and begging Melquiades, at Pete's prompting, for forgiveness at his final grave). He is seen as at peace in the penultimate sequence where he is sleeping deeply. It is through this journey and character development, atypical of the Western Villain, that we see how *The Three*

Burials of Melquiades Estrada can be seen as a unique case study of the Western genre. Fojas writes that "it is Mike who undergoes forced migration to face his racialized prejudices and imperial chauvinism" ("Border Media," 39). Fojas elucidates this at greater length, writing, "Mike is literally dragged through the desert to face all of his prejudices about Mexicans; for instance, he meets one of the migrants whom he beat up and debased as a border patrol agent and accepts his fate when she returns the favor. We sense that he is changing at various points in the journey and at the end, when Pete demands that he ask Melquiades for forgiveness, Mike is truly contrite" (Fojas, *Border Bandits*, 194). However, the characterological inconsistencies of the Hero, and the inversion of character development of the Villain are only evidence of how the film approaches the male characters. The female characters are, in very subtle but significant ways, both examples of Western character archetypes and subversions of generic conceptions of Western female characters.

Lou Ann

As many commentators have indicated, the Western is overwhelmingly the province of the male.[3] It either concentrates on masculinity or features a cast largely comprised of men. However, in writing about the characters in *Shane* (George Stevens, 1953), John Saunders writes, "The roles allotted to women in the western are painfully circumscribed, and it is fitting that we should meet her indoors, the 'Angel of the House,' leaving the outside world to men and their doings."[4] Saunders here identifies one of the archetypes typically attributed to female characters in the classical western: the Housewife.

Furthermore, French also identifies archetypal female characters that frequently appear in Western films including the Housewife: "the unsullied pioneer heroine: virtuous wife, rancher's virginal daughter, schoolteacher, etc." (38). French claims these characters "are in short supply, to be treated with respect and protected" (38). Lou Ann fits this description at the film's outset. As the pioneer, she travels with her husband, Mike, from Cincinnati, Ohio to Texas as he starts his new job. She may not be happy, but in the beginning she quietly and steadfastly helps keep and decorate their home. She complains little, though the film regularly highlights her loneliness. She is shown sitting in the local diner in the middle of the day, reading a magazine and smoking a cigarette. Her investment in her reading material appears limited as she regularly looks out of the window, and at her surroundings.

The film reframes this archetype early on: not only is Lou Ann seen as bored and lonely, but she even stands by her man, so to speak, by quietly staying still and bending over her counter top while Mike quickly, artlessly, and without a hint of romance or love, fucks her from behind. The fact that when he first touches her, she says, "Stop it," indicates this as an instance of rape.[5] She continues to watch television, showing alternating expressions of boredom and discomfort, while he finishes, smacks her on her behind and walks back to his chair. She is doing what this generic character type is supposed to do, due to generic mandate, and clearly does not enjoy it, a position framed by the film to elicit identification and sympathy with the audience. Her husband, after all, is both appropriately and ironically the Villain.

To complicate this position, Lou Ann later, and quite suddenly, appears as an escort for Melquiades. Pete's implication that she is one of the "girls" he has hired for sexual favors for Melquiades comes as a surprise, considering the generic conventions surrounding this character. However, the film doesn't explicitly imply that they had sex, and the screen time spent with them privately shows Melquiades nervous, and Lou Ann kindly trying to calm him. The viewer only witnesses the two talking and dancing. This does not fully undercut the fact that she seems fully prepared to sleep with Melquiades, but the film appears to attempt both justification and identification with Lou Ann—she is not only unhappily married, but unhappily married to the Villain. The same Villain who has killed the man we see her, in flashback, showing kindness and tenderness toward. While this sequence, on a moment-to-moment basis provides a complex experience, undermining the expected behavior of a character archetype while establishing a justification and identification with the character, it also functions as a significant step in the character's story arc: this event informs her character, her potential (and unseen) response to the news that her husband has killed the man who she was kind to, and he to her in turn, and her dissatisfaction with her married life all point toward her final scene.

Toward the end of the film, Lou Ann returns to the diner and talks to the waitress Rachel, whom she has befriended, and tells her that she is leaving to return to Ohio. Though little dialogue occurs in this sequence, Lou Ann makes it clear she is dissatisfied with her life and feels no loyalty to her husband, who she has not seen for a long time. Lou Ann is then seen, bag packed, getting onto a bus and leaving. This is diametrically opposed to the fundamental function of the Housewife archetype, to support her husband.[6] However, her husband has mistreated her, harmed others, and killed an innocent man. So when Lou Ann leaves, as surprising as it is due to this uncharacteristic deviance from the genre's character formula, it is consistent with the specific character's trajectory, and even potentially meets not only with viewer sympathy, but viewer relief. Similarly, the other key female character archetype in the film benefits from the contextual reframing of the generic elements.

Rachel

There is one other type of woman in what French calls the "model traditional western woman": the Saloon Girl, "with her entourage of dancers," and such characters are "reasonably plentiful, sexually available and community property" (French 38). In *The Three Burials of Melquiades Estrada*, this role is filled by Rachel, the waitress at the local diner owned and operated by her husband, Bob.

The diner, like the saloon in classical period westerns, is a place of refreshment and sustenance. It is owned by a male figure, who hires a woman to interface with the customers. Rachel, as the Saloon Girl, also engages in sex with at least two people apart from her husband. Rachel is seen arranging to meet the sheriff, Belmont (Dwight Yokam) while he openly gropes her as she serves him at the diner. Furthermore, she is twice shown with him, sitting on a couch, both completely undressed (save his socks and a pillow). However, on both occasions, Belmont has apparently had difficulty getting an erection, and Rachel attempts to comfort him. When she tries to tell him that this happens sometimes to Bob, he mainly responds in frustration, saying, "Fuck Bob."

Rachel is also seen with Pete, who seems to engage in regular encounters with her.[7] It appears to be Rachel who has recruited Lou Ann to be a companion for Melquiades when Pete claims to have found sexual partners for himself and Melquiades. Whether these interactions involve a monetary exchange or not, which is never made entirely clear, it seems to be a regular occurrence for Rachel, and something that she is both familiar and comfortable with. However, the film resists objectifying her, or settling her comfortably into the archetype, instead opting to present her as a sympathetic character.

The fact of her promiscuity, unbeknownst to her husband, initially establishes this archetype and calls into question her likeability. The first hint of a sympathetic framing comes with her revelation that her husband regularly has erectile dysfunction in the first sequence with Belmont. This clearly suggests sexual loneliness and dissatisfaction, which to an extent at least explains her sleeping, seemingly regularly, with two other men. However, the sequence that most strongly elicits sympathy from the viewer, takes place in the diner, at a point when Lou Ann is the only patron. Rachel, sweeping the floor, stops and looks pointedly at Lou Ann. Then she calls, "Hey Bob? How long we been married now?" Bob responds, "Twelve...," followed by a long pause, then, "Hell, I don't know. What is it?" Rachel doesn't respond to this, only maintains eye contact with Lou Ann throughout and then begins working again. In this moment, the viewer not only sees how unappreciated Rachel feels by her husband, but gains sympathy and understanding for her, and this

"Hey Bob? How long we been married now?" Bob, (Richard Andrew Jones, left), Rachel (Melissa Leo, center), and Lou Ann (January Jones) in *The Three Burials of Melquiades Estrada* (EuropaCorp and Javelina Film Company, 2005).

moment of identification not only explains her actions, but develops the character past generic archetypal configuration.

Lou Ann and Pete appear to be the closest thing that Rachel has to friends: Rachel treats Lou Ann apparently with admiration and respect, Rachel seeming to fill a maternal role with respect to her; and Pete, who may act macho in front of Melquiades when Rachel is there, is set at odds with Belmont. Pete and Rachel appear to have fun together (as opposed to the lecherous/glum dynamic presented by Belmont), and while we are not privy to their sexual relationship, at the very least Pete doesn't openly grope her in view of her husband. Furthermore, it is Rachel that informs Pete of the identity of Melquiades' killer, suggesting a relationship that goes beyond sexual. This relationship culminates when Pete ultimately asks Rachel to marry him. However, Rachel doesn't just choose to stay with Bob, but responds as though she had never considered doing so; when Pete asks her why she won't marry him, she responds in a bemused tone "I love Bob, Pete," as though she's surprised she even has to explain it. She expresses love for her husband—in generic terms, the Saloon Owner—and appears confident in her decision to stay with him.

Interestingly, the genre encourages the expectation that Rachel will say yes to Pete. While the coupling of the Hero, Ringo Kid (John Wayne) and the Saloon Girl, Dallas (Claire Trevor) in *Stagecoach* (John Ford, 1939) subtly undermined the Hays Code, and gently subverted contemporary genre expectation, the development of the Western since that time has presented many such romantic pairings, successful or no.[8] Therefore, when Pete telephones Rachel from Mexico, the viewer is coaxed into expecting acceptance; not only because Rachel has demonstrated dissatisfaction with her life, but as part of a generic mandate. Her refusal elicits a sense of admiration from the viewer, while at the same time seeming at odds with the narrative information regarding her character to that point. It is through these spare characterological inconsistencies that Rachel, the Saloon Girl, closes the door on the dictates of the genre for female characters.

Conclusion

These four archetypes in *The Three Burials of Melquiades Estrada*—the Hero, the Villain, the Housewife, and the Saloon Girl—according to French's definitions, all initially establish consistency with their generic heritage, before complicating, subverting, or rendering incoherent viewer experience and expectation. This is consistent with other research on the film, such as work done by Carter, Fojas, and Mitchell, which identifies the uneasy and knowing relationship *The Three Burials of Melquiades Estrada* has with the Western genre, whether playing with gender and racial representation, or narrative ambiguity.

Whether this film can be conceived as revisionist, postmodern, post-postmodern, post-classical-revival revisionism, or deconstructive modernism, the film still clearly utilizes tropes and character archetypes seen throughout the Western. However, the re-situation of this Western from the nineteenth century west, the typical temporal framing of the Western, to contemporary (mid–2000s) borderland Texas, creates a complication for these traditional tropes. The development of legal systems to prevent lawlessness; increasing and developing population, housing, and common technological usage; and the relative liberation of women (despite a continued climate of institutionalized misogyny and racism), results ultimately in re-representation of the classical tropes as stale and less believable. Furthermore it provides a fertile groundwork for believably subverting these tropes. The brilliance of *The Three Burials of Melquiades Estrada*, then, lies not in its wholesale discarding of generic elements and expectations, but through establishing and subsequently undermining what we have been generically guided to anticipate.

Notes

1. It should be noted that the "revisionist" Western did not wholly replace traditional genre offerings. Films like *Silverado* (Lawrence Kasdan, 1985), *Tombstone* (George P. Cosmatos, 1993), *Wyatt Earp* (Lawrence Kasdan, 1994) and, one of my personal favorites, *Open Range* (Kevin Costner, 2003) do not so much re-establish classic genre tropes and update them for a more contemporary aesthetic, as simply use the classic genre as a model. They appear less a reaction to revisionism than generic exercises.

2. We see this dynamic, with a different character framing, in *The Searchers* (John Ford, 1956)—Ethan is a hero who is extremely well versed in Native American culture. However,

in *The Searchers*, Ethan's cultural awareness doesn't alter the fact that he is quite an exceptional racist.

3. See Mitchell 446, French 41, Saunders 16, Hayward 503–4, and Neale 59–60.

4. Saunders 16. It should be noted that *Shane* is a very interesting case study here. While the character is, in fact, bound to the home, this particular character seems to be screaming for agency in an overwhelmingly patriarchal structure. Or, to put it more truthfully, this female character is shown and written, albeit subtly, to have much more complexity than other such characters within the genre. It's arguably one of the reasons *Shane* is widely considered (see number 69 on the 2007 updated American Film Institute list "100 Years ... 100 Movies" [n.p.]) a great American film.

5. In addition to the quote by Aaron in the previous section, Susanne Kord and Elisabeth Krimmer similarly discuss this sequence:

> Mike's casual rape of Lou Ann at the kitchen counter while she is watching a TV soap opera and chopping vegetables for dinner expresses in one succinct scene the nature of the relationship. As he pushes into her from behind, showing as much concern for her as he does for the porn magazines he regularly masturbates over or the toilet that he masturbates into, she endures, rolling her eyes, her gaze fixed on the TV on which another marital drama unfolds [Kord and Krimmer 81].

6. One could draw attention to the example of *High Noon* (Fred Zinnemann, 1952), where the new wife of the hero is vocally opposed to his taking action against the villains. I argue that this is keenly opposed to generic trend, which heightens the narrative tension, and contributes to the film's highly regarded status (again, see the AFI's 2007 "100 Years ... 100 Movies" list at number 33).

7. Rachel's relationship to Bob, Belmont, and Pete is also briefly discussed by Kord and Krimmer (81).

8. See *Rio Bravo* (Howard Hawks, 1959) for a straightforward example, *McCabe and Mrs. Miller* (Robert Altman, 1971) provides an example from the Western's highly revisionist wing, and the television mini-series *Lonesome Dove* (Simon Wincer, 1989) proves a more traditional example.

Filmography

The Candidate (1972). Dir. Michael Ritchie. Warner Home Video. 1997. DVD.
Dead Man (1995). Dir. Jim Jarmusch. Universal Home Video. 2005. DVD.
High Noon (1952). Dir. Fred Zinnemann. Republic Home Entertainment. 1997. VHS.
Lonesome Dove (1989). Dir. Simon Wincer. Rhi Entertainment. 2008. DVD.
McCabe and Mrs. Miller (1971). Dir. Robert Altman. Warner Home Video. 2002. DVD.
Open Range (2003). Dir. Kevin Costner. Touchstone Home Entertainment. 2004. DVD.
Rio Bravo (1959). Dir. Howard Hawks. Warner Home Video. 2010. DVD.
The Searchers (1956). Dir. John Ford. Warner Home Video. 2006. BluRay.
Shane (1953). Dir. George Stevens. Warner Home Video. 1998. VHS.
Silverado (1985). Dir. Lawrence Kasdan. Sony Pictures Home Entertainment. 2009. DVD.
Stagecoach (1939). Dir. John Ford. Warner Home Video. 2005. DVD.
The Three Burials of Melquiades Estrada (2005). Dir. Tommy Lee Jones. Sony Pictures Home Entertainment. 2006. DVD.
Tombstone (1993). Dir. George P. Cosmatos. Hollywood Pictures Home Video. 1997. DVD.
Wyatt Earp (1994). Dir. Lawrence Kasdan. Warner Home Video. 2011. DVD.

Works Cited

Aaron, Michele. *Death and the Moving Image: Ideology, Iconography and I*. Edinburgh: Edinburgh University Press, 2014. Print.
American Film Institute. "100 Years ... 100 Movies." *American Film Institute*. American Film Institute, 2007. Web. 31 August 2015. http://www.afi.com/100years/movies.aspx.
Berliner, Todd. *Hollywood Incoherent: Narration in Seventies Cinema*. Austin: The University of Texas Press, 2010. Print.

Carter, Matthew. *Myth of the Western: New Perspectives on Hollywood's Frontier Narrative.* Edinburgh: Edinburgh University Press, 2014, 2015. Print.
Fojas, Camilla. *Border Bandits: Hollywood on the Southern Frontier.* Austin: The University of Texas Press, 2008. Print. Cited parenthetically as *Border Bandits.*
Fojas, Camilla. "Border Media and New Spaces of *Latinidad.*" *Latinos and Narrative Media: Participation and Portrayal.* Ed. Frederick Luis Aldama. Houndmills: Palgrave Macmillan, 2013. 35–48. Print. Cited parenthetically as "Border Media."
French, Philip. *Westerns: Aspects of a Movie Genre* and *Westerns Revisited.* Manchester: Carcanet, 2005. Print.
Gorbman, Claudia. "Musical Worlds of the Millennial Western: *Dead Man* and *The Three Burials of Melquiades Estrada.*" *Music in the Western: Notes from the Frontier.* Ed. Kathryn Kalinak. New York: Routledge, 2012. 203–13. Print.
Hayward, Susan. *Cinema Studies: The Key Concepts, Third Edition.* Abingdon: Routledge, 2006. Print.
Kord, Susanne and Elisabeth Krimmer. *Contemporary Hollywood Masculinities: Gender, Genre, and Politics.* Houndmills: Palgrave Macmillan, 2011. Print.
Mitchell, Lee. "'Is There Actually Any Jiménez?': Believing as Seeing in *The Three Burials of Melquiades Estrada.*" *Quarterly Review of Film and Video* 32.5 (2015). 446–55. Print.
Neale, Stephen. *Genre.* Chippenham: British Film Institute, 1980. Print.
Saunders, John. *The Western Genre: From Lordsburg to Big Whiskey.* London: Wallflower Press, 2001. Print.
Zimmermann, David H. "The Walking Dead: The Role of the Corpse in Western Myths." *Death Lore: Texas Rituals, Superstitions, and Legends of the Hereafter.* Ed. Kenneth L. Untiedt. Denton: University of North Texas Press/Texas Folklore Society no. LXV, 2008. 217–24. Print.

About the Contributors

Richmond B. **Adams** is an assistant professor of English at Northwestern Oklahoma State University. He has published on various aspects of American literature, film and culture. Other research interests include the function of physicians in American literature and film in the years after the Civil War as well as the relationship between manners and power across the 19th and 20th centuries.

David **Blanke**, professor of history at Texas A&M University–Corpus Christi, has written three books and many essays on U.S. popular culture in the late nineteenth and early twentieth centuries, including *Hell on Wheels* (2007). He is the coeditor of *A Destiny of Choice?* (2013).

Gilles **Chamerois** is a senior lecturer at the University of Brest, France. He has published on various filmmakers (Robert Kramer, Ken Loach, John Huston, Jacques Rozier, among others), coauthored two books on adaptation, and edited or coedited two collections of essays on Thomas Pynchon.

Wickham **Clayton** is a lecturer in film production at the University for the Creative Arts in Farnham, UK. He is the editor of *Style and Form in the Hollywood Slasher Film* (2015) and coeditor of *Screening Twilight* (2014). He has also published a range of work on film form, adaptation, and genre.

Maria Cecília de Miranda N. **Coelho** is an associate professor of philosophy at the Universidade Federal de Minas Gerais, Brazil. She is the coeditor of *Cinema* (2009), and has published articles on Gorgias, rhetoric, Euripidean tragedy and the reception of classics in cinema.

Jim **Daems** is an assistant professor of English at the University College of the North, Canada, and teaches pre–nineteenth-century English literature. He has published books on seventeenth-century literature, culture and John Milton, coedited Charles I's *Eikon Basilike*, and edited a collection of essays on *RuPaul's Drag Race* (2014). He has also published essays on a wide range of literary and popular culture topics, from Edmund Spenser to *Harry Potter*.

Alexander **Davis** is a doctoral candidate in cinema studies at New York University's Tisch School of the Arts. In addition to psychedelic, counterculture westerns, he has also researched and published on the use of intertextuality in Jim Jarmusch's films, the western persona of Jimmy Stewart, and the aesthetic influences of Bonnie and Clyde.

Monica Montelongo **Flores** is an assistant professor of multiethnic American literature in the Department of English at California State University–Stanislaus. Her specializations include U.S. literature, film and media studies, and Latina/o cultural studies. Her research often highlights the dialogues between the construction of the American West and Chicana/o cultural productions.

Stella **Hockenhull** is a reader in film and television studies and codirector of the Research Centre for Film and Media at the University of Wolverhampton, UK. Apart from various publications on British cinema and landscape, she has written widely on animals and animal performance in film, in particular horses on screen.

Martin **Holtz** studied English and mathematics at Greifswald University in Germany, where he teaches American literature and film. He is the author of *American Cinema in Transition* (2011), and his research interests include war and agency in American literature.

Andrew **Howe** is a professor of history at La Sierra University, where he teaches courses in American history, film studies, and popular culture studies. He has published on Manifest Destiny and the extinction of the Passenger Pigeon, and *Avatar* as a re-working of the Mohican myth. His research interests also include how biological invasions, extinctions, and reintroductions are packaged by the media to resonate with contemporary social issues.

Katherine A. **Johnson** is a doctoral candidate specializing in film and media in the Department of Communication and Culture at Indiana University. Her research broadly focuses on Hollywood, gender, and genre. Along with examining the iconography of the Western, her work specifically explores the representation of women and femininity within the genre.

Deborah L. **Kitchen-Døderlein** is an associate professor of American history and culture in the Department of Literature, Area Studies and European Languages at the University of Oslo, Norway. Her research interests concern interracial sex and romance in the movies from the silent era to the present.

Helen M. **Lewis** teaches English and humanities at Western Iowa Tech Community College and has taught English and humanity courses since 1971. She has served as Area Chair of Westerns and the West for the Popular Culture Association / American Culture Association since 2002.

Kelly C. **MacPhail** is an assistant professor of English at the University of Minnesota–Duluth. His primary research has been on Anglo-American literary Modernism and the resignification of spiritual belief systems by a transatlantic group of writers and poets. His other interests include poetics, cinema, and narrative analysis of popular genres such as film noir, detective fiction, and Westerns.

Sue **Matheson** is an associate professor of English at the University College of the North, Canada. She has published more than 40 essays on film, culture, and literature in a wide range of books and scholarly journals. She is the editor of *Love in*

Western Film and Television (2013) and the author of *The Westerns and War Films of John Ford* (2016).

Robert E. **Meyer** is an associate professor at DePaul University, where he has taught such courses as Literature and Film, the Literature of Baseball, and History of the English Language. His primary research interests are the Western in literature, film and television, and baseball in American culture.

Cynthia J. **Miller** is a cultural anthropologist, specializing in popular culture and visual media. She is the editor or coeditor of 11 volumes, including *Steaming into a Victorian Future* (2012), *Undead in the West* and its sequel *Undead in the West II* (2012, 2013), and *International Westerns* (2014).

Christopher **Minz** is a doctoral candidate at Georgia State University. His research focuses are genre (especially the Western and James Bond films), Eastern European cinema, formal aesthetics, and psychoanalysis. He has presented papers at SCMS, Film & History, and the International Melodrama Conference.

Fran **Pheasant-Kelly** is the MA film studies course leader and reader in screen studies at the University of Wolverhampton, UK. Her research spans terrorism, space, science and abjection in film and television. She is the author of numerous publications including two monographs, *Abject Spaces in American Cinema* (2013) and *Fantasy Film Post 9/11* (2013).

Ashley Sufflé **Robinson** is a specialist on the nineteenth century. Her most recent article, "Go West, Young Woman," was published in *CEA: Critic*. Her research interests include gender theory, nineteenth-century English and American literature, the American West and popular culture.

Index

absurdity 124, 234, 240, 263
The Ace of the Saddle (film) 227n12
Across the Wide Missouri (film) 5, 75, 77, 78, 80, 81–82, 84
Alamo 26, 30
The Alamo (film) 31
alcohol 6, 39, 55, 153, 154; *see also* iconography
All the Pretty Horses (film) 99
Altman, Robert 17, 30, 36, 49, 50, 161, 164, 210n5, 241n4, 283n8
ambush 129, 137, 159, 206
Ambush at Cimarron Pass (film) 121n4
American Character 2, 14, 19, 30, 34, 199
American Outlaws (film) 227n19
animation 244, 245, 246, 254, 255n1, 262
Annie Get Your Gun (film) 16
Annie Oakley 12, 16, 18
Annie Oakley (1894) (film) 14
Annie Oakley (1935) (film) 31, 34, 121n7
anti-hero 5, 32, 62, 275
Apache Ambush (film) 226n6
Appaloosa (film) 53
archetype 2, 16, 17, 18, 19, 20, 36, 37, 64, 71, 75, 85, 113, 115, 120, 122n18, 271, 273, 274, 275, 276, 278, 279, 280, 282
The Arizona Cowboy (film) 215
Autry, Gene 1, 17, 21n5, 89, 98, 100, 103, 109n3

The Ballad of Josie (film) 5, 86, 88, 90, 91, 92, 97n3 119
The Ballad of Little Jo (film) 114, 118, 119, 120, 122n17
Battling with Buffalo Bill (film) 34
Belasco, David 38
The Big Trees (film) 216, 218, 221, 222, 224
Billy the Kid 117, 120n3, 170, 239, 240
Blade Runner (film) 63
Blowing Wild (film) 215
boarding house 68, 170, 171, 175n1; *see also* hotel
Boetticher, Bud, Jr. 6, 117, 152–55, 158, 159, 161, 162, 163–64, 164n2

Bonanza (TV series) 72n11, 168, 169
Bonanza: The Next Generation (TV series) 171
Borgnine, Ernest 32, 137, 210n7
bounty hunter 1, 5, 62–71, 71n2, 72n3, 72n6, 72n7, 72n8, 72n9, 264, 265; *see also* iconography
"The Bounty Hunter" (TV episode) 63, 772n4, 72n10
Brokeback Mountain (film) 5, 86–87, 89–94, 96, 97n6, 173
Broken Arrow (film) 4, 5, 75, 76, 77, 78, 79, 80, 81, 82, 84, 85n1
Broken Lance (film) 75, 76, 77, 78, 79, 80, 82, 84
Bronco Billy 17
Bronco Billy (film) 17, 19, 20
Bronson, Charles 268n5
Brooks, Peter 153, 155, 162
Brooks, Richard 117
brothel 110n5, 170, 171, 172, 208; *see also* prostitute
Bucking Bronco (film) 14
buckskin 1, 4, 23–33, 34n1; *see also* iconography
buffalo 11, 12, 13, 26, 27, 85, 264, 266
Buffalo Bill (1894) (film) 14, 21, 29
Buffalo Bill (1941) (film) 30
Buffalo Bill (1944) (film) 30
Buffalo Bill and Escort (film) 14
Buffalo Bill and the Indians, or Sitting Bull's History Lesson (film) 30
Buffalo Bill, Jr. (film) 31–32
Buffalo Bill Cody 1, 4, 9–10, 12–17, 23, 24, 26, 29, 30, 31, 32, 146, 147, 210
Buffalo, Bill, Jr. (TV series) 31
Buffalo Bill, l'oeroe del far west (film) 30
Buffalo Bill Rides Again (film) 30
buffalo hunter 26, 29
A Bullet for the General (film) 227n15
Buntline, Ned 20, 21n2, 29
Butler, Judith 75
Butch Cassidy and the Sundance Kid (film)

289

290   Index

97n3, 127, 207, 210n3, 213, 226, 232, 233, 237, 239, 240, 241

Calamity Jane 31, 32, 44
Calamity Jane (film) 31, 44, 97n3, 111, 119
The Call of the North (film) 38
Canadian Pacific (film) 216, 218, 222, 224
The Candidate (film) 276
capitalism 6, 45, 166, 199, 209, 265, 268n9
Carson City (film) 215
Casino Royale (film) 124
Cat Ballou (film) 30
cattle 5, 31, 39, 86–94, 103, 119, 128, 131, 132, 143, 153, 154, 159, 204, 205, 258, 260; baron 59, 87, 89, 91, 92, 223; drive 260, 261; *see also* iconography; livestock
Cattle Queen of Montana (film) 121n7
cavalier 4, 23, 26–27, 29, 31–33, 34
cavalry 26, 27, 35, 106; cavalryman 23, 28, 29
cemetery 7, 257, 258, 259, 260, 262, 263, 267, 268, 268n9 269n20; *see also* graveyard; iconography
Cemetery Without Crosses (film) 268n9
Champion, the Wonder Horse 100
China 9 Liberty 37 (film) 219, 226
cigarette 1, 5, 28, 51–53, 55–59, 60, 154, 222, 277; *see also* iconography
Cimino, Michael 223
La Cirque Buffalo Bill (film) 14
Civil War 26, 27, 34n1, 52, 62, 113, 125, 147, 215, 257, 261, 266
civilization 5, 6, 13, 28, 37, 39, 40, 43, 47, 49, 52, 53, 56, 58, 67, 155, 166, 167, 172, 183, 187, 199, 200, 202, 204, 205, 206, 207, 208, 215, 237, 245, 248, 258, 267, 273
Cody of the Pony Express (film) 16
Coen Brothers 4, 33, 126
coffee 1, 6, 152–62, 164, 164n1, 164n2; *see also* iconography
Cold War 6, 48, 74, 85n1, 94, 151n14
Colorado Sunset (film) 89
Comanche Station (film) 117
The Comancheros (film) 217, 227n8
Come On, Rangers (film) 102
comedy 30, 68, 109n4, 110n4, 119, 169, 170, 210, 202, 205, 211n9
competence 84, 105, 114, 204, 205, 208
cowboy 1, 5, 6, 7, 9, 11, 12, 17, 18, 20, 21, 21n1, 21n5, 29, 32, 34, 75, 87, 89, 90, 92, 93, 94, 95, 97n5, 99, 100, 101, 104, 105, 107, 108, 109, 109n3, 109n4, 110n4, 116, 117, 119, 125, 130, 133, 136, 137, 153, 160, 164n1, 164n2, 166, 173, 174, 203, 205, 210n5, 215, 232, 233, 236, 237, 238, 246, 247, 248, 249, 250, 254, 272; *see also* iconography
Crazy Horse 28
criminality 6, 166, 168, 173, 174
Crockett, Davey 24, 30
Cupid's Round Up (film) 99

Custer, George Armstrong 11, 26–29, 30, 34n1, 47

Dallas (film) 100
Davey Crockett: King of the Wild Frontier (film) 24
Dawn Rider (film) 227n19
Dead Man (film) 231, 235, 241, 242, 247, 260, 263, 265, 266, 270, 272, 283
Dead Man's Walk (film) 260
deconstruction 32, 110, 112, 275
DeMille, Cecil 5, 24, 37–49, 49n1, 49n2, 49n3, 49n5, 49n6
desert 6, 49, 53, 184, 188–96, 197, 197n3, 202, 203, 206, 210n6, 238, 239, 262, 266, 272, 278; *see also* iconography
dime novel 4, 20, 21n2, 48, 246, 247, 248
Django 210n9, 219, 223, 224
Django Unchained (film) 223, 224, 225
domesticity 6, 42, 57, 109, 156, 157, 161, 166, 169
Drums Along the Mohawk (film) 227n12
Duck, You Sucker! (film) 213, 218, 220, 222, 223, 227n18
The Duel at Silver Creek (film) 215
dynamite 1, 7, 117, 193, 207, 213–226, 226n2, 226n6, 226n7, 227n8, 227n12, 227n13, 227n15, 227n16, 227n18, 227n19; *see also* iconography
Dynamite Joe (film) 219
Dynamite Pass (film) 215

Earp, Wyatt 97n2, 146, 166, 167, 170, 172, 181, 282n1
Eastwood, Clint 1, 17, 21, 32, 100, 108, 116, 135, 181, 219, 223, 224, 261, 268n5, 268n9
Easy Rider (film) 170, 239
Edison, Thomas 14
El Dorado (film) 122n15, 217, 226n8
El Topo (film) 268n10
The Electric Horseman (film) 20
epic 46, 50, 113, 120, 121, 272; historical 48, 272; Homeric 121n3
etiquette 6, 52, 55, 153, 156, 157, 160, 163, 164
expansion 20, 166, 215, 242, 261; capitalist 206; continental 266; westward 1, 6, 148, 166, 199, 206, 215, 261

F Troop (TV series) 16
fantasy 11, 13, 26, 69, 96, 99, 101, 111, 125, 186, 209, 220, 235, 275
Fantasy Island (TV series) 20
The Far Horizons (film) 5, 75, 78, 79, 80, 82, 83, 84
femininity 75, 82, 83, 136; *see also* gender
fetish 6, 124, 145
Fighting with Buffalo Bill (film) 29
A Fistful of Dollars (film) 4, 210n9, 218, 219, 224
For a Few Dollars More (film) 32, 63, 227n13

Index 291

Ford, John 4, 5, 6, 51–52, 60, 86, 97n, 98, 121n3, 122n14, 161, 162, 167, 189, 191, 192, 196, 227n12, 238, 281, 282n2
Forty Guns (film) 114, 116, 119, 120, 121n8, 126, 127, 130–31, 135, 137, 139
The 400 Blows (film) 241
freedom 3, 5, 11, 18, 30, 39, 41, 43, 47, 48, 49, 65, 66, 67, 70–71, 99, 105, 109, 113, 114, 192, 194, 195, 203, 204, 245, 246, 249, 255n1, 267
frontier 1, 2, 3, 4, 6, 7, 11–21, 23–36, 32–33, 39, 41, 43, 44, 46–48, 62, 64, 71, 75, 86, 102, 110, 125, 126, 137, 147, 148, 154, 156, 160, 161, 167, 199, 202, 203, 205, 209, 210n1, 214, 215, 224, 225, 226, 227n9, 244, 245–252, 254, 257, 258, 259, 260, 263, 264, 266, 267; frontiersman 14, 16, 17, 23, 25, 26, 30, 48, 250
Frontier Pony Express (film) 102
Fuller, Samuel 14, 121n9
funeral 59, 80, 120, 204, 257, 261, 267, 269n20
The Furies (film) 114, 115–116, 119, 120, 121n6, 121n12

The Gabby Hayes Show (TV series) 104
gender 5, 6, 7, 21, 31, 38, 42, 43, 55, 74–76, 80–84, 85n3, 86, 88, 90–94, 114, 115, 120–21, 123, 125–27, 138, 139, 157, 257, 282; see also femininity; masculinity
Geronimo 12, 18, 32
ghost town 170, 184, 268
Ghost Town Gold (film) 103
Giant (film) 269n20
The Girl of the Golden West (film) 38, 41
The Good, the Bad and the Ugly (film) 32, 63, 151n13 189, 218, 257, 261, 266, 268n9
graveyard 7, 257, 259, 260, 261; grave 204, 258, 263, 267, 271, 272, 277; see also cemetery; iconography
Greaser's Palace (film) 231, 232, 236, 239, 240
The Great Silence (film) 63
The Great Train Robbery (film) 213, 214, 219, 226
guns 6, 28, 51, 65, 66, 67, 70, 91, 92, 93, 97, 106, 108, 110, 115, 121, 122, 124–39, 142–49, 150n9, 151n9,, 156, 159, 160, 167–187, 189, 190, 191, 195, 198, 217, 221, 223, 226n5, 227n9, 237, 240, 248, 262, 263, 264, 265, 267, 275; Gatling gun 135; handgun 90, 126, 147, 149; machine gun 210n9, 211n9, 211n10, 218, 219, 220, 221; see also iconography; rifle; technology, Winchester
Guns of the Magnificent Seven (film) 220
gunslinger 100, 137, 189
Gunsmoke (radio) 181
Gunsmoke (TV series) 67, 181

Hathaway, Henry 4, 33, 122n14
Hawks, Howard 122n15, 152, 216, 226n8, 238, 283n8

Heaven's Gate (film) 223
Heldorado (film) 102
Hellfighters (film) 217, 226n8
Hellman, Monte 6, 189, 197, 219, 225, 228, 232, 236, 238, 242
hero 1, 4, 5, 6, 17, 18, 19, 20, 23, 30, 32, 35, 40, 45, 53, 60, 62, 65, 68, 71, 74, 75, 76, 77, 80, 81, 83, 84, 86, 99, 101–9, 113, 122n17, 123, 124, 126, 129, 130, 143, 145, 146, 148, 149–50, 152, 153, 154, 156, 158, 160, 161, 163, 164, 168, 177, 178, 179, 180, 160, 161, 163, 164, 168, 177, 178, 179, 180, 181, 184, 186, 187, 194, 200, 205, 209, 210, 216, 219, 220, 221, 226, 231, 238, 239, 240, 241, 245, 246, 247, 248, 249, 252, 254, 262, 271, 272, 273, 274, 275, 276, 277, 278, 281, 282n2, 283n6
heroine 101, 162, 278
Hidalgo (film) 16, 19
High Noon (film) 5, 75, 76, 77, 79, 80, 83, 84, 85, 85n1, 110n6, 168, 171, 175n2, 217, 283n6
High Plains Drifter (film) 262, 268n9
Homer 113, 121n3, 122n13
The Homesteader (film) 215, 218
homoerotic 6, 92, 93, 95, 97, 126, 127, 131, 132
homosexuality 95, 96, 173
homosocial 87, 93, 95, 97n2, 132, 135
horse 1, 3, 5, 11, 13, 23, 27, 29, 51, 53, 56, 66, 80, 81, 82, 85, 93, 99–109, 109n1, 109n3, 110n5, 110n6, 113–20, 121n3, 121n4, 121n5, 121n8, 121n9, 121n11, 122n14, 122n16, 122n18, 128, 129, 132, 142, 143, 144, 159, 182, 185, 190, 191, 194, 198, 200, 202, 203, 304, 205, 206, 207, 210n1, 210n4, 211n10, 226, 236, 259, 266, 267, 268, 274, 276; see also iconography; livestock
hotel 6, 166–75, 175n2, 175n3, 177–79, 182, 184, 185, 247; see also boarding house; iconography
HUAC 44, 74
The Hunter (film) 72n3

I Am Sartana, Trade Your Guns for a Coffin (film) 219
iconography 2, 3, 4, 7, 9, 11, 13, 14, 15, 17, 18, 19, 28, 29, 33, 36, 51, 65, 66, 86, 101, 104, 113, 114, 126, 143, 149, 150, 166, 167, 170, 198, 199, 200, 241, 246, 266; see also alcohol; bounty hunter; buckskin; cattle; cemetery; cigarette; coffee; desert; dynamite; graveyard; gun; horse; hotel; sheep
identity 6, 17, 18, 41, 60, 75, 76, 81, 130, 142, 148, 150, 167, 177, 178, 190, 195, 198, 222, 270, 281; national 7, 12, 20, 231, 245, 251
immorality 171, 194
In the Days of Buffalo Bill (film) 29
Indian 4, 7, 11, 12, 17, 18, 19, 20, 23, 25, 29, 31, 33, 39, 41, 45, 75, 76, 77, 79–80, 81–82, 85n2, 121n3, 142, 143, 147, 151, 153, 159, 167, 172, 252, 255, 265, 266; Apache 54, 84,

121n4, 186; Comanche 259; Kiowa 258, 259; Pawnee 71; Sioux 14, 26, 28
Indian War 9, 15, 19, 20, 22, 29, 30
The Indian Wars (film) 15, 29
individualism 3, 5, 25, 33, 37, 71, 89, 93, 159, 163, 200, 211n9
Inglorious Basterds (film) 225

Jarmusch, Jim 23, 235, 241, 263, 264, 265, 266, 269n16, 272
Jesse James 225
Jesse James (film) 199, 218, 227n19
Johnny Guitar (film) 121n8, 126, 127, 136–37, 213, 218
Jones, Tommy Lee 173, 258, 269n20, 271, 273
justice 70, 71, 81, 127, 135, 139, 170, 187, 198, 205, 222, 225, 238, 248, 272, 274

"Keepin' It Real with Sitting Bull" (TV episode) 20
Kit Carson 29
Kit Carson (film) 226n6
Kitses, Jim 116, 157, 159, 160, 199, 202, 239, 241

landscape 1, 6, 37, 56, 84, 107, 113, 142, 143, 147, 155, 166, 167, 170, 172, 174, 175, 188, 189, 191, 196, 199, 203, 204, 216, 218, 222, 232, 236, 238–40, 241n4, 250, 262, 263, 267, 268n9; see also desert; Sublime
Lasky, Jesse 37, 38, 40, 41, 49n1
Lasseter, John 7, 244–54, 255n2
"The Last Cowboy" (TV episode) 20
The Last Frontier (film) 16
The Last Movie (film) 232, 239
Last of the Comanches (film) 226n6
The Last of the Mohicans (1932) (film) 4, 24, 25
The Last of the Mohicans (1992) (film) 31, 267
The Last Stand 11, 28, 29
law 66, 25, 30, 32, 43, 44, 45, 53, 62, 63–66, 73, 186, 187, 205, 210n1, 210n8, 211n9, 237, 248, 272, 273, 274, 277; lawman 53, 63, 66, 67, 155, 170, 248, 249, 276
Leone, Sergio 4, 32, 67, 72n8, 126, 189, 211, 218, 219, 220, 222, 227n18, 261, 262, 263, 266, 268n3, 272
The Life of Buffalo Bill (film) 15
Little Big Man (film) 28
Little Bighorn 20, 27, 28
Little House on the Prairie (TV series) 72n11, 171
livestock 5, 86, 87, 88, 91, 93, 96; cattle 5, 31, 39, 86–94, 103, 119, 128, 131, 132, 143, 153, 154, 159, 204, 205, 258, 260; horse 1, 3, 5, 11, 13, 23, 27, 29, 51, 53, 56, 66, 80, 81, 82, 85, 93, 99–109, 109n1, 109n3, 110n5, 110n6, 113–20, 121n3, 121n4, 121n5, 121n8, 121n9,

121n11, 122n14, 122n16, 122n18, 128, 129, 132, 142, 143, 144, 159, 182, 185, 190, 191, 194, 198, 200, 202, 203, 304, 205, 206, 207, 210n1, 210n4, 211n10, 226, 236, 259, 266, 267, 268, 274, 276; sheep 5, 65, 86–96, 119, 247
the Lone Ranger 167, 175n4, 177
The Lone Ranger (1956) (film) 31
The Lone Ranger (TV series) 31
The Lone Ranger (2013) (film) 31
The Lone Ranger and the Lost City of Gold (film) 31
The Lonely Man (film) 121n9
Lonesome Cowboys (film) 237, 283
Lonesome Dove (TV series) 257–61, 283n8

The Magnificent Seven (film) 220
male power 6, 124, 139
The Man from Hell's Edge (film) 97n5
The Man Who Shot Liberty Valance (film) 51, 52, 58, 110n6, 266
Manifest Destiny 7, 19, 21, 76, 245, 257, 261, 262, 263, 264, 265, 266, 267, 268
Mann, Anthony 114, 117, 121n10, 139, 142, 143, 145, 149, 150n5, 153
Marked for Murder (film) 5, 86, 90, 92
Marlboro Man 89, 94, 95, 97n6
Marvin, Lee 44, 47, 79, 187, 249
masculinity 2, 4, 6, 7, 11, 23, 32, 34, 40, 47, 52, 53, 54, 56, 57, 58, 59, 60, 75, 76, 77, 85–87, 89–93, 95, 97n2, 97n3, 99, 100, 104, 105, 109, 124, 126, 126, 127, 128, 129, 130, 131, 132, 133, 136, 137, 143, 149, 152, 186, 257, 259, 278; manliness 104; white masculinity 5, 74, 81, 84; see also gender
Massacre Canyon (film) 226n6
The Maverick Queen (film) 121n7
McLintock! (film) 169
McQueen, Steve 5, 62, 63, 71, 72n3, 180, 181
melodrama 6, 37, 39, 41, 75, 96, 152, 153, 154, 155, 161, 162, 163
MGM 43
"Mild, Mild West" 16
Milius, John 52–53, 60
Milland, Ray 6, 198, 194, 196
morality 5, 6, 32, 94, 100, 113, 120, 162, 169, 196, 237, 245, 248
A Mule for the Marquesa (film) 117
My Darling Clementine (film) 4, 52, 55, 56, 58, 167, 170
My Name Is Nobody (film) 219
My Pal Trigger (film) 102

Night at the Museum (film trilogy) 16
1960s 7, 59, 90, 94, 162, 170, 172, 180, 198, 199, 200, 206, 209, 211n9, 213, 214, 225, 231, 233, 246, 249, 274; see also politics
No Country for Old Men (film) 174
North to Alaska (film) 122n14
nostalgia 4, 26, 94, 97n6, 217, 247, 273

Index 293

Oakley, Annie 12, 16, 18, 31
The Odyssey 13, 121*n*3
Once Upon a Time in the West (film) 126, 206, 207, 262, 268*n*3, 268*n*5
One-Eyed Jacks (film) 172, 175*n*3
100 Rifles (film) 211*n*9, 220, 221
Only the Valiant (film) 226*n*6
open range 152
Open Range (film) 282*n*1
outlaw 30, 39, 40, 42, 53, 69, 97*n*3, 128, 130, 134, 135, 136, 142, 173, 191, 205–8, 213, 237, 239, 260
The Outlaw (film) 117, 122
The Outlaw Josey Wales (film) 127, 135, 136

Paladin 6, 177–87
Pale Rider (film) 223, 224, 227*n*18, 262
The Paleface (film) 226*n*6
Paramount Pictures 43, 49*n*1
pastoral 87–88, 94, 95, 96, 97*n*2, 199, 200, 209
Pat Garrett and Billy the Kid (film) 231, 235, 238, 241, 242
Pawnee Bill 12, 15, 18
Peckinpah, Sam 97*n*2, 109*n*4, 168, 198, 200, 202, 203, 210*n*9, 221, 222, 239, 240, 272
Pickford, Mary 41–42
pig 108, 234, 235, 241, 250; *see also* iconography
Pixar 7, 244–47, 254, 255*n*2, 256
Plains 19, 23, 26, 28, 29, 40, 45, 46, 105, 238, 239, 269*n*16
Plainsman 26, 29
The Plainsman (film) 30, 43, 44, 45, 46, 47
Plato 97*n*2
politics 1, 37, 64, 96, 97*n*3, 154, 170, 238, 240, 261, 269*n*20, 273; political injustice 21, 198; *see also* 1960s
The Pony Express (1950) (film) 16
The Pony Express (1953) (film) 23, 24
The Professionals (film) 32, 114, 117, 118, 120, 210*n*9, 220, 222, 227*n*18, 238
progress 6, 45, 49, 156, 161, 166, 199, 200, 201, 202, 207, 209, 210, 210*n*2, 215–16, 245, 246, 251, 252, 254, 262, 264, 269*n*20
prostitute 108, 116, 117, 118, 119, 157, 171, 172, 173, 208

Queen Victoria 29
The Quick and the Dead (film) 126, 127, 136, 137, 139

railroad 43, 44, 45, 136, 192, 199, 205–7, 210*n*7, 211*n*10, 215, 216, 227*n*19, 264, 266, 268*n*3; *see also* train
Rainbow Valley (film) 215
Rancho Notorious (film) 121*n*8
Ray, Nicholas 121*n*8, 126, 218, 225, 227*n*12
Red River (film) 31, 126–27, 131, 161

Remington, Frederic 4, 147
Return of the Seven (film) 220
Return to Lonesome Dove (TV series) 260
revenge 7, 103, 108, 114, 139, 143, 190, 201, 241, 257, 258, 268*n*9
revision 1, 30, 79, 117, 172, 248; revisionist 17, 19, 28, 162, 231, 282*n*1, 283*n*8
revolution 162, 220, 221, 222, 234; revolutionary 117, 118, 227*n*17, 233, 245, 246
Ride in the Whirlwind (film) 232, 236–38
Ride Lonesome (film) 117
Ride the High Country (film) 32, 198, 200, 201
Riders of Destiny (film) 100, 105, 226*n*4
rifle 1, 6, 32, 107, 124, 125, 128, 129, 131, 134, 135, 136, 142–50, 150*n*2, 150*n*3, 150*n*6, 150*n*7, 150*n*9, 151*n*13, 151*n*14, 159, 185, 211*n*9, 220, 221; *see also* technology; Winchester
The Rifleman 151*n*13, 151*n*14, 168
Rio Bravo (film) 4, 164*n*2, 216, 217, 226*n*8, 227*n*8, 283*n*8
Rio Lobo (film) 207, 217, 227*n*8, 283*n*8
rodeo 11, 16, 33, 87, 94, 102, 202, 203
Rogers, Roy 1, 17, 89, 92, 100–4, 109*n*2
romance 9, 26, 52, 70, 74–76, 78–79, 81, 99, 100, 279; doomed 152; forbidden 173; interracial 74–76, 79
A Romance of the Redwoods (film) 40–41, 42, 43
romanticism 32, 39
Roosevelt, Franklin 47
Roosevelt, Theodore 1, 5, 26, 147
Rooster Cogburn...and the Lady (film) 217
Rose of the Rancho (film) 38
Roy Rogers Rodeo: TV Special 104
The Roy Rogers Show (TV series) 103
The Roy Rogers Rodeo: TV Special 104
Run, Man, Run (film) 219
Rustlers' Rhapsody (film) 5, 86, 89, 92, 93, 95, 97*n*5

sacrifice 27, 28, 30, 60, 71, 80, 81, 82, 83, 90, 192, 193, 194, 196, 259, 263, 264, 267
saloon 40, 42, 43, 45, 46, 51, 56, 92, 97*n*5, 116, 136, 137, 152, 153, 171, 172, 182, 184, 185, 186, 207, 247, 268*n*2, 271, 273, 280–82
saloon girl 184, 185, 186, 271, 273, 280, 281, 282
Scorsese, Martin 46, 52, 59, 60
Scott, Randolph 24, 32, 117, 155, 210*n*1
The Searchers (film) 5, 52, 53, 56–60, 75, 76, 77, 78, 79, 81, 82, 84, 121*n*3, 187, 189, 191, 282*n*2, 283*n*2
Seitz, George B. 23, 24
Seven Men from Now (film) 6, 153, 155, 159, 163
Shane (film) 4, 30, 100, 106–7, 124, 134, 223, 244, 266, 278, 283*n*4
sharpshooter 9, 18, 19, 147

294 Index

sheep 5, 65, 86–96, 119, 247; *see also* iconography; livestock
The Sheepman (film) 5, 86, 89, 91, 92
sheriff 42, 53, 56, 60, 67, 68, 69, 70, 71, 108, 110n3, 116, 124, 154, 172, 184, 192–95, 210n3, 247, 248, 258, 268n9, 274, 280
The Shooting (film) 6, 189, 192–94, 196, 232, 236–38, 241
The Sign of the Cross (film) 43, 44
Silver 99
Silverado (film) 282n1
Sioux Ghost Dance (film) 14
Sitting Bull 12, 16, 18, 20, 22, 30, 31
Slotkin, Richard 1, 199, 206, 210n2, 217, 220, 221, 227n12, 230
Son of Paleface (film) 102, 103
The Sons of Katie Elder (film) 217, 226n5
Spaghetti Western 4, 32, 67, 93, 214, 217–20, 222, 226, 262, 268n9
The Squaw Man (film) 38–40
Stanwyck, Barbara 31, 44, 114, 115, 116, 121n7, 130
Stewart, James 51, 76, 77, 78, 81, 84, 143, 144, 170
Streets of Laredo (film) 260
the Sublime 6, 188–94, 196, 197n2, 241n4, 267
Supernatural (TV series) 63, 174
Support Your Local Sheriff (film) 210n3
Susanna Pass (film) 102
Symposium 97n2

Tarantino, Quentin, 172, 173, 224, 225, 227n22
technology 6, 32, 125, 147, 198, 210n1, 211n9, 214, 215, 219, 226n6, 227n17, 244, 254; car 12, 198, 199, 200–7, 210, 213, 215, 250, 254, 266, 273; Gatling gun 135; machine 6, 7, 125, 198-2-10, 210n5, 210n8, 210n9, 211n9, 211n10, 218, 219, 220, 264, 265; truck 95, 202, 203, 204, 205, 210, 253, 273, 275; *see also* gun; rifle; train
Theocritus 87, 88
They Died with Their Boots On (film) 28
This Is the West That Was (film) 17
Those Dirty Dogs (film) 219
The Three Burials of Melquiades Estrada (film) 173, 269n20, 271–73, 275, 280–82
3:10 to Yuma (film) 126, 127, 130, 131, 227n19
A Ticket to Tomahawk (film) 215
tobacco 5, 51–60; cigarette 1, 5, 28, 51–53, 55–59, 154, 222, 277, 278
Tom Horn (film) 72n3
Tombstone 55, 56, 130, 172
Tombstone (film) 130, 166, 172, 282n1
Tompkins, Jane 105, 107, 109, 143, 198, 200, 204
Tonto 31, 53, 167, 171, 175n4, 227n21; hotel 167, 171; town 53
Toy Story (film) 7, 244–54, 255n1, 255n2

tragedy 259; domestic 170; Washita 28
train 6, 12, 42, 51, 128, 198, 199, 200, 205, 206–8, 210n6, 210n9, 213, 214, 216–19, 222, 227n17, 247, 264, 265
The Train Robbers (film) 210n6, 217
Trigger 5, 99, 100–4, 109n2, 128, 135, 138, 198, 222
True Grit (1969) (film) 4, 32, 33, 35, 170
True Grit (2010) (film) 4, 33, 35, 126, 133, 134, 139
The True Story of Jesse James 218
Turner, Frederick Jackson 1, 14, 21n3, 199, 245, 251, 266, 267
Twentieth Century-Fox 17
Twin Peaks (TV series) 171–72
Two Lane Blacktop (film) 236
Two Mules for Sister Sara (film) 227n16

Unconquered (film) 44, 47–48
Under California Stars (film) 103
Under Western Stars (film) 102
Unforgiven (film) 100, 108–9, 110n5, 114, 116, 117, 119, 120, 122, 122n13, 124, 133, 139
Universal 148

Van Cleef, Lee 32, 68, 261
Verbinski, Gore 4, 225
Vidor, King 6, 189, 191, 192, 196
villain 59, 62, 66, 72n11, 92, 145, 152, 156, 157, 160, 161, 187, 210, 211, 216, 226n4, 247, 248, 262, 271, 273,–79, 282, 283n6
The Virginian (book) 154
The Virginian (1914) (film) 38–40, 43, 45
Viva Zapata! (film) 220

Walker (film) 231, 235
Wanted: Dead or Alive (TV series) 5, 62–71, 72n3
war 25, 28, 37, 148, 149, 205, 206, 220, 223, 257, 261, 263; American Revolution 25; Civil War 26, 27, 34n1, 52, 62, 113, 125, 147, 215, 257, 261, 266; Cold War 6, 48, 74, 85n1, 94, 151n14; Indian War 9, 15, 19, 20, 30, 34; Johnson County War 223; range 86, 90, 92, 94; Trojan 113; Vietnam 199, 211n9, 220, 231; World War I 201; World War II 20, 44, 52, 58, 59, 144, 148, 210n4, 223, 269n20; Wounded Knee 15, 20
The War Wagon (film) 210n9, 211n10, 226n6
Washita 28; *see also* tragedy
Wayne, John 30, 31, 32, 51, 52, 53, 56, 60, 76, 80, 81, 84, 89, 97, 100, 122n14, 131, 169, 187, 200, 205, 210n2, 215, 217, 223, 226n4, 227n10, 281
"Where the Buffalo Bill Roams" 20
Wild Bill (film) 16
Wild Bill Hickok 16, 17, 26, 31, 44
The Wild Bunch (film) 32, 97n2, 109n4, 200, 201, 202, 206, 210n4, 210n9, 211n9, 219, 220, 221, 226,, 262

Wild West Show 4, 9–21, 26, 29, 33, 246
wilderness 23, 24, 25, 40, 47, 53, 58, 60, 99, 100, 107, 109, 189, 191, 192, 196, 199, 237, 245, 246, 266
Winchester 1, 67, 88, 142, 144, 146, 147, 148, 149, 150, 150n7, 150n9
Winchester '73 (film) 6, 142–50
women 5, 9, 11, 13, 23, 24, 30, 31, 37, 40, 42, 45, 53, 54, 63, 70, 74, 75, 77–85, 89–92, 97n6, 104, 109, 110n5, 113–14, 116–17, 119–20, 122n18, 125–27, 132–33, 136, 138, 139, 154, 156, 162, 168, 171, 173, 178, 183, 185, 194, 195, 196, 209, 220, 245, 254, 273, 274, 276, 277, 278, 282; *see also* saloon girl
World War I 201; *see also* war
World War II 20, 44, 52, 58, 59, 144, 148, 210n4, 223, 269n20; *see also* war
Wounded Knee 15, 20; *see also* war
Wright, Will 32, 236–37, 241n3, 247–48

Young Buffalo Bill (film) 17, 30

Zachariah (film) 231, 232, 239, 240
Zinnemann, Fred 85, 110n6, 283n6

www.ingramcontent.com/pod-product-compliance
Lightning Source LLC
Chambersburg PA
CBHW021339230426
43666CB00006B/340